Remembering Cable
Fascism and Anti-Fascism i

Parkes–Wiener Series on Jewish Studies
Series Editors: David Cesarani and Tony Kushner
ISSN 1368-5449

The field of Jewish Studies is one of the youngest, but fastest growing and most exciting areas of scholarship in the academic world today. Named after James Parkes and Alfred Wiener and recognising the co-operative relationship between the Parkes Centre at the University of Southampton and the Wiener Library in London, this series aims to publish new research in the field and student materials for use in the seminar room, to disseminate the latest work of established scholars and to re-issue classic studies which are currently out of print.

The selection of publications reflects the international character and diversity of Jewish Studies; it ranges over Jewish history from Abraham to modern Zionism, and Jewish culture from Moses to post-modernism. The series also reflects the interdisciplinary approach inherent in Jewish Studies and at the cutting edge of contemporary scholarship, and provides an outlet for innovative work on the interface between Judaism and ethnicity, popular culture, gender, class, space and memory.

Other Books in the Series

The Berlin Haskalah and German Religious Thought: Orphans of Knowledge
David Sorkin

Holocaust Literature: Schulz, Levi, Spiegelman and the Memory of the Offence
Gillian Banner

Sir Sidney Hamburger and Manchester Jewry: Religion, City and Community
Bill Williams

The Making of Manchester Jewry 1740–1875, Revised Edition
Bill Williams

Anglo-Jewry in Changing Times: Studies in Diversity 1840–1914
Israel Finestein

Double Jeopardy: Gender and the Holocaust
Judith Tydor Baumel

Cultures of Ambivalence and Contempt: Studies in Jewish–Non-Jewish Relations
edited by Siân Jones, Tony Kushner and Sarah Pearce

Alfred Wiener and the Making of the Wiener Library
Ben Barkow

Remembering Cable Street: Fascism and Anti-Fascism in British Society

Editors

Tony Kushner and Nadia Valman

VALLENTINE MITCHELL
LONDON • PORTLAND, OR

First published in 2000 in Great Britain by
VALLENTINE MITCHELL
Newbury House, 900 Eastern Avenue
London IG2 7HH

and in the United States of America by
VALLENTINE MITCHELL
c/o ISBS
5804 N.E. Hassalo Street
Portland, Oregon 97213-3644

Website: www.vmbooks.com

This collection copyright © 2000 Vallentine Mitchell & Co. Ltd

British Library Cataloguing in Publication Data

Remembering Cable Street : fascism and anti-fascism in
British society. – (Parkes-Wiener series on Jewish studies)
1. Jews – England – London – History – 1789-1945 2. Fascism –
England – London – History – 20th century 3. London
(England) – Social conditions – 20th century
I. Kushner, Tony II. Valman, Nadia
941'.004924
ISBN 0 85303 361 7 (cloth)
ISBN 0 85303 362 5 (paper)

Library of Congress Cataloging-in-Publication Data

Remembering Cable Street: fascism and anti-fascism in British Society
/ edited by Tony Kushner and Nadia Valman.
   p. cm. – (Parkes-Wiener series on Jewish studies)
'First appeared in a special issue on "Remembering Cable Street:
fascism and anti-fascism in British society" of Jewish culture and history,
1/2 Winter, 1998' – T.p. verso.
   Includes bibliographical references and index.
   ISBN 0-85303-361-7 (cloth: alk. paper). – ISBN 0-85303-362-5 (pbk.: alk. paper)
   1. Great Britain – Politics and government – 20th century. 2. Anti-fascist
movement – Great Britain – History – 20th century. 3. Fascism – Great Britain
– History – 20th century. 4. Jews – Great Britain – History – 20th century.
5. Jews – Great Britain – Political activity. I. Kushner, Tony (Antony Robin Jeremy)
II. Valman, Nadia. III. Series.
DA566.7.R44 1999   99-37495
941.084 – dc21   CIP

This group of studies first appeared in a Special Issue on
'Remembering Cable Street: Fascism and Anti-Fascism in British Society' of
Jewish Culture and History 1/2 (Winter 1998) ISSN 1462–169X

All rights reserved. No part of this publication may be reproduced, stored in or introduced into a retrieval system or transmitted in any form or by any means, electronic, mechanical, photocopying, recording or otherwise, without the prior written permission of the publisher of the book

Printed in Great Britain by
Antony Rowe Ltd., Chippenham, Wilts.

In memory of David Englander (1949–1999),
an East Ender and a fine historian of British Jewry

Contents

Introduction:
Minorities, Fascism and Anti-Fascism   **Tony Kushner**
    Nadia Valman   1

Fascist Perceptions of Cable Street   **Thomas P. Linehan**   23

Women and Fascism in the East End   **Julie Gottlieb**   31

But What Did They Do?
Contemporary Jewish Responses to Cable Street   **Elaine R. Smith**   48

The Threat of the British Union of Fascists
in Manchester   **Neil Barrett**   56

The Straw that Broke the Camel's Back:
Public Order, Civil Liberties
and the Battle of Cable Street   **Richard C. Thurlow**   74

Docker and Garment Worker,
Railwayman and Cabinet Maker:
The Class Memory of Cable Street   **David Renton**   95

'Long May its Memory Live!': Writing
and Rewriting 'the Battle of Cable Street'   **Tony Kushner**   109

DOCUMENTS

Jewish Girls and the Battle of Cable Street   **Nadia Valman**   181

A. L. Cohen's 'The Memorable Sunday'   **David Mazower**   195

DRAMA

The Battle of Cable Street and *No Pasaran*   **Simon Blumenfeld**   203

Conclusion   **Tony Kushner and Nadia Valman**   280

Abstracts to Articles   282

Notes on Contributors   284

Index   286

Introduction: Minorities, Fascism and Anti-Fascism

REMEMBERING THE BATTLE OF CABLE STREET

Remembering Cable Street: Fascism and Anti-Fascism in British Society grew out of a conference commemorating the sixtieth anniversary of the historic confrontation between fascists, anti-fascists and the police in London's East End on 4 October 1936. This collection of essays and documents aims to continue that commemoration, but also to explore further what has become a highly contested memory. While it has been variously mythologised as a victory for working-class solidarity, political radicalism, cultural pluralism or local pride, the 'Battle of Cable Street' remains a complex event. Drawing on a variety of sources from public records to oral history to literary texts, the following essays provide a range of perspectives on 4 October, locating it in the different contexts of Jewish history and historiography, British social and political history, the history of fascism and racism, and the relationships between policing, minorities and the state – and interpreting it through the prisms of ideology, class, gender and language.

If recent work in British Jewish history has identified the social and ideological conflicts which fractured the Jewish community in the modern period, the 'Battle of Cable Street' could be cited as paradigmatic. Responding to the threat of fascism in the mid-1930s, the Board of Deputies of British Jews, Jewry's 'unofficial' governing elite, maintained a conservative, non-confrontational position that was increasingly at odds with the needs and wishes of many of those it purported to represent. Such was the Board's concern to maintain a uniform and coherent communal image, as Neil Barrett's essay in this volume shows, that it sought to suppress both dissenting voices and regional differences in Jewish responses to fascism. 4 October, in this respect, represented not only a battle against fascist provocation in a predominantly Jewish neighbourhood; it also represented a battle between Jews themselves over the terms of their public representation. When thousands of working-class Jews defied the advice of their middle and upper-class leadership to maintain a low profile and 'stay off the streets', it signalled a crisis of communal authority in British Jewry.

The conflict between fascism and anti-fascism itself has frequently been interpreted in terms of class conflict. As David Renton argues, recent research suggests that the events around the 'Battle of Cable Street' call for a more nuanced analysis, which attends to the interacting factors of class, ethnicity and economic interest. Renton nevertheless points to the dangers of losing 'class' as a category of analysis for these events, particularly in the era of post-Communist history. The diversity of Jewish responses to the impact of fascism is examined in greater detail by Elaine Smith. Underlying the different forms of defence activity pursued by elite, Communist, socialist and ex-servicemen's organisations – from disseminating counter-propaganda to trades union organising to surveillance of Jewish business practices – were conflicting attitudes to the politics of Jewish defence. While some organisations, such as the Jewish Ex-Servicemen's Legion, were concerned with combatting anti-semitism in particular rather than fascism in general, others, like the Communist Party, the Jewish People's Council and the Jewish Labour Council, assumed that fascist anti-semitism constituted a wider threat to democratic values and was therefore the concern of the British people as a whole. Such conflicts of approach also indicate the myriad socio-political backgrounds and differing life-experiences of Jews in the East End of London. Smith's examination of the responses to fascism reveals that there was no simple division between 'East End' and 'West End' Jewry but inside a multiplicity of internal differences of interest and aspiration.

A second focus of several of the contributions to this volume is the rhetoric and representation of 'Cable Street'. As Thomas Linehan strikingly shows, fascist violence against Jews was verbal as well as physical. Indeed, he makes a strong case for the power of propaganda in recasting the defeat of the BUF on 4 October. Linehan's analysis of the metaphors and allusive language used to describe anti-fascists demonstrates the BUF's ability to draw on a wide range of contemporary social, political and religious anxieties in order to appeal to the widest possible constituency. But the transformation of the events of 4 October into a recognisable narrative happened not only in the fascist press. For anti-fascists as well as the BUF, the 'Battle' had both local and international resonance in terms of contemporary European, and particularly Spanish fascism. Thus, as Tony Kushner's study suggests, the story of 'the Battle of Cable Street' began to be constructed in anti-fascist rhetoric well ahead of the day itself. Kushner shows how the meanings ascribed to 4 October have changed significantly over the past sixty years, as the 'Battle' has become 'usable history' for those who have written and rewritten its narrative.

Kushner's cultural history of 'the Battle' suggests that narratives of 'Cable Street' are important not only for what they tell us about the day itself but also for the ways in which they are told. Included in this volume are two examples of 'Cable Street' literature which participate in the complex process of constructing history through testimony, memory and myth. The first, an eye-witness account by the Workers' Circle activist A. L. Cohen, places equal emphasis on the exhilaration of participating in Jewish self-defence, and the shock of witnessing the brutality of the mounted police against the demonstrators whom they were supposed to be protecting. The second, by the East End novelist and playwright Simon Blumenfeld, represents the drama of the day's events literally as drama. Like Cohen, Blumenfeld stresses the effort and organisation which went into anti-fascist resistance, but the dialogic form of drama enables him to suggest debate, dissent and uncertainty. However, unlike Cohen, Blumenfeld, also a demonstrator at Gardiner's Corner, wrote *The Battle of Cable Street* from a distance of fifty years. The play's sequel, *No Pasaran*, imagines Cable Street veterans in the context of the East End in the early 1990s, where, Blumenfeld insists, the fading memory of the 'Battle' continues to be 'usable'.

Blumenfeld's *Battle of Cable Street* is one of the few accounts of 4 October to give prominence to the role of women in anti-fascist activism, and likewise the importance and problematics of Communism for women in the East End. More explicitly, Julie Gottlieb's essay raises the important question of what happens when we gender the history of fascism and anti-fascism. Gottlieb suggests the centrality of the notion of 'woman' to fascist rhetoric, a notion which both enabled and belied the actual participation of women in the BUF. But while her account clearly demonstrates the importance of examining the specific roles and representations of women within fascism, her research also draws into focus the unacknowledged parallels between women on both sides of the barricades. Like the upper-class fascist women whose apprenticeships in political organisation were served in philanthropic social work in the East End, upper-class Anglo-Jewish women, as Nadia Valman shows, shared similar maternalistic aspirations and assumptions about their poorer 'sisters'. One effect of interpreting Cable Street through the lens of gender, then, is to illuminate unexpected congruences as well as differences.

Considering 4 October from another perspective, that of the broader question of public order, produces a notably different interpretation of the day's significance. Richard Thurlow's account of the complicated relationship between Home Office, Home Secretary, Metropolitan Police Commissioner and police officers, suggests the array of conflicting interests that resulted in both the 'Battle' and its dramatic legislative after-effect, the Public Order Act. Like the conflict over Anglo-Jewish leadership, this battle was a sign of historical change: it was a battle between perceived traditions of British government, which emphasised maximum civil liberties and minimum state intervention, and the new circumstances of 1930s popular politics. Cable Street, according to Thurlow, was the crisis point at which the state intervened to prevent the confrontation between fascists and anti-fascists from becoming a challenge to law and order.

But at the same time the 'Battle of Cable Street' was a demonstration *against* the police, who were widely perceived to have failed in ensuring the safety of the Jewish population of east London from harassment and injury. A. L. Cohen's report of the 'Battle' is scathingly ironic about the betrayal by the police of their role as protectors; as much as his anger has been provoked by the Jew-baiting of the fascists, it is pushed to the limit by the behaviour of the police. In this sense, the 'Battle' can be interpreted as a watershed for British-Jewish identity politics, a Jewish Stonewall. In directly confronting not only the BUF but the representatives of the State, demonstrators at Cable Street were asserting both their integration within the local community and its politics, and their demand for respect as Jews. If the 'Battle of Cable Street' did not have the instantaneous effect of destroying British fascism that some accounts have ascribed to it, its resonance both for local activism and for British-Jewish identity may have been more long lasting.

As the 'Battle of Cable Street' moves increasingly beyond living memory and into the realm of the imaginary, it is the subject of more and more representations in both literary and visual texts and scholarly studies. Indeed, as Kushner's chapter in this collection suggests, within the writing of British-Jewish history and in the celebration of its heritage, the 'Battle of Cable Street' has gained privileged status. It would seem churlish, therefore, to make a plea for further intensive research on this specific, if extraordinary, day of action. Yet there are many important themes and ares of study emerging out of 4 October 1936 that merit further consideration.

FUTURE DIRECTIONS

Policing, Crime and Ethnicity

The 'Battle' of 4 October 1936 is an important focal point for the exploration of the sensitive issue of the policing of ethnic minorities. Just as the Rodney King affair in Los Angeles prompted a major rethink of the importance of institutiónal racism in the American police force, so the murder of Stephen Lawrence has had a similar impact in breaking through

Introduction

complacency in Britain. It has taken five years since the black teenager's death in 1993 to begin the process of recognising the appalling failures of the Metropolitan Police in dealing with what was a brutal racist murder. Nevertheless, for the first time some major figures in the police world in Britain have begun to accept that, rather than reflecting the behaviour of a 'few bad apples', racism is a serious, institutionalised problem affecting the way Afro-Caribbean and Asian people are treated on an everyday level. Through the prism of the 'Battle', earlier police-minority conflict can be traced, helping to cast light on the way many ethnic groups perceived as a menace have been criminalised by the agents of law and order. Police attitudes during the 1930s also bring into question the widespread assumption that the state apparatus in Britain has been free of bias against the Jews. Indeed the issue brings closer together the experiences of second generation Jews whose parents came from eastern Europe before 1914 and those whose parents came after the war from the Caribbean.[1]

David Cesarani has written that

> From the 1890s onwards, the construction of an Anglo-Jewish heritage was not merely an exercise in the establishment and perpetuation of Jewish values: it was also part of a continuing struggle with the taxonomy of Englishness. Anglo-Jewish history was part of the weaponry deployed by English Jews in the struggle against exclusionary tendencies in English culture and politics. Indeed, Anglo-Jewish historiography has for most of its existence been overdetermined by these strategic ends: it has been part of communal defence.[2]

It is ironic, therefore, that the most remembered day in twentieth century British Jewish history should be the 'Battle of Cable Street', whose very title commemorates a pitched and bloody street fight between young Jews and others against the combined forces of the Metropolitan Police. The writing and representation of British Jewish history was designed, at least initially, to provide the non-Jewish world with an image of Jews that was the very opposite of that on 4 October: law-abiding and respectable. As Cesarani continues, 'For years [after the first Anglo-Jewish exhibitions and the formation of the Jewish Historical Society of England or JHSE] there was almost nothing in books or exhibitions that referred to poor Jews, unsuccessful Jews, Jews engaged in crime or prostitution...'[3] It was, however, in a conference in 1980, partly sponsored by the JHSE, that the first tentative exploration of the 'Battle' was made within a Jewish historiographical context. But it was significant that this encounter with a potentially controversial past came through group discussion, when the testimonies of those who had lived in the Jewish East End were given an outlet, rather than through a specific paper on the topic. Moreover, the validation of oral history was provided by the conference co-sponsors, the Jewish East End Project of the Association for Jewish Youth, who wanted to explore 'the rich Jewish culture that evolved in the East End', rather than the JHSE.[4]

The conference and the volume emerging from it marked a key development in Jewish historiography, a crossroads reflecting the meeting of older and newer approaches. Historians of a Whiggish outlook, focussing on institutions, still dominated the proceedings but the voices of ordinary Jews who had been at the receiving end of these Jewish agencies and a younger generation of researchers opening up fresh perspectives and areas of interest, whose work would come to fruition later in the decade, provided alternative perspectives. The result, as Aubrey Newman put it, was 'a very lively discussion and, in the words of diplomacy, a "frank exchange of views". Not everyone agreed with each other, but then no one wanted a bland "establishment" view.'[5]

The tension was neatly exposed within the conference proceedings in the two papers dealing with criminality and policing. The first was an important study of 'East End Crime and the Jewish Community' at the turn of the century by Colin Holmes, who, at this stage, was beginning to establish himself as the leading authority on the history of immigration in Britain and, more specifically, British anti-semitism. Holmes' essay represented a pioneer study which concluded with a plea for further work. Holmes highlighted how 'we still do not have much information about the criminal behaviour of immigrant Jews at this time' and nearly two decades later this remains the case. The identity of criminals amongst the immigrant generation and beyond is a fascinating area of study, involving the complexity of extreme marginality through double outsider status. Through oral history and other sources it is possible to recover the intriguing experiences of those whose lives reveal much about the internal dynamics of Jewish communities as well as the minority within the minority itself.[6] Holmes also pointed out the gaps in knowledge concerning anti-semitism in Britain, although in this respect much more progress has been made since he wrote. But the bringing together of the two strands – the social *and* cultural construction of alien Jews as being inherently deviant, and therefore prone to violent crimes such as the 'Ripper murders' of 1888 – still needs a great deal more exploration.[7]

The alternative approach to law enforcement and Jewish history in the conference volume was provided in a short tribute to Inspector Thomas Eveson, who was a policeman in the heart of the Jewish East End at the turn of the century:

> His care and understanding of the immigrants flocking into the East End was limitless – for them he acquired a fluent knowledge of Yiddish and some Hebrew, and he had a close acquaintance with Jewish tradition and customs... He must, in his time, and with his unique qualities, have helped hundreds of the foreign Jews pouring into London at the time and he was honoured and loved by them.

On his retirement, Eveson was presented by 'leading members of the Jewish Community... with a heartfelt testimonial... The centenary of his birth was celebrated in nearly a whole page of the *Jewish Chronicle* in 1948.'[8]

There could have been few non-Jewish policemen like Eveson who knew 'a good deal of Talmud and some rabbinics' (it is also suggested that 'A *mezuzah* [box containing sacred scrolls attached to doorpost of Jewish houses] lived in his pocket and he possessed a *talles* [prayer shawl] and *tefillin* [phylacteries]).[9] Nevertheless, testimony from some veterans of the 'Battle' suggest that relations between East End Jews and the local police were generally friendly and sympathetic. Bill Fishman, both a witness to the events of 4 October 1936 and a historian of them, concludes that

> One important factor, omitted by both sides, that is, those accusing the police of pro-fascist bias, as against the proponents of police 'neutrality', is the locally-stationed (H Division) constable on the beat, who lived and worked among the immigrants, and was, therefore, disposed to be friendly towards the law-abiding Jews.

Fishman adds that 'There is a wealth of evidence, written and oral, to sustain this, if some of the "historians" of the area and the period had been perceptive enough to delve deeper into such sources'.[10] Such comments are an important reminder that it is rare for hostility to a minority group to be unrelieved. Indeed, the approach of Eveson and other 'local' police needs to be set alongside those in the same force who accused alien Jews of controlling the vice of London, so that the full complexity of relationships can be assessed. Some evidence of the type suggested by Fishman indicate a more ambiguous response by the East End police to the immigrants and their children. Bernard Kops recalled that 'We in the East End had no doubt that the police were loaded against us... I grew up with a healthy hatred for the law', concluding that it was 'excellent, at an early age, to differentiate between the police force and justice'. Nevertheless, there is evidence to suggest that familiarity more often than not brought the opposite of contempt.[11] There is little doubt, however, that the non-local Metropolitan Police are remembered by Jewish veterans of the 'Battle' for the vehemence of the anti-semitism which they expressed and enacted on the day itself and in subsequent proceedings.

At the 1980 Jewish East End conference, all those giving personal testimony in a workshop devoted to 'Anti-Semitism, Fascism and Anti-Fascism' were united regarding the hostile attitude of the police at the 'Battle'. One eyewitness suggested that 'the police were... very antisemitic and in his view there was some evidence of corruption by police officers to obtain convictions against Jews after Cable Street'. Others 'agreed that Jews felt victimised by the police' and 'that the police were not sympathetic to anti-Fascists'.[12]

Later oral testimony has provided frightening accounts of brutal police anti-semitism on 4 October 1936. One witness recalled three bus loads of police arriving in Commercial Road with some of those inside giving 'Hitler salutes' and shouting 'Jew bastards'.[13] Charlie Goodman was arrested and given a four month prison sentence. His friend, Jack Shaw, in explaining the violence and anti-semitic abuse they received at Leman Street station (ironically the same one occupied earlier by Thomas Eveson), put the blame firmly on police from outside the area:

> four policemen dragged me to Leman Street police station, my head went through the door and the shout was 'Another Jew bastard', and I have still got the scar on my head where I was given a belting. One of the old-time coppers was so shocked he dragged me away and he said 'keep quiet sonny, these bastards'll kill you'. He was so shocked at these plain-clothes boys from Lord Trenchard's school, from Hendon, and what they were doing. And Charlie was brought in the same time, and they nigh killed him. Blood flowed all over the floor and then they dragged him away, and then the late Georgie Peck, a docker, they were hitting him, calling him 'Jew bastard, you don't like Mosley', and they nearly killed him. And there was a Christian girl brought in, and it was 'You Jewish whore'.

It is not surprising that Shaw was anxious to 'put paid to the idea that the police were so great', adding 'they were pro-Mosley all the time'.[14] The reality was more complex, although there were undoubtedly individual police officers who were sympathetic to or members of the British Union of Fascists. But it is important to move beyond specific police attitudes towards the Mosleyites and onto the broader issue of their responses to the Jews as a whole during the 'devil's decade'.

In progressive police circles during the 1930s, most notably a group of men whom C. H. Rolph labelled the 'Turneymen' (after their mentor, Bob Turney), fascism and anti-semitism were anathema. Rolph himself, a Chief Inspector in the City of London police,

> always felt warmly pro-Jewish... I believe I can trace my feelings back to a time when I was a kind of self-appointed guardian of a small Jewish

Introduction 9

boy who was much persecuted, for no other reason than that he was a Jew [and] since that time I have hated anti-Semitism and 'Jew-baiting' with an intensity that sometimes startles even myself.[15]

The *New Statesman*-reading Turneymen and their fellow travellers, such as Rolph, were few in numbers, however – even if their very existence is an important reminder that generalisations about the ideological outlook of any organisation are inherently dangerous.[16] But an indication that the punishment meted out to individuals such as Charlie Goodman and Jack Shaw came out of a widespread culture within the police during the 1930s is provided in the unusually frank testimony of a retired officer reflecting half a century later, in Brighton, on the 'periods in my life when I've practised discrimination against a fellow human being':

> When I first joined the Metropolitan Police in London in 1934, anti-Semitism was rife at every level in the Force, and very soon I was as rabid[ly] anti-Jewish as the next officer. I was surrounded by it, and at twenty, vulnerable to the attitudes and opinions of men whom I subconsciously accepted as my superiors because of their age and experience. In 1948 I was posted to Willesden Green Police Station in North-West London, a predominantly Jewish district, where the High Street on a Saturday morning was as quiet as a funeral parlour, and on a Sunday, for obvious reasons, as busy and noisy as a Fair ground. My daily contact with Jews, plus the fact that I became more tolerant and maybe wiser, as I grew older, cured me of my anti-Semitism, a cure which has lasted to this day.

His postscript that 'I do hope anti-black feelings in the Police service in the 1980s have not taken over from [the] anti-Semitism of the 1930s. I do hope so', implies, by its repetition, the obvious answer.[17]

Thousands of police officers were on duty on 4 October 1936 but only fragments of testimony exist to give shape to their memories of the day. Of the three policemen interviewed in 1969 by the BBC's *Yesterday's Witness* documentary on the 'Battle' (sections of which were suppressed and never shown), 'their story was mostly one of waiting and confusion'.[18] A policeman commenting some 17 years later after this programme stated that he 'was at that time a PC on 'L' Div[ision] and like many others was drafted to the East End trouble spots practically every evening and Saturdays and Sundays all day. Being so long ago I cannot specifically remember Oct[ober] 4 1936 for most days and nights were the same down there, one street fight was the same as another.'[19] Another commented that he did not see the 'Battle' as a particularly important or significant event during the 1930s.[20] For the police as a whole, the fatigue brought about by the enormous extra duties in 1936, as well as the humiliations and injuries that were inflicted on them, made it not a day to remember in any detail or with any affection. Prejudicial and stereotyped attitudes may also have played their part in hindering police understanding that for others the day might have a special significance, and that fascism, for its opponents, was not just a movement 'pass[ing] in the night'. Instead, a rather crude reading of the conflicts during the 1930s was provided: 'Jews are a very industrious people and when people are industrious and they make money they create jealousy and [that's] why people were against them and so had sympathy with Mosley. It's as simple as that.'[21]

From the released files in the Public Record Office, we now have detailed evidence relating to the response of the police hierarchy to politicised anti-semitism, as analysed in this volume by Richard Thurlow. But what is needed to supplement this elite approach is detailed work on policing at all levels relating to the Jews of Britain in the pre-1939 era, confirming (or not) whether institutionalised racism – a specific and negative mode of behaviour towards a minority – existed against this particular ethnic group. It is possible, as the retired policeman from Brighton implied, that police antipathy has more recently shifted from one minority group to another. Some caution is, however, in order regarding the appropriateness of this analysis. First, it is frequently the case that discrimination can exist against more than one group at any one time. The small black communities of inter-war Britain, for example, faced intense police hostility. Evidence of local police empathy for the Jews was rarely replicated in the case of those of colour. The black communities in ports such as Cardiff were often regarded as a criminal entity *en masse,* whose presence the agents of the state tried, with some success, to remove.[22] Second, it is not clear when tensions between Jews and the police disappeared. In the immediate post-1945 period accusations of police bias against Jewish anti-fascists and of sympathy with those trying to revive Mosleyism were frequently made. There was also a strong feeling that the police were unwilling to take seriously physical assaults against Jews, unease that continued into the 1960s. In the late 1980s and early 1990s Jewish youth congregating outside London underground stations in the evenings led to friction with the police. These have been faint echoes of the major confrontations between the police and black youth in the post-war era and accusations that racially motivated crime is not taken seriously by the forces of law and order. Nevertheless, these post-war strains, as well as the tendency to draw upon the Jewishness of those accused of financial dishonesty, in scandals ranging from the Lynskey Tribunal of the 1940s through to the Guinness affair and most recently the downfall of Peter Mandelson, suggest that the proclivity to criminalise

Introduction

sections of the Jewish community has not yet abated. Glib assumptions that the British Jew is now 'one of us' and thus integrated into the mainstream of British society, including its legal enforcement agencies, need to be explored in a sceptical manner, requiring detailed research to discover what may, in fact, be a much more complex reality. There are, however, several other key areas in which the study of the 'Battle' may provide insights and a stimulus to further work.

Women and Children Last

The comments of the police dealing with an arrested female (non-Jewish) anti-fascist that she was a 'Jewish whore' illustrates that gender themes, as well as those of 'race', run through the 'Battle', shaping the experiences of the day and later representations of it. On a basic level, the involvement of women on 4 October 1936 needs further recognition. Recent scholarship has considered the role of women in fascist movements, including its British manifestations, and Julie Gottlieb's contribution in this collection adds further nuance and sophistication to this process of historicisation. But the involvement of women in anti-fascist activities, and their place in organisational structures, has received little or no attention.[23]

Writing fifty years later, Lady Janner, by then an esteemed member of the British Jewish establishment, explained her absence from the 'Battle' by suggesting that 'in those days women did not go into demonstrating crowds'.[24] Her remarks sparked furious correspondence in the columns of the *Jewish Chronicle*: Jeanne Freeman wrote that 'Numerous groups of women – and I was in the crowd – did demonstrate on that October day, so women *were* there to fight' and Hannah Grant pointed out that contemporary photographs told 'another story' to that of Lady Janner:

> I, with hundreds of other women, did demonstrate against the evils of fascism. Fortunately, there were enough of us, together with the men, to ensure that Mosley did not pass.[25]

The large scale presence of women prompted contemporary comment by those in authority responding to the day's events. Special Branch, in an attempt to downplay the significance and purpose of the anti-fascist turnout, issued a statement late on 4 October 1936 that 'A fascist assembly was held in the East End today, and largely owing to one of the finest days of the year, many people were attracted to it including a large number of women and children.'[26] In fact, Special Branch's own statistics of the day – that of 79 anti-fascists arrested, eight were women – confirm, as Jeanne Freeman and Hannah Grant suggested, that women, Jewish and non-Jewish, were there to ensure that the East End should be barred from the

Mosleyites.[27] Special Branch had their own reasons for denying that the organised anti-fascists, whom they saw as subversive radicals, had popular support. Their official statement was part of a general campaign to undermine the importance of the 'Battle', one which has had much success in influencing subsequent historians. But for their well-respected contemporaries in the Jewish establishment, the involvement of women, or more specifically, girls, on 4 October 1936 had to be taken seriously.

Rose Henriques, leader of the Oxford and St George's Girls Clubs and a major figure in the world of organisations for Jewish girls in the East End as a whole, was clearly alarmed at the attraction politics had for those under her control. Her attempt, after the 'Battle', to ensure the reputation of Jewish girls, is explored by Nadia Valman elsewhere in this volume. For Henriques 'Excessive painting of the face' was, in terms of respectability, as dangerous as communism. Indeed, the two were mutually reinforcing. The possibility of the forces of law and order screaming 'Jewish whore' at an arrested protestor would have been the realisation of Rose Henriques' worst nightmare.[28] It is the case, however, that in spite of the wealth of personal testimony concerning the 'Battle' there is little evidence relating to the involvement of women that day. It is an unfortunate lacuna, and makes it hard to tease out further whether the passivity suggested by Special Branch or the militancy feared by Henriques was the more accurate analysis.

It is ironic that later patriarchal tendencies within the Communist Party should be partly responsible for the marginalisation of women at the 'Battle'. At the time the role of women as anti-fascist fighters was at the forefront of Communist propaganda. Its leaflet advertising the march first in solidarity with the Republican cause, and then amended to 'answer Mosley's provocation', depicted a young woman, alongside a man, loading a rifle behind the barricades.[29] The slogan of 4 October 1936, 'They Shall Not Pass!', was that of the legendary Spanish female Communist Deputy, 'La Passionara', or Dolores Ibarruri. Moreover, the *Daily Worker*'s tribute to the day, published on 6 October 1936, showed, through sketches and photographs, women proudly marching and joining the barricades.[30] Yet in subsequent Communist writing, especially the testimony which became the most dominant of the 'Battle' – that of Phil Piratin – the role of women, and of individuals more generally, became lost in the dominant political narrative.

The military style of Piratin's account is dissected in Kushner's contribution to this volume. Here it is important to highlight the gender implications of Piratin's description, first published in 1948, particularly relating to the events at Cable Street itself and the involvement of 'the lads'. Piratin's repeated use of this term is such that he glossed it himself:

Cable Street was a great scene. I have referred to 'the lads'. Never was there such unity of all sections of the working class as was seen on the barricades at Cable Street. People whose lives were poles apart, though living within a few hundred yards of each other; bearded Orthodox Jews and rough-and-ready Irish Catholic dockers – these were the workers that the fascists were trying to stir up against each other.[31]

Piratin did not totally ignore the role of women in the demonstration, but limited it to one sentence and also confined it within the domestic sphere: 'Some of the housewives began to drop milk bottles from the roof tops [on the police]'.[32] In later Communist accounts, as the Party attempted to re-establish its credibility as a respectable, British movement, its actions on 4 October 1936 were re-written within a patriarchal framework – they were necessary to defend women and children from the evils of fascism. Subsequent artistic interpretations of the 'Battle', especially in literature (like Simon Blumenfeld's *The Battle of Cable Street*, included in this volume), have attempted to reinstate the importance of women as activists on the street, although the striking mural in Cable Street itself is male-dominated with women largely in the background and, following Piratin's account, largely limited to the domestic arena. The most powerful gender-related influence of Piratin's narrative, however, has been in shaping oral and written testimony of 4 October.

The autobiography/memoir of Sylvia Scaffardi provides one of the few printed accounts by women of 4 October 1936. It is frustrating, however, that her own experiences, along with her partner, Ronald Kidd (secretary of the National Council for Civil Liberties during the 1930s) are abandoned early in the text in favour of the story as 'told from the inside by Phil Piratin'. Her experiences of the day were not particularly heroic, but they were, perhaps, typical of many. Scaffardi and Kidd initially overslept on the Sunday morning, worn out by their constant monitoring of the stream of public demonstrations and meetings in the summer of 1936. Nevertheless, Scaffardi was determined to witness and observe the threatened march: 'My impatient vehemence, my repulsion at the daily diet of injustice, clamoured for cries of rage, anger at the turpitude of the times.' They made for the fascist rallying point as this was normally where trouble manifested itself but this time they were wrong: 'We found ourselves impacted into a police enclave, a static scene dominated and controlled by officialdom.'[33] By the time Scaffardi and Kidd reached Gardiner's Corner, the huge crowds were beginning to disperse and her account switches from autobiographical reflections to the impersonal, triumphalist and macho narrative of Piratin.

The testimony of Joyce Goodman is similarly constructed to tell us more of male involvement than of her own. Joyce, who went to Gardiner's Corner with her friend, was only twelve years old at the time of the 'Battle', and it left a deep impact on her:

> It has been described as non-violent, but I did not find it so. The violence was not coming from us, it is true we went there as peaceful demonstrators, but for two young girls it was an absolute terror. The police first tried just to clear the roadway so that the traffic could get through. They were pushing us on to Gardiner's windows, there were people going straight through the plate glass windows… We never saw a fascist all that day, we never fought with the fascists. You were fighting the police. They were just hitting everyone, there were women going down under the horses' hooves. Absolute terror.[34]

It is, however, the connection to her husband, Charlie Goodman, perhaps next to Phil Piratin the most famous 'veteran' of Cable Street, that is the central focus of her narrative. The two met later with, she remembers, one of his first questions being 'Where were you on October 4th?' It was Charlie's role in climbing a lamp post and shouting at the police, which Joyce recalled from the day itself, that is at the heart of her account.[35]

A third female testimony that, yet again, only provides tantalising glimpses of personal experiences and then rests on the involvement of men was provided by Bertha Sokoloff, later secretary of the Stepney Communist Party and a local councillor in the district, in her biography of Edith Ramsay:

> Every East Ender has his memories of that October 4th, 1936. Whenever I read of great upsurges in other countries, I think of the excitement and determination of the people at Aldgate on that day, the feeling of not knowing exactly where the action is, being part of the throng, frightened and yet exhilarated. Above all, the picture I remember is of earlier in the day, when I left home to go west towards Aldgate – it was the men, young and middle-aged, men who one could tell had probably never demonstrated before, moving out in ones and twos, little groups of neighbours, seriously and purposefully.[36]

Scaffardi, Goodman and Sokoloff all had close links to the Communist Party. Testimony from women not linked to the extreme left are even rarer, with only brief snippets in the public domain. Women played a key role in the anti-fascist actions of 4 October 1936 but subsequent gendered constructions of the day, including from the female participants themselves, have undermined the significance of their contribution and the impact this may have had on their future self-confidence in the public

Introduction

and private domain. More generally, this omission raises questions of the broader involvement of Jewish women in communal, local, national and international politics. The intervention of Rose Henriques revealed clearly that female solidarity in the Jewish community had its limits. Her futile attempts to depoliticise and domesticate the Jewish 'girls' in her clubs reveal the dynamic and contested versions of Englishness being fought out in the worlds of Jewish women in inter-war Britain. Nevertheless, in subsequent historiography Rose Henriques has shared the fate of those whose lives she tried to shape in the East End – at best, marginality and more frequently, total obscurity. The 'Battle', as privileged but radical British Jewish history, has not managed to shake off a bias towards the experience of men. The same is true, largely, of issues relating to the age and identity of those who took part on 4 October 1936.

Benjamin Lammers has suggested that 'Politics was [one of the most important areas] which helped to construct the new form of English-Jewish identity, and this was most vividly demonstrated at the Battle of Cable Street. On October 4, 1936, young Jews confronted both the fascists and the Metropolitan Police in order to defend their place in the nation.' Although not ignoring the role of older East End Jews, Lammers sees the greater significance of the day as resting with the younger generation: 'By focusing on such a defiant and assertive action, young Jews demonstrated their rejection of the passive, almost hidden, Jewishness favored by the Anglo-Jewish elite. By stressing an event noted for its diverse participant base, they also demonstrated their vision of an inclusive Englishness.'[37]

Lammers' contribution is to be greatly welcomed in an area of research (identity) and chronology (the post-1918 period) largely absent in existing British Jewish historiography. A more inclusive interpretation of the correlation between age, ethnicity and identity could, however, be offered which, whilst not undermining the importance the day had for the younger participants, would tentatively suggest that it marked a decisive moment in the sense of belonging of adult Jews in the East End. The presence of the very young on 4 October 1936 (including the fascists – one ex-BUF member recalls that there were 'some 300 children, some as young as ten, [who] were lined up in the road outside the Tower of London and as far back as the Monument') has received almost no attention by historians although, as with the participation of women, early representations of the 'Battle' stressed their presence.[38] On the anti-fascist side, some, such as the four-year-old Arnold Wesker, later to write the most important literary work incorporating the 'Battle', were, at the time, 'aware of nothing'.[39] But its influence was great on Bernard Kops, also to emerge as a major literary figure during the 1950s, who was six years older than Wesker. Kops was bewildered by the sheer chaos and violence of the 'Battle' but ultimately exhilarated by the 'victory':

> From my small height I could see marbles being thrown under the hooves of the horses, and horses going over, and I could hear people screaming and shouting, and the terrible urgency of fire engines and ambulances...
>
> 'They shall not pass! They shall not pass!' Over and over again. And they did not pass. That was the beginning of the end of Sir Oswald Mosley and his under-privileged boys.
>
> 'But who stopped them? Who stopped them?' I kept asking my father on the way home.
>
> 'The dockers did,' he replied proudly. 'It was the dockers.'
>
> I had seen many dockers on my walks past St George's Docks and East India Docks.
>
> 'But dockers aren't Jewish, dad, are they? I mean, Jews are tailors and furriers, aren't they?'
>
> My father agreed.
>
> 'But I thought you said the world was divided between Jews and Jew-haters?'
>
> I asked the question twice, and he seemed confused. I felt sorry for him – and very, very pleased with myself. Not for my question, but because of the events of that day.[40]

The testimony of Joyce Goodman, just two years older than Kops, highlights the enforced political maturity of many in the area: 'if you were a youngster brought up in the East End in the 1930s you were no stranger to politics because there were political meetings on every corner... If you were a Jewish kid and you stood there listening to [the fascists] belting out their message of hate, you learned to hate back, because you heard of all the attacks in the East End.' As we have seen, Joyce and her friend decided to be part of the 'human wall' at Gardiner's Corner. It was a seminal moment in her young life, providing a foundation for a life of activism in the trade union, tenement and anti-racist movements: 'We stood there all that day, and I can remember that as young kids we were very proud that we had taken part in that demonstration.'[41]

For those brought up in Communist Party families or for young people joining the movement in the 1930s, memories of the 'Battle' were a crucial part of political and personal identities. But it is perhaps too tempting to overstate the significance of 4 October 1936 for the younger generation. In the years immediately after 1945, for example, those young and militant Jews in the '43 Group' fighting the neo-fascists referred to the war and to the Jewish catastrophe (as well as Jewish resistance in the

Introduction

Warsaw ghetto revolt) rather than to the 'Battle' as a usable past. Significantly the rare references to 4 October 1936 in the 43 Group were to praise the efforts of an older generation of anti-fascists. Not until the 1970s was there a widespread rediscovery of the 'Battle' and a bringing together of various generations of anti-fascists.

The dominant interpretation of the 1930s was that, for the first time, Jewish passivity was being challenged, as stated eloquently in the memoirs of Leonard Sanitt:

> We were the first generation who were taught to stand up and fight for ourselves. Our parents and families in Eastern Europe had to learn that it was wiser to bend with the wind in order to survive. We were the first generation brought up in a free society, instilled with the English traditions and spirit which formed our characters. This was most severely tested during the period of Oswald Mosley and his blackshirt thugs in the East End of London. We resolved that under no circumstances would we allow Fascists and their propaganda, together with their insults and attacks, to come along to our community where our people were living and working in peace... We were adamant that we were going to stand and fight – and we succeeded.[42]

Similarly, Cyril Spector, born in 1921, considered that his parents 'felt they were still visitors. They had to keep quiet in order to stay. What they were haunted with was the memory of the pogroms in Eastern Europe.'[43]

In parliamentary and press discussion in the weeks following 4 October, the 'paranoia' of older East End Jews was put down to such memories. Edith Ramsay continued this tradition in her contribution to the *Yesterday's Witness* documentary shown in 1970, which acted as a focal point in the revival of interest on the 'Battle'. Ramsay was on her way to a Sunday School and she 'had to go round backyards by Brunswick Buildings':

> and there sitting on an old box was an old Jewish woman with her wig all askew and I tapped her on the shoulder and said 'Oh Granny, granny, it is all right. It can't happen, don't worry.' And she said to me 'Oh lady, lady, I have seen it in Poland. It is coming here.'[44]

There were, however, different memories of eastern Europe that were at play for an older generation during the 1930s – that of Jewish militancy and self-defence against anti-semitism. Those in the Workers' Circle, for example, an organisation of great importance in mobilising popular response at the 'Battle', were heavily influenced by the Communist, Bundist and anarchist traditions that were brought by east European Jews westwards at the turn of the century. The memory of persecution was powerful for some. But its extent was probably exaggerated by contemporaries who wanted to downplay the reality of BUF anti-semitism, and distorted in later autobiographical writings of the younger generation anxious to explain tension with their parents' generation – as has been suggested, many Jews came to Britain at the turn of the century from parts of eastern Europe where there was an absence of pogroms.[45] Yet for other older Jews in the East End, the fact that they had experienced 'the real thing' helped provide a different perspective on the threat posed by the Mosleyites. As the Jewish East End writer Willy Goldman, describing responses to inter-war anti-semitism, put it: 'We children took it less philosophically. We hadn't the memory of Tsarist pogroms to help us appreciate the comparative harmlessness of the current attacks. We felt ourselves English and outraged.' But for other young Jews, as David Mazower's contribution to this volume makes clear, a lack of confidence in the future for Jews anywhere in the world, including Britain, was a powerful factor in shaping their identities and day to day concerns.[46]

For those older Jews who were less politicised, 4 October 1936 was important, as for Bernard Kops' father, in showing them that they were not isolated and that public protest could bring success. As Bertha Sokoloff wrote of the adult males present: 'There was no mistaking their grim determination, Mosley was that day to be denied the streets of Stepney.'[47] Returning to Kops' father, the presence of the dockers helping the Jews, which so surprised him, is explained in inter-generational terms by Bill Fishman. Fishman's account may have a romantic tinge, but it provides an important reminder that, by the time of the 'Battle', a large proportion of the original generation of east European immigrants had been present in the East End for the majority of their lives. Fishman describes the help given to the striking dockers in the East End in 1912 and its long term consequences:

> Dockers, trade unionists and social workers spoke of the warmth and hospitality shown to their unfortunate charges [of dockers' families] by East End Jews... Over three hundred children were taken into Jewish homes. Such action was in accord with [Rudolph] Rocker's [the non-Jewish leader of the Jewish anarchist movement] aim of bringing about a more congenial relationship between Jewish and Gentile workers, and in this instance, it laid the foundations of many friendships which neither time nor circumstance could erase. The dockland slogan, 'No Jews allowed down Wapping', might persist. But it was the dockers of Wapping and St George's who constituted the militant vanguard of the movement which, in 1936, forcibly prevented the Mosleyite incursions into East London.[48]

Introduction

It is perhaps wisest to conclude at this stage that Jews of all ages facing the fascist threat in the East End and elsewhere in Britain did so with a mixture on the one hand of fear (even terror, especially in the months before and after the 'Battle' when BUF anti-semitism was most intensive) and insecurity and, on the other, of excitement and growing self-confidence. Generalisations in this area of study must take account of the fact that the generational structure of the inter-war Jewish community was complex. Aside from the nucleus of the old established Anglo-Jewish community and the more recently-arrived refugees from Nazism, there was the fast disappearing generation of immigrants who had come as adults before 1914 and their children who, even if born in eastern Europe, had few memories of it, or were born in Britain itself. Much more detailed and precise work is required on all these groups, taking account of age, gender and politics, but also acknowledging the importance of place in the formation of personal and collective identity.

Geography and Identity

It is not surprising that establishment Jewish historiography, in its nervous attempt at proving Jewish loyalty to the nation, failed to stress the global affinities of Jews in Britain. Such defensive tendencies are not limited to the Jewish community. In its *Roots of the Future: Ethnic Diversity in the Making of Britain* (1996), the Commission for Racial Equality highlights the contribution made to Britain by immigrant and minority groups in the past and present. That many of those featured were and are still part of diaspora communities is glossed over.[49] Yet even within recent writing on British Jewry from a new generation of scholars, place identity has featured little. 'The Battle of Cable Street' presents an example of the potential of incorporating geographical perspectives on identity. First, the 'Battle' was very much part of a struggle for local belonging. Whatever their differences and lingering prejudices, as Bill Fishman argues, Jew and non-Jew combined to stop the 'alien' fascists passing through 'their' territory. Second, it was a significantly national day of action – anti-fascists gathered from across the country, including from within the provincial Jewish communities. Third, 4 October 1936 for the Jews was part of a wider network of international struggles. Most obviously, it was connected to the Spanish Civil War (and to a much lesser extent other anti-fascist struggles in countries such as France).[50] But it was also a way of identifying, if at one remove, with the persecuted Jews of Nazi Germany. By their radicalism, Jews were fighting back against the global menace of fascism. Jews in Britain may have identified particularly with the East End and other areas of mass settlement, but, as Doreen Massey writes, '"local uniqueness" is always already a product of wider contacts; the local is always already a product of "global" forces'.[51]

Moving beyond the specific context of the 1930s, we need to explore further the relationship between the place of origin and the place of settlement for immigrant Jews in Britain from the medieval period to the present – Jews who have come from almost all parts of the globe. What did the concept of 'home' mean to them? Was it contested and how did it evolve? Such knowledge is also important for our understanding of these immigrants' descendants. To the Jewish observer William Zukerman, writing in a somewhat apologetic vein a few months after the 'Battle': 'The truth is that what goes under the name of the East End Jew is in reality no specific Jewish type at all. It is but the general East End London Labour type with which the young East End Jew has assimilated so thoroughly that it is difficult to differentiate the two.'[52] Much more research is needed on the East End and other areas of mass Jewish concentration to tease out the accuracy of such assumptions.

The attention devoted to the Jewish East End has been to the detriment of Jewish settlements elsewhere in London and in the provinces. In this sense, the focus on the 'Battle' has had a negative impact, excluding other fascist/anti-fascist struggles across Britain. As David Cesarani suggests:

> The problem was not just in London: the same thing was happening in Leeds and Manchester. It should be remembered that the rioting in East London was preceded by rioting in Leeds, on Holbeck Moor, which was just as nasty in its own way – in fact far more bloody than what occurred in Cable Street ... That was one of the things which inspired a dread of what was going to happen in [the East End].[53]

In the next largest concentration of Jewish settlement, Glasgow, there was also extreme anti-semitism in the form of Mosleyites but also extreme Protestantism, especially Alexander Ratcliffe's Scottish Protestant League.[54] It remains the case, however, in spite of the recent extensive work on anti-semitism in Britain that, aside from in its organised form, we still know very little about local cultures and their construction of the 'Jew'. It is also true that local traditions of anti-fascism and anti-racism remain largely neglected. Such work, however, if it is carried out, will need to take on the advice of the anthropologist Clifford Geertz: 'We need, in the end, something rather more than local knowledge. We need a way of turning its varieties into commentaries upon another, the one lighting what the other darkens.'[55]

TONY KUSHNER AND NADIA VALMAN

Introduction

NOTES

1. Leah Chapman, a PhD student at the University of Southampton, is exploring these issues further from a comparative perspective.
2. David Cesarani, 'Dual Heritage or Duel of Heritages? Englishness and Jewishness in the Heritage Industry', in Tony Kushner (ed.), *The Jewish Heritage in British History* (London: Frank Cass, 1992), p.30.
3. Ibid, p.37.
4. Aubrey Newman (ed.), *The Jewish East End 1840-1939* (London: Jewish Historical Society of England, 1981), pp.309-10 in a panel discussing 'Anti-Semitism, Fascism and Anti-Fascism'; Harriet Karsh, 'The Jewish East End Project', loc.cit., pp.323-6.
5. Newman, 'Introduction', in *The Jewish East End* (see note 4), p.ix.
6. Colin Holmes, 'East End Crime and the Jewish Community, 1887-1911', in Newman, *The Jewish East End*, ibid, p.109; Bill Williams has been carrying out a long term project on Jewish marginality in Manchester based on oral history evidence.
7. Holmes, 'East End Crime' (see note 6), p.109. Bryan Cheyette was present at the Jewish East End conference. For Cheyette's later work, which provides a model of the research that needs to be carried out, see his *Constructions of 'the Jew' in English Literature and Society;. Racial Representations 1875-1945* (Cambridge: Cambridge University Press, 1993).
8. Joyce Weiner, 'Inspector Thomas Eveson', in Newman, *The Jewish East End* (see note 4), p.349.
9. Ibid.
10. William Fishman, 'A People's Journée: The Battle of Cable Street (October 4th 1936)', in Frederick Krantz (ed), *History from Below: Studies in Popular Protest and Popular Ideology in Honour of George Rudé* (Montreal: Concordia University Press, 1985), p.391.
11. See, for example, Ralph Finn, *No Tears in Aldgate* (London: Robert Hale, 1963), p.121 which refers to petty police corruption in seeking bribes from Jewish market stall owners; Bernard Kops, *The World is a Wedding* (London: Vallentine Mitchell, 1963), p.37.
12. In Newman, *The Jewish East End* (see note 4), pp.309-10.
13. Testimony in *The Red and the Black*, Radio 4, 4 March 1994.
14. For Charlie Goodman's testimony in relation to the police, see 'Cable Street: 60th Anniversary Reminiscences' (Marx Memorial Library video, 1996); Shaw testimony in 'The Battle of Cable Street: Witness Seminar', *Contemporary Record* 8:1 (Summer 1994), pp.129.
15. C. H. Rolph, *Further Particulars* (Oxford: Oxford University Press, 1987), p.112.
16. C. H. Rolph, *Living Twice* (London: Victor Gollancz, 1974), chapter 5.
17. Mass-Observation Archive: Spring 1990, DR 1389, University of Sussex.
18. Michael Rabiger, video on the making of the documentary in the possession of Tony Kushner.
19. R. Lymon, letter of 8 April 1986, in London Museum of Jewish Life, 61-1987/7.
20. David Fox, interview in London Museum of Jewish Life, 61-1987/4.
21. Ibid.
22. See Neil Evans, 'Regulating the Reserve Army: Arabs, Blacks and the Local State in Cardiff, 1919-45', *Immigrants and Minorities* 4 (July 1985), pp.68-106.
23. See the brief coverage in Pamela Graves, *Labour Women: Women in British Working-Class Politics 1918-1939* (Cambridge: Cambridge University Press: 1994), pp.209-11.
24. *Jewish Chronicle*, 3 October 1986.
25. Letters in *Jewish Chronicle*, 17 October 1986.
26. Sylvia Scaffardi, *Fire Under the Carpet: Working for Civil Liberties in the 1930s* (London: Lawrence and Wishart, 1986), p.159.
27. Special Branch report, 4 October 1936, in PRO MEPO 3/551.
28. See her guidelines and related correspondence in MS 60/17/16, University of Southampton archives.
29. 'All out against Fascism', leaflet in Communist Party archives, National Labour Museum.
30. *Daily Worker*, 6 October 1936.
31. Phil Piratin, *Our Flag Stays Red* (London: Lawrence and Wishart, 1978 edition), pp.23-4.
32. Ibid., p.23.

33. Scaffardi (see note 26), pp.154-6.
34. Joyce Goodman testimony in 'The Battle of Cable Street', *Contemporary Record* 8:1 (Summer 1994), p.127, reproduced in part in The Cable Street Group, *The Battle of Cable Street 1936* (London: Cable Street Group, 1995).
35. Ibid, pp.127-8.
36. Bertha Sokoloff, *Edith and Stepney: The Life of Edith Ramsay* (London: Stepney Books, 1987), p.82.
37. Benjamin Lammers, '"A Superior Kind of English": Jewish Ethnicity and English Identity in London's East End' (unpublished PhD dissertation, Rutgers University, 1997), chapter 6, esp. pp.318-20, 324.
38. Len Wise, testimony in 'The Battle of Cable Street', *Contemporary* Record 8:1 (Summer 1994), p.117; *Daily Worker*, 6 October 1936 has a sketch with a child defiantly behind a barricade.
39. Arnold Wesker, *As Much As I Dare* (London: Century, 1994), p.497.
40. Kops (see note 11), p.38.
41. Goodman testimony in 'The Battle of Cable Street' (see note 34), pp.127-8.
42. Leonard Sanitt, *On Parade: Memoirs of a Jewish Sergeant-Major in World War II* (Stevenage, Herts: Spa Books, 1990), pp.53-4.
43. Cyril Spector, *Volla Volla Jew Boy* (London: Centerprise, 1988), p.49.
44. Transcript of 'The Battle of Cable Street', broadcast on 4 January 1970, BBC, in Tower Hamlets Local History Library.
45. David Cesarani, 'The Myth of Origins: Ethnic Memory and the Experience of Migration' in Aubrey Newman and Stephen Massil (eds), *Patterns of Migration, 1850-1914* (London: Jewish Historical Society of England, 1996), pp.247-54.
46. Jack Pearce, 'The Fascist Threat', in *The Circle Golden Jubilee 1909-1959* (London: Workers' Circle Friendly Society, 1959), pp.20-1; Willy Goldman, *East End My Cradle: Portrait of an Environment* (London: Robson Books, 1988 edition, originally published in 1940).
47. Sokoloff (see note 36), p.82.
48. William Fishman, *East End Jewish Radicals 1875-1914* (London: Duckworth, 1975), p.300.
49. Mayerlene Frow, *Roots of the Future: Ethnic Diversity in the Making of Britain* (London: Commission for Racial Equality, 1996).
50. Julian Jackson, *The Popular Front in France: Defending Democracy 1934-38* (Cambridge: Cambridge University Press; 1988), chapter 9.
51. Doreen Massey, 'Places and Their Pasts', *History Workshop Journal* 39 (Spring 1995), p.183.
52. William Zukerman, *The Jew in Revolt* (London: Martin Secker and Warburg, 1937), pp.72-3.
53. David Cesarani in 'The Battle of Cable Street' *Contemporary Record* 8:1 (Summer 1994), p.124.
54. Colin Holmes, 'Alexander Ratcliffe: Militant Protestant and Antisemite' in Tony Kushner and Kenneth Lunn (eds), *Traditions of Intolerance: Historical Perspectives on Fascism and Race Discourse in Britain* (Manchester: Manchester University Press, 1989), pp.196-217; Henry Maitles, 'Confronting Fascism: attitudes of the Glasgow Jewish community in the 1930', *Local History* 27:2 (May 1997), pp.106-117.
55. Clifford Geertz, *Local Knowledge* (London: Fontana, 1993), p.233.

Fascist Perceptions of Cable Street

THOMAS P. LINEHAN

On 4 October 1936 a large anti-fascist gathering physically obstructed Oswald Mosley's attempt to conduct a series of propaganda marches in the East End to celebrate the fourth anniversary of the foundation of his fascist party, the British Union of Fascists. The popular local interpretation of the 'Cable Street' events, and one that surfaces in much of the historical literature on British fascism, suggests that this mobilisation represented a major victory for the anti-fascist forces, the repercussions of which irreversibly damaged Mosley's political campaign in east London.[1] This interpretation requires some qualification. Contrary to the above view, the immediate portents for the BUF following the 4 October affair were extremely favourable.

In the following week, the Mosleyites held their most successful series of propaganda meetings since the BUF's inception.[2] Audiences estimated in the several thousands attended BUF meetings in Stepney, Shoreditch, Bethnal Green and Stoke Newington.[3] Just as significant was the mood of these audiences, which was enthusiastic and manifestly pro-fascist in orientation. The BUF's membership also increased substantially immediately subsequent to the Cable Street affair. A police report confirmed that in the following three weeks the BUF's 'London Command' enrolled 2,000 new members, the majority recruited by its East End branches.[4]

Oral evidence also supports these Special Branch figures. The former Bethnal Green North East District Leader recalled that members 'poured in' to his branch after the disturbance, while the former District Leader of Limehouse Branch remembered that as a result of the Cable Street backlash, the branch enrolled '800 odd members in the next two weeks'.[5] We have a contemporary figure for this latter branch. Based on an inspection of a book register of members for Limehouse Branch, a November 1937 Special Branch report stated that a total of 1,700 individuals were listed as members.[6] Although the report also stated 'that it is certain that a great number of these have ceased to be members long ago', the figure probably reflects the rapid influx of 'Cable Street fascists' into the branch, thus supporting the oral evidence provided by its former

District Leader. Both the written and oral evidence suggests, therefore, that contrary to much of the prevailing wisdom on this subject, the BUF profited significantly from the Cable Street events in terms of its East End recruitment. The question that we need to address is: how did the BUF bring about this impressive upsurge in support in the wake of the physical defeat of 4 October? The first explanation for this, and what proved an irony of Cable Street, is that the anti-fascist mobilisation, rather than driving Mosley out of the East End, had the effect of intensifying his activities in this area. Wounded by the 4 October reversal, Mosley felt obliged to take up the challenge posed by 'Red Terror', 'Jewry', 'lawless anarchy' and all the other forces he imagined were behind the anti-fascist mobilisation. This resulted in the diverting of the greater part of his resources to the East End, a propaganda effort that produced the impressive recruitment gains outlined above and which culminated in the BUF's substantial electoral returns at the March 1937 London County Council elections, when it attained 23 per cent of the vote in Bethnal Green North East, 16 per cent in Limehouse and 14 per cent in Shoreditch.[7] The potentially damaging effects of this accelerating development in the direction of east London in terms of the BUF's national profile was noted early; a 17 October editorial in the Mosleyite press was at pains to reassure its other regional formations that they had no less an important role to play than their East End comrades in the building of fascism in Britain.[8]

However, in order to re-enter the East End after the 4 October set-back, and thus continue its campaign there with confidence, the BUF had first to challenge and undermine the emerging anti-fascist interpretation of Cable Street, and subvert its political and moral message. This meant that the authenticity of the Cable Street gathering had to be denied, and its moral credibility stripped away. Any claims to nobility, heroism and virtue that the Cable Street crowd might have had were to be ruthlessly renounced. This process of deconstruction was to be underwritten by a partial and biased perception of the Cable Street gathering which, in many cases, drew on a stock of representations of the role of the *crowd* in recent history. The anti-fascist emphasis on the moral grandeur of the Cable Street crowd – the crowd as the embodiment of virtue and decency – was to be replaced by a notion of the crowd as essentially *negative* and *destructive*.

At one level the Cable Street crowd was maligned by the BUF as an illegitimate expression of subversive political forces that challenged the authority of government and the rule of law. This notion of the crowd as *political*, as an instrument of political sedition seeking to undermine the State was a common theme in Mosleyite Cable Street propaganda. The prominent fascist, William Joyce, deplored the 'campaign of incitement' to defeat the law on 4 October and the insidious attempt 'to thrust the Home Office into the mud of humiliation'.[9] Joyce foresaw a disturbing future if these seditious trends were not checked, commenting that 'the mob which demanded the head of Mosley' on 4 October 'will demand the head of our Monarch should opportunity arise'.[10] John Beckett, another leading BUF official, was equally alarmed. Pointing out that 'the Communist Party's chief revolutionary tactic is to mass the workers on the streets for street fighting', he suggested that the 4 October anti-fascist mobilisation was 'used by the Communist Party as a revolutionary dress rehearsal'.[11] This is Taine's revolutionary crowd, the spectre of the Bastille mob that had haunted European conservatives since 1789, the crowd with latent revolutionary designs that presaged a horrible future of insurrectionary violence and bloodshed, and the eventual overthrow of order and decency.[12] The BUF's message to its East End supporters, and the Government, was clear. The Cable Street 'mob riot' was a portent of a far greater convulsion to come, unless the forces of 'order and decency' mobilised to avert the threat.

This perception of the Cable Street crowd as *political* and *subversive* had another dimension. The crowd was also imagined as the agent of powerful outside forces. Conspiracy theory explanations were brought to bear. The opposition to Mosley's march was of such intensity that William Joyce wondered whether the whole affair was orchestrated by 'the combined resources of Jewish Finance and Muscovite subversion'.[13] The spectre of 'Moscow gold' and 'Jewish Finance' was also raised by other Mosleyites. John Beckett proclaimed that the Communist Party, boosted by 'large sums' arriving 'specially from Moscow for this purpose', 'poured out money in an endless stream', while 'prominent Jews' also donated 'large sums'.[14]

The notion of the 4 October crowd as political and subversive was also utilised to undermine the anti-fascist contention that the 'East End' had risen spontaneously against Mosley. The 'stream of gold' from wealthy subversive external sources was utilised, according to Beckett, to import 'anything up to 10,000 hooligans' from 'every industrial town in the country' into Aldgate, where they then joined forces with 'anti-patriotic' local Jewish youths.[15] The unrepresentative nature of the Cable Street gathering was to become a recurring theme in Mosleyite discourse. Oswald Mosley informed his pro-fascist audience at Salmon Lane, Limehouse, ten days after Cable Street, of the 'Red army mobilised from all over Britain' who were 'brought into East London' on 4 October.[16] This was to become an enduring feature of the Mosleyite memory of Cable Street. The oral testimony of a former Hackney Mosleyite contained the recollection that 'Cable Street was not the people of the East End. It was the people from Manchester ... Glasgow ... from all over the country! And it was all paid for by the big Jews.'[17]

If the BUF's *political* crowd had a rational project, a set of clear political objectives and goals, at another level the Cable Street crowd was perceived by the Mosleyites to be dangerously *irrational*. This notion of the crowd as a descent into primitive barbarism, a 'regression to an animal past', was to underwrite much of the BUF's perception of the crowd's activities on 4 October. The idea of the crowd as essentially a primitive collective phenomenon has its origins in late nineteenth and early twentieth century psychological theories of crowd mentality that we find in the work of the French crowd theorist Gustave Le Bon, and in the writings of Freud on group psychology.[18] According to these pessimistic theories of crowd behaviour, the individual, on entering the crowd, dissolves into the undifferentiated uncultivated mass, shedding his reason and conscious personality and giving himself over completely to the collective or group mind. A crucial characteristic of the irrational group mind, driven as it supposedly is by repressed desires emanating from the unconscious, is a propensity to destruction and *violence*. It is also infantile, impulsive, and extremely vulnerable to the power of suggestion.

A 'descent into primitive barbarism', and particularly the inclination to violence, was an integral feature of the Cable Street 'mob' for the BUF. For one fascist, writing in the BUF press, the Cable Street crowd, 'inspired and infuriated' by Jewish agitators, was a 'motley rabble armed with improvised weapons and amenable to no other discipline than the herd instinct'.[19] Another correspondent contrasted the order and discipline of the Blackshirt ranks assembled at Royal Mint Street with the 'howling, yelling, sadistic mob' that opposed them, while A. K. Chesterton, a senior BUF official, referred to 'the insensate mobs of Red terrorists' of 4 October who 'seek everywhere in the world to overthrow civilisation'.[20] The violence of the Cable Street affair particularly outraged the BUF. It was perceived to transcend the boundaries of legitimate political and moral behaviour. On occasions the perception of the violence took on exaggerated proportions. A BUF editorial wrote of the 'daggers, bombs, pieces of wood studded with rusty nails, chair legs wrapped round with barbed wire, razor blades', and 'every device of the gutter and ghetto' used 'against a procession of unarmed men'.[21] A vein of intense moral indignation underpins this perception. The rhetoric of moral outrage was to become a core element in the BUF's denunciation of the Cable Street crowd.

The crowd as 'regression to an animal past', or journey into primitive barbarism, overlapped with another negative Mosleyite depiction of the

Cable Street crowd: the crowd as descent into criminality. One BUF writer referred to the 'gangsters and razor slashers' in the 4 October gathering, while another stated that the people imported into East London by the Communists that day were 'thugs and hooligans, cut-throats and razor slashers'.[22] For the Mosleyites, it was 'gangsters armed with truncheons and chair legs' who waylaid their 'heroic' Blackshirt comrade, 'Tommy' Moran, as he attempted to make his way to the BUF column assembled at Royal Mint Street.[23] The alleged criminal character of the Cable Street 'mob' was shared by many on the conservative and fascist right. In a letter to the pro-fascist journal *The Patriot*, a Mosleyite sympathiser was convinced that a sizeable section of the 4 October 'mob' was composed of the 'hooligan, criminal or corner-boy', while another believed that the opposition in the East End to Mosley's march was a 'sign of the degraded condition' of its inhabitants.[24]

The latter view that urban centres harboured and nourished a degraded criminal element who could be utilised by the forces of political sedition and anarchy was a phobia of the far right. For Viscount Lymington, an associate of John Beckett and other prominent fascists in the pro-Nazi *The New Pioneer*, there was a 'scum of subhuman population' in 'every great city' that was 'willing to take any chance of a breakdown in law and order'. Having 'neither respect for property or persons, they are the willing tools of the communist, since revolution means an opportunity to gratify their lusts'.[25] The alleged criminal composition of the Cable Street gathering was to become another enduring theme in the Mosleyite memory of 4 October, a recent Mosleyite newsletter referring to the 'nucleus of Soho and Stepney gangsters' in the anti-fascist 'mob'.[26]

The moral credibility of the Cable Street gathering could be denied through other discursive processes. Alongside the idea of the crowd as the expression of subversive political forces or a psychopathological phenomenon harbouring degraded criminal elements, we also have the crowd, or more aptly the 'mob', as *metaphor*. John Carey has noted that for many twentieth century intellectuals, the deployment of the term 'masses' to describe the people who comprised twentieth century society often reflected a profound contempt for ordinary persons.[27] Moreover, the 'masses', because the term was 'a metaphor for the unknowable and invisible', a blanket expression that ignored and disregarded the rich diversity of modern life, and as such did not exist in reality, served to deny ordinary people their *individuality*. So also with the BUF's 'mob', employed to denote the collective crowd that gathered at Cable Street. The metaphor of the 'mob', as a metaphor for the vast 'unknowable' 4 October crowd, denies the individual members of that crowd *their* individuality. The individuals who made up the crowd had no identity other than as a negative element of the 'mob'. The rich complexity of the Cable Street gathering and the moral credibility of its individual members is thus denied.

But the 'mob' as metaphor can serve more sinister purposes. As with Carey's 'masses', the 'mob', because it only exists in the imagination and not in reality, can easily be substituted by other imaginary constructs of a more extreme and vulgar nature. In the more excessive moments of this rhetorical process the effect would be to progressively *dehumanise* the anti-fascist demonstrator. Metaphors associated with health, disease and dirt were in evidence. A Mosleyite likened the 'Bolshevik'-inspired 'terrorism' of 4 October to a 'latent ulcer among healthy tissues'.[28] For William Joyce, the vast gathering that opposed Mosley was a 'human barrier of obstruction and *filth*', while another Blackshirt referred to the 'Red *scum*' of 4 October [my emphasis].[29] Animal metaphors also stripped the crowd of its humanity, the Mosleyite cited above comparing the anti-fascist demonstrators to 'blind cattle' acting at the behest of 'the negroid Oriental' that Britons rashly cherished in their midst.[30]

Of all the rhetoric of 4 October, however, it was the rhetoric of the Spanish Civil War that enabled the BUF to construct the most damning critique of the Cable Street crowd. It was another irony of Cable Street that one of the central mobilising themes of the anti-fascist opposition, the link between the struggle against Mosley in east London and the confrontation in Spain between the Republic and Franco, was appropriated and subverted to great effect by the Mosleyites in their subsequent post-Cable Street propaganda. Moreover, within the BUF's Spanish Civil War rhetoric we can observe all the negative features of the Cable Street crowd that have been alluded to above. For a Mosleyite who witnessed the 4 October disturbances, the scene was one of 'unprovoked treachery' perpetrated by 'inhuman, church-burning, soul-destroying monsters, who prefer to call themselves Communists'.[31] Allusions such as this, to the darker, anti-clerical, features of the Spanish conflict, the physical attacks by 'Godless' Spanish Leftists on Spain's Catholic churches, were destined to find a favourable response in locations of the East End that harboured a significant Irish-Catholic population, such as a number of wards in Stepney.[32] In this context, it is interesting to note that of all the BUF's East End branches it was the Limehouse Branch, in Stepney, as referred to earlier, that achieved the most impressive growth rate in the months following the Cable Street affair.

The anti-fascist Cable Street mobilisation justifiably stands as a monument to one of the most impressive and remarkable displays of solidarity by ordinary people against the forces of reaction during the inter-war years. As such, the Cable Street crowd has rightly been

Fascist Perceptions

conceptualised as an instrument of nobility and virtue by many. But to the BUF, desperately anxious to avoid the humiliation of terminating its East End campaign after the 4 October setback, it had to be depicted as something far more sinister and seditious. It was through the various representations, metaphorical images and rhetorical devices discussed in this chapter that the BUF maligned the anti-fascist gathering of 4 October and made its successful appeal to what it imagined to be the more authentic 'East End' of honest, law-abiding, God-fearing, patriotic, respectable 'British' working men and women whom it confidently believed lay outside the boundaries of the Cable Street crowd.

NOTES

1. On the popular local 'legends' inspired by 'Cable Street', see N. Deakin, 'The Vitality of a Tradition' in C. Holmes, (ed.), *Immigrants and Minorities in British Society* (London: Allen & Unwin, 1978), p.167.
2. P[ublic] R[ecord] O[ffice] MEPOL 2/3043/253-261. Report for October 1936.
3. Ibid.
4. PRO H[ome] O[ffice] 144/21062/256. Commissioner. Minutes. Disturbances. British Union of Fascists and National Socialists. 27 October 1936.
5. A.G.P. BUF Assistant District Leader, Bethnal Green North East Branch, 1935-37; District Leader, Bethnal Green North East Branch, 1937-39; District Inspector, 8th London Area, 1939-40. Taped interview. A.L.M. BUF District Leader, Limehouse Branch, 1936-38; BUF Active Division 1 Member, Limehouse Branch, 1938-40. Correspondence. Response to questionnaire.
6. PRO HO144/21064/43-50. Special Branch Report. 11 November 1937.
7. See R. Skidelsky, *Oswald Mosley* (London: MacMillan, 1975), p.409.
8. *Blackshirt*, 17 October 1936.
9. *Action*, 10 October 1936.
10. Ibid.
11. Ibid.
12. See J.S. McClelland, *The Crowd and the Mob: from Plato to Canetti* (London: Unwin Hyman, 1989).
13. *Action*, 10 October 1936.
14. Ibid.
15. Ibid.
16. *Action*, 24 October 1936.
17. K.H. BUF Active Division 1 Member, Central Hackney Branch, 1933-37; Propaganda Officer, Central Hackney Branch, c. 1936; District Leader, Walthamstow West Branch, 1937; Registered Branch Speaker, Epping Branch, 1938-40. Taped interview.
18. Gustave Le Bon, *The Crowd: a Study of the Popular Mind* (London: Fisher Unwin, 1895). See also J. Carey, *The Intellectuals and the Masses* (London: Faber and Faber, 1992), pp.26-30, and McClelland (see note 12).
19. *Blackshirt*, 17 October 1936.
20. Ibid, and *Blackshirt*, 10 October 1936, on Chesterton.
21. *Action*, 10 October 1936.
22. *Action*, 24 October 1936 and 19 June 1937.
23. *Action*, 27 March 1937.
24. *The Patriot*, 8 October 1936 and 15 October 1936.
25. Viscount Lymington, *Famine in England* (London: Witherby, 1938), pp.42-3. On Lymington see also R. Griffiths, *Fellow Travellers of the Right: British Enthusiasts for Nazi Germany*

1933-39 (Oxford: Oxford University Press, 1983), pp. 317-328.
26. *Comrade*, October-November 1986.
27. Carey (see note 18), p.21.
28. *Blackshirt*, 17 October 1936.
29. *Action*, 10 October 1936 and 19 June 1937.
30. *Blackshirt*, 17 October 1936.
31. *Action*, 10 October 1936.
32. On the sense of outrage felt by Stepney's Catholic population at the left-wing anti-clerical violence in Spain and how this mood was generally exploited by the local Mosleyites, see T. Linehan, *East London for Mosley: The British Union of Fascists in East London and South-West Essex 1933-40* (London: Frank Cass, 1996), pp.81-5.

Women and Fascism in the East End

JULIE GOTTLIEB

The British Union of Fascists (BUF) was consistent in claiming that it adhered to the principle of the equality of the sexes, that women would be granted unprecedented political representation in the utopian Corporate State, and that fascism was the ideal home for the patriotic but independent and active woman. That the BUF's model for organising women was the continental Fascist or Nazi one was denied, and it was in the context of differentiating the treatment of women in his movement from the German example that Sir Oswald Mosley declared that

> we have a higher percentage of women candidates than any other party in this country and they play a part of basic equality. We are pledged to complete sex equality. The German attitude towards women has always been different from the British, and my movement has been largely built up by the fanaticism of women; they hold ideals with tremendous passion. Without the women I could not have got a quarter of the way.[1]

The prominence of women in Britain's fascist movement, their importance at the level of organisation, and their particular vigorous commitment, reveal the many differences between the stereotyped portrayals of women's political subordination under European fascist regimes and the mobilisation of women in the BUF.[2] The British Union of Fascists was never reluctant to place its women members in positions of potentially violent confrontation, both physical and verbal, and this chapter will explore how women's *fanaticism* was harnessed by the BUF in their campaign in London's East End.

The role of women in the politics of the East End during the inter-war period exemplified the many functions and representations of female activism in the British fascist movement. BUF women acted as stewards and delivered speeches at meetings. The Women's Section organised its own marches and the movement fully profited from women's willingness to fulfil the role of publicists for Mosley's 'Greater Britain'. Women's propaganda, directed at the plight of the working woman and the victims of sweatshop bosses, bolstered the BUF's industrial policy and added fuel to the movement's attacks on National Government inaction on unemployment. Women served as catalysts for the movement's electoral machine and stood as candidates for the London County Council (LCC) and Municipal elections, which the BUF contested in 1937. They also participated in the movement's anti-semitic campaign, as they contributed a veneer of decency to a racist and exclusionary ideology which promised to protect female virtue from alien interference. In both the fascist and anti-fascist campaigns, the pro-active role of women in demonstrations and counter-demonstrations in London's East End was tempered by the exploitation of the image of women and children, and the urgent call to protect the 'weaker sex' from hooliganism and sexual aggression. Most significantly in relation to the Battle of Cable Street, the image of and love for one woman in particular probably had more of an influence on the events of 4 October 1936 than did any other factor: two days after the BUF's anticipated march through Cable Street, Sir Oswald Mosley was due in Berlin for his wedding to his long-time mistress, Diana Guinness (née Mitford).

PRECEDENTS AND PIONEERS: LINTORN-ORMAN AND THE BRITISH FASCISTS IN THE EAST END

The story of female fascist activism in the East End predated the formation of Mosley's BUF. Britain's first fascist movement, the British Fascisti (the British Fascists after 1924) were the real pioneers of fascism in the poverty-stricken area, and their approach to East End politics set a precedent for the BUF. Founded on 6 May 1923 by the ultra-patriotic ex-servicewoman, Miss Rotha Lintorn-Orman, the BF appealed mainly to middle and upper-class men and women, many of whom had experience in running the empire, feared the proliferation of socialist thought, and tended to regard the Conservative Party as too heterogenous to speak for their radical Right agenda.

In the case of the BF, women members from more affluent backgrounds went down to the area in order to perform philanthropic work and gain experience with the constituents they were ostensibly to shield from Communist teachings and the imminent 'Red terror'. In fact, BF women played such a leading role in the movement's early campaign in the East End, holding meetings in East Ham, Forest Gate and Walthamstow, that in 1927 the editor of the movement's newspaper, *The British Lion,* felt compelled to urge: 'Wake Up, London Men. Are you going to allow the Women's Units to carry on the work of the men in East

London? See to it that in the future men lead the way in the Eastern Divisions. It is not Fascism to make the women do men's work in addition to their own.'[3]

Like the BUF after it, the British Fascists claimed that theirs was a cross-class movement. However, when the organisation tried to put these cross-class ideals into practice, their actions revealed snobbery and distance from the working classes. This was best exemplified by the work of the Women's Units in the East End where they held kitchen meetings, attracting those Lintorn-Orman described as 'the poorest kind of women, who were among the keenest members'.[4] Lintorn-Orman attributed the attraction of fascism to poor women to the fact that the uniform was worn by all members which had the effect of breaking down class distinctions. The British Fascists set up 'Helping Hand Funds' for 'our poorer fascist sisters',[5] and the central task of women members was the organisation and running of the Fascist Children's Clubs, established to counter the detrimental effects of the Socialist Sunday Schools on young minds.

Not only did the British Fascists predate the BUF in its mobilisation of women's welfare work in the East End, but women members of this early movement also inspired the kind of anti-fascist opposition that became concerted by the mid-1930s. For instance, in May 1927 Lintorn-Orman went down to Silvertown East with 15 members of her Women's Units to organise the campaign for the Fascist Children's Clubs. At this same event, where a man struck Lintorn-Orman on the face with a life preserver, she told a reporter that 'We took up our position outside Silvertown Station. Nearest the platform there were about 200 children, and the Reds behind kept on pushing at the back, so the children were driven towards us. After a while the children started throwing things at us.'[6] Considering the small membership, marginality and overall eccentricity of the BF, in the late 1920s the force of children was sufficient to fend off the infiltration of fascism in the East End.

THE EAST END IN BUF IMAGINATION: WOMEN'S DISCOURSES ON PHILANTHROPY, POVERTY, WORK AND HOUSING

The East End served as a potent symbol for fascist women, and for those women on the periphery of Mosley's movement. The history of fascist women in the East End must also take into consideration the fact that welfare work in the area was a focal point for female charity, and the concentration of philanthropic efforts can offer some clues to the class composition and the class cleavages within the BUF. Consistent in the background of many BUF women was charitable work in the East End. Mosley's sister-in-law, the Baroness Ravensdale, had been very involved with the Charity Organisation Society during the First World War, and in 1917 she started her work with the Highway Clubs of East London, 'helping these splendid young people through adolescent years to become good citizens'.[7] Similarly, Cynthia Mosley, Sir Oswald's first wife, had spent the latter part of the war taking 'a short welfare course at the London School of Economics including social work in the East End'.[8] Mercedes Barrington, one of the BUF's prospective parliamentary candidates, was credited with spending the last two years of the war engaged in 'welfare work in East London and slum areas'.[9] Yolande McShane, daughter of a captain on the Cunard line and Women's Branch Leader in the BUF's Wirral Hoylake/West Kirby branch, remembered that she was first attracted to Mosley's ideas because she saw in them the fulfilment of her concerns for the improvement of conditions for the very poor. She recalled,

> Since I was twelve I had been sending half my weekly pocket money to an organization called the East End Mission, run by the Reverend Percy Inesen. The Mission took the children of the East End of London for a day trip to the country or sea, if enough people sent donations... Joining the Blackshirts seemed to bring nearer the day when all children would have enough to eat, and also be able to enjoy the country and sea I loved so much myself.[10]

As these examples imply, fascist activism was more likely to be driven by a maternalistic middle- and upper-class attitude 'for the people', rather than support emanating 'from the people'.

The voices of BUF women in the movement's newspapers at the time of the East End campaign also exemplified the direction of policy-making from above. While a certain detachment was in evidence, it must be emphasised that articles concerning the plight of the woman worker and propaganda which echoed contemporary welfare feminism were plentiful precisely during the years 1935 to 1937, and many were directly addressed to East End women.

The women who wrote articles on the East End and on the conditions of women's labour were, however, rarely themselves East Enders or manual labourers. In the years 1935 to 1937, the chief propagandist on the problem of female employment and the related feminine issues of slum clearance, housing, diet, child care and maternity was Anne Brock Griggs. Brock Griggs was the wife of an architect, and she was praised by the movement for combining 'the best type of intelligent woman with the motherhood of two charming children'.[11] She had first gained notoriety in the BUF as a speaker, holding outdoor meetings in parts of London and the Home Counties. She joined the staff of the BUF as Women's

Propaganda Officer early in 1935; with the reorganisation of the movement in 1936 she became Women's Organizer of the Southern half of the country; and in March 1937 she stood as the British Union candidate for Limehouse.

In her survey of the BUF's women's policy, written in 1936, Brock Griggs pointed out that 'since their entry into industry women have received lower wages than men for the same work. This amounts to victimization and, apart from the injustice to women, causes the displacement of men ... Sweated wages for women reduce the standard of living for the whole country.'[12] The BUF's solution to the sex war in industry which arose from these facts was to advocate 'Equal Pay for Equal Work', with one foreseeable result being the liberation of women from the obligation to work.[13] Brock Griggs lamented the failure of Ellen Wilkinson's bill for equal pay in the civil service, debated in the House of Commons on 1 April 1936, but she emphasised that 'it is not a feminist question, nor should it be viewed from that angle and exposed to the flippancy and back-chat in Westminster. The sweated labour of women in industry to-day is a serious menace to the standard of living. Red petticoats swirling in the House have unwittingly raised a storm.'[14] That the BUF did not regard equal pay for equal work as a feminist issue is indicative of the fact that women were not intended to be the main beneficiaries.

Special appeals were made to the factory girl, the nurse, the domestic servant and especially to the textile worker who had to contend with competition from cheaper Japanese female labour.[15] Each category of female worker was assured that her status and opportunities would be ameliorated in a British fascist state. The model of the Corporate State recognised the role of women in the labour market as consumers and as wives, but it was the celebration of domestic government that was considered to be the most ingenious and marketable aspect of the fascist plan. It was explained that 'in the Home Corporation women who run a home or are employed in domestic work will be represented. This will be recognized as one of the most vital corporations in the Fascist State, and will give the career of home-maker the status of a profession.'[16] By raising the occupation of mother and housewife to the status of profession in the state, the BUF was, in fact, professionalising domesticity, rather than offering the means for women to liberate themselves from the psychological and financial constraints of their private sphere.

While Anne Brock Griggs spoke of the condition of female labour from a more detached perspective, one of the BUF's keenest and most active young members spoke from experience. Olive Hawks, formerly an employee in the research department of the Amalgamated Press and then a reader for the Wellington Press before she joined the BUF's research department, claimed first-hand experience of factory conditions. Hawks argued:

> Fascism, with its ideal of national unity, appeals to every British man and woman alike, but as one who has worked long hours under hard conditions in a 'rat' workshop, I can speak best to you, the young woman in whom blind spirit of revolt is being bred by the injustices under which you work and live ... Would it not be better for people with a direct knowledge of your conditions, men and women who have 'been through the mill' to have their say in the scheme of things?[17]

Hawks was particularly disappointed by the fact that women workers failed to organise and unionise. In her novel set in the East End, *What Hope for Green Street?* – written while she was interned as a member of the British Union under Defence Regulation 18B(1a) – her main protagonist is engaged in the following discussion at her place of employment in the catering trade:

> 'Exploitation will always go on so long as we don't keep together. That's what's wrong with the working class — especially the women. No solidarity.'
>
> 'Oh, and that's what you think, is it? Well, how the hell are we going to keep together when there's always somebody ready to step into your job, or take it for less wages if they can?' ...
>
> 'That's the trouble. We've got to find the spirit to stick together, even at the cost of going through it.'[18]

In the East London campaign, British Union writers emphasised their knowledge of the condition of the working poor and tended to make the most sentimental appeals to recruit women.

This emotional appeal was most marked when BUF women discussed housing conditions and advocated slum clearance. Brock Griggs described how,

> within a stone's throw of the Houses of Parliament, where ministers talk of prosperity (to the tune of 80%), we may walk into humble homes where our feet crush through the flimsy boards rotten under the shabby linoleum. There may be six people, the parents, three children and a baby, living in two miserable rooms and a scullery... Everyday we read of suicides and despair, of citizens housed in hovels, where farmers would not put their pigs.[19]

It was the feminine narrative voice in BUF propaganda that described desolate living conditions most dramatically: 'The narrow streets of

Bethnal Green straggle across East London, hidden like a shameful secret behind the City's facade of wealth. The tiny box-like houses were hastily flung up years ago, without thought, without plan, without consideration of beauty or regard to health, to accommodate the unhappy population which manufactures the City's goods.'[20] While fascist propaganda was ambivalent about many aspects of women's employment, the BUF consistently accepted that women could play the largest part in town planning and housing. As early as 1933, Elizabeth Winch argued that contrary to popular apprehensions, fascism would not send women back to the home as 'the presence of women architects and advisers in new building schemes could be of inestimable value. While such opportunities are open to women – under a Fascist State – surely it cannot be said that women are being "forced back to drudgery."'[21] As the wife of an architect, Brock Griggs emphasised that women should enter the fields of architecture and planning and occupy all those professional positions which had the greatest impact on the private sphere of which they were the rightful directors and dictators.[22]

'MOTHERLY HATE': SEX AND ANTISEMITISM

The emotional appeals female propagandists made to East End women did by no means exclude the attempt to awaken racist sentiments. Anti-semitism was one of the main planks supporting the women's platform. The women were apparently as uninhibited as their male counterparts in making anti-semitic references in their discourses, and for tactical reasons they had to be entreated to censor their speeches. As Neville Laski, President of the Board of Deputies of British Jews, reported to the Under-Secretary of State at the Home Office in September of 1936, 'Mrs Anne Brock Griggs is now to concentrate upon East End women, and will NOT mention the word "Jew"(as all speakers have now been warned). There will be plain clothes members at all meetings to use the word instead, as coming from the public, and to rouse others.'[23]

The anti-fascist Lionel Birch assumed that the 'Fascists have adopted Colonel Blimp's assumption that tolerance and the desire to reconcile are feminine un-British qualities.' As the following survey of opinion will indicate, there was nothing tolerant or conciliatory about the way in which women fascists rhetorically denigrated those they stigmatised as 'other'.

Women MPs were considered as 'Other' in that the 'M' was missing. Parliamentary democracy failed women because those few women who did sit in the House of Commons were seen collectively as unmarried and childless and thus effectively abnormal. Mosley set the tone when he wrote: 'the field of women's interests is left clear to the professional spinster politician who used irreverently to be described as a member of "No Man's Land". It will not be surprising to those familiar with this distressing type that the interests of the "normal women" occupy no great place in the attention of Parliament.'[24] Abnormality could refer to either sexual or national out-groups, and Norah Elam, the ex-suffragette who had stood as an Independent in 1918, was disturbed by the fact that the first woman elected to the House of Commons was 'the Sinn Fein Countess Markieviecz, who though a notorious and avowed enemy of Britain, found it a perfectly simple matter under the democratic system to secure election to the Parliament of the country which she had openly boasted that she would destroy, disintegrate and discredit'.[25] To add insult to injury, the attack on the political woman was more truly an assault on democracy itself and an ethnically heterogenous national community.

As much as the unrepresentative woman politician, the feminist had betrayed British womanhood. The feminist had done so not so much by serving only her sex to the exclusion of men, but paradoxically, when we consider the source, by selling out to party interests. Elam condemned post-enfranchisement women for having

> allied themselves with the very parties in the state which had treated them with such unprecedented contempt. They once again wear the primrose of the Jew Disraeli, the rosette in honour of Sir Herbert Samuel, the red emblem in commemoration of Karl Marx; they have turned again as handmaidens to the hewing of wood and drawing of water for the Party wirepullers.[26]

Elam did not seem to see the irony in her condemnation, and disregarded the fact that BUF women were wearing the Blackshirt in honour of Mosley, the former Labour MP, and acting as handmaidens to Mars by engaging in and condoning fascist violence. However, that emancipated women should join the democratic parties was less the point than that they unwittingly served the Jewish interest. When Brock Griggs declared that the 'ping-pong at Westminster will not breed an athletic race', perhaps she was being more candid by exposing feminised fascism's essential marriage between racialism and anti-democratic sentiment.[27]

Tony Kushner has asked: 'was anti-Semitism linked to patriarchy or was it gender blind?'[28] Pondering the same problem from the perspective of women in the BUF, the questions that must be posed are as follows: Were women in the BUF anti-semitic? Were they as anti-semitic as the men? Was the nature of women's anti-semitism in any way distinctive? And, how were women represented in anti-semitic propaganda?

The answer to the first question is readily apparent, as women in the BUF indulged in some of the most malignant forms of hate propaganda.

However, while the BUF's anti-semitism was blatant, it was not necessarily part of the attraction of fascism for some women. Yolande McShane remembered that 'Mosley's policies were not racist; he was anti-Jew, but as I knew no Jew and Mosley seemed to object to their apparent monopoly of British money and business, it did not seem to me very important, compared with the promise of "equal opportunities for all"'.[29] And yet fascism was a package deal, and scapegoating, xenophobia, and rhetorical violence against the Jews were inextricable from the British fascist ideological discourse.

There also seems to be little reason to doubt that women could be as racist as men. Women fascists did highlight certain areas of the anti-semitic discourse, and particularly rampant were stereotypes of the predatory Jew exploiting women workers in the sweat shops, perpetrating sex crimes, and disseminating indecent literature. The evil machinations of Jewish interests were identified behind each area of social crisis that affected the women's sphere. The self-ascribed role of fascist woman as mother of the race meant that women were considered the most vulnerable to the Jewish corruption of culture, the desecration of the Christian family and the thinning of the British racial blood line. One BUF critic asked: 'The instability of our homes, the pseudo-scientific study called psychoanalysis, the discontents occasioned in British families by the falsity of Hollywood sex-filled entertainment, the pernicious doctrine of Marxism, the destruction of the family by use of contraceptives: can it be seriously denied that all these things have originated from the Jew?'[30] Anti-semitism was always reinforced by arousing anxieties about sexual potency, and women were portrayed as the symbolic victims of a Jew-ravaged Britain.

In the feminine fascist imagination, the Jew was always male and in a position of authority over British women (there were significantly fewer derogatory images of the Jewish woman). Mosley explained the origins of the BUF's anti-semitism by the fact that 'our girls were dismissed from shops owned by Jews. Our people were persecuted. Our supporters were blackmailed by Jewish interests.'[31] The undue influence of the Jew was only possible in a Financial Democracy, but his power transcended democracy and rendered the parliamentary system a farce. Eileen Lyons pointed out that 'one may be an ardent Tory, Socialist, or even Liberal, but is it going to get "Our Mary" out of the Jewish sweat-shop? Is it going to make the old Jew pay decent wages? No! Is not Financial Democracy afraid of the Rosenbaums, or perhaps it would be truer to say are not the Rosenbaums Financial Democracy?'[32] The use of 'Our Mary' connoted Jewish corruption both of the helpless common woman, and the first Christian mother. Women weakened and prematurely aged by work outside the home for 'slave wages' were described as 'broken on the financial rack', as the Jew became woman's captor and torturer.[33] The allusion to torture administered by the Jew suggested a reliance on the medieval gallery of images, and, in particular, reawakened the (false) memory of blood libel. Jewish employers were also held responsible for preventing sympathetic British women from joining the BUF, and when Dinah Parkinson had a short exchange with a typist on the bus, the young woman scoffed: 'They held a Blackshirt meeting in Cheetham Hill recently. I longed to go, but I daren't. I know nothing about the policy, but I do know all the Jewish employers are scared stiff.'[34] Her article displayed some sadistic pleasure in the fact that Britain's working women could arouse the fears of their Jewish employers.

In the East End, the discourse surrounding slum clearance was buttressed by reference to Jewish corruption and domination: 'Fascism does not need the poisoned blood money of aliens to rehouse British people.'[35] Brock Griggs referred to the 'evil force of finance, which flourishes as weeds do in the garden they destroy'.[36] At one of her meetings during her LCC election campaign, Brock Griggs spoke of corruption in housing, and argued that 'when the Tories were in power ... the head of the Housing Committee was a Jew – Levita, but 3 years ago when Labour came into office a great change took place, another Jew – Silkin was the head'.[37] BUF women contributed their voices to the movement's line of argument that only Jews should be conscripted for service as 'British life and wealth must not be sacrificed in Palestine'.[38] In regard to the same issue, the BUF played on male fears of the alien's sexual licentiousness and threat to white women by claiming that 'Jews are the international enemy, that Arabs are complaining that Jewish men are outraging Arab women in Palestine'.[39]

As Claudia Koonz has pointed out in the case of women in the Third Reich, 'at the grassroots of daily life, in a social world populated by women, we begin to discover how war and genocide happened by asking who made it happen'.[40] In Britain too, fascist women were by no means victims, and their Jew-baiting activities, their appeals to motherly protectiveness and their fear-mongering, drove the anti-semitic campaign at every turn. In its reaction to the 'Other', feminine fascism transformed motherly love into motherly hate.

PREACHING AS THEY PRACTISED: THE ROLES OF BUF WOMEN IN THE EAST END

While BUF propaganda focused on a mild extension of the notion of women's private sphere to appeal to women of the East End, the activities of women in the area tell a story of female participation in the public sphere. The BUF mobilised its women members for marching, speaking, canvassing, and organising meetings and bazaars in East London. Women were to be the salespersons and soft-sellers of fascism in Britain, and the movement exploited female participation for maximum publicity in the rough street politics of the East End. Women members were responsible for advertising Mosley as 'the People's Man', Anne Cutmore applauding the Leader's consistency as 'the friend of the underdog'. At a Blackshirt march in Bethnal Green in June 1936, Cutmore remarked how 'onlookers cheer as the Leader passes and a woman throws a flower from a window'.[41] In May 1936 the women Blackshirts of London took part in the first 'Propaganda March' ever held, following a route through Bethnal Green to Victoria Park where they attended a meeting addressed by Anne Brock Griggs. Led by Miss Olga Shore, Women's Executive Officer, they 'marched in perfect step, with commendable order and discipline, the more praiseworthy because they had no band or drums to lead them'.[42] While this march was reported to have attracted much positive attention from local women as 'thousands stopped to watch them and comment on their pluck in marching through a Red stronghold and gave applause to lighten the road', the second women's propaganda march aroused more antagonism.[43] In June, in Balham, the women's meeting was disturbed by heckling, a barrage of questions and facetious remarks. On this occasion the *Blackshirt* reported the following exchange: 'Throughout the interruptions were frequent. They were good-humoured but the speaker's humour was better. Someone asked why we wore blackshirts. "Because they don't run," came the instant reply. "We all know what happens when you wash a red shirt."'[44] By September 1936 the women's pluck and occasional wit facilitated the intensification of their campaign in the East End, and they were reported to have stimulated interest among women. The main speakers in their campaign, Mrs. Brock Griggs, Doreen Bell, Olive Hawks, Mrs Carruthers and Ann Good, were credited with having 'a very stimulating effect upon massed audiences. Record collections and paper sales have been accompanied by a gratifying flow of new members of both sexes.'[45] While women were infiltrating the public sphere through the unlikely route of fascism, it must be emphasised that men's and women's work within the movement was more often than not segregated. We will see how this segregation had some impact on the Cable Street rally some weeks later.

Following the Battle of Cable Street, BUF women intensified their activity in the East End. On Sunday morning, 11 October, Brock Griggs spoke at Bethnal Green. When the women marched up to join the men's meeting, the male speaker, S. O. Clarke 'called upon his audience to look at the English women who are reviled in the gutter Press and to judge for themselves', illustrating the BUF's use of its women as exemplars of British fascism's civility and discipline.[46] An estimated 70 mothers of Bethnal Green, some accompanied by their children, attended a meeting at the BUF's Green Street headquarters on 29 October to hear Blackshirt policy explained to them by the W.A.O. (Southern) Mrs Brock Griggs.

By the winter of 1936, the thrust of the women's campaign was directed towards preparations for the LCC elections. Attention was now turned to indoor meetings and the *Blackshirt* made an appeal to women members who were free in the afternoon, in order to 'catch the fires of enthusiasm kindled by the great events of the past week and translated into action in the form of hard slogging canvas work'.[47] The *Blackshirt* was not telling tales when it spoke of the enthusiasm for British fascism aroused among women by the events of October in the East End. Even the *Manchester Guardian* remarked on the crowds of onlookers at a BUF procession and how 'it was noticeable that almost all those who saluted were women, many of them girls of 16 or 17'.[48]

There is also some evidence for the view that the dramatic events of 4 October 1936 stimulated female recruitment, regardless of the fact that the Battle of Cable Street was widely regarded as the anti-fascists' victory. The young Gladys Walsh (née Libiter) had been instantly attracted to Blackshirt policy after hearing a BUF speaker at an outdoor meeting in Limehouse during the summer of 1936, but she only joined as a non-active member, giving as her reason that she and her two sisters worked for a Jewish firm. However, as she recalled, after seeing 'for ourselves the communists, their clenched fists, rolling marbles under the horses feet and stuffing glass up their noses to bring the police down ... we were really disgusted. I made up my mind from then on to be an active member.'[49] Walsh went on to become Women's District Leader, and during the first phase of the war, District Leader of the British Union's Limehouse branch.

The BUF's East London campaign culminated in the LCC elections of March 1937 and, again, women played a prominent part. In late December 1936, Mosley announced that the BUF would contest the LCC elections, Anne Brock Griggs being one of the six BUF candidates. 'The Women's Section received a considerable boost in its prestige as the BUF began building its election machinery because of Mosley's personal belief that at the constituency level women were absolutely invaluable in election winning, because of their persuasive abilities and more flexible daytime hours of work.'[50] In campaigning for the elections the movement organised 420 meetings, 18 of which were addressed by women speakers.[51] While all six candidates failed to be elected, Brock Griggs received 2,086 votes (16.3 per cent). In November 1937, 56 BUF members stood for the Municipal elections, including 4 women.[52]

DID FASCIST WOMEN PASS?: THE PRESENCE AND ABSENCE OF BUF WOMEN AT CABLE STREET

Women played an integral part in the BUF's East London campaign, with their voices integrated into the movement's anti-semitic diatribes and members of the Women's Section involved in every form of political activity that the BUF pursued. On 4 October 1936 women joined the ranks of Mosley's troops, but it is not clear what percentage they made up of the estimated 1,900 Blackshirt marchers.[53] It is still less clear how many of these women marchers were themselves East Enders.[54] The type of BUF women who attended were described by Anthony Crossley MP as 'rather grim middle-aged spinsters and some pretty young women'.[55] Notably, on this same day, the BUF's fourth anniversary was being celebrated in Manchester by a women's march and an outdoor meeting, the first all female march in that region. Therefore, while the Battle of Cable Street was in progress many of the most prominent BUF women, including Olga Shore and Doreen Bell, were carrying on their work undisturbed by the events in London. This coincidence of marches brings into question whether the Cable Street march was considered paramount by BUF supporters, or whether the Manchester march was only a regional show of force in commemoration of the founding of the movement.

In the events surrounding the Battle of Cable Street, women contributed yet another dimension to East End political discourse: the image of women and children was exploited by both fascists and anti-fascists to excite the male protective instinct. The poster disseminated by the Ex-Servicemen's Movement Against Fascism calling all ex-servicemen 'to stop Mosley putting the clock back to barbarism', also exclaimed: 'protect women and children from Fascist hooliganism'.[56] The fascists retaliated by questioning the masculinity of anti-fascist protesters, calling them 'she-males', and reserving special insults for the Red woman or the 'sub-woman' who was permitted by her emasculated colleague to stand in the front line of battle.[57]

While rank-and-file fascist women did not play an extraordinary role in the events of 4 October, the image of one woman in particular may well have had an enormous influence on the conduct of the fascist rally. In 1932 Sir Oswald Mosley had met Mrs Diana Guinness, the luminary of the Bright Young Things, heir apparent to Emerald Cunard's Society throne, and herself a major player in the social and sexual intrigues surrounding European fascism and relations with the dictators. Although Mosley was married to Lord Curzon's second daughter, Cynthia, Diana soon became Sir Oswald's mistress. Diana left her husband, Bryan Guinness, and set up house with her two infant sons while awaiting Mosley's sporadic visits, a shocking arrangement even among her own smart-set circle. While Lady Cynthia Mosley's death in May 1933 should have left the way open for Sir Oswald's and Diana's affair to be made open and for the couple to seek public acceptance, they did not rush to do so.

It was male protective instinct that was partially responsible for Diana's inadvertent influence on the events of October 1936. As Diana remembered, Mosley 'thought it was wise to keep our marriage a secret, as I was living at Wootton, often alone, and politics were rough'.[58] Also significant was Mosley's second excuse for keeping their marriage secret. As he later explained to the 18B Advisory Committee, 'there is a legend in the movement that if you marry you cease to do any work. I therefore meant to keep it quiet for some time so that if they find it out they could say "well, you see I have not changed at all, the movement has been just the same," and that period of annoyance and disappointment about my marriage would have passed over.'[59] To shield both his future wife and his own masculine and macho reputation, Mosley went to some trouble to plan a secret wedding. If they were to marry in Britain, or even at the Paris Consulate, their marriage would have been publicised and Diana would have been vulnerable to attack. Diana thus arranged that they should have their nuptials in Berlin, where Hitler would ask the registrar to keep the marriage quiet.

On 4 October Mosley was rallying his followers in the East End, and on 6 October he was due in Berlin for his secret marriage ceremony, to be held at the Goebbels' residence with Hitler in attendance. Is it not more than possible that Mosley obeyed the Commissioner of the Metropolitan Police, Sir Philip Game's command that the BUF march should be redirected, due to his anxiety that he should not miss his plane the next day?

Nicholas Mosley has also made the connection between these two events. He has said:

> What did my father think he was doing. A big demonstration in the East End and then due to be married in Goebbels' house ... which would obviously be very difficult if he didn't turn up. It would be difficult on the personal level, very hard on Diana if he didn't turn up for the wedding, but it would also be a bit awkward if Goebbels had fixed the whole thing, and Goebbels had fixed it all up so the press wouldn't let it out, it wouldn't be known ... Why didn't he just march through Cable Street? ... But then, of course, had he been arrested he wouldn't have been able to get to Berlin the next day for his wedding.[60]

Nicholas Mosley avers that the decision to turn around, to obey the police and react meekly, was out of character for his father. Therefore, while for the anti-fascists the events of 4 October inevitably recall memories of hatred and successful opposition to Mosley's Blackshirts, for the fascists themselves the myth of the Battle of Cable Street was also part love story.

The role and influence of women is inextricable from the progress of the fascist movement in the East End of London. On both the personal and political levels, women fascists animated disturbances, added fuel to the fire of anti-semitism, and inspired their men to action, or as the case may be, to inaction. In the perspective of the long history of fascist women's involvement in the East End, the Battle of Cable Street was only one of many events in which they participated, and only one of many failures to which they contributed their particular colour and spectacle.

NOTES

1. Advisory Committee to Consider Appeals Against Orders of Internment, 3 July 1940, Public Records Office (PRO), HO283/14/2-117.
2. While praising most aspects of Gertrud Scholtz-Klink's Nazi women's organisation, as well as the Italian Fascist provisions for women's welfare, BUF women went to great lengths to emphasise Britain's fundamental difference and progression on the issue of women in politics. Brock Griggs gave voice to this opinion when she wrote that 'we do not as a rule compare British Fascism, especially in this respect, with the continental manifestations; for as you are aware from your first hand experience of Italy and Germany, a differing racial tradition in their attitude towards women makes comparison between these two countries impossible'. *Fascist Quarterly*, 1:3 (July 1935), p.164.
3. *The British Lion*, 24 (December 1927).
4. *The Fascist Bulletin*, 13 June 1925.
5. *The Fascist Bulletin*, 20 June 1925.
6. Quoted in 'Women Fascists Attacked: Rowdy Scenes at the East End Meeting', *Evening News,* 7 May 1927.
7. Baroness Ravensdale, *In Many Rhythms* (London: Weidenfeld & Nicholson, 1953), p.101.
8. Nicholas Mosley, *Rules of the Game* (London: Secker & Warburg, 1982), p.17.
9. *Action*, 23 January 1937.
10. Yolande McShane, *Daughter of Evil* (London: Star, 1980), pp.29-30.
11. *Action*, 21 November 1936.
12. Anne Brock Griggs, *Women and Fascism: 10 Important Points* (London: BUF Publications, 1936).
13. Ibid.
14. Anne Brock Griggs, 'Red Petticoats and Blue Stockings: Equal Pay – A Trivial Debate which Raises Major Issues', *Action*, 16 April 1936.
15. Examples of these articles at the time of the East London campaign are: 'Girls Lured to London for Domestic Work', *Blackshirt,* 16 May 1936; 'What About the Nurse?: The Women in White by Eileen Dewis', *Blackshirt*, 22 August 1936; 'The Distaff Side: Give Our Women Workers a Chance, Says Eileen Dewis', *Blackshirt*, 19 September 1936; 'The Problem of the Woman Worker: National Socialism will Solve it', *Blackshirt*, 23 January 1937. For Anne Brock Griggs on Japanese competition see 'Alice in Cottonland: The Adventure with the "Red" Queen: A Phantasy with a Moral', *Blackshirt*, 2 May 1936.
16. Brock Griggs, *Women and Fascism* (see note 12).
17. Olive Hawks, 'Freedom and the Factory Girl', *Blackshirt*, 19 September 1936.
18. Olive Hawks, *What Hope for Green Street?* (London: Jarrolds, 1945), p.28.

19. 'How Britons Live: Anne Brock Griggs Describes the Building of a Super Race', *Action*, 28 May 1936.
20. Anne Cutmore, 'In the Heart of an Empire: Great East London Welcome to Sir Oswald Mosley', *Action*, 11 June 1936.
21. *The Fascist Week*, 8 (29 December 1933).
22. Women were presumed to be especially well-qualified for power in a *fascist* state as a consequence of their experience in domestic management. Agnes Booth wondered 'when will they realize that women are, in a quiet way, the Dictators of this or any country? In their youth they are subject to and later become the mistress of the home, and so in turn, Dictators'. Agnes Booth, 'Women and Dictatorship', *Action*, 13 January 1938.
23. Letter from Neville Laski to Sir Russell Scott, Under-Secretary of State, 10 September 1936. HO144/21060/207.
24. Oswald Mosley, 'Fascism will End the Battle of the Sexes', *Fascist Week* 10 (12-18 January 1934).
25. Norah Elam, 'Fascism, Women and Democracy', *Fascist Quarterly* 1:3 (July 1935), pp.290-98.
26. Norah Elam, 'Women and the Vote', *Action*, 26 March 1936.
27. Anne Brock Griggs, 'Food or Usury?' *Fascist Quarterly* 2:2 (April 1936), pp.237-44.
28. Tony Kushner, 'Sex and Semitism: Jewish Women in Britain in War and Peace', in Panikos Panayi (ed.), *Minorities in Wartime* (Oxford: Berg, 1993), p.119.
29. McShane (see note 10), p.30. At her first, and indeed her last, visit to the Carlisle Branch, Eugenia Wright described the form of the BUF meeting: 'Then we were invited – no! –instructed to march around the room chanting "The Yids, the Yids, we've gotta get rid of the Yids!" and when told, refused to say it as I felt it was not the right thing to do.' Letter from Eugenia Wright to the author, 6 May 1997.
30. *The British Union Quarterly* 1:3 (September 1937), p.105.
31. Advisory Committee to Hear Appeals Against Orders of Internment, 2 July 1940, HO283/13/2-125.
32. Eileen Lyons, 'Women Fought for the Vote: What Have They Got – Nothing', *Action*, 24 April 1937.
33. Brock Griggs, 'Women Must Work: The Labour International Will Sell Them into Slavery', *Blackshirt*, 25 April 1936.
34. Quoted in Dinah Parkinson, 'In a Manchester Sweat Shop', *Blackshirt*, 18 April 1936.
35. 'How Britons Live' (see note 19).
36. Anne Brock Griggs, 'Food or Usury' (see note 27).
37. Special Branch report of a BUF meeting at Piggott Street, Limehouse, HO 144/21063/365-68.
38. Anne Cutmore, 'Conscript the Jews', *Blackshirt*, 26 September 1936. In a more unguarded moment, one BUF woman expressed the opinion that 'As far as driving the Jews goes, I expect that many know nothing about them or their powerful mischief. Very apparently nobody likes, or wants them, therefore they should be shipped to a distant no-man's land and get on together, which they appear able to do, and certainly not be dumped, by the informal interference of Britain, on the unfortunate Arabs, for whom we have the greatest liking and sympathy.' Letter from Mrs Mabel Helen Sanford to Robert Saunders, December 1936, Saunders Collection, Sheffield University, File A.4. Certainly there were many women among the 'Jew-wise' in such organisations as the Imperial Fascist League, the Nordic League and the Right Club.
39. HO144/21378/307.
40. Claudia Koonz, *Mothers in the Fatherland* (London: Jonathan Cape, 1987), p.3.
41. *Action*, 11 June 1936.
42. *Blackshirt*, 23 May 1936.
43. Ibid.
44. *Blackshirt*, 20 June 1936.
45. *Blackshirt*, 12 September 1936.
46. *Blackshirt*, 17 October 1936.
47. *Blackshirt*, 31 October 1936.

48. *Manchester Guardian*, 15 October 1936.
49. Inteview with Gladys Walsh, from the Archive of the Friends of O. M. Transcribed by author.
50. D. S. Lewis, *Illusions of Grandeur: Mosley Fascism and British Society* (Manchester: Manchester University Press, 1987), p.78.
51. Speakers included Mrs Carruthers, Mrs Bowie, Mrs Thomas, Miss Barrington, Olive Hawks and Mrs Whinefield. See HO144/21063/379-387.
52. 56 Fascist candidates were nominated in 10 Boroughs (18 Wards), all in East London with the exception of St. Pancras, Mitcham and Croydon. Of these 56 candidates, four were women: Mrs Margaret Warnett, Kingsland Ward, 110 votes; Mrs Margaret Catherine Tisler, St. Pancras No.1 Ward, 113 votes; Lilian Wilson, Bethnal Green North Ward, 665 votes; and Margaret M. E. Johnston, Bethnal Green West Ward, 354 votes. A total of 1242 votes were cast for fascist women candidates, average of 311 votes.
53. Special Branch reports estimated that 1,900 fascists assembled for the march as opposed to approximately 100,000 counter-demonstrators (HO144/21068/53). It is interesting that the breakdown according to gender was not given for this event while Special Branch frequently counted men to woman at fascist meetings. On average, Mosley's audiences were 28 per cent female, and women stewardesses constituted 25 per cent. For a more complete statistical analysis and an examination of the women's organisation and forms of participation in the BUF see Julie V. Gottlieb, 'Women and Fascism in Inter-war Britain' (unpublished PhD dissertation, University of Cambridge, 1998).
54. Also see Thomas P. Linehan, *East London for Mosley* (London: Frank Cass, 1996) for a detailed study of the regional manifestations of the BUF and for some examples of East End women who were active in the movement.
55. Letter to Geoffrey Lloyd from Anthony Crossley MP, 14 October 1936. HO144/20161/293.
56. HO144/21060/360.
57. 'More Skirted Shouting at Hampstead', *Blackshirt*, 31 October 1936.
58. Diana Mosley, *A Life of Contrasts* (London: Hamish Hamilton, 1977), p.141.
59. HO283/13/2-125.
60. Interview with Nicholas Mosley, Lord Ravensdale, by the author, 25 September 1996.

But What Did They Do? Contemporary Jewish Responses to Cable Street

ELAINE R. SMITH

Nobody would doubt that during the 1930s fascist anti-semitism presented a direct physical threat to Jews in the East End, who increasingly felt abandoned by the community's official leadership, the Board of Deputies of British Jews. East End Jewry's geographical isolation from the Anglo-Jewish leadership was compounded by the huge social and economic differences between the two sections of the community. The leadership consisted of middle-class Jews. By contrast, the Jewish population in the East End, especially after 1918, was primarily working class. Conflicting ideas on how best to tackle the issue of communal defence led to clashes between Jewish political leaders in the East End and the Board of Deputies.

In the Jewish East End, local councillors, trade unionists and Communist activists, as well as specifically Jewish defence groups, each had their own distinct identity and political complexion. Cable Street was located in the borough of Stepney, and in 1936 the council was governed by the Labour group which controlled all the seats on the council. However, the Stepney Labour Council's record in 1936, when Fascist disturbances in the borough were at their height, did little to endear it to the East End Jewish community. This was because the members of the ruling Labour group were mainly on the right-wing of the party. As the Jewish Communist Phil Piratin later noted in his memoir *Our Flag Stays Red,* only a minority could be described as socialist.[1]

Jewish councillors, such as Morry Davis and Dan Frankel, were regarded with considerable scepticism by many of the more radically-inclined Jewish workers in the East End. Davis was one of the founders of the Whitechapel Labour Party, becoming mayor of Stepney in 1930 and leader of the council in 1935.[2] He was also active in Jewish communal life and was perhaps best known as President of the Federation of Synagogues.[3] Despite these activities, the extent of his personal involvement in anti-fascist initiatives was extremely limited. Indeed, there is remarkably little evidence of his willingness to provide leadership to East End Jews on the issue of BUF anti-semitism. Dan Frankel's record was, if anything, even weaker. Like Morry Davis, he also was on the right-wing of the Labour Party. As well as being a councillor in Mile End, Frankel was elected Mile End's Labour MP in 1935.

Throughout 1936, his advice to the Jewish population was unequivocal: under no circumstances should Jews confront the fascists on the streets. But in the tense atmosphere of 1936 this was not the sort of advice that many young East End Jews were willing to heed. Many of the East End Jews who searched for a more radical solution to political anti-semitism and fascism believed that the defeat of the BUF could only be achieved by a strong trade union movement and a strong Communist Party.[4] In line with the Popular Front policy being pursued by European Communist parties under instruction from Moscow, the Stepney Communist Party actively encouraged the creation of a united front against fascism. This was the thrust of the plea made by Joe Jacobs, secretary of the Stepney Communist Party in 1936, in a letter which he addressed to East End Labour parties and to Stepney's three MPs.[5] The offer to form a united front was rejected outright by the Stepney Labour Party largely because the Communist Party's policy of direct confrontation on the streets with the Blackshirts was anathema to the Labour Party.

The Communist Party's tactic of direct confrontation with the Blackshirts had the effect of attracting large numbers of Jewish youth to the Party in Stepney during the 1930s.[6] This was a source of considerable concern both to Anglo-Jewish establishment figures engaged in youth and social work in the East End and to the Board of Deputies. Basil and Rose Henriques, wardens of the two largest Jewish youth clubs in the East End, both expressed dismay about the number of club members joining the Communist Party, 'not because they are Communists, but because they feel that the Communists were the only people who were trying to fight the Fascists'.[7]

The events of 4 October 1936, which subsequently became known as the Battle of Cable Street, epitomised the diversity of opinion within the Jewish community about how fascism should be tackled. Two days before the demonstration the *Jewish Chronicle* published a warning urging Jews to stay away from the route of the Blackshirt march.[8] In addition, Neville Laski, the President of the Board of Deputies of British Jews, had posters displayed in the East End warning the local Jewish community against the danger of becoming involved in disorders in connection with the march. He also circulated similar messages to East End synagogues.[9] By contrast, the Communist Party advertised the counter-demonstration and urged the participation of trades councils, trade unions and local Labour parties.[10] This pro-active strategy was undoubtedly more in tune with the sentiments of Jewish East Enders, who regarded the planned BUF march through the East End as an act of extreme provocation.

However, even within the Communist Party opinion was not monolithic. A small group of Jewish communists in Stepney centred around Joe Jacobs did not believe that the party was sincere in its efforts to oppose fascism in the East End. As evidence of this, Jacobs later pointed out in his autobiography that the London leadership of the party put all its energy into organising a Young Communist League rally in support of the anti-fascist cause in Spain, which was also due to be held on 4 October. According to Jacobs, it was only as a result of continual pressure from the Stepney branch that the leadership was eventually persuaded to cancel the Young Communist League rally in Trafalgar Square and instead rally communists to Cable Street.[11] However, this tension between the local branch in Stepney and the London leadership of the Communist Party should not be treated as a conflict between Jewish political interests and Communist interests. In fact, Jacobs' policies were opposed by other Jews within the Stepney Communist Party, notably the group around Phil Piratin. In his account of the events, Piratin stated that he had no doubt that the London District Committee of the Party had taken the lead in initiating a plan of action to combat the Fascists.[12]

The disagreements between Piratin and Jacobs over the Communist Party's response to the Battle of Cable Street was part of a wider schism within the Stepney Communist Party. Jacobs was the leader of the faction which favoured 'street work'. According to Piratin this meant 'Bash the fascists wherever you see them'.[13] By contrast, Piratin's idea of 'street work' involved developing links in the local community by, for example, helping people to form tenants' committees.[14] It was these different approaches to tactics which led to the power struggle within the Stepney Communist Party in 1936 between the followers of Jacobs and those of Piratin. The defeat of the Jacobs faction in this struggle led other Communist Party members to claim that Jacobs had an axe to grind when he later criticised the London District Committee of the party for leaving preparations of the Cable Street demonstration to the last moment. Whatever the truth, there is no doubt that the Communist Party played a leading role at Cable Street. It was the Communist-inspired slogan 'They Shall Not Pass' which served as the rallying cry for the demonstrators.

The call to demonstrate was answered by a wide variety of groups and individuals, not all of whom were Communists. It has been estimated that 100,000 people rallied to oppose the fascists while the Communist Party nationally had just 11,500 members.[15] In addition, it would be inaccurate to suggest that only Jews participated. Irish dockers and ex-servicemen's organisations both played a prominent role in the Battle of Cable Street. However, as far as the Anglo-Jewish establishment was concerned, numbers were irrelevant: it was the fact of Jewish participation that was so worrying. An editorial in the *Jewish Chronicle*, criticising the actions of those Jews who had taken part in the demonstration, believed their actions to have been 'profoundly mistaken'.[16]

The trade union movement in the East End also played a part in mobilising workers against fascism. Like Jewish Communists, Jewish trade unionists did not treat anti-semitism as a specifically Jewish problem but as a threat to democracy in general. They insisted that Jewish workers could only fight fascism effectively by joining a trade union and uniting with non-Jewish workers. The Jewish Labour Council, formed out of a conference of Jewish trade unionists in 1934 was one such initiative which aimed at bringing Jewish workers into the wider anti-fascist movement.[17] However, even one of the Council's leading lights was later forced to admit that support for the Council remained lacklustre.[18]

As well as Jewish involvement in general anti-fascist initiatives, there were also specifically Jewish organisations which specialised in communal defence work. Among the more significant of these were the two ex-servicemen's organisations: the Jewish Ex-Servicemen's Legion and the Ex-Servicemen's Movement against Fascism and Anti-Semitism. Both organisations were based in Whitechapel. The Legion, which was regarded as the official representative body of Jewish ex-servicemen, had been active in the fight against Mosley since 1934.[19] It enjoyed the approval of the Board of Deputies, which was not surprising since it advocated the centralisation of defence work in the hands of the Board.[20] The Legion's assertion that its only concern was with anti-semitism and not with fascism further endeared it to the Board.[21] The Ex-Servicemen's Movement against Fascism and Anti-Semitism was formed in the summer of 1936 at the Whitechapel headquarters of the Workers' Circle Friendly Society, a Jewish socialist organisation rooted firmly in the Russian Bundist tradition.[22] Although the Movement claimed to be non-political and non-sectarian, it was in practice left-wing and predominantly Jewish. Reports in the Metropolitan Police files suggest that the organisation was 'controlled by Jews, most of whom were in close contact with the Communist Party'.[23] In the summer and autumn of 1936, the Ex-Servicemen's Movement held large outdoor meetings at Duckett Street in Mile End and Mansford Street in Bethnal Green, both BUF strongholds.[24] The Jewish People's Council against Fascism and Anti-Semitism (JPC) was the most controversial of all the Jewish defence groups and the one which provoked the greatest opposition from the Board of Deputies. This was because, more than any other Jewish defence group in the East End, it challenged the legitimacy of the Board in its claim to be the sole official representative of the Anglo-Jewish community. At the founding conference of the Council in July 1936, it was contended that the 'Board of Deputies, constituted as it still is, on an obsolete and often farcical basis of representation, does not represent the widest elements of the Jewish people in this country'.[25] In other words, it was felt that the Board excluded working-class Jews.

The JPC was formed from a conference convened by two Jewish Labour Council activists.[26] Nearly 200 delegates attended, representing 86 Jewish organisations including Workers' Circle branches, trade unions, friendly societies, synagogues, Zionist bodies, youth organisations and ex-servicemen's organisations.[27] All seven members of the first executive committee of the JPC were Workers' Circle members. Support from Circle branches was crucial for the survival of the JPC. A number of historians have labelled the JPC a Communist front body.[28] Although individual Communists, notably Jack Pearce, Julius Jacobs and Israel Rennap, were the key figures in the JPC, it is impossible to state with any degree of certainty that the Council was a Communist front organisation. In common with the line taken by trade unionists and other anti-fascists, the JPC firmly believed that the attack on the Jews was 'only a prelude to the attack on the rights and liberties of all the democratic people in the country'. Anti-semitism was therefore as much the concern of 'the British people as a whole as of the Jews'.[29] The Council's most spectacular achievement was to collect 100,000 signatures in 48 hours for a petition to the Home Secretary urging him to ban the BUF march through Stepney on 4 October 1936.[30] The JPC's actions during the turbulent month of October won it considerable popular appeal among Jewish East Enders. For example, after the Battle of Cable Street, the *Jewish Chronicle* reported that shopkeepers were very grateful to the JPC for providing them with legal aid.[31]

The JPC's activities were a source of considerable concern to the Board of Deputies and did nothing to allay the Board's fears that the JPC was presenting itself as a serious rival to the Board. Neville Laski, the Board's President, was particularly critical of the JPC for sending a deputation to the Home Office. The Board was prepared to go to extraordinary lengths to de-legitimise the JPC, even urging the Central Committee of the Workers' Circle to ignore it as 'independent, sporadic and undisciplined'; something which the Workers' Circle was hardly likely to do.[32] The Board's Co-ordinating Committee, which was set up in the summer of 1936 to unify the Board's defence campaign, also decided that if reports of the JPC's activities appeared in the press, the Board should issue a communiqué denying their claim to represent the Jewish community.[33]

For its part, the JPC made it clear that it believed that the Jewish community should be united in the fight against fascism and to this end advocated co-ordinating its work with the Board. However, its approaches were rejected.[34] According to Jack Pearce, the JPC's secretary, the major reason for this was that the Board found the JPC's attitude to fascism unacceptable. The Board believed that organised anti-semitism, propagated by the BUF, could be fought by concentrating solely on the defamation of the Jews.[35] Indeed the Board believed that Jews themselves were largely responsible for creating anti-semitism by their own actions and behaviour. Jewish communal leaders such as Neville Laski and Hannah Cohen, President of the Jewish Board of Guardians, asserted that vulgar displays of ostentation and 'crowding' of Jews in certain professions were a major contributory cause of anti-semitism. By contrast, the JPC argued that political anti-semitism was an integral part of fascism and therefore a struggle had to be waged against the BUF.[36]

One major reason for the Board's reluctance to oppose fascism was its determination to remain neutral in British party politics. In other words, the Board wanted to avoid any action which might suggest a Jewish attitude to a political party.[37] In addition, Board leaders were anxious not to antagonise the fascist powers and pointed to Italy where, at the time, Jews were not persecuted. A further reason for the Board's reluctance to co-ordinate its defence work with the JPC was the Council's connections with the Communist Party.[38]

More acceptable to the Board's leadership than the JPC's political campaign was the anti-defamation campaign conducted by the Association of Jewish Friendly Societies. The friendly societies' meetings campaign was, in many senses, bolder than the JPC's campaign because the societies held their open-air meetings in BUF strongholds such as Duckett Street in Stepney and Victoria Park Square in Bethnal Green.[39] By contrast, the JPC held the majority of its meetings in predominantly Jewish areas such as Bloom's Corner and Philpot Street in Whitechapel.

The variety of actions taken by the East End Jewish community to organise their own defence against the BUF indicates a strong degree of political pluralism in the community. This may at first seem surprising in such a solidly working-class community. However, even within the East End Jewish working class there were gradations of social status and wealth. This helps to explain why local political leaders such as Morry Davis and Dan Frankel, who were professional politicians and wished to cultivate a moderate, 'respectable' image, had no desire to be associated with the more radical Jewish political activists in the East End. These Jewish radicals ignored the advice of right-wing Jewish Labour leaders. Prompted largely by the perceived unwillingness and inability of the Board of Deputies to act effectively in the face of fascist attacks, and by the passivity of the elected local leaders, left-wing Jews mounted their own defence campaigns.

As this article has tried to show, dissatisfaction with the Anglo-Jewish establishment, as represented by the Board of Deputies, was conducive to the fostering of a local autonomous political leadership in the Jewish East End. This leadership was itself divided between Labour moderates and Communist radicals. It was these radical leaders who challenged the power and authority of the Board. In this way, political anti-semitism and fascism, instead of uniting the Jewish community, highlighted the sharp social, economic and ideological divisions between working-class Jews in the East End and middle-class Jews in the West End and the suburbs.

NOTES

1. P. Piratin, *Our Flag Stays Red,* 2nd ed. (London: Lawrence and Wishart, 1980), p.14.
2. For profiles of Davis see *East London Observer (ELO),* 15 November 1930; *East London Advertiser (ELA),* 15 November 1930; 28 December 1935.
3. On Davis's Jewish communal work see *The Jewish Graphic,* 30 March 1928; *ELA,* 15 November 1930; *ELO,* 15 November 1930. For published accounts of Davis's career see G. Alderman, *The Federation of Synagogues 1887-1987* (London: Federation of Synagogues, 1987), pp.56-68; G. Alderman, 'M.H. Davis: The Rise and Fall of a Communal Upstart', *Transactions of the Jewish Historical Society of England* 31 (1988-1990), 249-65.
4. *ELA,* 18 September 1937.
5. *ELO,* 13 June 1936.
6. J. Jacobs, *Out of the Ghetto: My Youth in the East End, Communism and Fascism, 1913-1939* (London: Janet Simon, 1978), pp.148, 170, 171.
7. Circular letter from Rose Henriques to the mothers of absentee girls of Oxford and St. George's Girls' Club, 28 October 1936, Southampton University archives and manuscripts MS 60/17/16. For a succinct explanation of the appeal of the Communist Party to Jewish youth in the East End see the memorandum prepared by the Association for Jewish Youth, 30 June 1936, HO 144/21378/502735/114.
8. *Jewish Chronicle (JC),* 2 October 1936.
9. Ibid. 9 October 1936.
10. Piratin (see note 1), p.20.
11. Jacobs, *Out of the Ghetto* (see note 6), p.237. See also S. Bornstein and A. Richardson, *Two Steps Back: Communists and the Wider Labour Movement, 1935-1945* (Ilford: Socialist Platform, 1982), p.47.
12. Piratin (see note 1), pp.18-19.
13. Ibid., p.18.
14. Interview with Phil Piratin (June 1985). For the conflict between Jacobs and Piratin see also N. Branson, *History of the Communist Party of Great Britain, 1927-1941* (London: Lawrence and Wishart, 1985), p.162; W. J. Fishman, 'A People's Journée: The Battle of Cable Street (October 4th 1936)', *History from Below: Studies in Popular Protest and Popular Ideology in Honour of George Rudé,* in F. Krantz (ed.) (Montreal: Concordia University, 1987), pp.385-7.
15. G. C. Lebzelter, *Political Anti-Semitism in England 1918-1939* (London: Macmillan, 1978)

p.163; R. Thurlow, *Fascism in Britain: A History, 1918 -1985* (Oxford: Basil Blackwell, 1987), p.111; Piratin, *Our Flag*, ibid, p.23; H. Pelling, *The British Communist Party: A Historical Profile*, 2nd ed. (London: A. and C. Black, 1975), p.192.
16. *JC*, 9 October 1936. This issue provides comprehensive coverage of the day's events. For detailed accounts of the Cable Street demonstration see also R. Benewick, *The Fascist Movement in Britain* (London: Allen Lane, 1972), pp.225-29; C. Cross, *The Fascists in Britain* (London: Barrie & Rockliff, 1961), pp.159-61; Lebzelter, *Political Anti-Semitism*, pp.39, 163.
17. *JC*, 25 October 1935; *The Circle,* December 1934, p.5. See also *The Workers' Circle Golden Jubilee Bulletin* (London, 1961), p.20.
18. *The Circle,* May 1937, p.8.
19. *The Jewish Ex-Servicemen* 1:1 (December 1934), 1, 10, 22.
20. L. Sarna (General Honorary Secretary of the Legion) to N. Laski (President of the Board of Deputies), 8 September 1936, Board of Deputies Archive (BDA), E1/11; *JC*, 10 July 1936.
21. Sarna to Laski, 14 September 1936, BDA, E1/11. On the Legion's participation in the Board's anti-defamation campaign see *JC*, 23 October 1936.
22. *ELO*, 1 August 1936.
23. Commissioner's Monthly Report, August 1936, Metropolitan Police files (MEPO) Public Record Office, 2/3043/10A. See also ibid., October 1936, MEPO 2/3043/21B; June 1937, MEPO 2/3043/61A.
24. *JC*, 4 September 1936.
25. *JC*, 31 July 1936. See also *JPC Conference Report,* 15 November 1936, University of Southampton archives and manuscripts MS 17/16, p.6.
26. *The Workers' Circle Golden Jubilee Bulletin* (see note 17), p.20; *ELO*, 25 July 1936; *Daily Herald (DH)*, 27 July 1936.
27. *JC*, 31 July 1936.
28. C. Holmes, *Anti-Semitism in British Society, 1876-1939* (London: Edward Arnold, 1979), p.193; Benewick (see note 16), p.223; R. Skidelsky, *Oswald Mosley* (London: Papermac, 1976), p.403.
29. *Is it True?*, JPC leaflet, n.d., uncatalogued, Communist Party of Great Britain Library (CPGBL). See also *What Fascism Means!*, JPC leaflet, n.d., uncatalogued, CPGBL.
30. *JC*, 2 October 1936. For a full discussion of the JPC's role in the anti-Fascist opposition to Cable Street see *The Workers' Circle Golden Jubilee Bulletin*, p.20; *Jewish People's Council against Fascism and Anti-Semitism and the Board of Deputies* (London: 1936), uncatalogued, CPGBL. See also *Stop Racial Incitement in East London!!* JPC leaflet, n.d., uncatalogued, CPGBL.
31. *JC*, 16 October 1936.
32. *The Circle*, May 1937, p.3. This instruction for the Workers' Circle to ignore the JPC first appeared in a circular letter from Neville Laski dated 5 November 1936, University of Southampton archives and manuscripts, MS 15/53.
33. Co-ordinating Committee minutes, 29 October 1936, BDA, C6/1/1.
34. *Jewish People's Council against Fascism and Anti-Semitism and the Board of Deputies* (see note 30).
35. For example, the Board produced two books; *Jewish Rights and Jewish Wrongs* (London: Soncino Press, 1939) by Neville Laski, and *The Jews of Britain* (London: Woburn Press, 1939) by Sidney Salamon, which aimed at refuting the charges made against the Jews.
36. 'JPC Statement of Policy', typescript, n.d., University of Southampton archives and manuscripts, MS 15/53; *JPC Conference Report,* 15 November 1936, p.3. University of Southampton archives and manuscripts, MS 17/16; Newsam memorandum, 11 June 1937, MEPO 2/3112; *Young Zionist* (YZ), September 1937, pp.10-11; *Jewish People's Council against Fascism and Anti-Semitism and the Board of Deputies* (see note 30).
37. See, for example, Percy Cohen memorandum, *Fascist Parliamentary Candidatures,* 23 November 1936, University of Southampton archives and manuscripts, MS 17/16.
38. Laski to Dr Redcliffe Salaman, 8 December 1936, University of Southampton archives and manuscripts, MS 15/53.
39. *The Leader,* November 1936, p.231; *JC,* 4 September 1936; 18 September 1936.

The Threat of the British Union of Fascists in Manchester

NEIL BARRETT

In Manchester as in London, the British Union of Fascists (BUF) were only too aware of the confrontational activism of sections of the Anglo-Jewish community. At an important BUF rally in September 1934 at Belle Vue, two miles south of the city centre, Oswald Mosley was quite clear about this, remarking 'look at the mobilisation of Jews from Cheetham Hill Road', and later adding: 'What they call today the will of the people is nothing but the organised corruption of the press, cinema and Parliament which is called democracy but which is ruled by alien Jewish finance – the same finance which has hired alien mobs to yell here tonight.'[1]

Richard Reynell Bellamy, often described as the unofficial chronicler of the BUF because of his unpublished *magnum opus* 'We Marched With Mosley', was even more blunt about Jewish opposition to the BUF, concluding that 'the simple fact was that Jews, often the same ones were to be seen more and more frequently in opposition to our meetings in London, Liverpool, Manchester and Leeds'.[2] On a more personal level, Bellamy recalled that anti-fascist opposition to the BUF at Hulme Town Hall in 1936 was led by 'a well known officer of the Young Communist League from Cheetham Hill, a particularly evil looking man and a Jew'.[3]

Yet in a letter to Felix Frankfurter, Harold Laski, a left-wing Professor of Political Science at the London School of Economics and a member of the Labour Party's National Executive Committee from 1935, condemned what he perceived to be 'the complete refusal of the Jews here to adopt a fighting attitude towards Mosley'.[4] It is this apparent contradiction between fascist and Jewish perceptions of the resistance to fascism that forms the basis of the following chapter. The response of the Jewish elite to the threat of the BUF is often dismissed as timid and half-hearted, without much discussion as to the nature of this response and the logic which underpinned it. This view of the Jewish elite was not necessarily shared by contemporaries. Victor Gollancz, writing to his cousin Hugh Harris, remarked exasperatedly that nothing would really induce me to meet the Managing Director of the *Jewish Chronicle* — unless he is going to have a very different policy from that of his predecessor.

I am bound to say that I regard the whole 'line' of the *Jewish Chronicle* — We are not against fascism, but simply against the anti-semitic element of Fascism'... as the last word in ... well let it be!⁵

By focusing on Neville and Nathan Laski in particular, it is possible to analyse the key elements which may be broadly seen to comprise both the national and local responses to the BUF, as well as the interplay between the two. Neville Laski KC, born in Manchester in 1890, was President of the Board of Deputies of British Jews (BoD) between 1933 and 1939. Neville's father, Nathan, had been born in Middlesbrough in 1863 and died in Manchester in 1941. Nathan, whose father had come to Britain from Poland in 1831, became an extremely successful businessman whose eminence had contributed significantly to putting Manchester Jewry on the wider communal map. He too had been a past President of the BoD and was President of the Council of Manchester and Salford Jews (CMSJ) between 1931 and 1940. The Laski family can be characterised as 'alrightniks', one of a number of families identified by Bill Williams as part of a group of more recent immigrants who had been absorbed into the older Jewish elite and readily espoused traditional values.⁶

A number of complementary approaches characterise the attitude of the BoD to the threat of the BUF. Geoffrey Alderman argues that there were two recognisable strategies linked to their aim of countering BUF slanders.⁷ Firstly, there was intelligence gathering, monitoring of the media and co-operation with the intelligence services, notably Special Branch. The second strategy revolved around the publication and distribution of literature which both emphasised the positive contribution of the Jews to British life and aimed to highlight the shortcomings of the BUF. The BoD were only too well aware that dealing with BUF slanders was far from straightforward. In his study of the development of the BUF in the East End of London, Thomas Linehan notes the residuum of anti-semitism from the earliest years of the century when the British Brothers League had been active there.⁸ He also highlights the existence of Jewish rackrent landlords, Jewish traders flouting Sunday trading laws, disquiet over cultural changes associated with perceived Jewish control of the cinema and Jewish dominance of the furniture trades. The existence of such people has led Alderman to conclude that the Jews of the East End 'had contributed much to anti-Jewish feeling in East London'.⁹

This interactionist approach has been criticised for downplaying the specificities and vitality of pre-existing racial stereotypes. According to Bryan Cheyette, this approach leads to conclusions that are little more than self-fulfilling prophecies – the perfidy of Jewish controlled international finance being perhaps the most obvious example.[10] Bill Williams notes that in the last decade of the nineteenth century, the growth in Manchester of a number of short-lived newspapers such as the *City Lantern*, *City Jackdaw* and the *Spy* sought to cash in on anti-Jewish feeling as competition within the labour market intensified.[11] Yet by the 1930s the Jewish community in Manchester seems to have been integrated into the wider community to the extent that questions of visibility, either cultural or geographical, or economic separation, do not seem to have loomed large for the wider community. As a consequence, the playing of the Jewish card by the BUF in Manchester failed to produce much of a popular response. The Jewish anti-fascists, who were often the BUF's most resolute opponents both in the city and beyond, wore their Jewishness most lightly. I would argue that this was very much a function of their distance from the local elite and of the influence of a variety of left-wing influences encountered in the household – most Jewish anti-fascists in Manchester were the sons and daughters of first generation immigrants. In her study of Jewish anti-fascist activism in Manchester, Sharon Gewirtz also highlights the enduring importance of political tradition, and this survey is heavily dependent on the oral testimony of those most involved in anti-fascist activism in the Challenge Club, the Cheetham Branch of the Young Communist League (YCL).[12] In the East End of London, as in Manchester, many Jewish anti-fascists on the front line in the campaign against the BUF seem to have accepted that the Communist Party was the most suitable vehicle for opposition to the Blackshirts. This is one conclusion drawn by Elaine Smith in her study of Jewish anti-fascist activism in the East End, where the perceived tardiness of the BoD to act was, she argues, a major factor in the formation of the Jewish People's Council Against Fascism and Anti-Semitism (JPC).[13]

The BoD were well aware of these accusations which, without doubt, influenced their response to BUF attacks. The *Jewish Chronicle* under the editorship of Ivan Greenberg highlighted the need for Jews to act as model citizens beyond reproach. The editorial of the New Year's Day edition of 1937, the first under Greenberg's editorship, argued that it was necessary to stamp out 'the materialism which is rampant among some of our people' and the 'vice of vulgar display'.[14] Having highlighted the three fronts which the national leadership identified as crucial in dealing with the threat of the BUF, namely intelligence gathering, the publication and distribution of literature and imploring Jews to act as model citizens, I will firstly examine these strategies as they were implemented at the national level before considering how these defence imperatives were interpreted and implemented in Manchester.

The existence, by the end of 1936, of fifteen Vigilance Committees, locally controlled bodies which looked to the BoD for direction, highlights the way in which national initiatives were implemented at the local level. These bodies appear to have had three main functions, all of which were linked closely to BoD concerns. Firstly, the Vigilance Committees were to watch for any anti-semitic activities or influences in their locality. Secondly, they were to keep an eye on the press and, if necessary, answer any letters or refute any charges locally or with reference to the Co-Ordinating Committee of the BoD. Thirdly, the Vigilance Committees had a remit to guard against anti-social behaviour by members of the Jewish community which might bring the Jewish people into disfavour.[15] The development of Vigilance Committees can be seen as having a dual function. Not only were they concerned with the threat of the BUF and with endeavours to bring errant co-religionists to heel in terms, for example, of eschewing ostentation and behaving as model employers, but these bodies can also be viewed as an attempt to calm frayed communal nerves. By the middle of 1936, the wider Jewish community was becoming increasingly fearful of the threat posed by the BUF and open divisions within the BoD were becoming more visible. Writing to the *Jewish Chronicle* at the end of July 1936, the Chairman of the Jewish Labour Committee decried the setting up of a Press and Information Committee by the BoD in order to counter BUF slurs as too little too late. He then proceeded to outline a more damning critique of the Board which, he argued, in no way represented the mass of Jews nationally, 'constituted as it still is, on an obsolete and often farcical basis of representation that does not represent the wider elements of Jewish people in the country'.[16]

Alderman notes that the production of leaflets and election material by the BoD and its local agencies had a marked political dimension.[17] The policy of supplying of election literature, which candidates passed off as their own, was begun at the municipal elections of 1937, when the BUF fielded a number of candidates in the East End of London. This tactic was used to good effect in two wartime by-elections at Leeds North East and Middleton and Prestwich, both of which had sizeable Jewish communities. Some BoD inspired pamphlets were used specifically to highlight the positive contribution of the Jewish community to British society. One example was a pamphlet entitled *The Jews of Britain*, published in September 1936. The pamphlet refuted the claim that Jewish interests controlled the British government or press and that the growth of Jewish immigration was becoming a problem. Moreover, it was emphatically denied that 'Jews had any motives for instigating the last war, and that they seek to embroil Britain in another war, [which] is a foul and baseless calumny'.[18] In final conclusion, it was vigorously asserted that

> **Charges are being spread with the object of undermining the good relations which exist between the Jews and non Jews in this country. What a contemptible campaign!**
>
> **The British Empire has been founded on the principle of toleration for all races and creeds. Why destroy this principle? The Jewish community in Britain is composed of law abiding and peaceful citizens, proud of their citizenship and just as mindful of their obligations and duties as any other class.**

JUDGE THE JEWS BY FACTS — NOT FABLES[19]

Another favoured tactic used by the communal leadership in their propaganda campaign revolved around exposing the anti-semitism of the BUF and drawing a number of differing conclusions from that fact. In this vein, the Jewish Defence Committee, another BoD vehicle, produced a number of pamphlets attacking the BUF that were not so easily traceable to the BoD, which usually used Woburn Press. *The BUF and Anti-Semitism. An Exposure* was published in 1937 by C. H. Lane as was *The BUF by the BUF* which was probably published the following year. The same publishers produced *True Blue Patriots of the BUF* which is undated, but was probably produced in the earliest months of the war, given its content. The first two pamphlets used material from those who, for differing reasons, had become disenchanted with the BUF. In *The BUF and Anti-Semitism*, the comments of Charles Wegg Prosser on leaving the organisation were noted. He had concluded:

> I renounce my political allegiance to you for the following reasons. Your methods have become increasingly dictatorial and un-English. You are sidetracking the whole issue of social betterment by the anti-Jewish campaign.
> I have watched with dismay the mentality which said, get rid of the Jews, and you will automatically get rid of unemployment, slums and sweating.[20]

This theme was aired again in *The BUF by the BUF* which quoted more of the words of Wegg Prosser.[21] The thoughts of A. C. Miles, formerly the Director of Propaganda in the BUF[22] were also noted, particularly concerning the Blackshirts' endeavour to be all things to all men – anti-semitic in East London, Leeds and Manchester, anti-Roman Catholic in Edinburgh and anti-Protestant in East Anglia.

Effective intelligence gathering was crucial to the BoD in its efforts not only to combat the threat of the BUF but also, perhaps more importantly, to maintain the fiction of its ability to articulate the concerns of the wider Anglo-Jewish community. Neville Laski frequently highlighted his close links with the Home Office and he seems to have assisted the intelligence services, regarding the activities of certain right-wing groups, on a number of occasions, for example, the BoD investigation into the activities of the Nordic League, the Right Club and the Pro-British Association. The Nordic League, one of a number of shadowy right-wing groups which operated in the 1930s, had been infiltrated by a former Special Branch Inspector employed by the BoD.[23] The League had amalgamated with Arnold Leese's Imperial Fascist League in 1934 and was openly committed to racial nationalism. Its leading member and publicist was the Conservative MP for Peebles, Archibald Maule Ramsay. By late 1939, the Nordic League was attempting to co-ordinate and direct the activities of all fascist groups, including the BUF, a Metropolitan Police Report noted.[24]

Yet, on closer inspection, the response of the communal elite seems to have been more concerned with gathering intelligence related to the activities of sections of the Jewish community, whilst at the same time also endeavouring to keep Jewish anti-fascist activism contained within tolerable bounds.[25] Two examples highlight this concern. Like Smith, David Cesarani concludes that the dilatory way in which the BoD was perceived to be acting in respect of BUF threats in the East End of London was a crucial factor in the formation of the JPC.[26] Unsurprisingly, the JPC was highly critical of the BoD. In a pamphlet entitled *Anti-Semitism and the Board of Deputies*, the Board noted JPC criticism for refusing to work with them in a co-ordinated fashion.[27] In reply to this charge, the Board concluded that it could not work with the JPC as it felt that it was self-appointed, sporadic and undisciplined. The accusation of being self-appointed was one which could just as easily be pointed at the Board, given its social composition and limited knowledge of the everyday experiences of the lives of many poorer co-religionists. It was undoubtedly the perceived indiscipline of the JPC which most bothered the communal elite as it endeavoured to maintain the appearance of communal respectability.

The meetings Neville Laski had with Herbert Morrison and Harry Pollitt highlight the concerns of the communal leadership that the good image of the Jewish community ought to be promoted and maintained at all costs. In a meeting with Herbert Morrison in the aftermath of the events at Cable Street early in October 1936, Laski noted that Morrison was seriously contemplating, if the Government did not take action of a vigorous character, of forming a defence corps out of his own Party for the East End, which would be truly defensive and in no way aggressive. He said he would like to have some contact with me on the question of certain Jewish employers, house agents and house owners. I said that anything brought to my notice would be investigated and, if possible, suitable action taken. His view was that the very best way to kill the Fascist Movement was to ignore it, and he was wholeheartedly with me in the discussion of the information I had got as to the views of the Home Office, the Police and the Press that if everyone would combine to stay away, no step more destructive to this Movement could be visualised.

He said he was prepared to instruct his people in categorical terms to stop away, but he was very doubtful if it was useful unless the Communists agreed also. He said he would like to meet Mr Harry Pollitt but that Party distinctions made it impossible for him to extend the invitation, but that if I procured the attendance of Mr Pollitt as on my own invitation and secured from Mr Pollitt a promise that nothing would be said and that it would be private, he would attend.[28]

The meeting between Laski, Morrison and Pollitt took place shortly thereafter, on 14 October 1936. Laski told Pollitt that he was of the opinion that Jewish activism in the Communist Party was damaging the good name of the wider community and that he, Laski, sought with the other two 'to consider with them whether there was any possibility of M. and his friends and P. and his friends in concert with myself and my friends using our joint and separate influences to keep those over whom we might be deemed to have control, off the streets and from meetings and processions of Mosley'.[29] Both Morrison and Pollitt were extremely critical of Jewish employers who sweated their workers – of course this included both Jewish and non-Jewish workers – and were concerned with the need to act against rackrent landlords, whom they seem to have seen as being predominantly Jewish. These concerns clearly highlight the pervasive nature of an interactionist perspective. For Morrison, 'Jews ought to be super-correct in their economic conduct. In any walk of life, at the present time, Jews should see that they should get a 100% corrective, indeed more than 100% if they could get it.' With a typically Morrisonian flourish he suggested that Jews ought to 'keep in the background – except for the more important figures in the community, whose names and position would command respect – and leave it to the Gentiles to fight for them'.[30]

The themes highlighted at the national level are readily observable in

Manchester in the responses of the CMSJ to the threat of the BUF locally. If the BoD was seemingly hamstrung by their acceptance that some BUF accusations had an element of truth in them, the Manchester community appears to have been similarly constrained. The police in the city concluded that it was the confrontational activism of Jewish anti-fascists that provided the catalyst for violence at BUF events. In a letter to the Home Secretary, Sir John Simon, written in 1936, Neville Laski noted the upset caused to his father by verbal attacks in his native Manchester. Laski was at pains to stress that when he visited Manchester shortly thereafter, he would reiterate that the wider community ought to be in no doubt as to the impartiality of the police in the city and the need to respect their authority.[31] In a letter from the Home Secretary to Nathan Laski, it was reported that the Chief Constable had assured Sir John Simon that anti-Jewish activities were being carefully monitored. However, in a letter to the Home Secretary related to these events, the Chief Constable of Manchester, John Maxwell, was far less emollient. He noted that BUF meetings in the city were, by and large, orderly except that 'when any meetings are held anywhere adjacent to the Jewish quarter, trouble usually arises due to the manner in which Jews attending the meeting interrupt and try to prevent the speaker from delivering his message'.[32]

This was not the only time concern was highlighted by the authorities. Later in the same year, the question of Jew-baiting in Manchester was again raised by Neville Laski in a letter to the Home Office. Responding to this concern, the Chief Constable made little mention of the tensions which inevitably resulted from BUF meetings being held at Marshall Croft in Cheetham, concluding that for the Jewish community there was 'nothing to which exception could be taken. From our experience a good deal of trouble which develops can be attributed to the action of certain Communist Jews in the crowd.'[33] Appended to this report was a further comment from R. Taylor, Superintendent of B Division, which covered that part of the city. In referring to the Blackshirt meetings of 13 and 20 November 1936, he concluded that at the first of these there had been little mention of the Jewish question until

> At question time several Jewish Communists, who are well known to the Police, asked some questions directly referring to Jews. Greenwood [BUF speaker] in some instances answered them very mildly and in other instances where questions were asked, particularly by D. Pollick and Leslie Starr, he [Greenwood] definitely refused to answer ...
> There was no reference at this meeting to Jewish Ex-Servicemen, nor was Jack White VC [Jewish holder of the Victoria Cross won with the

Manchester Regiment during the First World War] present, but I understand that he did stay for a short while at the meeting on 20 November 1936.[34]

At the latter meeting, it was reported that a general melee had occurred during question time, after the commencement of offensive Jewish heckling. Five people were arrested for causing a breach of the peace, two fascists and three who were 'of Jewish persuasion and well known Communists'.[35]

It therefore appears that the fears of the communal elite in Manchester that Jewish activism against the BUF could bring the wider community into disrepute were well-founded. One of the many more general slanders the BUF aimed at the Jewish community related to an alleged lack of patriotism which was linked to service in the armed forces in the Great War. Writing to Sir Russell Scott at the Home Office on behalf of the CMSJ, Neville Laski indicated that Jewish ex-servicemen in Manchester were becoming exceedingly agitated by BUF slurs regarding their war service. Laski had been made aware of this tension by the Co-Ordinating Defence Committee of the CMSJ, which claimed that the general melee that engulfed the BUF meeting at Marshall Croft on 20 November 1936 came after a comment from the platform decrying Jewish war service and concluding: 'Yes they went to war – plenty of Jews went to war – with bullets in their backs.' Laski was informed that Jewish ex-servicemen were incensed by this slander and were

> determined to take action of some kind, legal or 'direct action'. They have first however, consulted my Committee and accordingly, I have been instructed by my Officers to ask your legal opinion, Sir, on this matter ...
> I might repeat that Jewish Ex-Servicemen are impatient of delay, and are fully determined to take some sort of action.[36]

The communal elite was concerned that it might be losing control of an important section of Jewish opinion, particularly given their potential for violent confrontational response. One response to this fear locally was the use of Jack White VC in addressing meetings sanctioned by the CMSJ. This tactic was part of a national initiative which used prominent notables, both Jewish and non-Jewish, to counter BUF propaganda using prepared texts. The usefulness of Jack White was that as a Jewish holder of the VC, he could be utilised to nail firmly the lie that Jews had avoided war service. However, White was something of a maverick and it appears that the communal leadership in Manchester were wary of making too public their links with him. A number of meetings at which he had been present had erupted in violence, and the communal leadership were concerned that they might be open to charges of inciting public disorder, the maintenance of respectability being a central part of their *raison d'être*. In its Annual Report for 1936, the CMSJ outlined its concerns regarding the spread of anti-semitism, and it was reported that a Co-Ordinating Committee for Defence Work against Anti-Semitism had been set up. This body augmented the functions of the Vigilance Committee and it was reported that numerous sub-Committees of this body had also been set up. For example, there were sub-Committees to deal with pamphlet distribution, attendance at meetings and the giving of lectures and addresses to non-Jewish organisations. Once more, however, the cautious nature of the communal leadership is readily apparent on closer inspection. The sub-Committee charged with replying to BUF slanders was to complement the work of the Press Council of the CMSJ, formed in June 1933.[37] The Press Council had been set up primarily to overcome the perceived problem of particular individuals rushing to print, which, it was feared, might increase anti-Jewish feeling. In a letter to all Jewish bodies in the area, it was stated that the Press Council was to be consulted prior to any interviews with the press.

The use of pamphlets, as has already been noted, was a favoured and relatively risk-free tactic. The charge that Anglo-Jewry had done little to aid the war effort was countered in *What the Jews of the British Empire Did in the Great War*.[38] In this pamphlet, it was reported that 12 per cent of British Jews had served in the Great War and that of these, fully 80 per cent had belonged to fighting units, the bulk of Jewish recruits being drawn from London, Manchester, Leeds, Birmingham, Liverpool and Hull, where the greatest concentrations of British Jews lived. The numbers of Jewish fatalities and casualties were recorded as was the fact that individual Jews had won five of the 650 VCs awarded. As a postscript to the fear that Jewish ex-servicemen might be drifting away from identifying with the communal leadership, the Annual Report of the CMSJ for 1938–39 noted that defence literature was being distributed by Jewish members of the British Legion, suggesting that the rift had only been a temporary one.

An example of a publication aimed specifically at the Manchester area was a pamphlet entitled *How Refugees Help Lancashire: New Industries With Secret New Processes*. The example of a Dr Kroch in Eccles was highlighted as a positive contribution to the depressed local economy.[39] It was pointed out that numerous Lancastrians had found employment after Kroch, fleeing Nazi tyranny, had set up a factory in the town which used a patent chemical developed by him for the tanning of leather.[40] The pamphlet served to highlight the positive contribution of the Jewish community to Britain but, given the date of its publication in mid-1939, refutation of the BUF campaign against Jewish refugees from Europe must also have been an important concern.[41] The CMSJ was also active at the wartime by-election at Middleton and Prestwich of May 1940 at which the BUF fielded a candidate.[42] At their 1940 Annual General Meeting, held on 17 July, it was reported with satisfaction that the efforts of the CMSJ had borne fruit. The CMSJ had produced significant amounts of literature for the Conservative candidate and the communal leadership was heavily involved in the monitoring of the BUF campaign. Tony Kushner points out that by the time of the Leeds North East by-election, the BoD was producing leaflets in support of the mainstream political parties.[43] For Kushner, the production of leaflets which warned Jews that the BUF meant 'Concentration Camps for You' heralded a change of emphasis by the BoD, in that by 1940 the communal elite felt able to denounce the BUF – and fascism more widely – as a threat to democracy and the British way of life.

The CMSJ, like the BoD, was only too happy to keep at arm's length those anti-fascist bodies it felt to be both radical and beyond communal control. In 1933 the CMSJ had set its face against the proposed boycott of German goods and manufacturers.[44] Any thought of co-operation with anti-fascist bodies was equally circumscribed. In 1936 the British Union of Democrats wrote to the CMSJ asking that the communal leadership give their blessing to a meeting planned in opposition to a BUF rally at Albert Croft, Miles Platting. True to form however, the Executive Committee of the CMSJ shied away from confronting their detractors openly, and Nathan Laski claimed that he had received assurances from the Chief Constable that the BUF would not be allowed to hold open air meetings in Jewish districts.[45] At this meeting of the Executive Committee of the CMSJ, specimens of BUF literature were examined and it was suggested that an official shorthand writer ought to be in attendance at the BUF rally so that an accurate record of Mosley's speech could be obtained.[46] At this time, Nathan Laski seems to have been in close contact with the city's Chief Constable. At a Quarterly Meeting dated 7 July he sought to calm fraying communal nerves assuring listeners that 'the Jewish people [ought] not to be alarmed at the activities of the Fascists. The Fascist question was not a Jewish question. The Police would use their best endeavours to see there was no breach of the peace.' Clearly, it seems, the Jewish community did have something to worry about. The communal leadership, in playing any such fears down whilst seeking to gain assurances from the authorities, seems to have been very anxious to hold the community together, albeit that part over which it exercised some control.

Faith in the ability and willingness of the authorities to deal with the threat posed by the BUF was highlighted at a meeting late in 1936, when it was resolved 'That all meetings for propaganda under the auspices of the Co-Ordinating Committee be suspended pending the passing into law of the Public Order Bill now before the House of Commons'.[47] This attitude seems rather complacent, especially as the National Council for Civil Liberties (NCCL) in Manchester was warning its London headquarters of the growth of anti-semitism in the city at the end of November 1936.[48] It was reported that on 13 November a pig's head had been tied to a synagogue door in Crumpsall and BUF leaflets strewn outside.[49] This had been kept out of the press, at the request of the synagogue, and represents clear evidence of the CMSJ's desire to keep the lid on such matters, especially as there was no mention of the incident in the communal records. There was, however, a letter from Nathan Laski to Canon Shimwell, the Chairman of the NCCL in Manchester, asking to join the organisation, though the NCCL in Manchester was linked to the CMSJ through the person of L. F. Behrens who served on the CMSJ at this time and was also listed by the NCCL as its Treasurer. It would appear, then, that the CMSJ was keen to extend its intelligence-gathering capacity to the extent of being willing to liaise with an organisation often seen as a front for the Communist Party of Great Britain (CPGB). It may also be the case that the communal leadership hoped to influence the activities of the NCCL, thus allowing it to serve a dual function both as intelligence-gatherer and as a possible link to certain elements outside communal control.

The belief that Jews ought to be model citizens was another national concern in Anglo-Jewry which was studiously replicated at local level. The beginning of 1935 saw increased efforts towards the maintenance of communal control as the CMSJ sought to liaise with the Clerks of the Justices in Manchester and Salford in order to ascertain how many Jewish boys and girls were coming before the Bench.[50] The latter part of 1938 saw the CMSJ endeavouring to put pressure on Jewish employers in the waterproof garment trade by publicising their view that these employers ought to recognise the principle of collective bargaining. It was also concluded that a resolution to this effect ought to appear in the local press, with the Manchester and Salford Trades Council also being made fully aware of the CMSJ position.[51] Early in the following year, it was further resolved that Jewish employers needed to be convinced of the virtue of allowing their employees to join trade unions, this representing 'a bulwark against Fascism'.[52]

What conclusions can be drawn from this survey of elite responses to the threat of the BUF? The Laski connection must surely have had some bearing on the congruence of the responses of the BoD and the CMSJ, and the evidence adduced certainly seems to point in that direction. It is not being suggested that the communal leadership nationally or locally was an undifferentiated whole without internal tensions or diversities of viewpoint. Indeed, as has been shown, in the summer of 1936 as fears of threat of the BUF reached their height, the *Jewish Chronicle*, often little more than a mouthpiece for the Board and its allies, openly criticised what it perceived to be the half-hearted response of the communal leadership. Criticism at this time was not limited to the pages of the *Jewish Chronicle*. A Special Branch Report of September 1936 noted that Barnett Janner, speaking after Neville Laski at a meeting organised by the BoD, had challenged the view expressed by the President of the BoD that Jews ought to keep away from BUF meetings.[53] Janner was extremely critical of what he perceived as the very timid approach of the Board, concluding: 'Why should a fascist speaker be allowed to slander Jewry and get away with it? Jews have a right to defend themselves in such circumstances.'[54]

Dissenting voices could also sometimes be detected amongst the Jewish leadership in Manchester. At an Executive Committee meeting of the CMSJ, with Mr L. Kletz in the Chair for the absent Nathan Laski, there was criticism of 'the ineffectiveness of steps being taken to prevent the insult and abuse of Jewry'.[55] The absence of the leading figure in local Jewry may well have emboldened dissenting voices to air their concerns but, given their appeal to the BoD, it would seem that radical solutions were probably not being sought. The local Jewish elite appear to have accepted, with misgivings, that there was a significant and active Jewish presence amongst the ranks of local anti-fascist activists. The Jewish elite, nationally and locally, do seem to have weathered the storm of the summer of 1936 without too many difficulties and thereafter internal dissent related to responses to the threat of the BUF seems to have disappeared almost completely. There is a notable congruence between local and national responses to the BUF with relatively few dissenting voices emanating from within that circle.

Harold Laski, in contrast to his father and brother, both noted leaders of Anglo-Jewish opinion, sought to highlight the dangers of fascism both at home and abroad. Harold was a leading light in the NCCL, as well as a Sponsor of the Left Book Club, and actively sought left-wing co-operation in the Socialist League and later the Unity Campaign. In a letter to Felix Frankfurter, dated 10 October 1936, Harold Laski spelled out in unequivocal terms the dangers facing England if it continued to act as if the menace of fascism could simply be ignored. He concluded:

> Add to all this the steady growth of anti-Semitism in the East End, and I predict soberly and cautiously that only a war in which we are anti-

German can save us from some kind of Fascism. I have never seen such blindness in a body of leaders since I began to be interested in politics. It is just pitiable ...[56]

The Laski family may usefully be viewed as a microcosm of the debate between those who favoured confrontation and those who preferred much less abrasive methods.

With regard to the overall communal response to the BUF, Geoffrey Alderman has concluded that the policy of the Board aimed 'not so much at protecting the Jews from their detractors, as at shielding the detractors from the Jews'.[57] He further considers that Board thinking was conditioned by their acceptance of traditional precepts of collective responsibility for the conduct of individual Jews.[58] The BUF was avowedly anti-semitic, bringing it into conflict with the BoD and its regional affiliates. Nationally and locally in Manchester, the communal leadership sought to work behind the scenes in what they perceived to be a considered and measured fashion, in an attempt to impose a unified communal response to the BUF. This approach hardly endeared it to co-religionists for whom the threat of the BUF was one of everyday fact and who undoubtedly felt, not without good reason, that the Board and its allies were too concerned about maintaining the good name of the community. Furthermore, it would appear that the communal hierarchy came uncomfortably close to accepting that BUF slanders had some basis in fact. Imploring Jews not to go in for shows of ostentation, and to act as model employers or landlords, for example, seemed to suggest that BUF propaganda had about it a ring of truth and was tantamount to asking Jews to accept second-class citizenship.

The Jewish elite was acutely conscious of a need to maintain some sort of communal control, and this seems to have been achieved fairly successfully. Yet how were those outside their purview to be channelled away from violence which not only brought potential disgrace on the wider community, but also lent credence to BUF claims that its most violent opponents were Bolshevist Jews who had no intention of allowing free speech – supposedly a basic tenet of 'English' cultural traditions of fair play? The communal leadership could implore Jews not to attend BUF meetings. Whilst this message may have worked for many co-religionists, clearly for some Jews it fell on deaf ears. Thus, different tactics had to be developed. The use of notable Jews, such as Jack White VC, in attending specific BUF meetings was one tactic, as was the use of counter meetings, trained speakers on the subject of Jewish defence, and the proliferation of literature answering BUF falsehoods or attacking that organisation. The communal leadership in Manchester also attempted to gain greater access to the NCCL. The two organisations certainly made unusual bedfellows. The motives of the Jewish elite probably had as much to do with keeping an eye on anti-fascist activities as increasing their intelligence-gathering capacity. More usually, links with anti-fascist organisations which were deemed to be both radical and confrontational were eschewed in favour of low-profile activism lest the name of the community as a whole be besmirched. There was undoubtedly an acceptance that certain sections of the wider Jewish community, largely outside the control of the communal leadership, were always likely to confront the BUF in a more active way than the Jewish elite, locally or nationally, deemed to be wise. The leadership therefore concluded that it was vital to keep this kind of activism to a minimum, and to deny, even though it was not self-evidently the case, that militant anti-fascists might be Jewish – in other words to engage in a damage limitation exercise. This exercise was buttressed by largely behind-the-scenes activity at various levels of everyday life, extending from fairly modest activism at the local level through to the development of closer links with the State apparatus. The line developed by the national elite appears to have been followed without much deviation or dissent by the Jewish leadership in Manchester.

NOTES

1. *Manchester Guardian*, 18 September, 1934. At this time, Cheetham, roughly a mile or so from the city centre at its north eastern extremity, was the stronghold of the Jewish proletariat in Manchester. A sizeable proportion of this section of the Jewish community consisted of first-generation immigrants and their children, this factor serving to accentuate the cultural distinctiveness of the area.
2. Richard Reynell Bellamy, 'We Marched With Mosley' (unpublished manuscript dated between 1958 and 1968), pp. 387-8. 'Dick' Bellamy was, at one time, the Northern Organiser for the BUF. In the interwar years, he was first a Black and Tan, later a jackaroo in the Australian outback and then a coffee grower in New Caledonia. He became active in the BUF after returning to Britain. Experiences such as these are not untypical of the feelings of rootlessness engendered by the First World War and in this vein, Bellamy remarked wistfully of his Blackshirt comrades that they were often those 'whose minds lay rooted in the halcyon past which had ended abruptly in 1914'. See p.517.
3. Bellamy, 'We Marched With Mosley', p.478. Given the relatively small size of the groups confronting each other on regular occasions, it is quite likely that both sides knew each other by sight, if not by name. The incident at Hulme, around a mile south-west of the city centre, saw an estimated two to three thousand persons rushing Mosley's car, booing and shouting (*The Times*, 29 June 1936). The police escorted Mosley to the local BUF headquarters and it was here that the violence reached its crescendo, with windows being broken and the BUF flag torn down. There were reports of skirmishes through the night, order being slow to return to the streets.
4. Letter from Harold Laski to Felix Frankfurter, 4 August 1934, quoted in I. Kramnick and B. Sheerman, *Harold Laski: A Life on the Left*, (London: Hamish Hamilton, 1993), p.352. Even more damningly, two years later when once again corresponding with Frankfurter, Laski

ventured that his richer co-religionists would 'risk Fascism in the hope of buying themselves off rather than strengthening the working-class cause'. Quoted in Kingsley Martin, *Harold Laski (1893-1950). A Biographical Memoir* (London: Victor Gollancz, 1953), p.106.
5. Letter from Victor Gollancz to his cousin Hugh Harris of the Jewish Peace Society, letter dated 9 March 1937, University of Southampton archives and manuscripts, MS 136, AJ 177/25.
6. Bill Williams, '"East and West": Class and Community in Manchester Jewry, 1850-1914', in David Cesarani (ed.), *The Making of Modern Anglo Jewry* (Oxford: Basil Blackwell, 1990), pp.15-33.
7. G. Alderman, *Modern British Jewry* (Oxford: Clarendon Press, 1993), p.285.
8. T. P. Linehan, *East London for Mosley: the British Union of Fascists in East London and South West Essex, 1933-1940* (London: Frank Cass, 1996), p.72.
9. Alderman, *Modern British Jewry* (see note 7), p.286.
10. B. Cheyette, 'Hilaire Belloc and the "Marconi Scandal" 1913-1914: A Reassessment of the Interactionist Model of Racial Hatred', in T. Kushner and K. Lunn (eds.), *The Politics of Marginality: Race, the Radical Right and Minorities in Twentieth Century Britain* (London: Frank Cass, 1990).
11. B. Williams, 'The Anti-Semitism of Tolerance: Middle Class Manchester and the Jews, 1870-1900', in A .J. Kidd and K.W.Roberts (eds.) *City, Class and Culture, Studies of Cultural Production and Social Policy in Victorian Manchester* (Manchester: Manchester University Press, 1985), p.86.
12. S. Gewirtz, 'Anti-Fascist Activity in Manchester's Jewish Community in the 1930s' in *Manchester Region History Review*, 4:1 (Spring/Summer 1990).
13. E. R. Smith, 'Jewish Responses to Political Anti-Semitism and Fascism in the East End of London, 1920-1939', in T. Kushner and K. Lunn (eds.), *Traditions of Intolerance. Historical Perspectives on Fascism and Race Discourse in Britain* (Manchester: Manchester University Press, 1989).
14. Both quotations from D. Cesarani, *The Jewish Chronicle and Anglo Jewry, 1841-1991* (Cambridge: Cambridge University Press, 1994) p.159. The East London correspondent of the *Jewish Chronicle*, Maurice Goldsmith, had been unstinting in his criticism of the timidity of the Board's leadership during the middle part of the previous year yet, under Greenberg, he readily engaged in the campaign to expose sweating in Jewish workshops.
15. These aims were listed in the Minutes of the Co-Ordinating Committee of the BoD, dated 12 November, 1936. By this time Manchester had its own Vigilance Committee. The Co-Ordinating Committee of the BoD was centrally involved in the Board's efforts at communal defence.
16. *Jewish Chronicle*, 31 July 1936. The writer was undoubtedly referring to the specific dominance of London Jewry coupled with the overwhelming influence of middle-class concerns. Many of their poorer co-religionists believed that these were Jews for whom the threat of the BUF was not one of everyday concern, living for the most part as they did well away from those areas of settlement, such as the East End of London and Cheetham, where the BUF might be physically encountered.
17. G. Alderman, *The Jewish Community in British Politics* (Oxford: Clarendon Press, 1983), p.122.
18. *The Jews of Britain* (London: Woburn Press, 1936), p.2.
19. Ibid, p.6. Bold in original and capitals and underlined as shown. The Jewish elite had made something of a fetish of the toleration and fair-mindedness of the British. Numerous examples of this are evident in Neville Laski's paean of praise for the English in his book *Jewish Rights and Jewish Wrongs* (London: Soncino Press, 1939). Laski constantly referred to English, rather than British, traditions, concluding, for example that 'Since the middle of the nineteenth century England has been a country ... where it was possible for the Jew to really feel at home. He has had, broadly speaking, equality of treatment and equality of opportunity, and the fact of his being a newcomer has rarely been made a matter of reproach or a ground of discrimination against him.' (p.113).
20. *The BUF and Anti Semitism: An Exposure*, (London: C. H. Lane, 1937), pp.1-2. Wegg Prosser had stood as a BUF candidate in Limehouse in the municipal elections of that year.

21. In this pamphlet, Wegg Prosser was quoted as remarking that '**Anti Jewish propaganda as you and Hitler use it, is a giant side tracking stunt, a smokescreen to cloud thought and divert action with regard to our real problems ... Hitler I cannot judge, but you, I know, are intelligent enough to agree that in places where no Jews exist (as in my home country) there may still exist injustice, poverty, bad housing, low wages dirt and degradation.**' [bold in original], *The BUF by the BUF* (London: C. H. Lane, n.d.), p.5.
22. Miles had also been an Industrial Organiser in Manchester in the earlier part of the decade.
23. HO144/21381/502735/371.
24. HO144/22454/820681. Fascist Organisations. Activities 1939. The report from the Metropolitan Police was dated 4 October 1939. Leaflets distributed by this loose confederation had an undeniable taint of anti-semitism. In early October 1939, it was noted that the BUF and the Nordic League had sunk their differences and merged and that members of the last named had also joined the Peace Pledge Union in late September 1939, as this organisation was, the Report concluded, 'presumably regarded as a useful cover for activities calculated to embarrass the government'.
25. This was all the more important given that an important element of BUF propaganda was related to the high profile nature of Jewish anti-Fascist activism which in turn could be seen to make the anti-semitism of the BUF more explicable.
26. Cesarani, *Jewish Chronicle* (see note 14), p.150.
27. Undated, Woburn Press.
28. University of Southampton archives and manuscripts, MS 134, AJ 33/89.
29. University of Southampton archives and manuscripts, AJ 33/90, p.1. This would seem to clearly indicate Laski's desire to see some control exerted over Jews who lay outside his sphere of influence and may possibly be taken as a sign of desperation. This desperation can be inferred from the fact that Laski was surprised by Pollitt's view that 'I sometimes wonder whether they think they might want to use Mosley one day', a line of argument that was central to many Communist analyses of fascism. These represented capitalism in the last ditch, with the Blackshirts perhaps being prepared for use as a paramilitary force on the streets, much as the SA and later the SS had been used in Germany (p.7). Both Pollitt and Morrison were seemingly of the opinion that 'part of the technique of Mosley in the putting up of Municipal candidates was to let the Tory in and thereby gain a footing in Tory ranks' (p.2). This line of analysis fitted well with left-wing mistrust of the National Government and the view of the BUF as the stormtroopers of the forces of reaction.
30. Ibid, p.3. Such a line of argument must have been music to Laski's ears as it chimed in perfectly with the exhortations of the BoD. Lebzelter believes, correctly it would seem, that this line of argument led the Board close to appealing to Jews to accept second-class status, at least temporarily, in order to dampen down anti-Jewish prejudices. See G. Lebzelter, *Political Anti-Semitism in England, 1918-1939* (London: Macmillan, 1976), pp. 147-9.
31. Oral evidence from Jewish activists suggests that they did not believe that the authorities dealt with them and the BUF evenhandedly, concluding that the authorities clearly favoured the Blackshirts.
32. HO 144/21378/502735/51-146.
33. HO 144/21379/502735/232.
34. Ibid.
35. Ibid. They were named as Monty Rosenfeld, aged 18, Abraham Rosenfeld, aged 24 and David Pollick, aged 25. All came from Cheetham and were each fined 20s. The first named served with the International Brigade in Spain and won the Military Medal in Italy in the Second World War, being killed just prior to its conclusion in that particular theatre. A short biographical note on him can be found in the CPGB special issue of *Lancashire News*, dated 1944.
36. HO 144/21379/502735/232.
37. Executive Committee Meeting of the CMSJ, 28 June 1933.
38. Undated, published by Woburn Press.
39. Roughly four miles west of Manchester city centre.
40. The name of his company was Lankro, probably an amalgam of *Lan*cashire and *Kro*ch.
41. The pamphlet was actually undated but was a reprint of an article taken from the *Manchester*

Evening Chronicle dated 16 May 1939.
42. The result of the election was as follows:

Result of the Middleton and Prestwich By-Election, May 1940
Candidate	Votes
Lieutenant F. E. Gates [Conservative]	32,036
F. Haslam [British Union]	418
Conservative Majority	31,618

Figures from F. W. S. Craig, *British Parliamentary Election Results, 1918-1949* (Chichester: Parliamentary Research Services, 1983), p.401.

43. T. Kushner, *The Persistence of Prejudice: Anti-Semitism in British Society During the Second World War* (Manchester: Manchester University Press, 1989), p.167.
44. Executive Committee Meeting of the CMSJ, 28 June 1933.
45. The Miles Platting district of the city, roughly a mile or so north-west of the city centre, was not a Jewish district, though it did adjoin some of them.
46. Executive Committee Meeting of the CMSJ, 15 July, 1936.
47. Executive Committee Minutes of the CMSJ, 18 November, 1936.
48. NCCL archive, University of Hull, reference DCL 37/4. Harold Laski was a leading figure in the NCCL.
49. Roughly 2 miles north-east of the city centre.
50. Executive Committee Meeting of the CMSJ, 2 February 1935.
51. Executive Committee Meeting of the CMSJ, 21 December 1938.
52. Quarterly Meeting of the CMSJ, 15 January 1939. It does not seem too churlish to question how much this new found interest in workers' rights had to do with self-interest rather than a paternalistic interest in their well being.
53. Liberal MP for Whitechapel 1931-5 and Labour MP for West Leicester, 1945-70.
54. HO 144/21379/502375/166.
55. Meeting dated 17 June 1936.
56. Martin (see note 4) pp.105-6.
57. Alderman, *Modern British Jewry*, (see note 7), p.286.
58. Ibid.

The Straw that Broke the Camel's Back: Public Order, Civil Liberties and the Battle of Cable Street

RICHARD C. THURLOW

The Battle of Cable Street on 4 October 1936 is usually remembered, particularly by the Left, as the day on which the labour movement, the Jewish working classes and the inhabitants of the boroughs decisively checked the incursions of Sir Oswald Mosley and his British Union of Fascists (BUF) into the East End of London. In fact that is a misreading of events, and the areas around North East Bethnal Green, Limehouse in Stepney, Shoreditch, Central Hackney, Stoke Newington, and the Ridley Road, Dalston were to remain centres of Mosleyite activity and political conflict up until the Second World War and beyond.[1] The Battle of Cable Street was to prove significant in other ways, however, which resulted in changes to the law and influenced national history; the difficulties experienced by the authorities were to act as a trigger mechanism for the decision by the National Government to introduce the Public Order Act, which was rushed through all its parliamentary stages by December 1936, and became law on 1 January 1937. Although this was far from the only cause of increasing the powers of the authorities, reducing civil liberties and strengthening the law on public order, the Battle of Cable Street was the last straw for the state. In spite of its reluctance to change the law, and nervousness about how such change would be perceived by public opinion, the government was convinced that police powers needed to be strengthened, in order to monitor and control more effectively state management of fascism and anti-fascism; or, as the authorities perceived it, political extremism in general. In that sense the Battle of Cable Street became the straw that broke the camel's back.

POLITICAL VIOLENCE AND PUBLIC ORDER

Since the mid-Victorian era Britain had gained an enviable reputation for stable constitutional government and lack of state interference in freedom of opinion, provided that incitement to violence or breaking the law had not been advocated. The principles for the maintenance of public order were based on minimal state interference; maximum freedom of expression, assembly and beliefs should be allowed within the law, as individual political opinions, provided they were pursued within a constitutional framework, were no concern of the authorities. As a result the British state had been slow to develop a political police; Special Branch had not been formed until the 1880s, and only then as a response to Irish Fenian terrorism.[2] What became MI5 developed from the need to monitor internal security as a result of worsening international tension and the popularity of the 'invasion scare' genre of spy novels before 1914.[3] Labour unrest, the suffragettes, and the constitutional crises over the Parliament Act and Home Rule between 1909 and 1914, had created increased public order difficulties for the authorities prior to the First World War, but that conflict severely weakened the nation's political, economic and social fabric. Although Britain was on the winning side in the war, the rise of militant trade unionism, the Irish insurrection, the hysteria over the emergence of the revolutionary Communist Party of Great Britain (CPGB) and industrial unrest between 1918 and 1922, culminating in the General Strike of 1926, severely undermined state complacency about the preservation of public order. Many parliamentary politicians in the 1920s also complained of an increase in disruption at political meetings, blamed on communists and other left-wing activists. This concern was not reduced by the diminishing resources available to counter increased unrest. Security and Defence were no more immune to deflationary cuts than welfare expenditure in the inter-war years. Military aid for the civil power was curtailed, expenditure on police was reduced, and means were sought to increase administrative efficiency and more centralised organisation without upsetting local control over the management of regional police forces.[4]

Such difficulties were highlighted by the effects of the accelerating economic and financial crisis between 1929 and 1933. The growth in unemployment from 1 million to more than 3 million in those years, accompanied by increased public order problems associated with the activities of the National Unemployed Workers Movement (NUWM), the militant communist front organisation which provided both successful reformist representation for many of the unemployed before National Assistance tribunals and effectively propagandised their plight in the 'Hunger Marches' of the 1930s, led to increased problems for the authorities. In 1931-2, riots in Belfast, Birkenhead and Bristol led to several fatalities, and the 'Hunger March' to London in 1932, for which contingents of the unemployed arrived from Wales and Scotland as well as most regions of England, caused the authorities to call more policemen on to the streets of London than at any time since 1848.[5] Although the authorities made life as difficult as possible for the NUWM, arranging for only minimal bread and water diets for those marchers who stayed at Poor Law institutions on their journey to London for example, and arrested many of the leaders on dubious charges, the violence associated with the movement caused the government to consider strengthening the law on public order.[6] However it was decided on the advice of the law officers that a greater use of binding over organisers of meetings and demonstrations to keep the peace should be introduced before permanent restrictions be enacted as this would affect traditional rights of freedom of assembly, limit the discretion of the authorities and would be opposed by the parliamentary opposition and public opinion.

FASCIST-COMMUNIST VIOLENCE

The need to strengthen the powers of the authorities with regard to maintaining public order became stronger as a result of fascist-communist confrontation in Britain from 1933. A specifically Jewish dimension to this problem became apparent as up to half of all those arrested as a result of disturbances at meetings and demonstrations in 1933 and 1934 came from the Jewish community. This resulted from the understandable fears of Jewish radicals that the development of fascism in Britain meant an increasing threat to the security of the community, given the introduction of discriminatory anti-semitic legislation and state sponsored persecution in Nazi Germany. This was a perceived threat, even though Mosley forbade the development of political anti-semitism in the early BUF. At the outset it should be stressed that such difficulties, although worrying at times for the National Government, were never on the same scale as the breakdown of state authority in Italy between 1919 and 1922, nor in Germany between 1930 and 1933. Thus there was no equivalent of the 55 socialists and trade unionists murdered by fascists in Grossetto, Tuscany on 30 June 1921, or the 70 Nazis killed in street violence in Germany in 1932.[7] In fact there was not one proven fatality from political violence, neither fascist nor anti-fascist, in Britain in the 1930s; there was no British Horst Wessel nor any anti-fascist martyr. This reflected the fact that, despite diminishing resources and increased political violence, the authority of the British state was not effectively challenged by political extremists in this period. In spite of increased political violence the authorities, through political surveillance and through strengthening the law, were able to manage effectively the problems posed by British fascism and communism.

The formation of the BUF by Sir Oswald Mosley in October 1932 soon led to increased political violence. While Mosley exhorted the necessity for voluntary self-discipline by members of the BUF, and always advocated that members should obey the demands of the police without question, the early days of the movement saw several examples of offensive violence by BUF members against rival fascist groups, and attempted disruption of CPGB meetings and processions. Although Stephen Cullen is correct to suggest that the BUF were far more sinned against than sinning with regard to instigating violence, and that the police arrested a much larger number of anti-fascists than fascists for violent behaviour in the 1930s, the authorities blamed the Blackshirts for the public order problems of the 1930s.[8] Marching through working-class districts and areas of ethnic concentration of British Jews was interpreted as attempting to intimidate and provoke the anger and wrath of the labour movement and the Jewish community. While the BUF insisted on its civil right to march where it pleased the authorities recognised the anger felt by inhabitants who felt their safety and homes threatened by the provocative tactics of the fascists. The potential conflict situation was in some ways analagous to the objections many Irish Catholics have to Orangemen marching in Catholic neighbourhoods in contemporary Northern Ireland.

As a result of increased political confrontation between fascists and anti-fascists the Home Office called a conference in November 1933, where it was decided that the BUF, like the CPGB, should be placed under political surveillance by Special Branch, and that MI5 should report on the results.[9] A sign of the times was that the implementation of that decision should be delayed six months because there was not the money to introduce it immediately. However, as a result of the increased political surveillance, Lord Trenchard, the Metropolitan Police Commissioner, was able to persuade the Home Office to expand Special Branch from 134 to 169 officers in July 1935. A temporary deployment of an extra 50 officers in 1936 was reduced, after the coronation of George VI in 1937, to a permament increase of a further six officers in the Special Branch establishment.[10]

If the activities of Blackshirts necessitated the expansion of secret policemen to monitor their activities, then this was merely the tip of the iceberg with regard to the visible presence of the uniformed branch in the great public order confrontations of the 1930s. Particularly in the East End of London in 1936 and 1937, large numbers of extra special constables were deployed for normal duties, while much of the police establishment was used to maintain order at the more than a thousand public meetings held in each of the summer months between 1936 and 1939, the great majority of them organised by fascists or anti-fascists.[11] The point was that such tactics worked; although Jewish radicals, communists and much of the community in the East End of London distrusted police impartiality, blanket saturation by the police of all potential disturbances, together with the restrictions imposed by the Public Order Act, and the banning of all marches and demonstrations in the East End after July 1937, effectively kept the lid on the seething confrontation between fascists and anti-fascists in the area. Although a considerable headache for both the Jewish community and the authorities in the East End of London, Mosley's espousal of political anti-semitism was counter-productive outside that area. Although political violence and confrontation between fascists, communists and Jewish radicals was a public order problem elsewhere, other areas of pronounced Jewish concentration such as Manchester and Leeds did not experience the same degree of fascist anti-semitism, nor a response in the local community, as did the East End of London. Whilst it would be an exaggeration to blame the introduction of the Public Order Act purely on the the breakdown of tolerance and political liberalism in a small area of east London, culminating in the Battle of Cable Street, the fact that elsewhere the authorities were able to contain political anti-semitism, and potential violence between fascists and communists, suggests that it was a drastic national over-reaction.

The problem for the authorities was that the Home Office was extremely nervous of regulating civil liberties in case the police overstepped their powers. It was very concerned that over-vigilant policing would be challenged successfully in the courts. This was the chief worry embodied in the Home Office response to the assumption of powers by the police, the legality of which was doubted when Manchester threatened, prior to the 1936 legislation, to ban a procession if uniforms were worn, and Leicester stopped Blackshirt meetings in the market place.[12] In fact, apart from the Metropolitan Police, the Home Office could only advise local constabularies about how they regulated marches and meetings. The issues included whether fascist meetings and processions were designed to intimidate or merely express an opinion in an attempt to convert (whether *Wise v Dunning* (1903) or *Beatty v Gilbanks* (1882) was the relevant case law), if there was a right of 'free born Englishmen' to demonstrate in public places, and whether special protection should be given to specific minority groups, such as the Jewish community in this case, who were subject to group libel or abuse. Fascist-communist violence and the Battle of Cable Street were the catalyst which convinced the state to increase the powers of the authorities in regulating public order and civil liberty. Matters pertaining to conflict situations, which had arisen as far back as the 'Skeleton Army' and Trafalgar Square riots of the 1880s, the Kensitite demonstrations of 1903-9 and the suffragette disturbances of 1906-14, were all dealt with under the new Public Order Act.[13] The reluctant authorities decided to regulate more general aspects of law and order, not just problems posed by contemporary extremist violence. Together with amendments to the Public Meetings Act (1908) in 1938, it was to provide the new legal framework for the control of mass political demonstrations until 1986.

THE RISE OF FASCIST ANTI-SEMITISM

Although the BUF, with its black shirts and fasces insignia, was originally modelled on Mussolini's movement, which did not become anti-semitic until 1938, it had nevertheless attracted fascist anti-semites from the outset. Mosley, after visits to Rome and the Brown House in Munich in 1932, and advice from New Party activists like Harold Nicolson, had apparently decided that an openly anti-semitic movement would be counter-productive, both in terms of attracting elements from the political establishment and of converting public opinion, given the philo-semitic liberal British political culture.[14] In his discussions with the smaller fascist movements in 1932, Mosley had come to the conclusion that Arnold Leese was an anti-semitic crank, with his obsessional Jew hatred, his fanatical belief in the authenticity of the *Protocols of the Elders of Zion*, and his nordic racial nationalism. Therefore, when the BUF was formed on 1 October 1932 there was no mention of anti-semitism. Neither was there any reference to it in the manifesto, Mosley's book *The Greater Britain*, published on the same day. Those who looked, however, would have found references to international finance and to alien influences in British life, remarks which could have been interpreted as coded language to attract anti-semites. Such attempts to ignore or downplay potential anti-semitism failed to convince either the CPGB or radicals in the Jewish community, and Mosley was opposed from the outset by both the labour movement and militant Jewish elements. Such opposition led to increasing confrontation and political violence at public meetings addressed by Mosley in Oxford, Hull, Manchester, Middlesbrough and Nottingham in 1933 and early 1934.[15]

From October 1932 until July 1934, Mosley tried to convert the British public to the necessity for 'fascist revolution' in Britain, along the lines outlined in *The Greater Britain*. Essentially, this meant electing a fascist majority in a general election on a geographical franchise, which would then give the executive (Mosley and a Cabinet of five members) the authority to act to cure unemployment. After re-election on an occupational franchise, the full Corporate State would be developed, whose aim would be a tripartite management of industry between capital, labour and the consumer/state. 'Politics' would be the responsibility of the executive. Yet although the BUF experienced spectacular growth in this period, due mainly to the support of Lord Rothermere and the *Daily Mail* between January and July 1934 when the movement grew from 12,000 to between 40-50,000, this had little to do with the attractions of the political programme.[16] It owed much more to the disillusionment felt by many Conservative voters over Baldwin's leadership of the party and the drift of the National Government under the National Labour Prime Minister, the woolly-minded Ramsay Macdonald, despite the large overall majority of the Conservatives. This was essentially the reason why Rothermere supported Mosley, as well as his protectionist plans for the British Empire. In fact the unemployed, whose fate had caused Mosley to revolt against the Party system in the first place, remained impervious to Mosley's campaign, as shown by the lack of BUF success in most areas of high unemployment, such as the North East of England, South Wales and Central Scotland. Only in parts of Lancashire, in some of the cotton towns in 1934-35 did the BUF recruit the unemployed in significant numbers.[17]

This rapid period of growth was followed by the near collapse of the BUF following the clashes between fascists and communists at the Olympia meeting on 7 June 1934. Mosley's Blackshirt stewards and their rough handling of interruptions and heckling were widely blamed for instigating the violence which erupted. Although this interpretation has been recently questioned by Martin Pugh, who rightly points out that the response of Conservative MPs and influential public opinion was far more ambiguous, the controversy over the issue, and the bad publicity for fascism generated by the 'Night of the Long Knives' on 30 June 1934, when Hitler had much of the SA leadership and several Conservative political opponents murdered, caused Rothermere to stop giving free publicity to the BUF, although he still remained on good terms with Mosley.[18] Fascists later claimed that threats by Jewish entrepreneurs to withdraw advertisements from the *Daily Mail* forced Rothermere's hand, although there is no evidence for this.

What is clear is that the National Government took the disturbances at Olympia very seriously. The Home Office had legislation drafted and the matter was discussed three times in Cabinet in 1934. The idea for new public order legislation was only dropped when it became clear that the parliamentary Opposition parties were lukewarm about the idea, and the incidence of fascist-communist confrontation declined in the summmer of 1934.[19]

With the near collapse of the BUF in the summer of 1934 Mosley changed his tactics. The attempt to rebuild the party was based on a reorganisation of the BUF between 1935 and 1938, with greater initiative being given to a grass roots movement which developed propaganda campaigns around local issues. At best this had only a limited impact in most areas of the country, with only partial and slow revival as a result of different local emphases – on the Cotton Campaign in Lancashire, on the restructuring of the shipping industry in Liverpool, on the expansion of the woollen industry in Yorkshire, and on self-sufficiency in British agricultural production in East Anglia. By far the most successful of these initiatives was the impact of political anti-semitism in the East End of London. Indeed it has been estimated that up to one half of the national membership of the BUF in the middle 1930s was concentrated in the four East End boroughs of Bethnal Green, Stepney, Shoreditch and Hackney.[20]

While there was evidence of some anti-semites joining the Mosley movement as early as the New Party, anti-semitism did not become official policy until September 1934. Following the Olympia debacle, Mosley asked A. K. Chesterton to conduct research into Jewish influence in British life; Chesterton, a second cousin to both G. K. and Cecil Chesterton, who had exposed alleged involvement by prominent Jews in the Marconi scandal and the Indian silver affair before 1914, had an anti-semitic family history, but there is no evidence of his notorious virulent cultural anti-semitism before he conducted his research for Mosley. It showed that more than half of those arrested for offences against the BUF were 'little Jews' with Jewish sounding names, while 'big Jews' purportedly dominated 'British' finance and industry.[21] This persuaded Mosley to take off the kid gloves, and in speeches at Manchester and the Royal Albert Hall in September and October 1934 Mosley criticised Jewish influence in British life. Yet this did not open the floodgates; Mosley and most of his propagandists were reticent on the issue for much of 1935. It was only when Richard Alistair 'Jock' Houston in Shoreditch, and E. G. 'Mick' Clarke at Victoria Park Square, Bethnal Green, began to gain receptive audiences in the summer of 1935, together with the public order response of the authorities, that the issue became seen as a fruitful one for the BUF.[22]

The East End of London had traditionally been a reception area for new immigrants. From the late nineteenth century it had acted as a first home for a large influx of refugees who either settled or were in transit to the USA. A campaign led by Tory MPs, parliamentary committees and by the British Brothers League had resulted in the passing of aliens legislation in 1905, which partially defused the question. Although there was a broad range of social, economic and political issues in the 'municipal particularisms' of the East End of London, and to a certain degree there were difficult economic and social problems associated with the activities and behaviour of a small minority, nevertheless alleged

Jewish 'cultural swamping' and behaviour was made the scapegoat for the difficulties of the East End, and emphasised by BUF speakers in the 1930s, some of them trained by William Joyce. Not surprisingly both the Labour movement and the Jewish community were appalled by the attempt to stir up a hornet's nest of resentment amongst East End communities, and the authorities were disturbed by signs of increasing conflict. However the working-class and ethnic responses were divided; the Labour party and the Jewish establishment thought the correct response was to ignore Mosley and deny him the oxygen of publicity. Even the leadership of the CPGB thought the real threat of fascism in the 1930s was from the National Government, who had passed the Incitement to Disaffection Act in 1934, which, as a result of pressure from MI5 and the experience of the Invergordon Mutiny in 1931, proposed draconian penalties for those trying to undermine discipline in the armed forces. The CPGB was more concerned about the threat posed by international fascism, the activities of Hitler and Mussolini, and the need to defend the Spanish Republic. Mosley was perceived as a renegade aristocratic dilettante, and a traitor to the labour movement, a figure of ridicule rather than a threat to the ability to protest.[23] However for the people of the East End, and for many Jewish radicals, action, rather than benign neglect was needed as the correct response to fascist political activity, and a militant anti-fascist grass roots organisation opposed Mosley on the streets.

The growth of East End anti-fascism was an important phenomenon which had greater significance than merely a local response to BUF political activity. Its importance stems from its role in the origins of community politics. Although anti-fascism was an alliance of radical groups and individuals, the role of Jewish communists was to be pivotal. It also forced the CPGB leadership to take over the organisation of the opposition to Mosley at the Battle of Cable Street. Although Special Branch, MI5, the Metropolitan Police Commissioners, and the Home Office were at one in denouncing Cable Street anti-fascism as a communist front, manipulated by the CPGB and its 'subterranean connections' to the National Council for Civil Liberties, it was to spawn a significant political movement which revitalised the politics of a decaying area. Local Jewish communists such as Phil Piratin (later CPGB MP for Mile End 1945-50) and the expelled Joe Jacobs, and radical organisations like the Workers' Circle, were to organise tenants' associations, women's groups, trade union activities and vigilance associations, as well as playing an active role in the campaign for a national charter and greater community involvement in defending working-class living standards during the Second World War.[24] Anti-fascism also both galvanised the CPGB and forced the Labour Party to address the issue of regeneration of the East End, a task which was to be made more urgent by the Blitz. Such political activity had its origins in East End anti-fascism – in the alleged 77,000 signatures to the petition gathered in a few days before 4 October 1936, and in the mobilisation of 100,000 people (at the conservative estimate of Special Branch) who ensured that Mosley did not pass at Cable Street.

FASCISM, ANTI-FASCISM AND THE POLICE

If the anti-fascist opposition to Mosley was to have more significance than the authorities were prepared to credit it with, then various other myths about the maintenance of law, the nature and attitudes of the police as well as the Battle of Cable Street also need re-examination. The conflict generated between Blackshirts and anti-fascists was merely the trigger mechanism for changes in the law which had been formulated in response to previous concerns. D. S. Lewis, echoing the contemporary concerns of the National Council for Civil Liberties (NCCL) has gone further and criticised the 'reactionary' and 'regressive' measures passed by the National Government with regard to public order and internal security issues in the 1930s.[25] Yet this may not be a particularly helpful way of interpreting a complex situation. The release of most of the Home Office public order documents, together with the Metropolitan Police Commissioner's files, now enable us to understand the rationale behind policy-making in this area, the prejudices and preconceptions of the authorities and the interpretation of these events by historians.

The problem of public order for the Home Office was further complicated in the 1930s by the personality of the Metropolitan Police Commissioner, Lord Trenchard (1931-35). Trenchard was brought in to reform a police force tainted by corruption and sleaze, and to restore military-style discipline, but the Home Office mandarins objected to the speed at which he wished to introduce graduate recruitment and a police college. By using his personal influence with the Home Secretary, Sir John Gilmour, Trenchard went above their heads and steamrollered through the changes. The sometimes fraught relations between Trenchard and senior civil servants also reflected differences in public order policy.[26]

These problems were shown quite clearly in 1934 in a response to Trenchard's call for banning the BUF. The Home Office replied that the same consideration still applied as when General Horwood wished to ban the CPGB in the 1920s: there was no argument for outlawing extremist beliefs provided the expression of such policies did not break the law. Only if the authorities' management of the situation under existing powers appeared to be threatened could changes in the law be contemplated. So long as public opinion believed that Britain had a fair and efficient government which upheld the law, the state should not attempt to restrict the holding of political beliefs, no matter how obnoxious they appeared to those who held democratic values. Political surveillance of such movements was necessary, but attempts to restrict liberty would drive political expression underground, and create worse problems in the long run.[27]

Trenchard's trenchant views on fascists were somewhat ironic given that the CPGB accused him of being a closet fascist himself, because of his autocratic style of management and the alleged close connections between Mosley and the RAF, of which the Metropolitan Police Commissioner had been the founder. Trenchard wished to ban fascists because of the public order problems they presented, and the waste of police resources associated with the management of processions and meetings. He particularly wanted to outlaw paramilitary organisations and the wearing of political uniforms. He did not want uniformed stewarding of meetings outside police control, neither did he want the police to be seen as protecting fascists. Trenchard was also concerned that 'respectable' people would appear on CPGB platforms in support of anti-fascist activities. He believed that police should also have the power to enter meetings to prevent disturbance even if they had not been invited by the organisers of the event.[28] Just before his retirement he began to advocate the view that fascist processions should be banned.

Trenchard's views developed in response to practical problems after it was made clear to him that restricting the rights of fascists outside the use of emergency powers was not a feasible political or legal option. He was succeeded as Metropolitan Police Commissioner in 1935 by Sir Philip Game, who, as his leading administrator in the RAF, had been personally selected to succeed him. However, although the Home Office officials found him more reasonable to deal with, he was even more anti-fascist than his predecessor. Game wished to outlaw political anti-semitism and to ban the fascist movement.[29] His experience as Governor-General of New South Wales in the early 1930s, when he had sacked the Prime Minister and experienced problems with fascist demonstrations, gave him the right background for dealing with the troubles in the East End of London.[30] Whilst maintaining civil relations with the Home Office, he was later to use his personal influence with the Home Secretary, Sir Samuel Hoare, to maintain the ban on marches against the advice of officials in 1938.[31] He wished to extend the ban to the whole of London, but this move was turned down by the Cabinet after objections from the Home Office officials and consultation with the Opposition.[32] Hoare had been Trenchard's closest political supporter in the inter-service battles of the

1920s, and the Home Office and Commissioner's files have several congratulatory notes from the Home Secretary relating to Game's efficient and hardline management of fascist disturbances in the later 1930s. Problems associated with the alleged partiality of the police in favour of the fascists in the 1930s most certainly did not originate in official policy.

In fact, Sir Philip Game insisted that his officers should err on the side of harshness with regard to cautioning and arresting anti-semitic speakers in the East End. In July 1936, at the request of the Home Secretary, Sir John Simon, Game began to submit monthly reports to the Home Office on anti-semitic disturbances in the East End.[33] These were supplied until the summer of 1944. Game also circulated at the same time a memorandum to all police divisions on the necessity to keep the peace, to curb the provocative tactics of anti-semitic speakers, and not to allow freedom of speech to degenerate into street brawls. However the police often experienced difficulty in differentiating between anti-semitic provocation and what was alleged to be humourous banter at the multitude of political meetings in the East End between 1936 and 1939. Whether this represented institutional racism, the suspicion that more trouble would be caused if meetings were terminated suddenly by the authorities, or the fact that many speakers were addressing audiences which agreed with or were neutral about the comments being made, was a moot point. There is evidence that all three reasons can be seen as causes of relative police inaction. Thus E. G. 'Mick' Clarke was not prosecuted following a speech at Chester Street, Bethnal Green on 4 October 1936, despite Special Branch shorthand notes which clearly quoted his words: 'It is about time the British people of the East End knew that East London's big pogrom is not far away now. The people who have caused the pogrom to come near in East London are the Yids.'[34] Interestingly, a private prosecution was later taken out against Clarke following a meeting at Stepney Green on 3 July 1938, when several anti-fascists complained about his alleged remarks about 'dirty rotten Jew bastards', to policemen present who claimed that they did not hear him utter those words.[35] The magistrate chose to believe the anti-fascists, fined Clarke ten pounds and awarded costs to the private prosecution. The case however was lost on appeal.

Yet given the literally thousands of political meetings held in the East End, and the many surviving Special Branch reports of anti-semitic speeches, what is surprising is the lack of action taken by the police, even where fascist and anti-fascist meetings were held adjacent to each other, given the clearly stated instructions of Sir Philip Game in his memorandum. What became quite clear was that the police on the ground were more concerned, provided that public order was not threatened, about the principle of free speech for fascists and communists than they were with protecting Jews or other minorities from verbal abuse. There also seemed to be a considerable discrepancy between anti-fascist and Jewish claims of physical assault instigated by fascists, and the lack of such incidence in the police records. Tom Linehan's *East London for Mosley*, for example, provides numerous examples of both fascist and anti-fascist unofficial violence, arson, desecration of Jewish synagogues and property, as well as much anecdotal evidence of the more dubious activities of both sides, a dimension which is lacking in the police records for the most part.[36] Certainly the Jewish working classes in the East End did not see the police as protecting their interests, and much of the tension arose from not only fascist/anti-fascist hostility, often based on reactions to provocative anti-semitic abuse or attempts to prevent its utterance, but also neighbourhood hostility to the massive police presence, which was often interpreted as protecting fascist attempts to insult and intimidate the Jewish ethnic population of the East End.

If the police were not seen as neutral arbiters of the peace by many East End inhabitants, it was also true that the authorities, the National Government and the leadership of the Labour Party and the Jewish community were equally critical of East End anti-fascism and what was perceived to be the alleged sinister role played by the CPGB in its development. Indeed the response of the authorities was partly conditioned by the political vacuum in the East End. Problems of political mismanagement in the Labour Party, particularly in Stepney, the collapse of the dominant Liberal Party in Bethnal Green in 1934, and the seething discontent over housing and working conditions, created the volatile mixture which provided political space for the development of BUF influence, and the anti-fascist reaction. The growing Jewish People's Council against Fascism and Anti-Semitism (JPC), which organised the Cable Street demonstration, was seen as a sinister CPGB front organisation by the authorities. The Home Office reported that Neville Laski of the Board of Deputies of British Jews had informed them that the JPC was a communist political organisation which did not contain any responsible element and was in no sense representative of Jewish opinion in this country.[37] Perhaps even more indicative of respectable opinion were the comments of Anthony Crossley MP, who acted as an 'impartial eye-witness' at the Battle of Cable Street, and reported his observations to the Home Office. With the help of the cover of a 'red bearded artist friend', Crossley provided an interesting, and reasonably objective account of the violence at Cable Street. However his covering letter left some room for doubt; in it he could not help vent his prejudice that 'it was very hard in that crowd to think of the demonstrators as other than a riff-raff of the foreign population of London'.[38] Many in the police had similar views, prejudices reinforced by the often obstreperous responses of anti-fascists to police requests, whilst Mosley informed fascists to obey all police orders without question. The lack of Jewish local policemen, and the hostility of much of the East End to figures of authority ensured that there would be little co-operation between the local community, either fascist or anti-fascist, and the forces of law and order.

THE BATTLE OF CABLE STREET

The Battle of Cable Street on 4 October 1936 represented the point where the state intervened to prevent fascist-communist confrontation from becoming a challenge to the maintenance of law and order. Reading the relevant documents today, the immediate response is why was it necessary to use a sledge-hammer to crack a nut, and why were most of the reactions so alarmist? In retrospect it is quite clear that although CPGB anti-fascist propaganda was successful in both mobilising mass hostility to Mosley on the streets and as an effective recruiting device for the party, it failed to alter public opinion, or influence, except negatively, the political establishment. The use of political anti-semitism by the BUF, although it galvanised support for fascism in a few localities in east and north-east London, proved to be highly counter-productive elsewhere. Mosley and the BUF, already perceived as political failures since Olympia, and often regarded with ridicule, were seen in Nicholas Mosley's account to be ignoring the *Rules of the Game* by going *Beyond the Pale*.[39] In fact the Battle of Cable Street was not a decisive setback for the BUF, and the evidence suggests that membership continued to increase slowly in London; but its impact on influential opinion elsewhere was disastrous and the pressures on the authorities forced the government to act.

The Battle of Cable Street represented the point where Jewish activists forced the CPGB leadership, against its will, to oppose Mosley on the streets, in a high profile campaign to destroy the BUF. After Olympia on 7 June 1934, the authorities had forced Mosley to abandon plans for a procession and demonstration at the White City in August 1934; its replacement, the Hyde Park demonstration in September 1934 was a fiasco, with most of the fascist speakers failing to make themselves heard as anti-fascist demonstrators effectively heckled the proceedings. The near collapse of the BUF in 1935 led to the decline of anti-fascist opposition, and the relatively trouble-free 'Mind Britain's Business' campaign in which Mosley indirectly advocated support for Mussolini's invasion of Abyssinia. However, the beginning of the BUF's incursion into the East End in late 1935, together with the onset of the Spanish Civil

War in 1936, reactivated CPGB concerns about fascism, including British fascism. Those radicals most concerned in the East End of London began to organise a grass roots campaign to oppose Mosley and the BUF, and to persuade the CPGB leadership to challenge Mosley's incursion into the area.

The first major confrontation occurred following Mosley's rally at the Royal Albert Hall on 22 March 1936. This was rowdy, but the main trouble flared up afterwards when Sir Philip Game, the new Metropolitan Police Commissioner, banned all meetings within a half-mile limit of the Albert Hall. At Thurloe Square, the CPGB defied this instruction and the attempted meeting was broken up when mounted police cleared the area, and a certain amount of disorder resulted. The CPGB had called for observers in advance of the meeting and the police interpreted this as an attempt to monitor police behaviour and to provide a slanted interpretation of the actions of the authorities if trouble should flare up. This it did and Ronald Kidd of the National Council for Civil Liberties set up an unofficial enquiry to study the violence at Thurloe Square. Needless to say the evidence of the enquiry and the police reports did not tally, and the Home Office viewed the former as a propaganda stunt by a CPGB front organisation.[40]

The deterioration of community relations in the East End, the fascist and anti-fascist campaigns in the summer of 1936, and the swamping of the East End with policemen to keep the two opposed factions apart and to maintain law and order at meetings led to increased tension. The Home Office was also perturbed by the outcome of *Rex v Leese* in September 1936. Leese was indicted on charges of seditious libel and creating a public mischief after alleging in *The Fascist* that Jews practised ritual murder against Christian children. The jury found Leese guilty of the lesser charge, but not guilty of seditious libel.[41] He still went to prison for six months because he refused to pay a small fine. The Attorney General was astonished at the verdict and concluded that the jury viewed Leese as a stupid crank with honest convictions who should be found not guilty of the serious charge of seditious libel. The Home Office was worried by the outcome, and this reinforced their resistance to specific clauses which would specifically outlaw racial incitement. Unless it could be proven to have fomented disorder, the authorities refused to prosecute even the worst cases of anti-semitic or racist libel. This proved to be the central issue in several blatant cases in the following years. Leese was not charged over the more detailed accusations expressed in *My Irrelevant Defence* in 1937, because a further acquittal might be misunderstood by the public.[42] A. K. Chesterton, following an alleged call to string up Jews on lamp-posts made at a Nordic League meeting in 1939, was not prosecuted in order to avoid publicity for the organisation and because of a slight discrepancy in the evidence;[43] and there was no prosecution of Alexander Ratcliffe's *Truth about the Jews* because, although it was deplorable, legislation protecting a particular group or person would set a dangerous precedent.[44] Fear of an alleged nativist reaction which could be used by both left and right-wing extremists proved a more potent influence on policy than the need to protect minorities from verbal abuse.[45] Even Sir Philip Game worried about a possible alliance between fascists and communists, between racists and those who wished to protect British employment against immigrant undercutting – a scenario which the Home Office, with good reason, thought most unlikely. Whitehall was anxious to avoid the impression of reacting to pressure from street politics. The denigration of extra-parliamentary pressure did not alter the fact that the authorities were as concerned to preserve civil liberties as their critics, and that they acted with hesitation and reluctance to alter the law.

It was the Battle of Cable Street that persuaded the government to change the law, as well as the perceived need for increased police powers given continued public order concerns including the Hunger March in November and the Abdication crisis in December 1936. The change in the law was a consequence of Sir Philip Game's inability to ban Mosley's proposed march in the East End on 4 October 1936. Game realised in advance that he did not have sufficient police resources to control the massive counter-demonstration. When the Home Office informed him that he had no powers to ban a perfectly legal march, and that it was inadvisable to make a martyr of Mosley and give him publicity, Game used the only legal power at his disposal, and re-routed Mosley's march to the West End of London. This would avoid a confrontation between 1,900 fascists and 100,000 anti-fascists. Although the police had drawn truncheons and cleared Cable Street of protestors before Mosley was forced to re-route his march, the fact that anti-fascists had erected barricades, and broken the windows of five shops in order to prevent mounted police from clearing the thoroughfare, meant the authorities found it necessary to improvise quickly in order to keep the two sides apart. Fortunately Mosley and the BUF obeyed police instructions and a very ugly incident was averted. Apart from the beating up of the Blackshirt Tommy Moran, the violence at Cable Street was confined to a confrontation between the police and anti-fascists over a wide part of the East End. Of the 85 people arrested, 79 were anti-fascists. The charges against the six fascists arose from disturbances at Trafalgar Square when the police refused to allow a fascist meeting. Forty police and 30 civilians were injured during the confrontations.[46]

The immediate aftermath of the Battle of Cable Street saw a considerable debate about the relationship between civil liberties and public order. During September and October 1936 Sir John Simon, the Home Secretary, had been under considerable pressure to ban fascist meetings and marches. The Manchester Watch Committee and a delegation of East End mayors and politicians had both been to the Home Office to emphasise the point. Between June 1934 and July 1936, various aspects of civil liberties had been discussed six times in the House of Commons as a result of fascist-communist confrontations and the resultant public disorder.[47] Following the disturbances at Cable Street, the Home Secretary used a speech at Spen Valley on 7 October 1936 to reiterate the basic commitment to civil liberties of the National Government. Simon argued that democracy did not mean that those we disapprove of must be dealt with by repressive measures. The Home Secretary did not have, and did not want to have, powers in advance to ban legal marches and meetings of which he disapproved. If the law was to be changed it had to apply to all, be it of the left or right. Although fascism and communism were intolerant creeds, those who advocated them had the right to expound their doctrines within the law, as this was the essence of British liberty. If we remained tolerant and preserved liberty then common sense suggested that such un-English doctrines would remain marginalised.[48]

If the Liberal Home Secretary was determined to withstand pressure, as far as possible, to restrict freedom of expression, provided that public order was maintained, then both the Labour Party, the wider labour movement, and many Jewish inhabitants of the East End saw the problem as one of specific restrictions against what was perceived as the cause of the problem, the anti-semitism of the BUF. This view was also reinforced by Sir Philip Game, who in a memorandum on the 14 October argued that if the BUF could not be banned then new powers were needed by the authorities to regulate public order. These included the necessity of outlawing paramilitary organisations, banning political uniforms and giving the police authority to regulate or stop marches and processions. Game was particularly insistent that the anti-semitic activities of the BUF were the cause of the problem, and that they were more culpable for creating public disorder than the communists or anti-fascists.[49] As a result of public concern, the Cabinet decided to set up a committee to formulate a Public Order Act, using previously proposed legislation discussed in 1932 and 1934. The bill was rushed through in December, at the height of the Abdication crisis, and just after the 1936 Hunger March. The emphasis in the proposed 1934 legislation on giving the police greater powers to close meetings and to ban demonstrations was dropped, as *Thomas v Sawkins* (1935) and *Duncan v Jones* (1936) both appeared to show that police powers were more extensive than the law officers and the Home

Office realised.⁵⁰ The former case showed that the courts would support the police if they entered a private meeting where they had reason to believe that a breach of the peace was threatened, and the latter that the police had extensive powers to ban meetings in public places, even if they were law abiding.

The legislation had three main objectives: the prohibition of political uniforms, the outlawing of paramilitary organisations and the regulation and control of public processions and assemblies. Section 1 made it an offence to wear a political uniform; Section 2 declared it illegal to manage or control a group designed to usurp the function of the police or armed forces; Section 3 gave the police powers to impose conditions on marches, or the chief of police to approach a local council (or in London, the Home Secretary) for an order to ban all political processions in a locality for up to three months; Section 4 made it illegal to possess an offensive weapon at a public meeting; Section 5 made into general law the Metropolitan Police Act of 1839 which established it as an offence to use threatening, abusive or insulting words with intent to provoke a breach of the peace; and Section 6 enabled chairmen of meetings to ask a constable to take the name and address of offenders, who if they refused or provided false information were liable to arrest.⁵¹ The aim was to increase police powers to regulate public order, and not to discriminate against any particular creed or party. In practice, Sections 1 and 2 had fascists particularly in mind; 5 and 6, communists and other left-wing groups; and 3 and 4, all forms of low politics.

Although the decision to introduce the Public Order Act arose as a direct result of fascist-communist confrontation and political anti-semitism, its implementation, somewhat ironically, affected anti-fascist politics rather more than fascist activities. Banning political uniforms and paramilitary groups did not impede the ability of the BUF to organise or hold meetings, although it did stop fascist processions in the East End of London between July 1937 and 1949. In practice, however, 'abusive words and behaviour' was almost entirely used against anti-fascist protestors, and only occasionally aimed at fascist libels against the Jewish community. This was partly because fascists very rarely named individual Jews, and fascists had instructions to follow police orders and advice without criticism. Thus the Public Order Act only worked because of the blanket police operation in 1937 in the East End of London, which succeeded in keeping the numerous fascist and anti-fascist meetings during the London County Council and Borough elections under political surveillance and control, and because of the banning of all political processions in the area.

Within the secret state, there was a constant battle between the liberal traditions of the Home Office and the more security conscious police and

MI5. With the failure of fascism after July 1934, this expressed itself mainly in public order concerns, and the Home Office was determined to maintain as much administrative flexibility as possible. After the Battle of Cable Street had made the introduction of the Public Order Act inevitable, a more complex battleground emerged between 1937 and 1939 over the regulation of processions in the East End of London under the terms of the new legislation. Whilst Game used his powers to limit the use of loudspeakers and banned torchlight processions, the Home Office controlled violence through the use of the Public Order Act to outlaw political uniforms and marches in much of the East End after July 1937.[52] It steadfastly resisted Game's attempt to extend the ban to the rest of London after the Bermondsey march in October 1937, although it unsuccessfully opposed the extension of the ban in the East End.[53] A combination of pressures from Game and the Labour Party led to the maintenance of the ban, which was lifted only in 1949. Local councils, particularly those under Labour control, also became increasingly hostile to the BUF and imposed bans which prevented the movement from using local government property for meetings. Councils also increasingly interfered with processions and demonstrations, even before the passing of the Public Order Act.

The Battle of Cable Street was important not only because it revealed significant disquiet in the Jewish community about the perceived inaction of the official institutions of British Jewry to the activities of the BUF, but it also proved to be the incident which strengthened the powers of the authorities to monitor and control fascism and anti-fascism. Although political anti-semitism was perceived as the chief cause of disturbance and disquiet, the eventual Public Order Act did little to curb its incidence. Indeed police at the operational level proved to be more concerned about free speech and civil liberties for fascists – provided they remained within the law with regard to threatening words and behaviour, and were not too abusive – than they were with protecting the Jewish community from verbal abuse. The Battle of Cable Street was, in some ways, a pyrrhic victory for the forces of anti-fascism, as they at least as much as the fascists were to be impeded by its terms and operation. Section 5 of the Public Order Act for example, after being used in the Harworth Colliery dispute, was increasingly applied to radical protests.[54] Revisionists see the public order problems of the 1930s deriving from a conflict between the two political extremes, with the state authorities attempting fairly successfully to regulate and control public order.[55] It was to be the public order and civil liberties problems of the post-1945 era that illustrated that Britain, despite its traditions of political asylum, liberalism, toleration and assimilation of immigrant groups, was as prone to outbreaks of racial violence, institutional racism, and prejudice and discrimination against immigrant groups including Jews, as most modern states. It was to be post-1945 racism and fascism that convinced the British state that specific Race Relations legislation was necessary to protect minority groups. The Battle of Cable Street showed that if the authorities, in trying to protect the principle of civil liberties within the law, would not stop fascist provocation, then the Jewish community would defy their leadership and insist that something positive needed to be done to check fascist incursion into the east London. The passing of the Public Order Act in fact hindered the possibility of protest as much as checking fascist provocation.

NOTES

The author would like to thank the Humanities Research Board of the British Academy for a small personal research award which funded the work for this article.

1. T. P. Linehan, *East London for Mosley* (London: Frank Cass, 1996).
2. B. Porter, *The Origins of the Vigilant State* (Woodbridge: Boydell, 1987).
3. C. Andrew, *Secret Service: The Making of the British Intelligence Community* (London: Heinemann, 1985); N. Hiley, 'The Failure of British Counter-Intelligence against Germany 1907-1914', *Historical Journal* 28:4 (1985), pp.835-62.
4. R. Thurlow, *The Secret State* (Oxford: Blackwell, 1994), pp.112-13.
5. J. Stevenson, 'The Politics of Violence' in G. Peele and C. Cook (eds.), *The Politics of Reappraisal 1918-39* (London: Macmillan,1975), p.149.
6. J. Morgan, *Conflict and Order: The Police and Labour Disputes in England and Wales, 1900-1939* (Oxford: Clarendon, 1987), p.160.
7. F. M. Snowdon, *The Fascist Revolution in Tuscany 1919-22* (Cambridge: Cambridge University Press, 1989) p.201; R. Bessel, *Political Violence and the Rise of Nazism* (London and New Haven: Yale University Press, 1984), p.77.
8. R. Thurlow, 'Blaming the Blackshirts: the Authorities and the Anti-Jewish Disturbances of the 1930s' in P. Panayi (ed.) *Racial Violence in Britain in the Nineteenth and Twentieth Centuries,* 2nd ed. (London: Leicester University Press, 1996), pp.112-30.
9. PRO HO 45/25386/54-59.
10. PRO HO 45/25479.
11. PRO MEPO 2/3043.
12. PRO HO 144/20158/272, HO 144/20143/107.
13. PRO HO 45/24996/13.
14. R. Skidelsky, *Oswald Mosley* (London: Papermac, 1975), pp.283-98.
15. R. R. Bellamy, 'We Marched with Mosley', unpublished MS, University of Sheffield, pp.469-493, D. Renton, *Red Shirts and Black: Fascists and Anti-Fascists in Oxford in the 1930s* (Oxford: Ruskin College Library, 1996).
16. G. Webber, 'Patterns of Membership and Support for the British Union of Fascists', *Journal of Contemporary History* 19 (1984), pp.575-606.
17. S. Rawnsley, 'The Membership of the British Union of Fascists' in K. Lunn and R. Thurlow (eds.) *British Fascism* (London: Croom Helm, 1980), pp.150-165.
18. R. Thurlow, *Fascism in Britain: From Oswald Mosley's Blackshirts to the National Front,* 2nd ed. (London: I B Tauris, 1998), p.72.
19. Ibid, pp.71-2.
20. Linehan (see note 1), pp.19-104.
21. D. Baker, *Ideology of Obsession: A. K. Chesterton and British Fascism* (London: Tauris

Academic Studies, 1996), p.129.
22. PRO HO 144/21060/20-23.
23. PRO HO 45/25383/306-309.
24. P. Piratin, *Our Flag Stays Red* (London: Thames Publications, 1948); J. Jacobs, *Out of the Ghetto: My Youth in the East End, Communism and Anti-Fascism, 1918-39* (London: Janet Simon, 1978).
25. D. S. Lewis, *Illusions of Grandeur* (Manchester: Manchester University Press, 1987), pp.149,159.
26. PRO HO 144/20158/350-357.
27. PRO HO 144/20158/162-163.
28. PRO HO 144/20158/186-187.
29. PRO HO 144/20159/155-162.
30. A. Moore, 'Sir Philip Game's Other Life: The Making of the 1936 Public Order Act in Britain', *Australian Journal of Politics and History* 36:1 (1990), pp.62-72.
31. PRO HO 144/21087/367-370.
32. PRO HO 144/21087/208-210, 215-219, 225-231.
33. PRO MEPO 2/3043 Aide Memore on Jew baiting, 22 July 1936, and Commissioner's memorandum 29 June 1936.
34. PRO MEPO 3/551 Special Branch report 4 October 1936, p.8.
35. PRO HO 144/21381/25 Home Office minute 12 August 1938.
36. Linehan (see note 1).
37. PRO HO 144/21060/314.
38. PRO MEPO 3/551, A.Crossley MP to Geoffrey Lloyd, Under-secretary of State, Home Office, 14 October 1936.
39. N. Mosley, *Rules of the Game* (London: Secker and Warburg, 1982); N. Mosley, *Beyond the Pale* (London: Secker and Warburg, 1983).
40. PRO MEPO 2/10655, Special Branch report 3 April 1936; PRO HO 45/25463/36-53, Report on Ronald Kidd.
41. PRO HO 45/24967/52.
42. PRO HO 45/24967/62.
43. PRO HO 144/21381/188-189.
44. PRO HO 45/25398/278-279.
45. Thurlow (see note 4), p.195.
46. PRO MEPO 3/551 Special Branch report 4 October 1936, Summary, HO 144/21061/101.
47. PRO HO 144/21060/24-30, 309-313, HO 144/21061.
48. PRO HO 144/20159/171-178 Sir John Simon 'Liberty and Liberalism' speech at Spen Valley, 7 October 1936.
49. PRO HO 144/20159/155-162, Memorandum from Sir Philip Game to Home Office 12 October 1936.
50. Morgan (see note 6), pp.265-66; Lewis (see note 25), pp.163-65; W. C. May, *Recollections and Reflections of a County Policeman* (Ilfracombe: Stockwell, 1979) pp.163-74; PRO MEPO 3/549.
51. G. D. Anderson, *Fascists, Communists and the National Government* (Columbia: University of Missouri Press, 1983), p.177; Lewis (see note 25), pp.145-180.
52. PRO HO 144/21086/245.
53. PRO HO 144/21087/201.
54. Morgan (see note 6), pp.229-75.
55. J. Stevenson and C. Cook, *The Slump* (London: Cape, 1977).

Docker and Garment Worker, Railwayman and Cabinet Maker: The Class Memory of Cable Street

DAVID RENTON

Why do we remember *Cable Street*? On 4 October 1936, it was not where the crowds assembled, nor where they dispersed. There were many more people at Gardiner's Corner, occupying the road, blocking the trams, and preventing the British Union of Fascists (BUF) from taking the route which it had originally planned. Harold Rosen has suggested that Cable Street gave the day its name because of the barricades that were placed there. In this way, he suggests, Cable Street fitted into the symbolism and existing mythology of the left.[1] I would like to argue differently. What contemporary anti-fascists found striking about Cable Street was not so much the barricades, but what they saw as its message of class solidarity, stretching across ethnic divides. Cable Street, a long narrow alleyway where the last and not the most important of the day's fighting took place, was a residential working-class area. According to anti-fascists, therefore, the BUF was not stopped at Gardiner's Corner, a busy junction near the City of London, but in the heart of the working-class East End. Thus anti-fascists saw Cable Street itself as a defining location, and the defeat of the police and the fascists was placed within the context of class conflict.

For anti-fascists, the Battle of Cable Street was immediately seen in terms of class. On 5 October the Communist paper, the *Daily Worker*, insisted that the Battle of Cable Street had been supported by all East End workers, across ethnic lines: 'the whole of East London's working-class rallied as one man (and as one woman) to bar the way to the Blackshirts. Jew and Gentile, docker and garment worker, railwayman and cabinet maker, turned out in their thousands to show that they have no use for Fascism.' A special commemorative booklet was also quickly produced, which again emphasised the class-based character of the protest: *THEY DID NOT PASS: 300,000 Workers Say No To Mosley*.[2] The first book-length history of the Battle of Cable Street was Phil Piratin's *Our Flag Stays Red* (1948). Written after Piratin became the Communist MP for

Stepney, his story fitted 4 October into a continuous narrative of working-class success. For Piratin, the lessons of Cable Street in terms of class struggle were clear. First, the fascists had come as a threat to the East End from outside. Fascism was originally a middle-class force, and it acted in the clear interests of capital. Second, the fascists had been defeated by working-class unity. The character of the Battle of Cable Street was symbolised for Phil Piratin in the visual unity of 'bearded orthodox Jews and rough-and-ready Irish Catholic dockers'. Third, Cable Street was a clear victory for the working-class against fascism, although its success was ensured by the united working-class campaign for better housing, which began with Paragon Mansions.[3] Piratin's account, the story of Cable Street as class confrontation, has been used as the basis for a range of commemorative activities, several plays, in poetry and television documentary, in at least one children's book, throughout the anniversary celebrations in 1976, 1986 and 1996, and in the large wall mural on Cable Street itself.[4]

The class memory has been the dominant memory of Cable Street, and it has influenced a surprising range of sources. In 1996, as part of research on the history of fascism and anti-fascism in Britain during the period of the 1945–51 Labour government, I interviewed Morris Beckman, the author of *The 43 Group*. I asked him to describe how post-war anti-fascists remembered Cable Street. What I was expecting to hear was a narrative which would justify the practice of his group of militant anti-fascists. The group's message was that fascism was above all a threat to Jews. Although the 43 Group claimed at the time that it 'adopts a completely neutral view in relation to the Zionist question', many of the group's supporters were strongly Zionist and thirty group members went to fight against the British in Palestine. The group's executive affiliated to the *Irgun*, and co-operated in Britain with Major Weiser, a founder of the Jewish Legion in Britain and a leading Zionist.[5] However, Beckman's account of Cable Street very much downplayed the Jewish character of the day's events, and concentrated instead on what he portrayed as the role of ordinary working-class people:

> South Wales miners, the slate workers, they sent contingents, Sheffield steel workers, Tyneside shipbuilders, and from London docks of course, a lot of seamen jumped off the ships and joined the anti-fascists. Also the nurses and doctors of London hospital, the Whitechapel hospital, turned out ...
>
> First, the mounted police came in. That day, every policeman in London, every single foot and mounted policeman was there. They charged twelve times. It was the most vicious thing. Tempers were

Docker and Garment Worker

absolutely out of control ... But the people started to throw marbles, and that stopped the police horses from charging ...

The fascists were waiting in four columns, with their bands and their flags, lined up across Tower Hill and the Embankment. Their officers had them all marshalled and the men were ready to march ... But what they had not taken into account, was that the people had built another barricade across Cable Street ...

The Commissioner of the Police took it upon himself, and Mosley was stopped ...

White-collar workers, blue-collar workers, some from further afield. They were saving democracy...[6]

Many of the themes here are familiar, and they are familiar because they are borrowed from class authorities. The notions that gentile working-class London 'turned out' to stop fascism, and that workers were faced by fascist 'officers' both fit closely to Phil Piratin's description of October 4.

This paper will examine the events of Cable Street and their aftermath from the perspective of class, asking whether the Left was correct to understand Cable Street in this way. The class model of Cable Street rests on three pillars, first, the idea that British fascism was a middle-class force, second, that anti-fascism was an authentic working-class response to it, and third, that the decisive outcome of the Battle of Cable Street was fascist defeat. Each of these claims will be evaluated in the light of recent research, before a conclusion is reached as to how far the class model still stands.

MIDDLE-CLASS FASCISM?

The flip side of the analysis which located Cable Street in the working-class East End was to describe fascism as a movement of the middle class. This was a common argument among the Left throughout the 1930s. John Strachey's book *The Coming Struggle for Power* described fascism as 'one of those methods which may be adopted by the capitalist class when the threat of the working class to the stability of the capitalist class becomes acute'. J. Cronin's *The Workers Next Step against Fascism* quoted favourably from a London Trades Council resolution, 'Fascism is the weapon of monopoly capital', while in Nancy Mitford's satirical novel *Wigs on the Green,* fascism was the natural language of the patriotic aristocracy, symbolised by the chocolate-guzzling blue-blood, Eugenia Malmains. In 1936 Arthur Horner, the miners' leader, coined the slogan 'scratch a capitalist and find a fascist'. W. A. Rudlin argued that the end of German democracy came about as a reflex response of capital, faced by economic crisis and determined to restore its profitability by crushing the organised working-class. Meanwhile A. C. Miles, a former senior propaganda officer in the BUF, gave a speech to the Southend Anti-Fascist Council in 1937, in which he outlined some of the links with business which the BUF undoubtedly did have. Sir Alliot Verdon Roe, founder of Avro the aeroplane manufacturers, was a supporter of the BUF, as was Major James Shearer, a director of Courtaulds. Maynard Mitchell, a BUF member, was a director of Mitchell's and Butler's, while Tony Twist, the son of the owner of Twist's breweries, was also in the BUF. So was J. L. Battersby, a director of Battersby's hats. J. T. Murphy put the argument in its simplest form: 'The Fascist Party ... is not dissimilar from a Tory Party of the Die-Hards, a party of the Lord Lloyds, Churchills, Beaverbrooks, Rothermeres and Hoggs ... It is impossible to regard the theories [of Fascism] as other than anti-working-class.'[7]

Recent evidence has tended to undermine some of this analysis, and it is certainly no longer clear that the BUF was composed of such men as Lords Rothermere and Hogg. In particular, Tom Linehan has argued that the BUF recruited relatively evenly from each different class in society: 'Fascism did not conform to the classic petit-bourgeois or bourgeois stereotype so beloved by many contemporary and post-war commentators.' He insists that the fascists were successful in recruiting workers, and he explains their success in terms of a 'strong radical or socialist current' which ran through BUF policy. According to Linehan, over half of all East End fascists (51 per cent) came from the 'lower' class. Thirty six per cent of his sample of 311 fascists were semi-skilled or unskilled workers, 15 per cent were skilled workers, while only 14 per cent were salaried, and only 14 per cent self-employed.[8] Such figures need to be taken seriously, as Linehan's work is the most complete and thorough sample of BUF membership to date. The possibility he has raised is that the BUF was a far more working-class party than the traditional class model of Cable Street would allow.

One response might be to take a closer look at Linehan's methodology. His sample was based on membership files and other records donated by a surviving fascist organisation, the Friends of Oswald Mosley, and it is impossible to know how their records were compiled. Linehan's survey also lacks any comparative element, and thus it is impossible to say how well or how badly the BUF's profile reflected the society around. The East End was a densely populated and poor area, and any neutral observer might expect the BUF to have recruited workers among the overwhelmingly working-class population that lived there. Twenty eight per cent of the BUF's East End membership, according to Linehan, worked as merchants or were self-employed, but he does not say what percentage of the population were in these positions, in Britain or in the East End. It is possible that any East End organisation which found that *only* fifty per cent of its membership came from the working class would have looked middle-class from the outside.

It is also clear that Linehan's evidence stands in marked contrast to what we know of the BUF from other sources. W. F. Mandle has examined the leadership of the BUF, which he describes as dominated by middle-class ex-officers: 'Time and again the prefix Captain or Colonel crops up before the names of BUF members of whom we know nothing than that they spoke at a local meeting reported only in the fascist press, or wrote an occasional article for it, or were arrested, or interned in 1940.'[9] Not one of Linehan's sample was a military man. One under-used source is the list of the 779 traceable fascists detained in 1940. If BUF full-timers and serving or former army officers are also excluded, then the remaining 52 fascists whose jobs are listed can be analysed. It is striking that this remainder were mostly employed in peripheral occupations. Although shop-keepers, teachers and police were all well-represented, there were no miners, neither dockers nor transport workers. There were more writers and novelists than civil servants, textile workers or printers. The detained fascists were unrepresentative of British society, and far more middle-class than Linehan's figures would suggest (see Table 1).

TABLE 1
OCCUPATIONS OF FASCISTS DETAINED IN 1940[10]

Shopkeepers 9	Boxers 2	Actress 1
Teachers 7	Anthropologist 1	Printer 1
Police 6	Architect 1	Professor 1
Farmers 4	Civil servant 1	School pupil 1
Racing motorists 3	Dentist 1	Ship's captain 1
Vicars 3	Driver 1	Solicitor 1
Managers 2	Explorer 1	Trawler owner 1
Writers 2		

Perhaps the best way to understand British fascism is by using class categories in a more subtle and dynamic way, looking at the function of fascism as well as the sociological character of its membership, and describing the two together in relationship with each other. Mechanical Marxists within the Communist Party of Great Britain (CP) tended to write in the 1930s as if all fascists were members of the bourgeoisie (petty or not). Indeed, in general terms, the CP tended to reduce politics to simple economics, as if all the players were mere mouthpieces for class interests. There was no dialectics in this Marxism, no space for contradiction, culture or consciousness. In his book, *A Proletarian Science*, Stuart Macintyre describes the method of J. T. Walton Newbold, C. H. Norman, Simon Haxey and other communists, who believed that they could trace the relationship between the state and big business simply by charting the directorships of various plutocrats:

> In Newbold's study there were various wall-charts, like genealogical tables, laying bare the hidden skeleton of the capitalist state: to write a study of foreign policy he would simply abstract information dealing with overseas trades and the armaments industry; for Middle East policy he would take the oil industry and so on.[11]

The connection between fascism and ownership was less simple than these Marxists tended to assume, but no less real. The BUF's membership was made up of a diverse and heterogenous collection of individuals, but with a middle-class core. During and after the recession fascism and British capital may have shared strategic interests. Many members of the establishment were happy to see Hitler profit at the expense of Stalin's Russia. Yet the majority of British capitalists found their interests expressed perfectly well by the Conservative Party, and any sympathies with fascism were expressed in terms of appeasement; sympathy with foreign fascism was typically combined with hostility to fascism at home. Meanwhile, the way in which the petty bourgeoisie helped to shape fascism was by providing a disproportionate share of the Fascist party's membership, as even Linehan's figures would suggest. The presence of a large petty-bourgeois membership fitted well with fascist ideology, and helped to shape it, but did so in a very complex way. It would be ludicrous to imagine that every fascist was a small capitalist, or that every small capitalist was a fascist. Yet it would surely be right to say that there was an overlap between the social position of the 1930s petty bourgeois, trapped between capital and labour, and the social ideology of fascism, which claimed to stand as a revolutionary alternative to both.

There were those at the time who put forward this sort of differentiated class analysis of fascism. In *Our Flag Stays Red*, Phil Piratin recalled opposing other members of the Stepney Communist Party who understood their enemies as being simply the dupes of capital, without also realising that fascism was a mass movement with an agenda of its own. In effect what he was arguing towards was an analysis which understood that fascism could be a contradictory, even Janus-faced phenomenon, *both* a class ideology, acting in the strategic interests of at least some members of the capitalist class, *and* also a mass movement, made up of ordinary people.[12] In an important and often neglected passage, Piratin described attending a fascist march through the East End, starting from Salmon Lane, some time before October 1936. What surprised him was the presence of workers, including several wearing trade union badges:

> I was curious to see who and what kind of people would march ... About 1,500 men, women (some with babies in their arms), and youngsters marched behind Mosley's banner. I knew some of these people, some of the men wore trade-union badges. This had a terrific effect on my attitude to the problem...[13]

Such insights did not make Piratin less concerned about the fascist threat. On the contrary, his realisation that fascism was a mass movement, capable of winning significant numbers of workers to its side, only made Piratin more convinced that fascism urgently needed to be stopped.

WORKING-CLASS ANTI-FASCISM?

If the notion that fascism was typically a middle-class phenomenon survives, but with some qualification, what of the argument that the Battle of Cable Street itself represented a working-class response to fascism? In general terms, it is clear that throughout the 1930s anti-fascism was most popular among members of the working class, typically the *organised* working-class. As Hywel Francis has shown, among South Wales miners in the 1930s there was a very large and powerful anti-fascist tradition, out of all proportion to the threat of the BUF. One way in which the tradition was expressed was through volunteering to fight in Spain. Another focus was the protests against Mosley's meetings, and seven large fascist meetings were stopped in South Wales without Mosley being able to speak. Anti-fascism was strongest where Communism was strongest, and British Communism, it is accepted, was an overwhelmingly working-class force. Indeed Raphael Samuel suggests in his retrospective on British Communism that the CP was more solidly proletarian than even the Russian Bolsheviks had been.[14]

When it comes to the details of the confrontation on 4 October 1936, however, the picture becomes more blurred. Sadly, there were no trained sociologists on hand to record their detailed observations of the class origins of the crowd. The size of the turnout suggests that people came from at least all over London to support the demonstration. It is not likely that over 70,000 protesters could have been found simply among the Jewish population of the East End. Clearly, there were dockers and many other workers present. Many of the dockers may have been motivated by support for the CP, others by a collective memory of Jewish support for the London dockers' unions in 1889 and 1926.[15] Jack Dash, the future dockers' leader, claims to have been at Gardiner's Corner, although strangely, he gets the date wrong. It is hard to imagine Phil Piratin or Joe Jacobs making the same mistake. It is also likely that numbers of London busworkers were there, although Ken Fuller, historian of the rank-and-file paper, the *Busman's Punch*, gives more attention to the presence of busworkers at the 1934 Hyde Park demonstration against the BUF. Noreen Branson points out that the majority of Communist Party branches across London were asked to support the blockade of Gardiner's Corner, although such was the size of the crowd that many 'never reached their destination'.[16]

Although the presence of many non-Jewish workers was important, at the heart of the anti-fascist movement was a layer of East End Jews who aligned themselves with the Communist Party. Many were members of the Jewish People's Council, which collected 100,000 signatures for a protest petition in just 48 hours. Some were members of the CP, others were anarchists or Zionists, who accepted the leadership of the Communist Party in the fight against fascism, while others still were active in explicitly Jewish socialist organisations, including the Jewish Workers' Circle.[17] Ethnicity was an important factor, working in the same direction here as class. Henry Srebrnik has done much to illuminate the Jewish Communist subculture of the East End. He argues that many of its members were 'left-wing Diaspora nationalists', keenly aware of racism, and enticed towards Communism insofar as it provided an expression of communal self-defence: 'one important factor for the Jewish attraction to the Communist Party in Britain was the CP's self-appointed role as a steadfast opponent to all manifestations of domestic fascism'.[18]

Clearly, there is some truth to Srebrnik's account. In an account of growing up as a young socialist in the 1960s with parents who had themselves come from this Jewish Communist milieu, Michael Rosen describes bringing home a young Trotskyist, Adam Westoby, one day for tea. His mother listened politely as Westoby criticised the Communist Party, before responding, using the language of ethnic memory:

> Who do you think was defending Jews in the East End of London in the 1930s? It's all very well for you to sit here in the 1960s and talk about the betrayals of the CP over the years, but for us, as Jews and socialists in the 1930s, there was no choice. The CP were the only organisation that had the power and the organisation to oppose Mosley. As YCL-ers that was the only possible route to take.[19]

It is likely that the Jewish Left adopted its values and its communal identity from the wider Jewish East End. And looking beyond the Jewish Communists, it seems clear that racism was an inescapable reality for all

Jews then living in East London. The novelist Emmanuel Litvinoff, who grew up in Bethnal Green around this time, has one of his characters say that 'Night after night I suffered with Mosley's fascists', while Ralph Finn, another writer, targeted his anger more against the polite racism of official British society: 'As long as you bring credit to the flag they will stand up and salute you and forget your background and hail you as one of their own. But overstep the mark ever so slightly, even to the extent of growing old, and they will put you back where you belong.'[20]

However, accepting that ethnicity was also an important aspect of the Jewish East End and of Jewish Communist identity does not mean that class should be ignored. For the Jewish Communists in particular, class was often the most important single factor in their political self-definition. Chimen Abramsky was a member of the party's National Jewish Committee in the 1940s, and he rejects the idea that Jewish Communism was in any way motivated by left-wing communal nationalism. Responding to the identification of Bundism with Jewish Communism in Srebrnik's book, he argues that prominent Jewish Communists were Jewish only in so far as they wanted to recruit Jews to Communism. The majority of Jewish Communists, he suggests, were atheists with little interest in religion; they were secular, fully assimilated Jews. Reuben Falber took 'very little interest in Jewish matters'. Jack Gaster 'was not interested' in Hebrew, the Jewish religion or organising among Jews. Bert Ramelson spent six years in Palestine and spoke Hebrew, but even he would have seen himself more as a worker and a Communist than as a Jew.[21]

It seems to me therefore that there is a need to retain a class analysis of the Cable Street protesters. The majority chose to be anti-fascists because for them it followed from their class identity. In many cases, this identity also contained a Jewish aspect, but it was an identity which combined ethnicity and class, and neither should be ignored. Jude Bloomfield's father, Alte Bloomfield, was another member of this milieu, and her description of him reflects the way he might have seen himself:

> My father was in the London East End Communist Party in the 1930s and he was part of the Jewish East End culture and anti-fascist movement. He was self-educated, very typical of a certain kind of working-class culture in the East End.
>
> He was a shop steward and a television tester and he was also a steward on the famous Cable Street march.[22]

Both Jewish *and* working-class: for Alte Bloomfield as for other members of his generation, there was no contradiction between the two. Evidence for this sort of differentiated class analysis of the Cable Street anti-fascists can also be found in Joe Jacobs' book, *Out of the Ghetto* (1978). Jacobs was a member of the branch committee of Stepney CP at the same time as Phil Piratin, and accused him and the rest of the London CP hierarchy of underestimating the importance of Jewish self-defence. One of the most important organisers of the Cable Street events, Jacobs accepted that ethnicity *was* an important part of the Jewish Communist culture, and he rejected the idea that Jews should assimilate into British society: 'We were and we are "different".' Still, however, he refused to reduce the Battle of Cable Street simply to ethnicity. In his narrative, the point is made that the support of Catholic working-class dockers was the crucial factor which guaranteed the success of the anti-fascist campaign.[23]

CABLE STREET AS A CLASS VICTORY?

The third pillar of the class history of Cable Street is the argument that Cable Street was a victory for the Left. As Phil Piratin wrote in *Our Flag Stays Red*, 'The working class had won the day ... The Communist Party had shown itself capable of leading the working class in keeping the fascists off the Stepney streets when the Government and the police ... had attempted to foist the fascists upon them.'[24] On the day, an acceptance of anti-fascist victory seems to have been shared by fascist and anti-fascist alike. Indeed, it is striking that fascist attempts to claim a success of Cable Street relied on an interpretation of the days that followed. In the fascist press, the actual events of 4 October faded out of sight. In the fascist paper, *Action*, John Beckett preferred to concentrate on the argument that popular support for fascism after 4 October had reversed the defeat which took place at Cable Street itself. The publicity following 4 October, he suggested, had helped the British Union of Fascists and National Socialists: 'the banning of the demonstration ... has secured the greatest amount of publicity yet given to Fascism in this country'. Beckett claimed that the Fascists had recruited 5000 new members within 48 hours.[25] More recently, some historians have gone along with Beckett's model of a resurgent fascism after 4 October, and the most important figure is again Tom Linehan, who takes the title of his book from a front-page article which appeared in the fascist paper *Blackshirt* in October 1936, 'East End for Mosley'. Linehan points out that in the immediate aftermath of the Battle of Cable Street, the British Union of Fascists remained buoyant and even won new recruits in the East End, with 650 new members joining after one meeting at Bethnal Green in April 1937.[26] Indeed, in the 1937 London County Council elections, the British Union of Fascists obtained a respectable 23 per cent of the vote, doing well in Stepney and North East Bethnal Green.

Again, this picture seems to rely too heavily on a small number of fascist sources. Although it is clear that the BUF recruited very heavily in the last few months of 1936, there is no certain evidence as to how far its successes were real, and how far they were exaggerated by the fascist press, determined as it was to prevent the organisation's morale from slipping. Linehan also fails to mention that some in the BUF expected their party to do much better than it actually did in the 1937 elections; indeed John Beckett remembers Mosley predicting that the BUF would win at least three or four seats outright.[27] The evidence from around the country also suggests that the BUF was generally in retreat by 1937, and this is certainly true for Oxford, Newcastle and the Medway Towns.[28] It is possible that the BUF responded to its reverse at Cable Street by throwing extra resources into the East End campaign – a strategy which would have prevented any short-term decline in morale, but in the long term would have weakened the organisation. If this was the strategy chosen, then its effect only put off the mood of decline and defeat; it did not prevent it from having an effect.

Richard Thurlow makes a useful comparison between the aftermath of Cable Street and the events following the fighting at Olympia in 1934:

> The first results of the demonstration and violence were much the same as after the Olympia meeting in 1934; there was an immediate stimulus to recruitment for both fascists and communists and Special Branch estimated the significant, if transient, boost to fascist membership in East London to be around 2000.[29]

After both Olympia and Cable Street, an immediate increase in fascist membership was followed by sharp decline. After Olympia, the BUF was seen by many to have been the victim of Communist protests, thus it enjoyed a brief moment of favourable publicity and recruited many new members, including Major-General 'Boney' Fuller, who was quickly brought into the leadership of the party. However, many existing middle-class supporters of fascism were disgusted by the violence they had witnessed and left. Thus, after Olympia the membership of the British Union of Fascists went into free-fall. Lord Rothermere withdrew his support for Mosley; Dr Robert Forgan, a prominent supporter who had followed Mosley from the New Party days, also left. Within a year, BUF membership fell from 40,000 to 5,000. Vernon Kell of MI5 went so far as to argue that 'Mosley has suffered a check which is likely to prove decisive'.[30]

Similarly, after the 1937 LCC election the BUF clearly went into crisis. The layer of Cable Street fascists who had joined in late 1936 quickly melted away. At the same time, the Communist Party became increasingly involved in local campaigns around issues such as housing, taking part in rent strikes, opposing evictions, and winning support in areas where the BUF thought it had a monopoly. The CP campaign weakened the BUF in its East End strongholds. With fascism already on the defensive, and possibly because the organisation was no longer recruiting on the expected scale, the British Union of Fascists went into financial crisis. The Northern Command HQ had to be closed down and the number of paid staff was reduced from 143 to 30. The BUF then suffered a debilitating split when William Joyce and John Beckett left, or were forced out, to form another rival party, the National Socialist League.

Again, the argument here is not that Linehan's evidence should be ignored, but rather that the brief fascist moment of success needs to be placed in a broader context, in which the BUF did go into decline in 1937 and 1938, and the Battle of Cable Street helped to hasten its demise. In this way, the actual events of the past can be seen to fit with the class model of contemporaries. Provided that the model is updated and used in a dynamic way, it enables the historian to find a coherent shape in the complex and contradictory patterns of the past.

CONCLUSION

The argument advanced here has been that the history of Cable Street as put forward by Piratin and other anti-fascists fits broadly to the shape of events. Like a much-loved vintage automobile, the class model of Cable Street does need some work, but the engine runs, and there is life in the old thing yet. Historians sympathetic to anti-fascism do need to take into account recent research, which has tended to stress the all-class character of fascist recruitment, the Jewish character of the Cable Street protesters, and the success which the BUF undoubtedly did enjoy in the autumn and winter of 1936-7. However, not of all this counter-evidence is compelling, and these reservations can certainly be incorporated into a more sophisticated and updated class model of what actually happened on 4 October 1936. The best and most compelling memory of Cable Street is still that provided by the class model which was first generated by those who took part in the day's events. Their testimony is not complete, and at points it needs revising, but there is still much there to treasure.

NOTES

1. H. Rosen, 'A Necessary Myth? Cable Street Revisited', *Changing English* 5:1 (1998), pp.27-34; also D. Renton, 'Necessary Myth or Collective Truth? Cable Street Revisited', *Changing English* 5:2 (1998), pp.189-94.

2. *Daily Worker*, 5 October 1936; Communist Party of Great Britain, *THEY DID NOT PASS: 300,000 Workers Say No To Mosley* (London: Communist Party of Great Britain, 1936).
3. P. Piratin, *Our Flag Stays Red* (London: Thames Publications, 1948), p.24.
4. The Cable Street Group, *The Battle of Cable Street 1936* (London: The Cable Street Group: 1996), p.30.
5. Interview with Len Rolnick, 9 December 1997; 'The Irgun and the Haganah', April 1948, in 43 Group Material, London Museum of Jewish Life (LMJL): LMJL/185/1990/5; also M. Beckman, *The Forty Three Group* (London: Centerprise, 1992).
6. Interview with Morris Beckman, 15 October 1996.
7. J. Strachey, *The Coming Struggle for Power* (London: Victor Gollancz, 1932), p. 261; J. Cronin, *The Workers Next Step Against Fascism* (London: Printing and Allied Trades Anti-Fascist Movement, 1934), p. 9; N. Mitford, *Wigs on the Green* (London: Thornton Butterworth, 1935), pp.16-22; K. Morgan, *Against Fascism and War: Ruptures and Continuities in British Communist Politics 1935-1941* (Manchester: Manchester University Press, 1989), p.19; W. A. Rudlin, *The Growth of Fascism in Great Britain* (London, G. Allen & Unwin, 1935), p.12; A. C. Miles, *Mosley in Motley* (Southend: Ex-Servicemen's National Movement, 1937), pp.8-10; J. T. Murphy, *Fascism! The Socialist Answer* (London: Socialist League, 1937?), pp.5-13.
8. T. P. Linehan, *East London for Mosley: The British Union of Fascists in East London and South-West Essex 1933-1940* (London: Frank Cass, 1996), pp.212-4, 224.
9. W. F. Mandle, 'The Leadership of the British Union of Fascists' *The Australian Journal Of Politics and History* 12:3 (1968), pp.360-83.
10. Taken from 'The Regulation 18B British Union Detainees List', unpublished manuscript in British Union collection in Sheffield University Library.
11. S. Macintyre, *A Proletarian Science: Marxism in Britain, 1917-1933* (London: Lawrence and Wishart, 1980), p.180.
12. Such a dialectical theory of fascism is outlined in the Introduction to D. Beetham, *Marxists in Face of Fascism: Writings from the Inter-War Period* (Manchester: Manchester University Press, 1983), pp.1-82; and in D. Renton, *Fascism: Theory and Practice* (London: Pluto, 1999).
13. Piratin, *Our Flag* (see note 3), p.18.
14. R. Samuel, 'The Lost World of British Communism: Part Three', *New Left Review* 165 (1987), pp.52-91.
15. H. Francis, *Miners against Fascism: Wales and the Spanish Civil War* (London: Lawrence and Wishart, 1984), pp.157-9; J. Charlton, '1889: The Rise and Fall of a Mass Movement', paper given to Alternative Futures and Popular Protest Conference, Manchester, March 1996.
16. K. Fuller, *Radical Aristocrats: London Busworkers from the 1880s to the 1980s* (London: Lawrence and Wishart, 1985), p.128; N. Branson, *History of the Communist Party of Great Britain 1927-1941* (London: Lawrence and Wishart, 1985), p.166.
17. One such was Harry Walters' father there is a brief description of him in H. Walters, *The Street* (London, Centerprise, 1975), 5-7.
18. H. F. Srebrnik, *London Jews and British Communism* (London: Vallentine Mitchell, 1995), p.15.
19. P. Cohen, *Children of the Revolution: Communist Childhood in Cold War Britain* (London: Lawrence and Wishart, 1997), p.61.
20. E. Litvinoff, *Journey through a Small Planet* (London: Joseph, 1972), p.157; R. L. Finn, *Spring in Aldgate* (London: Robert Hale, 1968), p.123.
21. Interview with Chimen Abramsky, 18 February 1997.
22. Cohen, *Children of the Revolution* (see note 19), p.66.
23. J. Jacobs, *Out of the Ghetto: My Youth in the East End, Communism and Fascism 1919-1939* (London: Janet Simon, 1978).
24. Piratin (see note 3), pp.24-5.
25. *Action*, 10 October 1936; Renton, 'Necessary Myth', pp. 190-1.
26. Linehan (see note 8), p.349.
27. J. Beckett, 'After My Fashion: Twenty Post War Years', unpublished manuscript, written

1938-40, in British Union collection, University of Sheffield, p. 395.
28. D. Renton, *Red Shirts And Black: Fascists And Anti-Fascists in Oxford in the 1930s* (Oxford: Ruskin College Library, 1996), pp.42-6; N. Todd, *In Excited Times: The People against the Blackshirts* (Tyne and Wear: Bewick Press, 1995); D. Turner, *Fascism and Anti-Fascism in the Medway Towns 1927-40* (Rochester, Kent: Kent Anti-Fascist Action Committee, 1993), p.27.
29. R. Thurlow, *Fascism in Britain: From Oswald Mosley's Blackshirts to the National Front* (London and New York: I. B. Tauris, 1998), p.81.
30. C. Andrew, *Secret Service: The Making of the British Intelligence Community* (London: Heinemann, 1985), pp.526-7.

'Long May Its Memory Live!': Writing and Rewriting 'the Battle of Cable Street'

TONY KUSHNER

Kenneth Leech, the radical Christian minister, social reformer and anti-racist campaigner, has said of 'The Battle of Cable Street' that it

> is a myth in the strict sense of the term: an event of imaginative power, a source of inspiration, a symbolic conflict with which those involved in subsequent struggles could identify.

On another level, as Leech adds, the power of this mythology has led to blatant distortions and even falsehoods, including that the 'Battle' destroyed fascism/Mosleyism in the East End, that it occurred in the heart of the Jewish East End, that it was masterminded by the Communist Party and finally, and most widely misconceived, that it consisted of a struggle between fascists and anti-fascists.[1] A classic example of the myth in action is provided within the autobiography of Joe Morgan, born in Canning Town (a largely non-Jewish part of the East End), who was later, in his own words, 'one of the labour movement's most active irritants of the 70s':

> Moseley [sic] announced that he was going to march through the East End. The communists and Cockney dockers were determined to stop him. There were running battles and barricades at places like Cable Street, but my part in all this, at ten years old, was to be a 'runner'.
> The Blackshirts intended to drive into Canning Town in lorries… The men of Canning Town were waiting as a human barrier… I was waiting on Canning Town Bridge, my goal being to run to the Beckton Arms pub with the news of the impending fascist invasion. The lorries were sighted. When it was my turn to pass on the message I set off as fast as I could, shouting 'The Blackshirts are coming!'… I had done my duty.
> The lorries turned up and the Blackshirts spilled out. The

Communists and dockers set on them immediately. As if from nowhere, a horde of policemen descended on the battle, trying to defend the Blackshirts. Truncheons were used left, right and centre to cosh those opposed to Moseley. The man himself travelled in a car, his whip in his hand. But it was Moseley who was whipped, his face scarred for life by someone in the crowd who struck him as he tried to get out of the car. Eventually the Blackshirts had had enough; even the police could not save them. Oswald Moseley never came to the East End again.[2]

In Morgan's testimony, so much history relating to the 1930s is squeezed into the confines of one single day. In terms of the who, what and where, his account is almost totally inaccurate. In encapsulating what for many was the 'truth' of the event in subsequent memory Morgan can equally claim that his account was faithful to the details of the day. The publication details stress that 'This autobiography states the absolute facts as determined by Joe Morgan'.[3] As late as the 1970s, many historians would have used Morgan's account to poke fun at the unreliability of 'ordinary people's' testimony, whether in written or oral form. But as Raphael Samuel and Paul Thompson wrote in 1990:

> When we listen now to a life story, the manner of its telling seems to us as important as what is told. We find ourselves exploring an interdisciplinary territory alongside others for whom the nature of narrative is a primary issue: among the anthropologists, psychoanalysts, historians like Hayden White who recognize history as itself a narrative construction, literary critics who read metaphors as clues to social consciousness.[4]

It has been suggested that 'The Battle of Cable Street has entered into the popular memory of the East End as one of the great events in the area's history.'[5] One can go further and suggest that the date of 4 October 1936 has become one of the most prominent, if not *the* most prominent, in what might be termed an alternative chronology of Britain during the twentieth century, excluding those events associated with world conflict and the Royal Family.

Any account of the 'Battle' that attempts to do justice to its full complexity has to explore the relationship between history, memory and myth. All three, in spite of the spurious claims of some practitioners of the first mentioned to 'objectivity', are intricately inter-related, if not always happy bedfellows. None of the three headings in relation to the 'Battle' remain uncontested. Indeed, the passion of the conflict on the day of 4 October 1936 has continued and even intensified subsequently. As Joe Jacobs, former secretary of Stepney Communist Party, put it decades later:

'The story of Cable Street is a story that has been mis-written, mis-recorded and historically fucked about.'[6] But linking the history, memory and myth of the 'Battle' are the narratives that have been constructed of the event, which, it could be argued, preceded 4 October 1936, were then articulated in a variety of ways immediately afterwards and show no signs of abating as the century draws to a close. This account will analyse the narrative strategies of those representing the 'Battle', charting its path over a sixty-year period into its recognisable, if still evolving, mythical form in the late 1990s. It will, however, always keep in mind that 'Oral [and for the purposes of the analysis here, other forms of] memory offers a double validity in understanding a past in which... myth was embedded in real experience: both growing from it, and helping to shape its perception.'[7] As Natasha Burchardt suggests, 'reality is more various, less tidy than myth'.[8] Tens, probably hundreds of thousands, of people, all with their own unique reasons for doing so, turned up on 4 October 1936, taking risks to stop the British Union of Fascists marching through the East End of London. That fundamental reality should not be lost amidst the exploration of narratives and counter-narratives, the myths, legends and contested memories of the 'Battle'.[9]

FORGETTING CABLE STREET

In Jonathan Boyarin's astute survey, *Storm from Paradise: The Politics of Jewish Memory*, the complex relationship between memory and forgetting in the context of New York's Lower East Side is explored. Rather than seeing these terms as simple opposites, such as plenty and famine, or in terms of inverse proportions, Boyarin suggests that the relationship between memory and forgetting is 'closer to that of direct proportion'. Indeed, at times, the processes of 'forgetting and memory [are] so intermingled as to become almost one'.[10] Such a process can be seen at work in the context of 'the Battle of Cable Street'. The growing power of its memory has led to a double process of forgetting: first with regard to the rest of the street's history and second, ironically, in relationship to the events of 4 October 1936 themselves. The bulk of this article will deal with the varying and ongoing forms of the latter, but it will turn first to the wider context and the representation of a street which, it has been suggested, has no rival in attaining 'notoriety' in Britain.[11]

In 1958, Kenneth Leech moved to Cable Street. Speaking at an event to mark the sixtieth anniversary of the 'Battle', he highlighted how the events of 4 October 1936 have overshadowed the later and earlier history and struggles of its diverse residents.[12] All that has been left for the record has been 'hostile and misleading publicity'; a pathological portrayal of the street which allows no place for the dignity and resistance to racism and poverty of its forgotten people. Leech's neighbour, Kathleen Wrsama, for example, helped set up a community organisation, the Stepney Coloured People's Association, during the 1950s, to fight these evils and died in her nineties in obscurity at a time when the legend of the 'Battle' had become firmly established. There is a brief glimpse of the Wrsama family in the biography of the Scottish teacher and unofficial social worker, Edith Ramsay, who settled in Stepney in 1920:

> The walls of Edith's flat offered historical documentation of another kind and bore a testimony to her friendships with the newcomers. There was a christening photograph of Mr and Mrs Wrsama's family. They ran a small lodging house off Cable Street, and later Mrs Wrsama fostered many children, remembering no doubt her own hard and prejudiced upbringing in Britain, of which she was later to speak so movingly on television.[13]

Cable Street had a reputation to those concerned about 'the question of England' for being a place where the 'dangerous classes' lived and congregated. By the late-nineteenth century, its inhabitants were mainly linked to the nearby docks, including large numbers of Irish workers and a smaller presence of Afro-Caribbeans. In inter-war Britain, the small black communities, which had grown largely around dock areas, totalled between 10,000 and 20,000, and were subject to the scrutiny of social workers and academics concerned about the 'problems' their presence was causing. The approach of these outsiders was generally pathological, viewing black deprivation as self-inflicted and arguing that the offspring of 'mixed' relations were likely to bring racial deterioration to the neighbourhoods they inhabited and beyond.[14] Slowly, in the 1930s and during the Second World War, a critique of this eugenics-inspired research developed.[15] Within the East End, a new approach to what would soon become known as 'race relations', one that was both more humane and more sensitive to the social context, was evident in the first major study of the local black population. It was published in 1944 by a group of local social reformers based around the East End 'settlement' Toynbee Hall, including Edith Ramsay, and researched by Phyliss Young. Although highlighting the problems of this community of at least 400 people around the Cable Street area (and though not free of a patronising tone), it suggested solutions that would ameliorate the poverty and insecurity of the 'coloured population' and did not recommend the solution, as had the inter-war surveys, of 'repatriation'. It saw the Africans, West Indians and Asians who had settled in the East End as problematic, but ultimately recognised that they were here to stay.[16]

'Long May Its Memory Live'

Michael Banton's research into the same area and topic, carried out six years later and published in 1955 as *The Coloured Quarter*, marked further progress away from the pathological approach. Even so, Banton was frank about the impact of his early encounters:

> At the beginning I found the coloured quarter a little frightening because of its strangeness and it took a little courage to enter one of the coloured men's cafes and public houses for the first time.

As with Young, Banton was confident that the problems of the 'coloured quarter' could be solved in the area, in spite of local antagonisms including an anti-black petition movement in 1947. Banton did not totally escape from the tendency to see the coloured population as potentially troublesome and to view the relationships between black men and white women that had developed as inherently unstable. Contemporary concerns that the Cable Street area might somehow become the English 'Harlem', dangerous and criminal, were largely dismissed by Banton. But his description of the 'cosmopolitan character of the neighbourhood' was ambivalent, rather than celebratory, reflecting perhaps how his initial unease was not fully overcome. It is revealing, for example, that he referred to particular buildings by the national background of those who owned them as if this somehow precluded a *local* sense of belonging. Nevertheless, his sketch did give a less prejudicial feel for the diversity of the area, contrasting markedly with Cable Street's frequent portrayal through lurid sensational journalism during the 1950s as a frightening alien 'other' whose alleged problem of 'vice' was intrinsically linked to the 'coloured' presence. Providing an overview of the first quarter mile of the street, Banton commented that

> Before the war the population was predominantly Jewish, and though most of these residents left during the war the Jewish element remains as large as that of any other group.... In this stretch of Cable Street there are... five Maltese cafes, each of which provides lodgings for six to twelve young males whose womanizing activities have given two of the cafes a particularly bad reputation. There is a Maltese-run fish and chip shop, an Italian restaurant which opens during the daytime for a white clientele, and a Greek cafe. Shops at the beginning of the street are of Jewish and *English* [my emphasis] ownership... A side turning leads down to a Somali cafe, a Greek cafe, and a Pakistani cafe-cum-lodging house. A little farther up the street is a general store run by a French family, two hairdressers – one an Arab, the other from Trinidad – a dyers and cleaners run by a Guianese, and a Pakistani cafe with an African and West Indian clientele. Another side turning leads to the Somali lodging

house and the premises of the club for coloured men run by the Anglican mission.[17]

A different perspective on the 1950s coming from *within* the Cable Street communities is provided by Caroline Adams in her collection of life stories of 'Pioneer Sylhetti Settlers in Britain' published thirty years after Banton's account. She represents the pioneers as being anything other than passive victims or problem people, highlighting their sense of local attachment *and* their continuing affinity to their birthplace. Adams estimates that by the early 1950s this community was 300 strong in London 'and they were conscious of the need to organize themselves'. Moktar Miah came to London in the early 1930s, opening a boarding house and later a cafe in Cable Street, and 'it was there in 1952 that the Pakistan Welfare Association was formed':

> In its first few months, the executive of the Welfare Association continued, in their sessions in the cafe and in restaurants... owned by members, to carry out the 'welfare' functions that had always been so important – the letterwriting, form-filling, etc. But increasingly also they began to lobby and organize on behalf of Sylhetti working people. Both in their welfare and in their political struggles they had the support of a succession of singularly dedicated and capable friends who devoted a great deal of time and effort to the cause of the East London settlers and with whom they had warm (if sometimes turbulent) relationships... The next few years were to see a significant politicization of the leaders of the community in London, through their growing consciousness of the mass movement for autonomy in East Pakistan.[18]

Ignored by the ruling local Labour council, the poverty of the area intensified in the 1950s and early 1960s and was hardly relieved by a slow and generally unsatisfactory demolition and redevelopment. This process gradually undermined – although it failed to destroy – what was left of the community spirit of this remarkable concentration of ethnic diversity.[19] Compared to the other multi-national ports of Britain, such as Cardiff and Liverpool, the 'foreign' dock community of the Cable Street area has been subject to particular historical amnesia. Social historians and others have been slow to incorporate immigrant and minority experiences in Britain and much, until recently, has rested in the hands of local enthusiasts and community groups. Typical in this respect was 'The Cable Street Group', which was formed to document the history of the locality, especially through the use of oral history. On the one hand, the 'Battle' has acted as a stimulus to study the less famous, or infamous, aspects of the street's history. On the other, the growing legend of the 'Battle' has sucked up energy and as yet the material produced by the Group, although impressive in its own right, has not moved beyond the event of 4 October 1936. Beyond the work of the Group, much more attention has been dedicated to the history and experiences of ethnic minorities in other parts of the East End, particularly around Spitalfields, many of whom would have been relatively unfamiliar with the specific groupings around Cable Street. Much contemporary reporting of 4 October 1936 focused on the conflict that occurred in Cable Street, although, as we will see, it took many years before the events became popularly known as a 'Battle' tied to the specific locality. But such place-naming, initially at least, did not break through the 'dangerous' image of Cable Street and its residents. Indeed, it created another barrier to comprehension of the ordinariness of its everyday reality and instead added to its violent reputation. For the most part, remembering the 'Battle' has meant forgetting the history of Cable Street.[20]

Doreen Massey has stressed that the 'local uniqueness' of places

> is always already a product of wider contacts; the local is always a product in part of 'global' forces, where global in this context refers not necessarily to the planetary scale, but to the geographical beyond, the world beyond the place itself.

In Cable Street, the many national origins of its inhabitants provided an obvious and direct connection between the local and the global. It was a community, or group of communities, whose shared transient nature paradoxically enabled a rootedness in the locality of Cable Street. To many outsiders, however, its internationalism made it ineligible to be considered as part of the nation, hence references to it as 'Harlem'. But as Massey adds:

> The attempt to align 'us' and 'them' with the general concepts of 'local' and 'global' is always deeply problematical. For in the historical and geographical construction of places, the 'other' in general terms is already within. The global is everywhere and already, in one way or another, implicated in the local.[21]

Moving away from the general history of Cable Street, the 'Battle' itself illustrated a struggle over 'belonging' and place – at one level concerning the East End of London, and at another, the international struggles of the 1930s.

CONSTRUCTING ENGLISHNESS: EARLY BATTLES OVER MEMORY

In his controversial biography of Oswald Mosley, Robert Skidelsky titled a chapter on Jewish-Fascist confrontation 'Who Was then the

Englishman?'. For Skidelsky, the answer was clear. Of the '150,000' Jews in the East End, he wrote:

> These were mainly foreign immigrants who had come in about the turn of the century and who remained largely unassimilated. Politicians talked about them as fellow-Britons, but to many of their Gentile neighbours they were foreigners ... There were Yiddish newspapers, Yiddish shops, a Yiddish theatre. It was as if a piece of Jewish East Europe had been torn up and put down again in the middle of East London.[22]

Here Skidelsky's portrayal was incorrect in its detail – the number of Jews is far too high and most Jews in the area by the 1930s, more than 70 per cent, were British born and on many levels highly integrated. As the Jewish commentator William Zuckerman argued at the time of the BUF struggles: 'There is ... so much in common between the young, post-War English Cockney and the young East End Jew, that much in them is easily interchangeable and confused.' Skidelsky, on the other hand, appeared to have imbibed much of the hostile discourse about Jews as ultimately 'alien' posited by Mosley and his followers at the time and subsequently. To the BUF, the 'Battle' reflected the power of the alien mob to influence British politics. Those who barred Mosley's way were not only un-British but also came from outside the East End.[23] The Jews' essential 'alienness' precluded them from either local or national belonging.

The *Jewish Chronicle*, whilst famously having advised Jews to stay away from the march on 4 October 1936, proclaimed in its issue after the 'Battle' in repeated banner headlines that 'Mosley [had] Receive[d] His Marching Orders'.[24] Turning round the BUF's image of the Jews as foreigners, on 16 October 1936 the *Chronicle* took great delight in pointing out in a 'boxed' feature entitled 'The "British" Union of Fascists' that Mosley had recently returned from a trip to visit Mussolini in Rome and Hitler in Berlin and throughout the summer and autumn of 1936 dismissed the ordinary fascist members as misfit louts.[25] Indeed, even before the 'Battle' had taken place, it was being constructed as a struggle over belonging. To the fascists the proposed march through the East End was not only a climax to many months of campaigning in the area but was also to mark the fourth anniversary of the founding of the BUF. The fact that such an early anniversary was being 'celebrated' highlights the desperate need of Mosley to prove how his movement was part of a British political tradition.[26]

Anti-fascists were equally prepared to highlight their national sense of belonging and the foreignness of the BUF. A leaflet from the 'Ex-Servicemen's Movement Against Fascism' called for a parade on 4

October 1936 with medals and decorations: 'If [the Union Jack] means as much to you now as in 1914, stop Mosley putting back the clock to barbarism.' Its Southwark and District branch called for the 'support [of] the Ex-Servicemen to Ensure that the Union Jack Stands for BRITISH Freedom and Democracy', adding that the people should 'Show Mosley You Don't Want His Roman Salute, Roman Sticks and Axe, Roman Dictatorship'.[27] Proving a local as well as a national sense of belonging was also crucial to the anti-fascists. In its special supplement, published on 3 October 1936, the *Daily Worker* stressed 'Save the East End of London from Fascism: Throng Streets in Protest... Let Gentiles and Jews Unite in Defence of Freedom'.[28] Similarly, the Jewish People's Council Against Fascism and Anti-Semitism (JPC), in its petition to the Home Office to call off the march, warned the government that the fascist movement 'aims to further ends which seek to destroy the harmony and good will which has existed for centuries among the East London population, irrespective of differences in race and creed'.[29]

Providing further layers of complexity to the 'Battle' was its international dimension which confirms, as a piece of concentrated micro-history and geography, Massey's contention that the 'local is always a product in part of "global" forces'. In a 'warning to British Jews', the Jewish labour leader J. L. Fine argued before the 'Battle' that 'once the international Fascists win in Spain, they will march on... Don't say we are unconcerned. Spain's fight is your fight'.[30] Within the anti-fascist movement, and more specifically inside the Communist Party, the importance of the Spanish Civil War was contested fiercely in the days before the 'Battle'. Initially, the London Communist Party, in its leaflets and other publicity, called for a march from the Embankment to Trafalgar Square 'where London's youth will vow their solidarity with Spain's people'. After that the march would continue through East London 'in opposition to the four meetings where Mosley will speak'. These rallies and marches were 'Against Fascism – the enemy of the people abroad and at home' as a demonstration against 'Fascism in Spain and Britain – The Butcher General Franco and the Jew Baiter Mosley'.[31]

In effect, through the campaigning of local Jewish activists, Communist and other, the issue was turned around so that the march against Mosley became the priority. Nevertheless, in many respects the struggles against fascism at home and abroad were, for the Communist Party, deemed to be inseparable. The slogans and discourse from Spain, most famously that of the Communist Deputy, Dolores Ibarruri, at the start of the rebellion – 'It is better to die on your feet than live on your knees. No Pasaran!' – were used not just at the 'Battle' but in the days leading up to the event.[32] Thus, on 1 October 1936, the *Daily Worker* pronounced that 'Mosley is provoking civil war in East London', calling upon people to 'assemble in scores of thousands' because they should 'remember the massacres at Badajoz and Irun'.[33] But this discussion also invoked the memory of anti-fascism at home. One of the banners carried at the demonstration bore the message 'Remember Olympia', the Mosley mass meeting in 1934 in which anti-fascists were viciously treated. On the evening of 4 October 1936, Ted Bramley of the Communist Party 'enjoined' his audience 'to remember Olympia, the Hyde Park affair, the Albert Hall [all representing sites of anti-fascist struggles] and above all the glorious victory of Cable Street, and to vow to themselves once more, "Fascism shall not pass"'.[34]

In the meetings on the evening of 4 October 1936 and in the following days a powerful narrative structure was constructed by the Communist Party to encapsulate the day. That it could be put together both quickly and coherently can be explained by the fact that many of the essential elements of the myth were already in place before the 'Battle' itself. First, the day represented Jew and gentile uniting for the good of East London. Second, the battle cry of 'They Shall Not Pass' was transferable from one antifascist struggle to another. Third, it represented the culmination of domestic Communist battles, whether for the rights of the unemployed in the hunger marches of the early 1930s or the struggles against the BUF from Olympia onwards. Harold Rosen has argued that 4 October 1936 was named after Cable Street rather than Gardiner's Corner (where most of the crowd gathered) because it

> was in Cable Street that a barricade was constructed. A barricade! That potent icon of urban revolution: 1848 across Europe, the Parisian Communards in 1871, the Russian Revolution.[35]

Rosen's analysis cannot be dismissed out of hand. Lazar Sheridan, who in 1939 was to write the first fictional account incorporating the 'Battle', recalled later 'that the thought in my mind when we stood behind the barricade in Cable Street was, "was this like the French revolution as the cobble stones were torn up?"'[36] Nevertheless, the more overarching metaphors utilised to describe the day were linked to war rather than to revolution. The 'victory' was achieved, in Communist rhetoric, by utilising military discipline and tactics. Earlier domestic narratives of physical conflict, including those against the BUF or the fights against the police in unemployed workers' struggles earlier in the decade, such as the 'Battle of Bexley Square', could be speedily utilised to describe the events of 4 October 1936.[37]

Even the exact topography of the day was foretold by the Communists – the *Daily Worker*'s special supplement on 3 October 1936 highlighted through the use of a map the centrality of Cable Street and Gardiner's Corner and reinforced in the text that these were the places that needed to be filled by the anti-fascists.[38] Speaking at a Communist mass meeting of 3000 people at Hoxton Square on the evening of the day itself, Pat Devine actually provided the narrative of the events that had just taken place with a title, expressing

> the hope that today's activities will encourage all sections of the working class to proceed with yet greater efforts. Today will go down in history as the Battle of Cable Street in the war against Fascism. The advance guard of the anti-fascists put up one of the greatest fights ever known, and succeeded in completely demoralising the Fascist ranks and stopping their proposed march to the East End... Mosley has sustained a crushing defeat today, and something he will remember for a long time, and in addition to this, great encouragement has been given to the comrades in Spain.[39]

In fact, although Devine proved an accurate prophet, it took at least a quarter of a century before 'the Battle of Cable Street' as a short hand for the events of 4 October 1936 was at all widely established. Whilst Rosen stresses that 'the very choice of name was a crucial part of the creation of a myth', the narrative structure established before, during and immediately after the event was enough to ensure that its imaginative cohesion would be maintained initially even without an agreed title.[40]

Lacking any ambiguity or hint of confusion about what was experienced on 4 October 1936, official Communist narratives of Cable Street changed little from the day of the 'Battle' to the demise of the Party in the 1990s. Aside from the 'victory' speeches given on the evening after the 'Battle', the *Daily Worker* did its best to ensure that it became part of collective memory. Two days after the 'Battle', it dedicated a full page of photographs, sketches and text to showing 'how East London barred Fascists' road'. Even more impressive was the 12 page pamphlet 'They Did Not Pass: 300,000 workers say NO to Mosley', put out by the Independent Labour Party (ILP) also within days of the event. Costing a penny, it provided an almost instant 'souvenir of the East London Workers' Victory over Fascism'. Its account, not surprisingly, stressed the role of the ILP and its leader, Fenner Brockway. The ILP had shown far less ambiguity about the need to oppose the Mosley march in the East End. Indeed, Brockway's appeal on behalf of the ILP for a mass turnout of 'workers to stop Mosley' was published on the front page of *The Star* the day before, the only non-Communist newspaper to lend its support for this course of action. Although Brockway and the ILP were deeply concerned about events in Spain, their Marxist rhetoric concerning the

'Battle' was much more domestically oriented than that of the Communist Party. Whilst pointing out the solidarity of those that took part 'irrespective of their race, or creed', less was made of inter-ethnic co-operation and more of class unity on 4 October 1936. The ILP's souvenir of the day concluded that whilst

> The Fascists did not pass... we must not be content with this. Mosley is the advance guard of Capitalism. We must now carry the offensive against Capitalism itself and against the National Government which represents it.[41]

Nevertheless, compared with the Communist Party, the role of Brockway and the ILP on 4 October 1936 has received relatively little attention in subsequent memory. The post-war demise of the ILP partly explains this lacuna, but it is also significant that whilst it featured in Brockway's first attempt at autobiography, published in 1942, it did not merit inclusion in his later reflections on a wide ranging political career. For him, clearly, the 'Battle' was less crucial and less valuable as usable history than for his Communist Party counterparts who also played a significant role on that day.[42] Nevertheless, what is perhaps still surprising, given the relative marginality of the Communist Party, is how dominant its narrative of the 'Battle' became in popular British culture. The power of Communist accounts of the 'Battle' has been seriously challenged on two occasions – first by contemporaries in what might be termed 'official' memory and more recently by those providing alternative readings of the event from anti-racist and radical Jewish perspectives.

'OFFICIAL' NARRATIVES OF CABLE STREET

Not surprisingly, the greatest concern of the government and the state apparatus related to issues of law and order. The most obvious outcome of the 'Battle' was the hastily concocted Public Order Act 1936, which came into force on 1 January 1937, and prohibited

> the wearing of uniforms in connection with political objects and the maintenance by private persons of associations of military or similar character; and to make further provision for the preservation of public order on the occasions of public processions and meetings in public places.[43]

Discussion in the House of Commons on the Public Order Bill focused almost exclusively on the East End disturbances involving fascists. As one MP put it 'it is no good disguising the fact that it was recent events concerning the black shirts which were the occasion of this Bill'.[44] It is significant, however, that in the Commons debate there was already vagueness about the specific events of 4 October 1936 just six weeks after they had taken place. Percy Harris, the Liberal MP for Bethnal Green, many of whose constituents would have taken part (as fascists and anti-fascists) referred to 'happenings last September or October in the East End of London [which] seemed to require some strengthening of the law'.[45] On 5 October 1936, an editorial in the *Manchester Guardian* commented that 'If the House of Commons had been sitting today a debate would almost certainly have been forced on the disorders in the East End', adding a warning that 'There are risks that yesterday's events will have been largely forgotten by October 29 when Parliament reassembles'. The *Guardian*'s concern was not without some foundation and, for those who had not taken part or were not directly affected, the event was, as early as November 1936, becoming subject to a process of amnesia.[46] But its impact on police authority was not so easily marginalised and it was through the perspective of the Police Commissioner, Sir Philip Game, that the first official detailed narrative of the 'Battle' was published.

Police perspectives on 4 October 1936 have received little attention from historians or others who have shaped the memory of the day. Witness seminars and oral history projects, whether in the form of publications or television documentaries, have all failed or have been refused permission to incorporate police voices.[47] Metropolitan Police files, released during the 1970s and beyond, have helped provide an account of high level discussions within the force, but, as Bill Fishman complains, 'there is a wealth of evidence' relating to the ordinary police that some historians have not 'been perceptive enough to delve' into.[48] The view that has now gained status as orthodoxy was put forward by Robert Skidelsky in 1975 and confirmed by John Stevenson in 1980:

> The police attitude ... was not pro-fascist or pro-socialist, but pro-police. Their chief concern was to maintain public order with the least expenditure of time and manpower; and the easiest way to do so was to ban any activities likely to lead to a breach of the peace, irrespective of the intentions of their organisers.

Skidelsky goes further and suggests that it is precisely because the police 'had little cause to love either fascists or their opponents that their evidence is the most reliable we have of the origins and causes of political disturbances involving both in the 1930s'.[49] But is this really the case?

C. H. Rolph, Chief Inspector in the City of London police during the 1930s, and arguably the most articulate, progressive and literate British law enforcer in the twentieth century, provided in his autobiographical writings support for Skidelsky's analysis:

We were often accused in the press of being pro-fascist, but my recollection [nearly forty years later] is that at first we thought the blackshirts slightly ... daft. We had no love for them, because they messed up our weekly leaves and involved us in long extra hours of duty. Then some of us began to see ... what fascism ... really would lead to ... But so would Communism... So we hated them both; those of us who had political natures hating the fascists more than the communists because they gave us less excuse for policemanly shoving around .... Contemplating the fascists and the poor unemployed stragglers we so stupidly called communists, we were ready to call down a plague on both their houses but some of us hoped that, if it came down, it would turn out nastier for the fascists.[50]

The Metropolitan Police report of the 'Battle', written the day after the event by A. G. Ralph, Deputy Assistant Commissioner, neutrally entitled 'Fascist Demonstration in East End on 4th October, 1936 and Counter Demonstrations by Communists and others', appears, on the surface, also to confirm Skidelsky's view. Inevitably of a factual nature, it described the events from a public order perspective at Royal Mint Street where the fascists gathered, the disturbances at Cable Street and the 'milder scenes of disorder [that] were occurring at Gardner's [sic] Corner'. Its narrative was then devoted to the fascist activities once the march through the East End had been banned by Sir Philip Game and to the anti-fascist meetings in the evening. It summarised the day's proceedings in numerical terms, estimating that 100,000 were present at 3.30pm 'in the neighbourhood of Royal Mint Street', 74 persons were arrested leading to 93 charges including 'assaulting the police, possessing offensive weapons, causing grievous bodily harm, wilful damage, throwing missiles etc'. In terms of violence, 33 police and 12 private individuals had reported injuries. In addition 'A number of shop windows [were] broken, 4 motor cars damaged [and] about thirty yards of pavement torn up in Cable Street'.[51]

Ralph's account to the Home Office passed no judgement on the participants and his only reference to Jews was to mention briefly a complaint by two Jewish men 'that they had been threatened and assaulted by Blackshirts'. In a later memorandum on the impact of the Public Order Act, he showed some empathy with those at the receiving end of BUF incursions: 'The unfortunate inhabitants are deprived of sleep, and some of them are more or less terror-stricken, for to the Jewish resident of the East End, the Fascist is a source of grave apprehension'. Although Ralph added that 'The activity is not all on one side, as the Jewish and Communist elements too are active, and their meetings and processions need quite as much policing', he acknowledged that 'offence breeds reprisal'.[52] But the apparently straightforward 'law and order' prism through which Ralph presented the events of 4 October 1936 provided almost no insights into the complex dynamics of the day. Indeed, he outlined a misleadingly simple chronology of how it unfolded, similar in this respect to Communist Party narratives, making little allowance for the confusion and chaos experienced amongst those participating or witnessing the day's events. More complicated, but at the same time more ideologically loaded, were the equivalent Special Branch reports on the 'Battle'.

Two lengthy reports, the first on the fascists and the second on their opponents, were written at the end of 4 October 1936. The picture that emerged from the account of the anti-fascists highlighted how throughout the day there had been a series of meetings by a variety of anti-fascist and radical Jewish organisations. It stressed the constant flow of people involved in the various events and the variety of places within the East End in which these meetings had taken place. The activities at Gardiner's Corner and Cable Street received particular attention but certainly did not dominate the Special Branch narrative as they did in Ralph's description.[53] The other major difference concerned Special Branch's approach to Jewish involvement in the 'Battle'.

In the account of fascist activities that day, its summary highlighted how 'A widespread counter-demonstration, chiefly organised by Jewish and Communist elements, supported by some 100,000 persons, was responsible for nearly all the disorder and arrests'.[54] Not surprisingly, a Special Branch report of 1 November 1936 provided a strongly anti-Communist analysis of the 'Battle', stating that 'there can be no doubt that the unruly element in the crowd which gathered in the East End on the 4 October was very largely Communist-inspired'. In particular, it emphasised the arrest of the Jewish Communist, Barnett Becow, at Cable Street, stressing that he was a notoriously violent and lawless figure.[55] The discourse identifying Jews as alien, Communist and disorderly was, of course, articulated strongest by the BUF but it was not absent, if in a modified tone, in more 'mainstream' British culture in 1936 – in society as a whole as well as in governmental circles. The Commissioner of Police himself appeared at least partially to subscribe to it. In September 1936, Game noted the hooligan element in the anti-fascist movement, stating that it included 'many Jews, the foreign Jews are far more anti-police than anti-fascist'. Game was certainly no blanket anti-semite – his views on Jews were classically ambivalent: 'The Jewish leaders [whom he regarded as sensible and reliable] do their best to restrain them but cannot control the young and hotheaded or the *lower type of foreign Jew* [my emphasis]'.[56] Game and other senior police figures were similarly ambivalent on the causes of anti-semitism which they put down to the activities of the BUF and other prejudiced people but also to the 'natural' resentment of alleged Jewish economic success in the East End. In this respect it should be noted that detailed surveys indicated that in reality Jews in the district suffered higher poverty than their non-Jewish neighbours. Further down the police hierarchy, the testimony of many anti-fascist campaigners, Jewish and non-Jewish, relating to the 'Battle', stressed how some of the 'boys from Hendon' tended to label all Communists as Jews, or, as was often articulated to those arrested, whatever their origin, 'Jew bastards' or 'Jewish whores'.[57]

Alongside the Metropolitan Police and Special Branch accounts of 4 October 1936, a third narrative was placed in the official records which further confirms the importance of anti-alienism in government and state discourse. Unsolicited, it came from the Scottish Conservative MP, Anthony Crossley, a witness to the events, especially around Royal Mint Street and Cable Street, who for his 'own entertainment [wrote down] my impressions of the October 4th disorders'. Crossley's gloss on his account, sent to Geoffrey Lloyd, Under Secretary of State at the Home Office, was indicative of its contents, again revealing a fundamental ambivalence about anti-semitism and the Jews:

> If it appears to be sympathetic with the Blackshirts I would have you know that I hate their movement probably as much as you do and in theory Anti-Semitism is intellectually repulsive to me. But it was very hard in that crowd to think of the demonstrators as other than a riff-raff of the foreign population of London.[58]

In another letter to Lloyd he stated that the 'Jew-Communist attitude was aggressive in the extreme'. His account made less blatant connections. Nevertheless, it subtly juxtaposed the fascists and their Jewish opponents, utilising notions of gender, partly complicated by age, in the process. The fascists featured only briefly in Crossley's narrative, but he introduced at the beginning a BUF standard bearer: 'a decent young man'. The fascist women were described as 'grim middle aged spinsters and some pretty young women'. In contrast, Crossley highlighted 'a particularly abusive Jewess' and another protester 'who was kicking [so] unscrupulously [that she had to] have her shoes removed by the police'. Crossley also commented that it 'struck [him] that the anti-fascists were mostly only small men'. As if to further emphasise their dubious masculinity, especially in relation to the policemen present, some of whom carried out 'herculean feat[s]', Crossley wrote that at Cable Street with the first appearance of the police *en masse* 'The barricades where we had seen numberless little Jews photographed with clenched fists and brandishing various weapons and missiles were deserted too!'.[59]

Lloyd responded to Crossley that 'You can have no idea how valuable it is to us to have an intelligent account by an impartial eye-witness'.[60] Similarly, a Home Office official minuted that it was 'A most valuable description of the scenes in Aldgate, Cable St. etc and a welcome testimony to the behaviour of the police'.[61] The day after the 'Battle', Frank Newsam of the Home Office wrote to Sir Philip Game asking if he would accept for himself 'and convey to all the ranks of the Metropolitan Police who were on duty yesterday, [his] congratulations on the way in which the difficult situation in East London was handled. It afforded me more proof, if one were needed, of the complete impartiality with which they discharge their duties.'[62] Crossley had concluded by stating that he 'heard many complaints about the brutality of the police, but saw no single instance of any conduct on their part to which any law abiding citizen could take exception'.[63] His comments, however, perhaps shed more light on popular attitudes than they did in confirming police impartiality. The police attitude was, inevitably, 'pro-police' and the state apparatus 'pro-state', but this tells us little about the complexity of their behaviour and the way in which their accounts of 4 October 1936, which still dominate many historical analyses of the day, were shaped. Rather than regarding them as uncomplicated narratives and the most 'reliable' evidence we have on their subject matter, we must view them critically, making particular allowance for the tendency to criminalise *sections* of the Jewish community at the time, which forms part of 'a long history of Britain perceiving herself to be in the grip of foreign criminals'. Such a perception is typified, it might be added, in the history of Cable Street itself and in the treatment of its minorities by the agents of law and order.[64] In turn, such accounts related to wider concerns in British society during the 1930s about the undermining of 'Englishness'.

THE 'BATTLE' IN THE CONTEMPORARY PUBLIC DOMAIN

In a speech on 'Liberty and Liberalism', the Home Secretary, Sir John Simon, referring to the events in the East End three days earlier, called fascism and communism 'utterly un-British in sentiment and creed'.[65] The reporting of the 'Battle' in the right-wing conservative press went further, identifying, as did the *Morning Post*, the 'real Fascists' as the alien East End mob who had denied the 'decent, clean-living young fellows' of the BUF the right to free speech.[66] Furthermore, the *Morning Post* later declared, echoing comments it had made after the First World War, that there was an established 'identity between Jewry, sedition and Socialist malpractice'.[67] The *Daily Sketch* claimed that alien criminals were creating and exploiting the violence in the East End and another newspaper suggested that the Jews were providing the money for the Communist campaign in East London.[68] Most of the contemporary reporting in the public domain which related to 4 October 1936 was most obviously concerned with law and order. It included a three-minute Paramount Newsreel entitled 'Fascists in the East End', which was shown the day after the event and met with the approval of the police. The newsreel commentary explained why mounted police and baton charges had been necessary: 'Communists, Labourites and Jews jammed the fascist route resisting the peaceful efforts of the police to clear the way.' The early photo-journalism confirmed the impression of police neutrality. *Weekly Illustrated* concluded its narrative of October, which was dedicated to the 'Trouble in the East End', with a photograph of four upright officers taking away a protestor, apparently cheerful and captioned 'The End of His Day', adding that 'The police, who had been strongly criticised for their conduct towards previous anti-Fascist gatherings, were generally felt to have held the balance fairly between both sides'. Unsurprisingly, Game's account in his annual published report as Commissioner praised the professionalism of his officers in handling the disturbances.[69] But the contents of an article in the *Morning Post* on 'Political Warfare in the East End', was indicative that across British politics, culture and society the issues raised by the 'Battle' involved much more complex, deeper issues involving the state of the nation and who ultimately 'belonged' to it. As its subheading put it: 'Fascist, Communist and Jew – How the Dangerous "Line-up" Came About'.[70]

The contemporary representation of Jews was, however, bifurcated, involving elements of both aggressor *and* victim. Horace Thorogood, a Fleet Street journalist and commentator, wrote that before the First World War, he and his colleagues could always rely on spicing up the front page, if news was short, by giving it 'the necessary lurid touch by "hitting up" the East End police-court reports, or sending a man down there to discover a "den" or a "gang" or a "thieves' kitchen"'. The Siege of Sidney Street in 1911 was a particular opportunity 'for sensational copy about secret societies and the ways and haunts of alien desperadoes'. Thorogood himself, as Benjamin Lammers has pointed out, was keen to problematise the Jews of the East End, referring to them in a book published the year before the 'Battle' as 'malignant bacilli' in the district.[71]

The tendency to view all that was wrong in 'England' as embodied by the East End, or sections of it, was still very powerful during the 1930s. A report in *The Times* on the 'causes of unrest' in the East End commented 'that most observers have seen what they would have liked to see and heard what they wanted to hear'.[72] Veteran reporter Trevor Wignall provided a typical example of such tendencies. Taking a taxi from Fleet

Street he related 'a plain presentation of the most remarkable night [he had] ever spent in the East End of London'. His report on one of Mosley's meetings was, in fact, remarkable only for its lack of content, clearly providing no evidence for his conclusion (of which he was 'certain') that 'A ready-made powder magazine is being prepared in the East End that will have disastrous consequences if a match is ever applied to it. The materials for a tremendous explosion are already there.' Wignall gave the game away in his attempt to provide local colour, recalling that the last time he 'had journeyed in a similar direction [his] mission was to tell a story of Sidney Street'.[73] Many other journalists without any knowledge of the area or its particular dynamics descended on the East End during the summer of 1936, their visits intensifying after the events of 4 October. One recurring word summarised their attempts to convey the feelings of East End Jewry – 'terror'.[74]

Attempting to minimise the impact of BUF anti-semitism, Robert Skidelsky suggests that in 1936 '"Fascist terror" became a press cliché'. Examining 'the facts', Skidelsky argues that fascists were subject to more violence than Jews and 'there is no doubt that some local Jewish communists were more violent than anything produced by the East London or any other branch of British fascism'. Skidelsky has been accused of blaming the victim, 'echo[ing] the Mosleyite position'. What is undoubted is his total failure to use historical evidence produced by the Jews at the time or subsequently. Instead, aside from the fascist sources, including Mosley himself, he relied on contemporary anti-alien journalism and police material which, as we have seen, was not always neutral to the Jews.[75]

Those who did listen to East End Jews found that fear permeated the community. The Reverend Zeffert of the East London Synagogue told one reporter that 'My people are terrified ... Bands of young men walk about the streets and molest individual Jews'. The *Jewish Chronicle* argued that what was happening amounted to a 'public scandal': 'Here a great population is sinking into something approaching panic. It finds itself assailed day and night by abuse and threats. It fears to leave its home after dark.'[76] Journalists, politicians and later historians have attempted to explain this fear as coming out of Jewish insecurity which resulted partly from memory of the persecutions in eastern Europe. Dan Frankel, the Liberal MP for Mile End, who showed himself throughout the 1930s to be out of touch with the concerns of his Jewish constituents, pleaded to the House of Commons in early November 1936 that

> The Jews in the East End of London are only one generation removed from those who were persecuted in Russia, Hungary and Poland. They

are the sons and daughters, and in many cases the same people. I ask you, then, not to be surprised if they are afraid or if it appears that they are unnecessarily excitable and hysterical.[77]

To outsiders to the Jewish East End this may have been reassuring – instead of concentrating on the British causes of minority unease, attention was focused on the victims themselves. In this case it could be explained away through the supposed Jewish tendency towards hysteria, utilising a strong discourse about 'the Jew' and especially, as Sander Gilman notes, 'a clear "feminization" of the male Jew in the context of the occurrence of hysteria'.[78] What some investigative journalists realised, however, was that Jewish East Enders were afraid because they were being attacked physically and reminded daily of the presence of fascist anti-semitism through racist graffiti, marches and meetings, which were designed to undermine their sense of belonging and security in the district. Moreover, Jewish fears were intensified by the success of political anti-semitism on the continent and Mosley's clear links to the Nazis in Germany. But for many contemporaries in Britain, including those in the hierarchy of the state, the BUF's anti-semitism – whatever their own ambivalence about the Jews – placed it beyond the pale. Thus the *Evening Standard*, which was vociferous in its anti-refugee campaign during the 1930s, arguing that refugees' Jewishness made them particularly undesirable, was willing to give prominence after the 'Battle' to a David Low anti-fascist cartoon. It depicted Mosley gaining an 'unhonourable mention' at a 'political rose show'. Amidst all the beautiful 'English' flowers, Mosley exhibits a distorted and monstrous growth labelled 'Anti-Semitism' which is dismissed with the 'Latin' tag 'Violentia Ignorami'.[79]

Nevertheless, the more sensitive reporting of East End Jewry which highlighted the real fears being experienced, tended to view the victims of anti-semitism as passive. Whilst countering the image of Jewish gangsterism and subversion in some right-wing journalism, it went to the other extreme of representing Jews as defenceless creatures. Particular attention was devoted in such reports to the children, women and old people unable or unwilling to go out into the streets for fear of violence. Such representations existed alongside those in contemporary anti-fascist portrayals of the 'Battle' which, in their desire to universalise the struggle and to emphasise Jewish/non-Jewish solidarity on the day, had the effect of downplaying Jewish activism.

Writing fifty years after the event, Lazar Sheridan recorded that 'The fact that there is little reference to Jewish participation saddens me, but does not surprise me'. Communist narratives which stressed that the 'Battle' had led to a defeat of Mosley also meant that subsequent BUF anti-semitism in the East End of London was forgotten, further undermining the Jewish memory of 4 October 1936. The Jewish People's Council was soon frustrated by the downplaying of its role on 4 October. In a conference in November 1936, one delegate argued that in his 'opinion, if it were not for the JPC the blackshirts would have marched in the East End of London'. He added that 'we must fight fascism to the last'. A leaflet produced after the 'Battle' indicated that the fears of East End Jewry and its experiences of fascist anti-semitism had by no means gone away: 'Violence in the East End of London! Windows smashed, shops looted, incendiarism, assaults on peaceful citizens on their doorsteps – even children are not safe from attack'.[80] It was, however, many decades before the specifics of ethnic memories of 4 October 1936 could challenge the dominant narrative of the 'Battle'. For the established Jewish community and its organisational structure had done its best to suppress the demonstration. In its aftermath, bodies such as the Jewish Board of Guardians used methods of social control to 'punish' those Jews who had transgressed – in prison after the 'Battle' Charlie Goodman was told that he would not be supported: 'you're the sort of Jew that gives us all a bad name'.[81] Subsequently the 'official' historiography of the British Jewish community has either ignored or given only the most passing reference to the disturbances of the 1930s and the 'Battle' in particular. The embarrassment caused to the Board of Deputies of British Jews and its advice to stay away on 4 October 1936 has lingered long in memory. Indeed, the Board's legitimacy in claiming authority in the fight against anti-semitism was undermined at the time and has still not recovered some sixty years later. It is perhaps significant that the Museum of the Jewish East End, established during the 1980s, which gave prominence to the 'Battle' in its early displays and education packs, has included no mention of it since the Museum's increased integration into the Jewish establishment as part of the London Museum of Jewish Life.[82]

Subsequently, for some of the participants, memories of the 'Battle' became essential to their identity. Joyce Goodman recalled how

> a few years later I met Charlie, my husband. And one of the first questions he asked me was: 'Where were you on October 4th?' Everybody laughs at this, but this is what East Enders asked themselves in those days ... And I said: 'I was at Gardiner's' and he said: 'I was there too'.[83]

It was, as a character in Frederic Raphael's novel, *The Limits of Love*, puts it: 'The proudest day of my life'.[84] Yet after the immediate reporting of the 'Battle' it was far from certain that a collective memory would emerge of 4 October 1936. The Jewish establishment, the police and the fascists had reasons for forgetting the day. For independent Jewish radical organisations such as the Jewish People's Council the day-to-day battles continued beyond the 'Battle'. This left the field of memory to be utilised almost freely by the Communist Party. Its suitability, however, as 'usable' history and culture was not unambiguous. The memory of the 'Battle' beyond 1936 was, therefore, unstable and uncertain to the extent that, just two or three years later, it was entering its first phase of obscurity.

USING THE 'BATTLE' IN WAR AND PEACE, 1937–45

In September 1937, Neil Francis-Hawkins of the BUF wrote to Game announcing that 'On Sunday October 3rd, it is our intention to celebrate the fifth anniversary of the foundation of the British Union, and it is our desire to mark the occasion by a march of our London members through the East End of London'. Not surprisingly the request was turned down under the provisions of the Public Order Act and instead the march was re-routed through Bermondsey in south London. Some 2-3000 fascists were met by at least 20,000 opponents and a large contingent of police. Representing a smaller, but more intensely violent version of the 'Battle', it is hardly surprising that the Communist Party utilised the victory of 1936 to muster support for its counter-demonstration. 'Mosley shall not pass' was the slogan of 3 October 1937. It was, to the Communists, the afterword to the 'Battle'. As their official historian put it: 'Bermondsey had shown that anti-fascism was as strong among the non-Jewish workers as it was among the Jews. Mosley's attempts to divide the workers on racial grounds had failed.'[85] Yet outside the specific confrontation with the BUF at Bermondsey, 4 October 1936 had not yet become a usable past for the Communists. An indirect allusion was made to it in the London County Council elections in the spring of 1937 but only in the context of the need to democratise the police. At a local level the Communists were broadening their appeal by campaigning on housing and employment issues which they hoped would remove the underlying problems which the fascists were exploiting to create support.[86]

The usefulness of the 'Battle' as political memory was further undermined by international events in the eighteen months before the start of the Second World War. Although its later title had yet to take hold, the most common words in the anti-fascist rhetoric concerning 4 October 1936 were 'victory', 'battle' and the 'defeat' of Mosley. In 1938 and 1939, street fascism waned in Britain but the 'Battle' had never been solely concerned with domestic matters. 'Cable Street' could never be a usable history for anti-fascists when the Civil War in Spain had been lost and the Third Reich had expanded its borders to include Austria and

Czechoslovakia. For members of the Communist Party, the Soviet-German Non-Aggression Pact of 23 August 1939 and the transformation of the war in the course of September 1939 from an anti-fascist crusade to a struggle between imperialist powers now to be opposed made the 'popular front' romance of 4 October 1936, temporarily, at least, redundant.

The near-despair of this period is illustrated strikingly by an individual who had been intimately connected to the Communist Party, Simon Blumenfeld. Blumenfeld was the most prominent of the working-class East End Jewish authors coming out of the sweatshops during the 1930s. In spite of his first-hand experience of the 'Battle' and his involvement in anti-fascist activities as a whole, it was significant that Blumenfeld did not write about 4 October 1936 until the 1980s. *Jew Boy*, published in 1935, was based on the individualistic Jewish communist, Sam Berkovitz, who later played a prominent role in the politics of the 'Battle'. Blumenfeld's second novel was published in 1937 – too soon for the 'Battle' to be incorporated – but this was not true of his third, *They Won't Let You Live*, published in 1939. In fact, Blumenfeld did include a fascist movement, the True Britons, clearly modelled on the BUF, in this novel. Nevertheless, its ordinary members were relatively harmless, simple but misguided people, who blame their misery on the Jews and are just as much victims of the economic system as their poor Jewish counterparts in the novel. The story is based on two small businessmen, Jewish and non-Jewish, whose debt grinds them down into suicide. In contrast, the True Britons' leaders are aristocrats who have 'influential friends on [their] side. They're not the lousy *schnorrers* [scroungers] who march about waving flags; they don't make much noise, but they're the people with the dough, the ones that count.' Such an analysis of the threat of fascism was a long way removed from the anti-fascist 'barricades' of Cable Street with its popular front message of how the movement was to be stopped. Nevertheless, the novel, whilst concluding with a litany of the disasters of recent years – China, Abyssinia and Spain and a warning, 'Yesterday Czecho-Slovakia, tomorrow Poland, the day after, who could tell?', ended on the characteristically optimistic note of the socialist writer. Considering the war ahead, it hoped that the novel's young protagonists, Jewish and non-Jewish, 'would establish a society where the whole of life could flower harmoniously, whose fabric would never more be endangered by one shrieking lunatic straddling Europe'. By the time *They Won't Let You Live* was published, however, the Communist line on the war had already changed.[87]

It is telling that for the next three years there would be no mention of the 'Battle' by the Communist Party or its supporters. Not until the war returned to becoming a fight that was not only against fascism, but also one that was successful, could it become a usable past. It was no accident, therefore, that the first major literary attempt to incorporate the 'Battle' was written by Lazar Shrensky (under the pen name of Barnett Sheridan) who was not directly influenced by the Communist line. Shrensky was educated at the Jews' Free School, where he was later helped by the influential English teacher, Samuel Rich, and he had also been a member of various Jewish youth clubs in the East End. Like many of the young Jewish writers at this time, he had finished his education early and had experienced working as a jewellery apprentice without seeing any future in the occupation. Shrensky was reliant on the Whitechapel Library for inspiration and a place to write. In contrast to the various sweatshops he encountered,

> I loved words … I enjoy[ed] working and playing with words. I wanted to write and it was as though spending my days in the workshop was akin to being in a prison, I was stifled within its confines and was only happy when the workday was over and I was free of it.

He was, as Joseph Leftwich suggested, part of a group of writers 'to which Simon Blumenfeld [and] Ashley Smith belonged'.[88] Shrensky, however, was, in his own words, 'very much my own person'. In 1937 a friend tried to get him to join the Communist Party. He recalls that he 'was already a member of the Labour Party and was not amenable to the Communist Party discipline … I was certainly revolted with the Russians when later Stalin and Hitler signed a pact of friendship through their ministers in Moscow!'.[89]

Shrensky had, in the pattern of many of the new East End writers, started submitting work to publishers at a very early age. His first manuscript was rejected, but in 1937 he started work on a novel, *King Sol*, which was published weeks after the start of the war. On one level it is a 'Boy's Own' adventure story of a young Jewish boxer whose Uncle Sol – a dreamer, but a good man at heart – is trying to exploit his talents. Some romance is thrown in as the boxer, Morry, falls in love with Alice, the daughter of an ageing and declining non-Jewish fighter, the 'Dane', whom he has just beaten in the ring. The Dane's family live in absolute poverty in the East End, though they have resisted the allure of fascist anti-semitism as an explanation of their plight. Picaresque figures add colour to a novel that provided interest through sport, a sentimental love story and the general pathos of its characters. But on another level *King Sol* has a strong political subtext. When writing it, Shrensky later reflected, 'The Spanish Civil War was constantly in my mind through hearing the news broadcasts daily on the radio, listening to the discussions in the cafe in Osborn Street and reading the reports in the press.'[90]

Shrensky had taken part in the events of 4 October 1936, an 'historic day which I shall always remember with pride'. In 1937 when he started writing *King Sol* the 'Battle' was 'still very fresh in [his] mind'.[91] The novel, published by the distinguished publishers Chatto & Windus, who used V. S. Pritchett as their reader, was published under the *nom de plume* of 'Barnett Sheridan' despite Shrensky's objections. 'The publishers said that they were worried that my name would appear to the reading public as though the book had been written by a foreigner and this might affect the sales.'[92] The tendency to universalise is also present in the book itself, particularly through the love affair between Morry and Alice. It also, however, has a strong underlying Jewish background, with references to the Jewish Board of Guardians, the Workers' Circle, acts of fascist violence against the Jews before and after the 'Battle' and descriptions of East End Jewish workshops. There is no doubt that the 'Battle' was introduced to the novel to add a degree of excitement to it. Yet much more was at stake. The need for individuals to stand up and fight fascism, wherever it manifests itself, runs throughout *King Sol*: 'Never in this country. We Englishmen would fight to the last man for our liberty.' As one character tells Sol, referring to the rise of Nazism in Germany: 'It's a serious thing ... and got to be taken seriously. They must be stopped now before they go any further.'[93]

It has been stressed here that in the days before, during and after the 'Battle', the events were constructed and reconstructed in order to provide its various narratives with cohesion. With *King Sol*, however, in spite of the closeness of the events to the novel's moment of publication, a new development had taken place – the transformation of the 'Battle' to the level of literary myth. Reflecting more than sixty years later, its author believed that 'The Cable Street battle halted the advance of fascism in this country'.[94] As early as 1939, Shrensky had written how 'The fire of the burning fight for liberty lit up the faces of those who stood shoulder to shoulder in the narrow, *now historic* [my emphasis], Cable Street'.[95] Shrensky was free from any Communist circumscription, but he desired to add vibrancy to a picture of ordinary people united against the forces of fascism. To do this he managed to utilise the image of notoriety, lawlessness and dangerous cosmopolitanism of the Cable Street neighbourhood and to subvert it for anti-racist purposes. Nevertheless, in the process he maintained the essential otherness of the street, which he later admitted he knew as little about as boxing.[96] He preceded his account, however, with a narrative of the 'Battle', representing it as a meeting of foreign-style war-revolution with Englishness:

Sol pushed through the crowd, eager to see if there was any truth in the news about Cable Street. After a terrific struggle, he gazed on a sight that left him speechless. Never in England would he have believed it possible.

At the beginning of Cable Street the pavement had been torn up. A gigantic lorry lay overturned across the narrow street. All manner of lumber was piled round and on the lorry. Glass and pebbles were strewn over the roadway. Men and women worked feverishly to make the barricade higher and stronger. Yes indeed; in Merry England; in the dirty, straggling, snobbish, slum-ridden centre of the world, the barricades were up.

From hundreds of tiny windows fragments of red cloth hung. The black men; the Chinese; Indians, the white foreign sailors; the Catholics from Prescot Street; the Jews; men without permanent address from ninepence-a-night houses; painted women from the shady cafes; the broad-shouldered dockers ... ; coster men from Petticoat Lane – all crowded the narrow, smelly slum that tore up the road for a barricade.

Shrensky had managed to meld the myth of the Cable Street neighbourhood and the myth of its 'Battle' into a powerful Dickensian style narrative. *King Sol* was well-received by contemporaries although its long-term impact was limited and now the novel has, undeservedly, been all but forgotten.[97] Nevertheless, as will be shown, the representation of the myth of Cable Street in terms of its 'Battle' proved to have renewed life under the influence of the anti-racist and multi-cultural influences of the 1970s and beyond, most obviously in the memorial in the street itself. Like *King Sol*, however, it appeared that the 'Battle' was heading for obscurity in collective memory. It was rescued from the threat of obscurity, however, mid-way through the Second World War, by Communists anxious to re-establish the Party's domestic credibility following the apparent defeatism of its war line and the subsequent banning of the *Daily Worker*.

On 4 October 1942 the Stepney Communist Party held a special meeting 'to commemorate the day when the people of Stepney stopped Mosley and his Fascists marching through London'. The secretary of the Stepney branch, Alf Rockman, made clear that it was the contemporary relevance that was being marked: 'He explained that the meeting had been called to link up the attitude of the people on October 4th, 1936, with the present situation.' It is significant that Charlie Goodman, who had 'fought' on 4 October and later in Spain, was only allowed a few words at the event, which remained unreported. Indeed, the first attempt to commemorate the 'Battle' revealed clearly how the process of remembering led simultaneously to the forgetting of the actual events of 4 October 1936. Rockman continued

> On that day success was achieved by the people making a united stand; they knew what was at stake, and were determined not to let the Fascists through Stepney, and didn't! Today the situation was far graver. The Communist Party were giving the lead to the workers in Britain to demand the immediate opening of a second front and the people of Stepney must do their bit to get the forces mobilised into some concrete form of action to this end.

Two other speakers, one from the trade union movement and the other from the Communist Party, provided a domestic and international chronology to fit what was referred to as 'a great day in British history'. It was, according to a Mr Ritman of the Transport and General Workers Union, one of three great working-class, Communist-inspired victories in Britain, following on from the dockers stopping the loading of a ship, the *Jolly George*, carrying arms against the Soviet Union in 1920, and then continued by the campaign to lift the ban on the *Daily Worker* in 1941. Gordon Cruickshank of the Communist Party provided an even more remarkable sequence of events in which to place the 'Battle'. 'There were', he suggested,

> three main phases in the growth of Fascism in Europe. In 1936 the question was 'will Fascism march through Stepney?' In 1938 'Will Fascism march through Spain?' and today 'Will Fascism march through Stalingrad?'

Cruickshank concluded by urging his audience 'to finish the job you started in October, 1936, when you drove the Nazis from the streets of London'.[98]

'The Battle' was entering its first major phase as a usable past, rediscovered by the Communist Party in its attempt to support a war which, it believed, could only be won by opening up a second front to stem the enormous losses of the Russian army. But the fulfilment of Cruickshank's final rallying call relating to the 'Battle', 'long may its memory live!', was dependent at this stage on 4 October 1936 being relevant to other contemporary concerns.[99] In 1943 the Communist Party added a theme in the commemoration of the 'Battle' which has been the most persistent and powerful in subsequent political utilisation of its memory – as a morality tale in mobilising against attempts to revive British fascism.

In the spring of 1940 many leading fascists in Britain, including Mosley, were interned under Defence Regulation 18B and the British

Union of Fascists was outlawed. In many respects the fascists and their successors never recovered from the blow to their prestige – especially the doubts on their loyalty and patriotism – caused by these government measures. Slowly, however, as releases were made and contacts re-established, groupuscules emerged during the war with the intention of paving the way for a post-war fascist revival. The opposition to this development from those connected to the Communist Party was both genuine and opportunistic. On the one hand there was real concern that such groups might become influential if the Western Allies teamed up with the Nazis to transform the war into an anti-Soviet crusade. On the other, their existence could be utilised to stress the credentials of the Communist Party, providing a link to the pre-war years and neatly obscuring the embarrassment of the period between September 1939 and June 1941: 'Here', as Douglas Hyde, who reported the fascist revival for the *Daily Worker*, put it, 'was the chance once again to come out as the great anti-fascist fighters'.[100]

It was almost inevitable that the 'Battle' would become prominent in the Communist Party campaign. In a Lancashire District Communist Party pamphlet celebrating '13 years of anti-fascist struggle', published in 1943, Pat Devine, now Lancashire District Organiser, provided a eulogy to 4 October 1936. There is no doubt that the events of the day made a deep impression on Devine, a founder member of the Communist Party. It was Devine, as we have seen, who had attempted to coin the title 'The Battle of Cable Street', though his early attempt at myth-making did not in this respect succeed. In 1943, however, his written testimony added a new dimension to the Communist Party narrative of the day's events:

> 1936: I WAS THERE. What a memory! What a fight! The Mosley Fascist blackguards flushed with seeming victory attending their attacks upon defenceless Jewish girls and old men, decided to invade the East End ... The aim to perpetrate an English pogrom upon the Jews. Consternation swept through Jewish circles. The Labour Party led by Herbert Morrison [who had been instrumental in continuing the ban against the *Daily Worker*] ... appealed to the people of East London and the Jews to stay off the streets and give the Fascists free passage.
>
> The London District Committee of the Communist Party met. We decided that, no matter what the cost, Mosley should not get free passage. We decided to rouse London's millions to action ... Our slogan for rallying the people was that coined by the immortal defenders of Madrid – 'They Shall Not Pass' ... On October 4, London's police, reinforced by police from all over the country, were there to preserve law and order by defending the Fascists from the wrath of the people! The

people were there too – 500,000 of them ... ready for anything.

I will never forget that day. The police charged, with the Fascists cowering behind them. The workers broke in face of the swinging batons of the policemen, but they rallied and fought back. I was in Cable Street directing operations. We threw up barricades by tearing up the streets, overturning lorries... anything to hold them up. Hand to hand fighting went on for hours. The police were exhausted. The workers determined. The Fascists afraid.
THEY DID NOT PASS.[101]

Similarly, in November 1943, the Communist Party was instrumental in the popular opposition to Home Secretary Morrison's decision to release Mosley from prison. Harry Pollitt in the *Daily Worker* evoked the 'Battle' and argued that freeing Mosley was 'a betrayal of the anti-Fascist war'.[102] In this, he was contributing to a wider wartime campaign against anti-semitism.

If the evidence for neo-fascism in Britain during the war was slight this could not be said for domestic hostility against the Jews. The Communist Party was keen to show that anti-semitism was a weapon of the fifth column and was a disguised way of bringing fascism and reaction to wartime Britain. It was also keen to bring the Communist message to its Jewish supporters and, once again, the 'Battle' could be employed for this purpose. In his polemic *Anti-Semitism and the Jewish Question* (1942), the Jewish Communist Issie Panner (writing under the pseudonym 'Rennap') argued that where strong working-class traditions existed, fascist anti-semitism could be defeated, as 'on that memorable day' when the BUF 'received a smashing defeat':

The hundreds of thousands of London citizens, Jews and Gentiles, of diverse political opinions, who packed the streets and prevented the Fascists from marching through, were a striking indication of how even the Government-protected forces of the Fascists can be defeated, provided the proletarian movement is strong, united, and determined to resist. These are the lessons which my own people, the Jews, must never overlook.[103]

As the conflict drew to a close and the Communist Party prepared for the post-war elections, its Stepney branch, the biggest in Britain, began to make a specific attempt to mobilise Jewish voters but to do so in a universalistic framework of 'Jew and Gentile together'. 'We Jews have the same enemies as our fellow-citizens who are Gentiles. On many occasions we have, by united action, defeated them. It was in unity that we defeated Mosley in 1936. It was in unity as tenants that we won our victories over the landlords.' The crowds on 4 October 1936, 'Jew and Gentile, docker and clothing worker, Labour Party member and Communist, seaman, housewife and small business man' were now being directly appealed to in an attempt to create 'a Stepney we can be proud of'. But the domestic use of the 'Battle' ran alongside its international significance:

> Today, when fascism is being pounded to the dust; when our country is allied to the Soviet Union, the USA and the other United Nations, we can take pride in the knowledge that our long years of struggle have borne fruit, that our defeat of Mosley at Cable Street was a milestone on a road which will include the handshakes that our boys will exchange with the men of the Red Army when they meet in Berlin.[104]

Not surprisingly, Phil Piratin, who was soon to create the most lasting legacy of Communist mythology of the 'Battle', utilised its memory among the Jewish constituents in his successful campaign to be elected member for Mile End – a particularly useful weapon given that his Labour opponent was Dan Frankel, who in 1936 had opposed the mass demonstration. As one of his leaflets exclaimed: 'Vote for Piratin: A Fighter Against Fascism'.[105]

The success of Piratin and of ten Communists elected onto Stepney Borough Council later in 1945 (of whom seven were Jewish)[106] marked the high point of their local influence and the peak of the triumphalist use of the 'Battle' for party political purposes. Thereafter it was utilised defensively by the Communists as the reality of the Cold War undermined their ability to claim that they had a place in Britain at either a national or a local level. There was, however, in spite of the dominant Communist narrative at the end of the war, a counter-use of the 'Battle' in 1945 which, as with Shrensky's *King Sol*, was indicative that its memory was constantly being contested.

Ralph Finn was another East End Jewish writer to emerge during the 1930s who became a teacher and then a journalist, his first work being published in 1940. He was perhaps the most mainstream of this new school, writing in a naturalistic style, often about non-Jewish subjects. During the 1960s he wrote two autobiographical accounts of his Jewish East End roots, which provided a nostalgic and sentimental picture of life in which 'the problem of anti-Semitism never arose'. Fascism is notable for its absence.[107] His realist novel, *Return to Earth* (1945), set in an East End shelter during the flying bomb raids of 1944, was of a very different nature. Its characters are hard and even though most are anti-fascist, Finn wrote in apologetic detail of how the widespread allegations made against the Jews during the war were factually wrong.[108]

The 'Battle' was written into the novel early by Finn, partly to introduce Hirst, a weak man who had joined the fascists before the war and who throughout *Return to Earth* 'was not just Hirst but Nazi-ism and Fascism and Totalitarianism and a whole lot of other rotten things'. The events of 4 October 1936 are presented in a heroic manner, romanticising the day by narrating it as a physical confrontation with the fascists as well as the police: 'With bare hands and stern hearts the East End stopped them ... They broke and fled with the tails of their black shirts sticking to their damp bottoms, with their beautifully creased flannels stained and their immaculate shirts ripped. They did not pass.' Yet in contrast to Communist Party accounts, his account of the 'Battle' was not ultimately triumphalist:

> I wept for the East End that day, in spite of its gallant victory. I wept for London, for England, for Britain, for the people everywhere. I saw the rule of the beast over the land, I saw its claws dripping blood, I saw its wicked heart in Berlin, its hind-paws in Rome, its fore-paws in London and its tongue out-thrust and its beady eyes gleaming.[109]

Although *Return to Earth* ends on a note of universal optimism, with 'Fascism being driven out of the earth by the free peoples of the world ... the victory of the common man [enabling] ... Freedom [to] walk abroad again', it recognises the damage inflicted in the process, especially to the Jewish people. It stresses the millions who had died in the death camps and, through the use of Yiddish, a rabbi and a refugee from Nazism, emphasises Jewish particularism throughout. Finn's vision of the 'common people' fighting to build the peace meshed neatly with the mood of the British people and the landslide victory of the Labour Party in 1945. Even though his account of the 'Battle' was distorted, however, Finn brought to it a pluralism and an understanding that for many Jews in 1945 the defeat of Nazi-fascism could be welcomed but not, because of the losses incurred, celebrated as a 'victory'.[110]

The specific 'Jewish' memory of the 'Battle' would eventually become less isolated. Nevertheless, Finn's nuanced acknowledgment that the defeat of fascism was not simply the conclusion of a straightforward war narrative with a happy ending (of which 4 October 1936 could be seen as a forerunner), has yet to be recognised fully. Indeed, the myth of 'Britain alone' has ensured that in post-war British culture, other experiences, such as that of the Jews during the Holocaust and even more so other victims of the Nazi genocidal machine, have been sidelined or, until recently, almost totally ignored.[111] In a similar vein, although less optimistic than Finn, the taxi driver turned writer Maurice Levinson described the 'Battle' in his episodic autobiographical writings, *The*

Trouble With Yesterday (1946). The sickening violence of the day was stressed by Levinson who was beaten up by the police. He left the conflict reflecting on 'the destructive energies of human nature. The urge to hate had become a mass-produced impulse'.[112] But in the years immediately after the end of the war, the 'Battle' would be remembered in far more simplistic terms than those outlined by Finn and Levinson.

REMEMBERING AND REMEMBERING TO FORGET: COMMUNISM, ANTI-COMMUNISM AND THE 'BATTLE', 1945–60

Late in 1945 and throughout 1946 the organisational revival of British fascism, of which the Communist Party and others had warned during the war, became a reality. The largest was the League of Ex-Servicemen, run by the Mosley sycophant, Jeffrey Hamm, who attempted to recreate the pre-war street meetings of the BUF in East London. The violence of these meetings and the rumours of Mosley's return to politics provoked a powerful anti-fascist response. It prompted a reassessment of the 'Battle', which had now come to be seen as an important stage in the fight against British fascism rather than, as in popular mythology, its moment of decisive destruction.

In 1946 the left-wing journalist Frederic Mullally was to write the first detailed history of 'Fascism Inside England', charting the rise of the BUF and its successors during and after the war. The 'Battle' received prominence – the first time it had been historicised in detail – but it was placed in a narrative which started with Olympia and was still ongoing. Mullally suggested that 'In the history of the British working classes, Olympia will remain as evocative and symbolic a word as Peterloo and Tolpuddle'. Out of the repression and violence of that day British complacency was for the first time challenged:

> the pulse of a fierce anti-fascist hatred beat in the hearts of the working-classes. It was beating for their comrades in Spain, locked at that moment in a death struggle with Franco's Moors, Mussolini's fascist divisions and Goering's Luftwaffe. And from their Republican comrades they borrowed that glorious phrase 'They Shall Not Pass', and threw it in the teeth of Mosley's 7,000 disciplined Blackshirts and the capital's entire police force.

Mullally, following a strongly Communist analysis, stressed how the mass of workers on 4 October 1936 had been marshalled 'according to a strategic plan'. In this respect his re-telling of the day's events fitted into a straightforward military epic. Unlike earlier left-wing versions, however, the story was not complete. He concluded his description of 4

October 1936 by arguing that 'Olympia had been partly avenged'. As his last chapter, covering the months after the end of the war, put it: 'The Thing is Dead: Long Live the Thing!'[113]

The anti-fascist movement that developed in response to the revival was not without its internal tensions. For some, the pre-war struggles against the BUF were more important than for others. For 'veterans' of 4 October 1936, the 'Battle' was immediately summoned as a call to 'Stop [Fascism] Now!'. Marking the day's tenth anniversary, the *Jewish Standard*, organ of the National Jewish Committee of the Communist Party, stressed how

> On that memorable day ... when the Fascists, under strong police protection, attempted to march through the London East End, where such strong working-class traditions exist, they received a smashing defeat. Key point was Aldgate. The people gathered there, Jew and Gentile, old and young, and nothing could shift them. They were an overflowing river, bursting its banks to wash away the filthy marks of the Fascists. That great day will never be forgotten.

Here the narrative almost possesses a mystical, religious character, although it was still to be completed with an agreed title. In this account the emphasis was on Gardiner's Corner, Aldgate, highlighting the numbers of people involved in stopping the Mosleyites rather than the fierceness of the fighting in Cable Street itself. The fascist revival was explained by the *Jewish Standard* as being caused by the reactionary policies of the Labour government at home and abroad.[114] For many non-Communist Jewish activists, however, this analysis was less relevant.

The '43 Group' which emerged in 1946, represented a remarkable development in the sociology of British Jewry. Many of its members were young men (and some women) just out of the forces who were deeply angered by the reappearance of fascism in the streets of Britain. Militant and aggressive, their point of reference was the war, rather than the 1930s, reflecting their own experiences of fighting fascism abroad and their anger at the destruction of European Jewry. Vidal Sassoon wrote of this time in 1992, and whilst adding a later understanding of the Holocaust to his testimony, explained the passion that led him to join the 43 Group as a seventeen year old:

> I do not know the exact day when we decided to return hate in kind, but the horror of the images coming from Auschwitz, Dachau, Buchenwald and seemingly so many other places triggered a sense of survival within the remaining Jewish population of Europe. Hearing of the heroics of Mordechai Anielewitz and his few thousand followers in the Warsaw

ghetto nurtured our mood ... 'Never again!' became a command not a slogan, and so the 43 Group was born.

More prosaically, one of the activists at the time stated 'I see this fascist in front of me and I think of the newsreels. I automatically put the bastard into a Nazi uniform in my mind and I go mad. I just want to hurt him!'[115] For these young Jews the war provided a reference point for their personal experiences in the forces and a new model of resistance in the form of the Warsaw ghetto revolt, the one episode of the Holocaust to gain widespread remembrance in the immediate post-war Jewish world.[116] If a link was occasionally made to the 'Battle' in the 43 Group's fights against the post-war fascists, it was generational – few had a direct connection to the earlier street battles. It is significant that those around the National Jewish Committee of the Communist Party (NJC) were generally antagonistic to the 43 Group: 'National Politics eluded [the NJC]. Their background was the fight against Mosley in the East End. They were still living in the 1930s in Cable Street.' In contrast, militant Jewish anti-fascism from the late 1940s through to the 1960s rarely made reference to the 'Battle' and the struggles of the 1930s.[117] The Second World War was now the central theme. The impact of the war, the horror of what had happened to European Jewry but also the bewilderment and irritation at the victims' apparent passivity, as well as an inter-generational link to earlier British anti-fascist struggles comes out powerfully in the testimony of a former member of the 43 Group:

> When I came home I was appalled. I just couldn't believe what was going on. I had been in a transport squadron, flying petrol up to the Typhoons and bringing back PoWs. I saw Belsen, devastation, displaced persons. We couldn't understand why so many Jews went to the gas chambers so meekly. And these bastards were back on the streets with their arms up, the same ones that my father had fought at Cable Street.[118]

The politics of the 43 Group ran across the ideological spectrum from communist to right-wing Zionist but they were united in their desire to use force against the newly-emerging fascists. Communist Party attempts to impose control on this movement had only limited success.[119] And it was for reasons of waning Communist influence that in 1948 the most influential personal narrative of the 'Battle' was published.

In his preface to the 1978 reprint of *Our Flag Stays Red*, Phil Piratin explained the genesis of the book:

> The book [was] in no way a [auto]biography... [It] was not my idea [but] came to be written as a result of discussions in the Communist

Party Executive and Political Committees. We noted the changes taking place in the political situation and the mood of the workers, which was also reflected in the ranks of the Communist Party.

Believing that the Labour government was following reactionary policies which were undermining Communist support, 'In 1948 a fresh campaign was launched ... involving the Party organisations conducting their activities on the mass issues in a vigorous and militant style ... The object was to restore the class-conscious, fighting tradition of the Labour Movement, and deepen political understanding in the course of the activity.'[120] *Our Flag Stays Red*, by relating the Communist struggles of the 1930s against fascism and in improving conditions in the East End before and during the war, was part of that process.

Piratin's account of the 'Battle' followed the epic approach of Frederic Mullally two years earlier but provided even more detail of the care and attention that had gone into the Communist planning of the event. His account was loaded with military terminology: 'plans were made', '[the fascists'] main objective', 'ensur[ing] strict discipline', 'at the front', 'headquarters', 'scenes of the battle', 'defeat for the fascists', and, of course, 'Victory'. According to Piratin's account, everything had been organised by the Communist Party – there was no uncertainty in the way that the day had unfolded and no doubt as to who should take the credit for it.[121] Not surprisingly, its influence at this stage hardly extended beyond Communist circles. The attempt of the *Daily Worker* around the same time that Piratin's book was published to utilise that 'great day in working-class history' to restore its fortunes was futile.[122] For the Communists, the impact of the Cold War and events in eastern Europe were undermining their moment of genuine popular support in Britain. For the Party's Jewish members, stories of anti-semitism and the suppression of Jewish anti-fascists in the Soviet Union created for many a crisis of confidence and identity. In all this uncertainty, the 'Battle' became a symbol of a less complicated world that had been clearly divided into good and evil. At this point, the only other group that cared passionately about the collective memory of the day were the fascists, now organised under Mosley's leadership as the Union Movement. In 1949 they attempted to march through the East End 'to celebrate the 13th anniversary of the victory of Cable Street'. What was even more remarkable about this fascist attempt to re-write history was the Union Movement's claim that the march would be welcomed as

> It is felt that many East London people would still like to have an opportunity to express their indignation, as they did so effectively at the time on this pitch at Cable Street, against the hooliganism of Communism and alien elements.

As one East End vicar said in response, 'This is a betrayal of what we fought the war for.'[123] The war acted as an impenetrable barrier for the fascists, but its aftermath was also highly problematic for the Communists. In the process, the 'Battle' was starting to enter its longest period of obscurity, interrupted only, significantly, in the late 1950s by one author who had broken with the Communist Party and another who was attempting to exploit for commercial gain the East End's unsavoury underworld reputation.

Arnold Wesker was four years old when the 'Battle' occurred. He was 'aware of nothing, but so electrifying had the riots been for my family, so full of anecdote, of little braveries and farce, of colourful personalities, that it was talked and talked about into my teens until I felt I had lived those days with them'. In 1956 Wesker left the Communist Party: 'I was a disillusioned socialist, not one who had come to believe socialist principles were unworkable, rather one who felt those principles had been betrayed, never allowed to show if they *could* work.... I was not a theoretician. My pleasure in, and capacity for, social action was limited. Human relationships mattered more.'[124] It was family and personal relationships that dominated Wesker's famous trilogy, the first of which, *Chicken Soup with Barley*, was written in the autumn of 1957.

Act I of the play, first performed in 1958, takes place with the 'Battle' in the background, the action concentrating on the basement of the Kahns, closely modelled on Wesker's own family. Phil Piratin claimed that his chapter in *Our Flag Stays Red* on the anti-fascist struggle was used by Wesker 'as the basis' for his own account.[125] On a superficial level, Piratin's claim for influence was justified. The Communist Party are portrayed as the instigators and organisers of the day, and even before the event it is assumed that Gardiner's Corner and Cable Street will be the dominant focal points. As Sarah, based on Wesker's mother, Leah, puts it: 'Everything happens in Cable Street.' Nevertheless, there is mention of the involvement of other groups, especially the Jewish People's Council, who had been written out of earlier accounts, including *King Sol*.[126] But, in total contrast to Piratin's account, it is the representation of the human dimension of the day – the fear, excitement, confusion and chaos, the bonding and conflict within the structure of family and friends – which makes the dialogue engaging and forceful. Indeed, it is those speeches which are employed to give the 'Battle' a clear narrative structure – based presumably on accounts such as Piratin's – that appear as the least authentic. When Harry, the father, asks to be told 'everything that happened', his friend, Prince, a Communist, provides an answer that would have been known to few if any of the participants on the afternoon of 4 October 1936: 'Sir Philip Game, the police commissioner, got the wind up and banned the march. He told Mosley to fight it out with the Home Secretary. He wasn't going to have any trouble.' It is worth contrasting this dialogue with the reported impressions of an American observer at Gardiner's Corner. Arriving at 'two o'clock [h]e stayed there until five, by which time the crowds had given up hope of blocking the Fascists (they did not know the parade had been called off)'.[127]

In the subsequent acts, set just after the end of the war and in the mid-1950s, the faith of the family and their friends in the communist cause is slowly undermined, some by prosperity and others through news of Soviet oppression and anti-semitism. Only Sarah remains firm, aware of the news from Hungary but unable to give up hope. As she tells her son, Ronnie, in response to his general despair and assertion that he does not 'see things in black and white any more':

> Socialism is my light ... A way of life. A man can be beautiful. I hate ugly people – I can't bear meanness and fighting and jealousy – I've got to have light. I'm a simple person, Ronnie, and I've got to have light and love.[128]

In his autobiography, Arnold Wesker's account of the gestation of the play highlights his desire to depict loss of faith, and how this loss could not be understood 'unless that faith was created in all its innocence':

> Which crisis more than any other in recent history presented itself as black and white? The days of the Spanish Civil War and the anti-fascist demonstrations in the East End, of course, when Jews and gentiles for an incandescent moment respected one another, held hands, shared angers, threw barricades across the intersection of Whitechapel Road and Commercial Road and rolled thousands of marbles into the paths of mounted policemen with batons, toppling their ferocious steeds; that thrilling day when Sir Oswald Mosley's blackshirts were thrown off their provocative route through the Jewish streets of London and many were lured to believe the end of capitalism was imminent, the millennium just across the road at Aldgate Pump.[129]

In the play the innocence of the left's struggle in the Spanish Civil War is punctured by a former Communist asking Sarah if Dave, one of those volunteering for the International Brigade after the 'Battle', ever told her 'the way some of the Party members refused to fight alongside the Trotskyists? And one or two of the Trotskyists didn't come back and they weren't killed in the fighting either?'[130] It would take a further twenty years before the unblemished memory of the Communist Party of 4 October 1936 would be publicly queried from within the left.

It was not long before the play, and the trilogy which was completed by 1960, gained classic status. Subsequently it has been revived, thus failing to fulfill Wesker's fears that, like William Goldman's *East End My Cradle*, it would be a victim of 'the literary establishment's brief flurry of enthusiasm for the exotic aspect of his Jewishness'. The play certainly helped project private family memories of the 'Battle' into the public domain, confounding his mother's belief, on hearing the first draft of the play in November 1957, that whilst it was 'very good ... it's a big work ... but who's going to be interested in any of it, silly boy? It's about us, it's between us. It won't mean anything to anyone else'.[131] *Chicken Soup with Barley* did not, however, spark off specific interest in the 'Battle' itself. In reviewing the work for the *New Statesman*, T. C. Worsley wrote of Act I: 'The Spanish war is at its height. It is the decade of hope. A successful anti-Mosley demonstration is at its height.' This vague reference to 4 October 1936 contrasts markedly with the same journal's enthusiastic contemporary response to the activities of that day, which it viewed as a progressive triumph made possible through Jewish-gentile co-operation.[132]

For many in the Jewish establishment by the 1950s, on the other hand, the 'Battle' and all it represented was a source of embarrassment. They were unwilling to dwell, as Wesker had done, on the attraction that communism had offered to East End Jews during the 1930s in terms of its idealism as well as its practical anti-fascism. In 1956, at the time of the extensive celebrations marking the tercentenary of the readmission of the Jews to England, the 1930s anti-fascist struggles were ignored and Mosley summarily dismissed as a friend of Julius Streicher, thereby stressing his unpatriotic and perverse nature. Max Beloff claimed that Mosley and other figures who tried to import anti-semitism to Britain were bound to fail as they were 'alien to the fundamentals of British thought or behaviour'. Those attacking Mosley, however, had made matters worse, particularly the small number of Jews who 'to their shame, were taking a prominent part in the Communist movement'.[133]

The militancy of the 1930s and of the late 1940s was marginalised and consciously forgotten in the attempt to show the integration of British Jewry after the painful years following 1945 and the clashes with the British government over Palestine. In addition, many Jews, as with some of the figures in Wesker's play, were settling for a quieter lower middle-class life in suburbia, or what Wesker's fellow 'new' writer, Bernard Kops, described as settling for the 'semi and the three piece suite'. The process of moving on from the East End, politically, economically and socially, with all the resultant tensions, were explored, again with reference to the 'Battle', by the emerging Anglo-American Jewish novelist, Frederic Raphael in *The Limits of Love* (1960). But few wanted to acknowledge the world of those still in the radical Yiddish-speaking milieu, such as members of the Workers' Circle, which in 1959 celebrated its golden jubilee. This event, however, was the first time that the specifically *Jewish* input into the 'Battle' received prominence, the Circle's celebratory brochure highlighting the role of the Jewish People's Council in the weeks leading up to 4 October 1936, and the rich diversity of Jewish bodies (including the Circle) which it represented. But the brochure's conclusion to the anti-fascist work of the 1930s, 'Let us hope that the day will not be far distant when the Circle will once again play an important role in the life of the Jewish people in this country', was, some quarter of a century later, unrealistic in the extreme.[134]

Coming from a very different Jewish angle to the Worker's Circle, another attempt was made in the late 1950s to break the Communist Party stranglehold on the narrative of the 'Battle'. With regard to the respectability demanded by Beloff and other conservative figures within British Jewry, it left left-wing accounts in the shade, though it matched that of Piratin for the simplicity of its plot and far outweighed the Communist in egomania. *Jack Spot: The Man of a Thousand Cuts* (1958) claimed on its cover to have sales of 13 million. This, like much of its contents, was probably fictitious, although the circulation of cheap, lurid paperbacks in the 1950s was enormous. Spot was a notorious East End criminal, although like many of these East End figures in the pre- and post-war period, the legend of his deeds was much greater than their reality. In his account of 4 October 1936, Spot himself is responsible for the large Jewish presence: 'They'll be there. You can stake your life on it. That big bastard Spot's getting a mob together!'

The 'Battle' in his version became one chiefly between Jews and fascists. The anti-fascist opposition of others is summarily dismissed: 'Our union leaders, the Communists, the left-wingers and the militants would all shout their heads off. But when it came down to brass tacks, shouting was all they ever did.' It needed Jack Spot to light the fuse: 'I'd start it off, and once it was started nothing would ever stop it. Nothing could ever stop that mob once it got out of hand.' Spot breaks up the fascists in 'a red, blood-mad haze' before launching an attack on the police which lands him with a six-month prison sentence. Not one to underestimate his own personal significance, Spot wrote that the failure of the government to follow 'the lead I'd given them' had 'cost a few billion pounds [and] a few million deaths'.[135] The appeal of Spot's gangsterland account has been lasting, playing into an East End mythology reproduced in film, soap opera and popular journalism. He repeated his story in newspaper articles in the following decade; it then became incorporated into histories of the infamous Kray brothers.[136] The overflowing machismo in his account of the 'Battle' appealed to a new generation of anti-fascists, commemorated and elaborated further by the left-wing folk rock band 'The Men They Couldn't Hang' in their 'Ghosts of Cable Street' (1986):

> The battle broke
> And the fists and the batons fell
> Through the barricades
> Passed the sound of a wounded yell.
> Jack Spot crept through
> With a chair leg made of lead
> Brought down a crushing blow
> On Mosley's head.[137]

For those who had participated in the 'Battle', the heroic accounts of Piratin and Spot simultaneously acted as an inclusive and exclusive framework of remembrance. On the one hand they gave meaning and structure to a day which had been of deep significance to many ordinary people but which had received no official recognition: as late as the 1950s, 4 October 1936 had still no agreed title. On the other, the elitism of such accounts, as well as their tendency to ignore the presence of those less easily placed into narratives of conflict, especially women and children, had the effect of marginalising the experiences of many present on the day. Through the complex interplay of remembering and forgetting during the 1950s, it was far from clear whether at a collective level the memory of the 'Battle' would survive into the following decade.

FORGETTING AND REDISCOVERING THE 'BATTLE': FROM THE 1960s TO THE 1970s

In 1961 the first full-length study of fascism in Britain was published. Its author, Colin Cross, arguing that the day marked 'the climax of all the East End disorders', referred to it as 'the so-called Battle of Cable Street', probably the first printed reference to the events of 4 October 1936 to use that title. Cross was clearly not very familiar with the 'Battle', getting the date wrong and providing the sketchiest of details relating to the day itself. What is significant, however, is that through the informal mechanisms of discussions between family and friends, reinforced by political discourse, popular culture and literary accounts over two decades, a name had been given to 4 October 1936 which had gained a degree of popular recognition.[138] Ironically, however, even with the advantage of a generally agreed title, at a public level the 'Battle of Cable Street' was hardly mentioned throughout the 1960s, and had to be rescued from the twilight zone between memory and amnesia at the end of the decade by *Yesterday's Witness*.[139]

Yesterday's Witness has been described as 'the world's first oral history TV series'. Starting in 1969, it was the inspiration of its producer, Stephen Peet, and owed much to the new form of 'history from below' represented in Britain by the History Workshop movement. The documentaries in the series, which ended in 1980, covered such topics as a school strike in 1914, industrial and other disasters, women's work from the 1890s, birth control during the 1920s, eye-witnesses to the testing of the first atomic bomb in the summer of 1945 and, in a film made in 1969 and shown in January 1970, 'The Battle of Cable Street'.[140]

Reflecting on the series, the journalist James Cameron who, after narrating 'The Battle of Cable Street' became closely involved, saw *Yesterday's Witness* as representing the experience between 'now' and 'history'. It was partly conceived as a form of rescue archaeology, interviewing witnesses before it was too late. But the series also had a more pro-active role in covering areas of history which others might have dismissed as unimportant:

> Yesterday's Witnesses were occasionally the witnesses of meaningful and momentous events, happenings that wrote themselves in the larger legends of the country; frequently their involvement was with something that only now seems dramatic, seminal, or even merely quaint, but which without their personal witness might easily have slipped through the net of history and become no more than folk-memory.[141]

In fact, this documentary on the 'Battle' was made at the same time that the first academic study of the British fascist movement, by Robert Benewick, was published.[142] Nevertheless, the documentary undoubtedly halted processes leading to the fading away of the 'folk memory' of 4 October 1936. Indeed, the director, Michael Rabiger, was deeply shocked when told about Mosley, his private 'army', the BUF and the 'Battle' itself by his friend Stephen Peet:

> I didn't know about this. As a World War Two child, brought up in the shadow of World War Two, we were not told about the Holocaust, we were not told about British anti-semitism and we were certainly not told that there had been a very large British fascist party ... I felt betrayed, I felt that my parents' generation had maintained a suspicious silence, the kind of silence that goes with denial and goes with guilt.[143]

Rabiger worked freelance, making films 'on the darker side of English history' and believing that 'if you went to history then you should find a subject with resonance for the present day'. Not surprisingly, 'the Battle' and the politics around it appealed to him. The film, whilst concentrating on the 'Battle', made explicit connections to the anti-black racism which was becoming increasingly politicised in Britain from the late 1960s onwards. As the narrator put it: 'That fight is over, but the malady lingers on.'[144] The documentary was a controversial one. Permission had to be granted from the BBC to interview Oswald Mosley, who had been refused access to any form of broadcasting in Britain since the late 1930s. Mosley had published his autobiography in 1968. In the film he was similarly anxious to continue his war of memory, blaming the alien-Jew-communist for the disturbances of the 1930s and arguing that his conflict with the Jews, rather than reflecting his own prejudices and political opportunism was, in fact, self-defence.[145] The film, whilst giving space to Mosley and his post-war supporters but not engaging in any dialogue with them, attempted to damn them in their own words alongside chilling newsreel images of the blackshirts marching in uniform, beating up opponents and mesmerised by the hypnotic and manic oratory of 'the leader' himself.[146]

Edith Ramsay and the local East End Jewish historian, Bill Fishman, provided testimony, giving the background which emphasised the poverty and despair of the area. In particular, Fishman movingly recalled the subtle, undermining impact of Mosley's anti-semitic propaganda:

> I often used to go away feeling 'Are we Jews like this?' and often when he used to call out that international finance, the alien domination of British politics, my mind used to go to my father who was a poor tailor wandering through the East End looking for work.[147]

The description of the 'Battle' itself, however, was dominated by the Communist Party activists, William Faulkner and Phil Piratin who developed the theme of 4 October 1936 as a precise military anti-fascist exercise – a narrative approach adopted since the day itself – to its most articulate and elaborate level. Piratin later claimed that the documentary was based on *Our Flag Stays Red,* and certainly the recounting of the day itself largely followed his earlier account. It was, however, taken even further by the testimony of Faulkner, who had infiltrated the fascist lines and from 'headquarters' spread word of the police's decision to shift the march to pass through Cable Street. Faulkner and Piratin appear in the documentary as two retired, self-satisfied generals, reliving a successful war campaign. Such tendencies were reinforced through the use of battle maps of the streets of east London, the two using batons to point to ground that was taken or successfully defended. Nothing was left to chance. In a moment that could have come straight out of the absurd discourse of *Monty Python's Flying Circus* (an exact contemporary of *Yesterday's Witness*), but was delivered without a hint of irony or any form of humour whatsoever, Piratin talked of the barricades at Cable Street 'where we had prepared to overturn a lorry which had been given to us by a local lorry firm for overturning purposes'.[148]

The aim of *Yesterday's Witness* was to provide testimony that was 'spontaneous and idiosyncratic'. In the case of Mosley and the Communist participants in the documentary this was far from the case with their rehearsed and polished memories. Piratin some years later told the *Morning Star* that it was pointless adding any 'spoken alternative' on the 'Battle' as he had written it all down in *Our Flag Stays Red*.[149] Nevertheless, the smoothness of the narrative was challenged, if not undermined, by the accounts of Fishman and Ramsay, who highlighted the terror experienced by some Jews on the day and the confusion felt by many of the protestors as to what was going on. Even Piratin's narrative came to life when describing the injuries inflicted on his

> own young sister-in-law... I helped her to get away to an ambulance, and her back was lacerated as a result [of broken glass]... she was not a grown person, she was then a kid of about 17.[150]

James Cameron, who had been brought in as an 'independent narrator' to act as a 'lightning rod' to deflect possible criticism – so concerned were BBC executives that they wanted to have the film vetted by the police – provided closure for the day itself: 'Then, suddenly, it was all over. The Battle of Cable Street was won.'[151] The film was clearly sympathetic to a left-wing analysis of fascism and its sympathies were with those who had stopped the march proceeding through the East End. Yet any hint of triumphalism was tempered by ending with a reference to the successors to Mosley on the streets of East London. Rabiger saw the film as a warning of the potential of the 'dark undercurrent in British life', the undercurrent of xenophobia which he saw fulfilled in the Thatcher years.[152]

As the first oral history of the 'Battle', the documentary had its strengths and weaknesses. The range of witnesses was limited, although this was partly beyond the producer and director's control. Former members of the BUF were reluctant to admit their affiliation and three policemen interviewed, whose testimony would have further reinforced the experience of confusion and chaos on the day, received threats that their pensions would be in danger if their accounts were broadcast.[153] The extensive use of Mosley and the two Communist Party members, alongside that of Edith Ramsay, who was a figure of some authority in the East End, meant that Bill Fishman was left to communicate the experience of the tens of thousands of ordinary Jews thirty five years earlier, which, even allowing for the eloquence of his testimony, was clearly impossible.

But, in spite of its limitations, the power of the *Yesterday's Witness* documentary established the 'Battle' as an event in history and memory that was important in its own right. In 1986 Piratin claimed that the name itself was 'coined ... by the BBC [documentary]' which, as has been shown, is not strictly accurate. Nevertheless, the former Communist MP was right to emphasise the importance of the programme's title in popularising the event outside the diminishing number of people who had direct memories of the day. Moreover, circumstances during the 1970s helped ensure that its recent obscurity would not be repeated. The life of 'The Battle of Cable Street' as an ever-increasing and self-sustaining myth was under way.[154]

There were three inter-linked developments which took hold from the late 1960s which at least partly explain the phenomenon of how the memory of the 'Battle' grew stronger as the event itself moved further into the past. The first was the return, in the form of the National Front, of a large scale fascist-inspired racist organisation which threatened, as had the BUF, to become a major political force in Britain. The connections between the BUF and the National Front extended across ideology – under its anti-black rhetoric and violence, the National Front maintained an anti-semitic world view – as well as leadership. The Front, whilst dabbling in national and local elections, was in essence, like its predecessor, a street movement whose major targets for physical assault were not Jews but Afro-Caribbeans and Asians.[155]

The anti-fascist response to this movement contained elements of continuity from the '43' and '62' Groups, emphasising the Nazi nature of the neo-fascists and using graphic imagery from the concentration camps liberated in 1945 to illustrate what fascism could lead to.[156] It also, however, moved back before the Second World War and utilised the 'victory' of the 'Battle' to show that fascism on Britain's streets could be defeated. One of the first cultural manifestations of this new approach was the publication in 1975 of *They Shall Not Pass*, 'a poetry anthology to celebrate the East Enders' victory over Fascism – October 1936', significantly subtitled 'They Shall Never Pass'. The anthology was put together by the Tower Hamlets Movement against Racism and Fascism and included the song 'Red Lion Square', by Jack Warshaw. Warshaw explicitly connected the events of the 1930s with the current situation; specifically the death in 1974 of Kevin Gately at an anti-National Front demonstration in Red Lion Square, it was rumoured by the use of a police baton. The poem provided a direct generational link in the anti-fascist struggle:

Oh father dear, the news just said,
There's a young man hurt, they think he's dead...

> Oh son, oh son, the things you see
> Bring back a long time memory.
> For I was young in '36
> When the fascists tried the same old tricks...
>
> In Cable Street we took our stand
> But the cops gave them a helping hand...
>
> The cry went up 'THEY SHALL NOT PASS!'
> We fought together and we held fast...
>
> And now they've banned their uniform
> But the hateful blackshirts have returned
> So son, remember Red Lion Square
> For it could happen anywhere

In the same volume, Jim Wolveridge, a 16-year-old button hole maker in Cable Street forty years earlier, added his own memories but finished by warning that 'Now we have a new gang – jolly Jack Tyndall and his National Front. Maybe one day they'll want to march through the East End. I hope they do – they'll get the same reception.' By the end of the decade Wolveridge's prediction had come true but with appalling results including the murder of Altab Ali and other serious injuries inflicted on East End Bengalis.[157] But, in these desperate and bloody days, the memory of the 'Battle' could be mobilised to show the power of collective resistance and, in particular, the strength gained when the minority group under attack was given support. Thus Charlie Goodman, recalling how 'catholic dockers the sons of Irish immigrants, orthodox Jews wearing long silk coats. Somali seamen [and] local cockneys joined ... to drive the hated blackshirts off the streets of the East End', concluded that 'We should remember the victory of October 4, 1936 if we have any doubts that [the racists] can be defeated.'[158]

The second development was the growth in interest and support for local studies, coming out of the same movement that had enabled the 'Yesterday's Witness' series and buttressed by the emergence of strong left-wing municipal government typified by the Greater London Council. Within the East End, individuals such as Jim Wolveridge were encouraged to write their memoirs and autobiographies through small local publishers and writers' collectives. Miriam Metz grew up in the East End after the Second World War. Her secondary school, typically for the time, was 'very narrow culturally':

> It didn't let us draw on our own culture. It did something which I suppose is counted as fairly radical: when you were in the second year

you had to write a local history essay, but what local history was interpreted as meaning was either the Tower of London or the Whitechapel Bell Foundry, where they made the Liberty Bell, or Chaucer's Stepney or something like that. It was never remotely signalled to us that what we could be doing was actually looking at the Jewish East End, or our own family histories.[159]

The new history from below enabled a different perspective, encouraging writing about everyday experiences and those formerly marginalised by professional historians such as women, the working class and ethnic minorities. Wolveridge and others from the 1970s onwards incorporated the 'Battle' into their life stories. In turn, these writings allowed different perspectives to emerge from those such as Piratin which had gained orthodoxy. These working-class autobiographies were often far less heroic but much more emotional in their outlook, referring to the fear and confusion experienced on the day itself and providing, in the process, more fragmented accounts. Yet so dominant had the narrative created by the Communist Party become that in the subsequent writing of 'ordinary people' a defensiveness has developed about the authenticity of experiences if they fail to match up to the mythology of the day.[160]

Alongside the greater respect and approbation given to ordinary people's experiences came a new form of radical teaching, typified by Chris Searle at Langton Park Secondary School in Limehouse (although earlier Searle had been sacked from another East End school for attempting a similar radical approach to the teaching of English, indicative that it was far from being universally accepted in the education world). Searle wrote in 1977 that

> Though our children were only a small portion of the human vastness of [the working] class all over the world, our work in the classroom had attempted to vindicate and sustain that feeling of belonging and oneness with oppressed humanity. And yet these children lived together in a particular country, a particular city and a particular neighbourhood. Their actual living relationships were fused with the streets, flats, canals and dockyards of East London, and their lives were taking place, moving forward and making sense in this particular concrete reality.[161]

He added that the children at his school, with their roots all over the world, had been pitched 'in the centre of an area of massive historical working class struggle and revolt'. This history would enfold them, just as it had earlier immigrant groups: 'It was up to us, the teachers, to make history work for us and nourish our children.' Searle devised a counter-history of the East End, one that would have been shocking to the teachers of Miriam

Metz, incorporating working-class struggle in which the 'The Battle of Cable Street' could be included both for its radicalism and for its use of inter-ethnic collaboration and anti-racism. 'With the current growth of organised racism in the neighbourhood, it was imperative for us, as teachers, to evoke the East End's inspiring anti-fascist history. Many would say that this had culminated in 1936 at Cable Street.' Searle's team collected testimony from veterans such as Jim Wolveridge, and found documents such as the 'Ballad' of 4 October 1936 written by the 'Tramp Poet' and sold in Oxford Street. The children themselves were then asked to imagine the day and wrote powerful poems on their perceptions of the 'Battle', bringing fresh insights combining their everyday experiences in the East End, their knowledge of the battle and their past family backgrounds in Africa, South America and Asia.[162]

The third element was the growth of multi-culturalism on a national and local level in Britain, building on the growing ethnic pride on both sides of the Atlantic in response to the assimilationist pressures that had previously operated on minority groups. In the case of the 'Battle' it enabled specifically Jewish memories to gain greater attention, countering the universalism running through Communist narratives of 4 October 1936 which, until the 1970s, were still dominant. The tendency to downplay Jewish activism in order to highlight the role of non-Jews in stopping Mosley was challenged, most notably by the former Communist, Joe Jacobs, in his posthumous memoir *Out of the Ghetto* (1978). For the first time a dissident Communist voice was heard detailing internal debates leading up to 4 October 1936 and especially the decision to abandon the rally in Trafalgar Square. Jacobs highlighted how it was Jewish activists such as himself and Sam Berkovitz who fought for confrontation on a street level, which many Jews in the area, inside and outside the Communist Party, demanded but were ignored by the national leaders.[163] Jacobs' account enabled a rediscovery of Jewish activism during the 1930s, including organisations such as the Jewish People's Council, which in turn stimulated radical groups such as the Jewish Socialists' Group, and its linked Greater London Council-funded Jewish Cultural and Anti-Racist Project, which emerged during the 1980s.[164] For the first time, 'the Battle of Cable Street' was prominent in a major memorialisation of Jewish life in Britain, the 'Festival of the Jewish East End' (1987). Aside from exhibitions which featured the 'Battle', the 'Festival' included Simon Blumenfeld's play on the theme. Revealingly, in respect of the growing recognition of the Jewish input to 4 October 1936, Blumenfeld's *The Battle of Cable Street*, whilst maintaining a universalist theme, nevertheless incorporated a character apparently melded out of the independent Jewish communists, Sam Berkovitz and Joe Jacobs.[165]

Taken together, the anti-fascism/anti-racism, the new history, progressive local politics and educational initiatives, alongside the multi-culturalism of the 1970s, allowed the 'Battle' to be commemorated as a critical 'rediscovered' piece of the British past. This particular history was always connected to contemporary issues and, in the process of historicisation, conflicts emerged, most notably over Jacobs' account of events.[166] But for the first time committees and groups were set up with the major purpose of memorialising the day.

MEMORIALISING 'THE BATTLE'

In February 1975 the anti-fascist journal, *Searchlight*, was launched, or more accurately, re-launched. Its new cover and editorial line made explicit the connection to 4 October 1936: '"They shall not pass" is really the motto of this publication'.[167] Under the direction of Maurice Ludmer and Gerry Gable, direct links were made between fascism at home and abroad during the Nazi era and the growth of the extreme right in Britain during the 1970s:

> We at SEARCHLIGHT hope to play our small part in the struggle against racism and extremism and in the defence of democracy by turning the light of day on those who would dig up the ghosts of the past and those who would raise up latter day Fuehrers. Mankind will never again tolerate those who would put us into chains and who would murder those who do not go along with their obscene ideas. They shall not pass.[168]

Searchlight had first appeared in the mid-1960s, representing a liberal-dominated, semi-assimilationist approach to 'race relations' as typified then by the Institute for Race Relations. Its attitude to the fascist groups of the 1960s was to connect them to the Nazis, who, it added for its readers' benefit, 'were, of course, Hitler's party in Germany' – reflecting fears that the genocidal nature of the Third Reich was already passing from memory in Britain. Apart from the pain caused to the specific minorities under attack, the threat offered by the neo-Nazis was viewed by the original *Searchlight* in terms of their future potential: 'Hitler was regarded as a harmless fool once, and yet he caused the death of millions of human beings, including 500,000 British men, women and children.' Images of Nazi atrocities were reproduced regularly in the *Searchlight* of the 1960s, as were references to the role of Britain in the Second World War. The neo-Nazis 'methods [were] dictatorial and un-British. They side-track the whole issue of social betterment by their anti-coloured and anti-Jewish campaigns' whereas the 'the people of Britain [were] decent, humane and tolerant'. 'The Battle', which represented the response to a mass British fascist movement and the fight against authority was not for the early *Searchlight*, in contrast to its successor, a usable past.[169]

The *Searchlight* of the 1970s was much more militant in its approach and, through Lumner and Gable, provided a direct connection to the physical response to fascism represented by the '43 Group' after the Second World War. The 'message' of 4 October 1936 was particularly important to its ethos and in October 1976 it dedicated a 'special anniversary issue to 'Cable Street', the first major journalistic commemoration of the 'Battle' since the production of Independent Labour Party and Communist Party 'souvenirs' at the time: 'We feel it is important forty years later to pay tribute to an earlier generation who engaged in an anti-fascist struggle and try and learn many valuable lessons from the events that took place that day.' It argued strongly against the position that ignoring the racists and fascists would make them go away: 'History has proved who was right in 1936. The 500,000 people who responded to the call for action struck a blow for democracy in Britain ... United action by wide sections of the people won the day.'[170]

Although crude in its presentation of the background and detail of the event, and lacking any first hand testimony, this special issue of the journal was important in establishing firmly the role of the 'Battle' in later anti-fascist discourse. Subsequently, *Searchlight* has played a vital role in the commemoration of the event, most significantly through the encouragement it has given to a new generation of militant campaigners, notably the organisation Anti-Fascist Action. In 1988, 'Cable Street Beat', later to be connected to Anti-Fascist Action, was formed:

> Firstly it was seen as a good way to get a militant anti-fascist message across to a wider audience and secondly, the threat posed by the fascists in respect of the way that they were organising in music, while at the same time attacking gigs, was something that could not go unchecked.[171]

Building on the more broadly defined 'Rock Against Racism' movement of the 1970s, those connected to 'Cable Street Beat' were able to utilise the specific memories of the 'Battle' which had become accessible to a younger generation, especially through the major fiftieth anniversary celebrations that had taken place in 1986. Indeed, some connected to Cable Street Beat, such as 'The Men They Couldn't Hang', contributed to the 1986 events. To these young, largely male, anti-fascists, the 'Battle' represented an unambiguous message:

> If Cable Street tells us anything, it is that the better organised this [anti-fascist] violence is, the more effective it will be. Fascists today must

learn what their forerunners in the BUF learned in 1936 – there is no easy target for their thugs, and there is a price to pay for advocating race hate.

The very title 'Cable Street Beat' can be, and was no doubt intended to be, understood in five ways – playing on references to history, music, violence, victory and the police. Through all five, the appeal of the 'Battle' could be broadened so that the street fight against neo-Nazis was at one with the confrontations with authority in Thatcher's Britain in industrial disputes and the 'poll tax' riots. Nevertheless, in this alternative left-wing universalisation, the specific history of the 'Battle' was never lost sight of. Thus the voices of 'veterans' of 4 October 1936 have been incorporated into Anti-Fascist Action and Cable Street Beat publications and other merchandise.[172]

Raphael Samuel in his *Theatres of Memory* was anxious to counter the tendency to regard the products of the 'Heritage Industry' as inherently conservative.[173] The marketing of the 'Battle' through the badges, T-shirts, videos and stickers of 'Cable Street Beat' alongside the postcards, posters and limited edition sixtieth anniversary plates (made by ex-miners) produced by the Cable Street Group provide ample evidence of the late historian's thesis (appropriately enough as Samuel was an East Ender and a founder of the History Workshop movement that helped stimulate the people's history approach to the anti-fascist struggle).[174] But the 'Battle', as product of heritage industry, has extended into the public realm, most prominently through one of Britain's largest murals, located in Cable Street itself.

In his important pioneer study of 'The Art of [the Battle of] Cable Street', Roger Mills argues that 'Not surprisingly, the occasion has become an emblem for the British left':

> What is surprising however, given the different factions and groupings involved, is just how little disagreement there is about interpretation of the facts surrounding the event. It is my opinion that, in part, it is this untroubled recollection that smoothed the way when a mural depicting the Battle was proposed. It had been, just about everybody agreed, a resounding success in the fight against British fascism.[175]

There is some truth in Mills' analysis, yet under the surface of consensus concerning 4 October 1936 were battles over memory, some of which were as old as the day in question itself. First, there were still some in the Jewish community who regarded the stance taken by the Labour Party and the Board of Deputies of British Jews as correct: 'What stopped the fascists was not violence against them, but the denial … of press and radio

'Long May Its Memory Live'

publicity, and of halls for public meetings.'[176] Others doubted whether it was appropriate for the 'Battle' to be commemorated, especially as it would be alongside those on the left who were deemed to be 'anti-Zionist' and thus hostile to real Jewish interests.[177] These were relatively isolated voices from an older generation within British Jewry, but they act as a reminder that responses to racism and attack are more likely to divide ethnic minorities than unite them. This is also true of those in the wider sphere of organisations against racism and fascism – the fragmentations in the neo-fascist world since the 1970s have been more than matched by those responding to them. Divisions over the 'correct' strategies to be employed in the present have extended into battles over the interpretation of the past and 4 October 1936, as an increasingly important site of inspirational memory, has not been exempt. In particular, those in Trotskyite organisations have criticised the 'Stalinist myth surround[ing] the Communist Party's role in the Battle of Cable Street' which has led to it 'untruthfully taking almost all the credit for the Battle of Cable Street'. Instead, they emphasis the popular nature of the working-class response and the initial failure of the Communist Party to pay heed to it, making particular use of Jacobs' testimony. The multi-ethnic composition of the crowds at Gardiner's Corner, and especially at Cable Street, has been highlighted by Trotskyites, utilising, though not directly referring to, the memories of Charlie Goodman: 'a virtual war was fought between the police and the defenders of the anti-fascist barricades. British, Irish and some Somali dockers fought the police'. But, as with the approach of Chris Searle, minority participation is incorporated into Trotskyite narratives in order to universalise 'Cable Street [as] working-class legend. It is rightly remembered as something the working class and its allies won against the combined might of the state and the fascists.'[178]

The contested memory, especially concerning the 'message' of the 'Battle', did not ultimately stand in the way of the mural's creation. Nevertheless, it is not surprising that contemporary concerns would inevitably shape the mural's content and that those continuing the BUF tradition of fascism and racism in the East End would attempt to destroy its presence. The mural was commissioned in 1976 by the Tower Hamlets Arts Project, founded that year and subsequently responsible for the dissemination of much people's history in the district, including that of the old Jewish East End.[179] Dave Binnington and Desmond Rochford of the Public Arts Workshop were

> chosen to carry out the work. Binnington ... conducted intense historical research. He looked at books, films and photographs of the event and worked much of what he found into his design: the dramatic uniforms of

the BUF, the eggs, milk bottles, tools and the contents of chamber-pots coming from the upper windows, the mounted police 'Cossacks' with long weighted clubs surging through the crowd, the use of marbles and ball bearings against the police horses, the overturned lorry, the chairs and mattresses of the barricade and the police autogyro flying overhead.

In keeping with the grassroots, public history approach, 'Binnington interviewed and drew many local characters, including them in the design'.[180] In 1978, the Cable Street Mural Project organised a special reunion party to celebrate the 42nd anniversary of the 'Battle'. 'Veterans' returned to the area to share their memories and to help raise the profile of the project to create 'a permanent landmark ... as a constant reminder of the battle'. There was, as the local paper commented, an apparent incongruity and dissonance between this friendly reunion of pensioners and their recapturing of a day of 'terror and excitement':

> Lorries overturned in the street ... slogans chalked on every corner ... battalions of truncheoned police facing a solid wall of anti-fascists. 'They shall not pass!' thundered the deafening roar. No, it's not a scene from a Brick Lane demo, but memories of a group of pensioners as they vividly recall their finest hour – The Battle of Cable Street.[181]

Repeated a year later in order to raise funds for the mural, the meeting of 'veterans' to commemorate the anniversary of the 'Battle' was, as many of them reached their seventies, becoming ritualised.[182] Work began on the mural in 1979 and was 'well advanced when, in 1980, fascists climbed the scaffolding and daubed the mural with the words "British Nationalism not Communism – Rights for Whites Stop the Race War" in six-foot-high letters. The bottom two-thirds of the painting [were] ruined. Dave Binnington immediately resigned from the Project.'[183] Throughout the 1980s and 1990s further fascist vandalism in the form of paint bomb 'attacks' on the mural continued this extreme war of memory against what they clearly internalised as the defeat of their predecessors in 1936.[184]

The radical artist Ray Walker was brought in, along with Paul Butler and Desmond Rochfort, to complete the mural, which was finished in October 1982, adding further layers of complexity to its representation of the 'Battle'. For the artists, the collaborative aspect of the last stages of the painting provided inspiration for their subject matter. As Rochfort recalled:

> In our many conversations throughout the twelve months we worked together Ray was constantly struck by the democratic and social character of mural painting, which the Cable Street work helped

underline for him. In its potential for collaborative and collective creativity, its public accessibility, and as a vehicle for the expression of social content, the mural represented for Ray the symbol of a truly democratic cultural intervention in an increasingly undemocratic society, and of a new pictorial aesthetic, equivalent to the socialist convictions that informed his political commitment.[185]

The mural – now protected against attack through a varnish covering, and having survived an attempt to create a disabled persons' entrance through it to St.George's Town Hall, the building of which it is part – remains an impressive tribute to the 'Battle'. Largely free of the Soviet heroic style which typifies so much of this genre from the 1970s and 1980s (indeed it should be noted that it has conscious echoes of Vorticism, a pre-war movement associated with fascist politics and aesthetics, it succeeds in showing the dynamism, fury and passion of the fighting in Cable Street but does not eschew representing the sheer terror that the police onslaught inflicted. And whilst the 'Cossack' police and the fascists are faceless and appear as sinister robots (only Hitler, exposed in his underwear, is a figure of fun), the detail on the faces of the anti-fascists, many modelled on people present on the day, such as Sam Berkovitz, helps to individualise what could easily have become an exercise in universalised socialist 'realism'.[186]

The anti-fascism of the mural is not party political and, whilst the message of a Communist Party banner is clearly represented, the presence and role of the Independent Labour Party is also acknowledged. The mural is also an important site of memory in relation to its representation of ethnicity, highlighting how memorialisation is as equally concerned with the present as with the past. Apart from the artists' attempt to represent 'veterans' of the 'Battle' they were keen to include contemporary inhabitants of Cable Street itself – indeed, it appears to owe much to futurist painters' interest in the street as an entity and their attempt to convey its dynamics by employing an aerial perspective and spiralling structure. As Roger Mills comments, 'Black and Asian faces were featured and although it is unlikely that it is this radical feature of the mural alone that sent fascists scurrying out with spraypaint and brushes in the dead of night …, it emphasised the modern parallel situation where people from these groups had supplanted Jews as the main object of fascist aggression.' Mills is at pains to emphasise that he is not implying that 'the mural purposely sets out to misrepresent and that none of the anti-fascists were black. Rather, as far as I am aware, that their presence had not been featured in representations until that point.'[187] In fact, as we have seen, Shrensky's *King Sol* had included the presence of Indians, 'black men' and Chinese as early as 1939. But whereas Shrensky was playing into the romanticised, 'dangerous' image of Cable Street, the reality of which he was unfamiliar with, the mural artists, through their local involvement in the late 1970s and early 1980s, had come to appreciate the ordinariness of the street's multi-culturalism.

The 'Battle of Cable Street' and Spanish Civil War veteran Charlie Goodman is the only contemporary to have highlighted the role of what he has on several occasions referred to as 'Somali seamen' who lived around Cable Street and took part on 4 October 1936 'shoulder to shoulder with Irish Catholics' and 'orthodox Jews with long silk coats and soft felt hats'.[188] There is clear romanticisation in Goodman's testimony, although there is no reason why the African and Asian communities, though tiny in number, should not have been present at the 'Battle'. We know, from a Special Branch report on anti-fascist activities, that a South African, Mr Fennell, described as a 'man of colour', spoke on the afternoon of 4 October 1936 in the East End.[189] The Communist Party, in particular, had forged links with black socialists and anti-imperialists across the world and so their presence at the 'Battle' would have been unsurprising. Nevertheless, the heavy emphasis in popular representations of the 'Battle' since the 1980s of black people also reflects contemporary concerns about the importance of multi-culturalism. Aside from the many black faces in the Cable Street mural, the Jewish presence is also clear, implicitly in the Jewish figures portrayed, and explicitly in the form of a shop sign for J.Wineburg, no.43 Cable Street.[190] The attempt to utilise the memory of the 'Battle' for multi-cultural, as well as explicitly anti-racist and anti-fascist purposes, began in earnest with the fiftieth anniversary celebrations in October 1986.

The expansion of the 'people's history' approach to the memory of the 'Battle', alongside the revival of interest in the day from contemporary anti-fascist movements, reached a climax in the series of events arranged to mark its golden anniversary. Along with the mural, it challenged the memory of the 'Battle' by placing it in the specific context of the history and present of the street that had become so intricately linked to its legend. Early in 1986 the residents of Cable Street started 'to organise appropriate celebrations of the rejection of fascism by the people of the East End on October 4th 1936'. Plans were drawn up 'for a major multi-racial neighbourhood festival in Stepney', incorporating local, national and international anti-racist organisations as well as 'Asian, Somali, Chinese and other minority ethnic community organisations'. Ironically, this attempt at multi-culturalism stopped short of considering Jewish religious sensitivities; 4 October 1986 fell on the Jewish New Year. In recognition of this problem, a Tower Hamlets Environment Trust plaque to commemorate the 'Battle' was

'Long May Its Memory Live'

unveiled later in the year. It was particularly unfortunate, therefore, that the launch of the Cable Street Group's booklet on the 'Battle', sponsored by Tower Hamlets council, some nine years later, should have been held on Yom Kippur, the Jewish Day of Atonement.[191]

The 1986 fiftieth anniversary celebrations represented, for the 'veterans', the high point of their recognition. In the commemoration rally itself, which 4,000 people attended, as well as in plays and exhibitions, their testimony was highlighted. Although male Communists were still prominent, more attention was given to other anti-fascist and local voices which, if not challenging the dominant heroic narrative of the day, at least provided material for future re-interpretations of who took part and why. Thus in a public exhibition on the 'Battle', the memories of May Smith, who had been out walking with her baby and accidently found herself in the middle of a police attack, were included. Having taken her baby out of its pram, May hid in an alleyway:

> There were policemen hitting everyone with truncheons ... I didn't scream ... the baby did though. We were in the doorway the best part of an hour, we couldn't get away. We were terrified, there must have been a lot of innocent people that were caught up in it ... Women were screaming and the road seemed to be covered in blood, the hospital was on red alert — you just can't hit people like that ... we had never seen anything like that before.[192]

Similarly, Anita Dobson, a star of the television soap opera 'East Enders', recalled that 'My Dad, who was in the East End at the time, said that everyone he knew did their best to avoid the riot'.[193]

Moreover, any tendency towards self-satisfaction at the 'victory' was challenged by the 1986 celebration's time and place: 'There was a little tension in the air. The previous night an Asian shop in the Brick Lane area had been burnt out and arson was suspected. The fascists had already desecrated the Cable Street memorial mural a few nights before.'[194] Indeed, in spite of the attendance and words of the 'veterans', including those from the Spanish Civil War, it was the lesson of the 'Battle' that was the dominant theme at the rally. Attention was focused on the racial attacks committed against Bengali and Asian communities in Tower Hamlets and the threat posed by the British National Party. Importantly, however, the battles taking place between the police and trade unionists picketing Rupert Murdoch's newspaper offices in Wapping were also frequently connected to those of fifty years earlier. As the memory of the 'Battle' intensified and became more accessible, it was inevitable that it would be utilised in political struggles which had less and less in common with the actual anti-fascist and anti-racist struggles of 1936.[195]

The very existence of celebrations in October 1996 for the sixtieth anniversary of the 'Battle' indicated that commemoration itself had become ritualised, with the mural and plaque in Cable Street enabling a focal point of remembrance. Further facilitating such memorialisation were the books, videos and other artifacts about the 'Battle', as well as the availability since the 1970s of plays written about the day. By 1996, however, the 'veterans' were getting old and infirm, which problematised the march from near the former site of Gardiner's Corner to Cable Street itself that had been a feature of earlier commemorations. Fascism in Britain during the mid-1990s was in retreat, although this could not be said for racial violence, which had, if anything, escalated in scale and intensity. Speakers emphasised the continuing violence faced by ethnic minorities in the East End and the need for solidarity against it. Indeed, symbolically, the march on 6 October 1996 started off from Altab Ali Park, named after the young local Asian who, as we have noted, was stabbed to death by racist thugs. Reference was also made to institutionalised racism in the form of the asylum legislation of the Conservative government. It showed how the commemoration was moving further away from being used only to make reference to the threat posed by organised extremists. 'Yesterday's Witness', for example, had limited its discussion of racism in contemporary Britain to Mosley's successors, not mentioning the impact of Enoch Powell or the discriminatory immigration control legislated by the Conservatives and Labour during the 1960s.[196]

The stress on multi-culturalism was even more pronounced than in 1986 although the poster for the event inadvertantly marginalised the place of ethnic minorities at the time of the 'Battle' and somewhat distorted the precise geography of East End Jewry in the inter-war years:

> In 1936 the whole community in East London – *local* workers [my emphasis], Irish, Jewish workers, dockers – turned out to stop Oswald Mosley's Blackshirt Fascists marching through Cable Street, the heart of the Jewish population. Today we march to ensure that all people can live together in a united, multi-ethnic society.[197]

In 1996 two separate tendencies concerning the memory of the 'Battle' were becoming more pronounced. The first was its place as a usable past for an ever-increasing range of contemporary issues, such as pensioners' rights and the abuse of prisoners and minorities in Turkey, as well as the more obviously connected problems of racism and fascism in Britain.[198] The second was for a more self-reflective approach to the memory and history of 4 October 1936, in which the subsequent shaping of the day has become increasingly scrutinised (this volume being a part of and a contribution to such a development).[199] The balance between diffusion and precision in the future commemoration of the 'Battle' can only be guessed at. Roger Mills is optimistic:

> Sixty years and still going strong. If anything, the Battle of Cable Street seems to be growing as a memory to rally round, as an event to be commemorated in word and image and song... There will almost certainly be a seventieth anniversary commemoration in [2006] and I suspect that there will be a hundredth anniversary event in 2036, by which time of course there will be no veterans left to remember it.

Because of the legacy of their testimony Mills does not believe this is a problem in itself and because, more pessimistically, as 'fascism in some shape or form will always be with us', he concludes that 'there will be artists for generations to come who will draw on the Battle of Cable Street's power for their inspiration'.[200] But is he right to suggest that the memory of the 'Battle' will live into the next millennium?

CONCLUSION

Commemorating the sixtieth anniversary of the 'Battle', Tower Hamlets Militant Labour exclaimed 'This fight is more than a memory: it continues today.'[201] The dominant tendency amongst those formally commemorating the 'Battle' since the 1970s has been to avoid the dangers of sentimentality, or as Arnold Wesker put it, 'looking back with dishonesty'.[202] The memory of the 'Battle' has always been contested within and outside the left-wing and progressive world in Britain. But for the first time the process of commemoration itself and the distance of time has given the potential for the 'Battle' to be remembered apolitically. This has been possible because in Britain since 1945 to be opposed to fascism may only imply a form of patriotism (which itself can exclude) rather than act necessarily as a commitment to human rights and anti-racism.[203] From the 1970s at least five left-wing plays on the anti-fascist, anti-racist and internationalist message of the 'Battle' were written and performed, including 'Shattersongs' by Alan Gilbey, once a pupil of Chris Searle in the East End, in addition to Steven Berkoff's version in *East*, told through the anger of an ex-East End fascist and continuing racist, Alan Gibbons' children's story of the 'Battle' published in 1995 and the radical cultures associated with militant anti-fascist groups.[204] It remains, however, that the post-war literature incorporating the 'Battle' with the biggest circulation has, in effect, de-politicised 4 October 1936. This was true of the autobiography of Jack Spot in the 1950s and more recently of the successful romantic novelist, Audrey Willsher.

Willsher's bestselling *All Shadows Fly Away* (1996) is set largely in the East End of London, telling the story of 'Fifteen-year-old Frances Henderson [who] is forever in the shadow of her beautiful sister, Kitty'. The tone of much of the book is typical of the genre:

> Kitty had never permitted a man to touch her breasts before, and she kept very still as he pulled down the straps on her petticoat. She could hear his jagged breathing and her own heart was pounding violently against her ribcage as he pulled her to her feet. With hungry kisses he lifted her on to the desk, then cupping her breasts in his hands he bent and gently took a nipple in his mouth. Almost swooning with ecstasy, Kitty closed her eyes.[205]

Just a few pages later, however, the novel provides a graphic description of the 'Battle' and, in particular, the role of local women at Cable Street as they attacked the police. In the process, Willsher challenges the submissive image of women which she had provided earlier:

> From behind the barricades, the besieged men were whooping their approval and support. 'Give it to 'em, gels,' they shouted. But the women were in no need of their encouragement. Store cupboards had already been raided and bottles of vinegar, camphor, ammonia ... exploded around the feet of the luckless policemen ... [who] surrender[ed] ... sheepishly aware that they'd been defeated by mere women.[206]

Willsher does not shy away from incorporating scenes of fascist intimidation and violence towards Jews and includes examples of police anti-semitism towards those arrested after the disturbances, utilising the radical testimony of Charlie and Joyce Goodman, whose help in describing the 'Battle' is acknowledged fully. Ultimately, however, the politics of the 'Battle' are neutralised and subsumed in the evolving love story of the narrative. The one fascist in the novel, whose marginality is reinforced by being an outsider to the East End, turns out to have been sexually abused as a child and is only attracted to the BUF because of its uniform. With the outbreak of war he is only too happy to change it for one of the British army. His Communist Party counterpart comes from the London suburbs and returns from the Spanish Civil War disillusioned with the left-wing struggle. But all the major characters in *All Shadows Fly Away* do their 'bit' during the war to fight the evil of Nazism.

In 1986 the Cable Street Anniversary Steering Committee emphasised that 'The battle of Cable Street which took place 50 years ago is still with us – the issues have not gone away.' Apart from the continuing racism in the area it highlighted how

Cable Street itself has seen pitched battles every weekend since January as police block off and barricade the street and the surrounding areas to make sure that Rupert Murdoch's papers get distributed. On May 3rd riot police on horseback galloped through our streets beating up trade unionists and local people peacefully protesting.[207]

From the local Communist Party in the 1940s through to Chris Searle's teaching initiatives during the 1970s and the commemorations thereafter, attempts have been made to place the 'Battle' within a radical chronology of the East End of London. Willsher makes use of one of the major sources in radical narratives of the 'Battle' – Charlie Goodman – but provides a very different 'history' of the East End in which to fit 4 October 1936. Her novel is set within an establishment framework; it starts with street celebrations to mark George V's Silver Jubilee and ends with similar parties to mark VE Day. More specifically to the East End it provides a classic case study of the potential of the 'heritage industry' to sanitise the past and render it safe for a mass audience. Just as there is now a flourishing trade in tours of the 'Ripper' murders in the East End, so the 'Battle' can be brought in to add excitement to descriptions of everyday life in the neighbourhood. In this respect it is no different to the use in *All Shadows Fly Away* of the razor-wielding gangsters, the Mantoni brothers, and the drunken Catholic who drives his wife, unable to support her many children, to suicide. In the acknowledgements, Willsher, alongside her tribute to the Goodmans, states that 'Robert Skidelsky's book *Oswald Mosley* also proved very useful'. *All Shadows Fly Away*, however, hardly exhibits the sympathy to the British fascist apparent in his biographer. Yet the juxtaposition of Skidelsky and the Goodmans is indicative of the apolitical nature of Willsher's narrative. Indeed, it is ironic but significant that it was published as part of Rupert Murdoch's empire which had been so prominently attacked ten years earlier in a very different form of heritage commemoration of the 'Battle'.

The apolitical use of the past is common to much romantic fiction, and it could be argued that, as James Young has done in relation to the Holocaust, 'Better abused memory ... which might then be critically qualified, than no memory at all'.[208] Undoubtedly, Willsher's well-constructed description of 4 October 1936 has made it accessible to many who would otherwise have no idea that it had occurred, as has Baron Moss's account of the 'Battle' written in a rags-to-riches adventure genre.[209] But constructing it in such a way as to hinder its relevance to the present, other than as entertainment, has inherent dangers when the problems faced by minorities continue and when attempts are being made to re-establish the reputation of Oswald Mosley and the BUF. As we have seen, this began with Mosley's autobiography in 1968, followed by Skidelsky's account in 1975, and biographies by Mosley's son in 1979 and 1983. The grassroots fascist members, whose loyalty to Mosley extended beyond 1945, have not surprisingly fostered this revisionist approach and have, as Dave Renton suggests, helped shape the work of later historians.[210] But the most remarkable triumph has been the influence of Nicholas Mosley on the Jewish television writers, Laurence Marks and Maurice Gran, whose four part epic, *Mosley*, was given national prominence in February-March 1998. As with Willsher's account, romance is more important than politics, the aristocratic origins of Mosley and his friends adding extra glamour and interest.[211] But as Nick Cohen argues, in the context of Britain during the 1990s 'Sir Oswald's reputation requires rougher handling' and in academic studies of the man, only D. S. Lewis has attempted to puncture the bubble of Mosley's pomposity and show it to be the result of 'Illusions of Grandeur'.[212] On a more popular level, few have been able to strip away the surface appeal of Mosley to reveal his sordid and malevolent influence on society in the manner of Elvis Costello who, in his debut single, 'Less Than Zero' (1977), described the Mosleyite fascist figure, 'Mr Oswald', as being quickly sucked into the corrupt 'English voodoo' in 'a caustic deconstruction of the establishment media's benign attitude to Oswald Mosley'. More politely, but no less caustically, Alan Bennett, referring to the reputation of the spy, Guy Burgess, suggests that

> You only have to survive in England for all to be forgiven. This was more or less what happened to Oswald Mosley, whose offence seems to me much greater, and would have happened to Burgess, had he lived.[213]

In many of these attempts to bring Mosley back into the fold, his opponents are rejected as radical alien Jews, unfamiliar with British ways. In Gran and Marks' version he is shown disgusted by discovering Nazi anti-semitism in 1936. This moment in their portrayal of the BUF leader was perhaps one of the most dishonest moments in British television history – even after the war Mosley denied that the persecution of the Jews had been deliberately murderous.[214] That this anti-semitic discourse is still in place is a reminder that Jews remain subject to antipathy in Britain alongside minorities more obviously and violently subject to attack. But as the memory of the 'Battle' is utilised increasingly to face contemporary concerns, there is a potential danger that in the process anti-semitism will be seen only as a problem of the past. Of even greater concern, however, are those, such as the neo-fascists who have attacked the mural, who want to obliterate the memory of the 'Battle', and others, through their pro-Mosley narratives, who claim that it depicts 'a "battle" which never took

'Long May Its Memory Live' 169

place'.[215] In this context, the work of those such as Audrey Willsher is essential. Out of ignorance denial can prosper but a neutered past that is only utilised for 'colour' brings forth its own risks of forgetting.

A process of self-reflection is required if the memory of the 'Battle', even if intended for radical purposes, is not to follow the conservative dynamics of the heritage industry. A possible counter-example was provided by the alternative guided tours created by the artist, Tim Brennan, working at 'Cameraworks' in 1994:

> What I did was to design and present a walk around Cable Street, entitled 'Insiders'. That Cable Street walk really did revolve around the street, it didn't necessarily appropriate what would be immediately obvious, the anti-fascist action in 1936, and focus on traditional narratives that might emerge out of Ray Walker's mural. But at the same time I wanted to make work that was very much aware of that. The walk involved replacing texts which could have been used for a touristic heritage mode of working, that might relate to the Jewish experience of the square mile.
>
> In order to do what I wanted to do I needed to replace some, not all, of those kinds of texts; what I came up with, just through looking sideways was a set of bread recipes that might relate to different social groups which have inhabited the locale ... This could form a skeleton around which other information could be brought in, so we might be standing in front of the mural, and I could then say: 'This is seeing it this way and commemorates this; but then aware of the fact that at this time, 1994, British fascists had defaced the mural with a black and white paint bomb, which looked in terms of its marking, very much like a Jackson Pollock splash mark ...
>
> So that would be the kind of discussion or kind of work, or delivery in front of the Cable Street mural, and then half way through, somebody who was at the bus stop said: 'Sorry to interrupt your guided walk, but I remember when the fascists ... I was there, I was at the end of the street, and I remember the day in 1936 when this happened'. I was involved in a way of working that would allow people to be involved, and it would certainly allow the passer-by to butt in.[216]

Writing sixty years after the event, it now seems that the memory of the 'Battle' has been firmly established, ritualised and even, as with Tim Brennan, counter-ritualised, in commemoration. Obituarists increasingly stress the role of their subjects if they took part in the 'Battle' and one of a veteran trade union leader, Ben Rubner, even offered sanctification at one remove, noting that 'his father fought in the 1936 battle of Cable

Street'.[217] The increasing frequency of these obituaries, however, is also an indication that the 'veterans' are fast disappearing. The 'Battle' is now no longer the 'secret history' it had become in 1970 when it was 'rediscovered' by *Yesterday's Witness*; attempts to put it in this category in a *Forbidden Britain* documentary in 1994 hardly rang true.[218]

Returning to Jonathan Boyarin, memory and forgetting cannot be regarded as 'simple opposites'. The remembering of 'the Battle' has often become oblique, its slogans recalled without explicit reference to the day itself in struggles varying from Communist opposition to the re-armament of Germany during the 1950s to protestors in the Christmas 1998 storyline of Britain's longest running soap opera, *Coronation Street*. In the latter, the programme's rather tame 'eco-warrior', with fist in the air, shouts 'They Shall Not Pass', whilst supporting the beleaguered ex-publicans (and very much the programme's comic characters) of the 'Rover's Return', who have barricaded themselves in the pub in protest at the activities of its new landlord.[219] Greater accessibility to the memory of the 'Battle' makes it both more prone to abuse through a lack of concern with what happened on 4 October 1936 *and* of greater interest to those who want to explore the particular dynamics of the day.

In his 1987 account of Mosley, the BUF and the anti-fascists, D. S. Lewis limits his narrative of 4 October 1936 to two sentences:

> On the day itself the CP divided responsibility for different streets amongst its members, as well as establishing first-aid posts, information posts, and runners to carry messages to other sectors of 'the front'. The rest, of course, is history.[220]

Although critical of the Communist Party, Lewis provides a recognisable military narrative of the 'Battle' that relies on the testimony of its members or former members such as Phil Piratin and Joe Jacobs. In contrast, what this overview of the writing and rewriting of the 'Battle' has attempted to show is that the 'history' of 4 October 1936 is far from complete or uncontested. The art that has come out of that day, especially the work of Arnold Wesker and the mural in the street itself (although its physical vulnerability has been all too clear), will make it easier for future generations to identify with the struggle the 'Battle' represented even when there are no 'veterans' left to give their testimony directly. But problems will remain, even with the wealth of accounts that now exist in the public domain. It will be hard for those visiting the East End and the sites of the day to realise that it was once home to well over 100,000 Jews as so little now remains of their physical heritage. This is in spite of the valiant efforts of those such as Bill Fishman (himself there at Gardiner's Corner) who have tried to preserve the secular and religious buildings which formed the focal points of the organised life of East End Jewry. The 'Battle of Cable Street' remains privileged memory in relation to the rest of the life and history of the area's Jewish minority, yet there remains much we do not know about those who took part on 4 October 1936. Issues such as the age, gender, ethnicity and politics of the ordinary participants need further exploration and the limitations of many oral history projects on the 'Battle' have rarely challenged the hegemony of the (largely) male Communist Party members who were prominent in the day's activities. 'The Battle of Cable Street' has now been established as a serious subject for historical research. If, as is possible, 300,000 took part, it would rank as the 'biggest demonstration in British history'.[221] But even if the 'Battle' is increasingly written into historical narratives of the period, it does not mean that this history is now worked through and done with. The memory and history of the 'Battle' will no doubt continue to be contested in the future as in the past. It is to be hoped, however, that 4 October 1936 will be remembered without distortion or sentimentality both for its relevance to the problems of the present and as a remarkable day in its own right – the latter not simply because of its size but because of who was there and why. As the veteran labour leader John Burns commented on 5 October 1936, 'yesterday was one of the greatest and most spontaneous manifestations of popular feeling [he] had ever seen'.[222] In a century when fascism, racism and genocide have rarely faced popular opposition, the 'Battle' is an example of grassroots resistance that should not be forgotten.

AKNOWLEDGEMENT

I would like to thank Nadia Valman and Greg Walker for kindly reading through drafts of this article. Nadia Valman provided more than generous support, stimulation and encouragement throughout its marathon evolution. Although the subject matter is very different, the approach adopted in James E. Young, *Writing and Rewriting the Holocaust: Narrative and the Consequences of Interpretation* (Bloomington and Indianapolis: Indiana University Press, 1988) has been influential in my exploration of the history and memory of Cable Street. Thanks also to Alan Dein for his interest in this project and for providing some obscure source references on the 'Battle' which have been of immense use.

NOTES

1. Ken Leech, 'Cable Street: The Making of a Myth', *Jewish Socialist* 11 (Autumn 1987), p.23.
2. Joe Morgan, *Eastenders Don't Cry* (London: New Author Publications: 1994), cover and p.18. For similar Jewish memory of the 'Battle' as one between fascists and anti-fascists see Benjamin Lammers, 'Jewish Ethnicity and English Identity in London's East End, 1905-1939' (unpublished PhD dissertation, Rutgers University, 1997), p.297.
3. Ibid.

4. Raphael Samuel and Paul Thompson (eds), *The Myths We Live By* (London: Routledge, 1990), 'Introduction', p.2.
5. Lammers (see note 2), p.297.
6. Joe Jacobs in a witness seminar quoted in Peter Grafton, *You, You and You: the People out of Step with World War II* (London: Pluto, 1991), p.3.
7. Samuel and Thompson (see note 4), 'Introduction', p.6.
8. Natasha Burchardt, 'Stepchildren's Memories: Myth, Understanding, and Forgiveness', in Samuel and Thompson, *The Myths We Live By* (see note 4), p.249.
9. This is not to imply agreement with the position adopted by Dave Renton, 'Necessary Myth or Collective Truth? Cable Street Revisited', *Changing English* 5:2 (1998), pp.189-94, esp. p.189 which argues that 'it is inappropriate to describe memory as myth' and crudely juxtaposes myth and truth as opposites.
10. Jonathan Boyarin, *Storm from Paradise: The Politics of Jewish Memory* (Minneapolis: University of Minnesota Press, 1992), pp.1,4.
11. Leech (see note 1), p.23.
12. Kenneth Leech of St. Botolph, Aldgate, speech at 'Sixty Years On ... Cable Street Revisited', 3 October 1996, Davenant Centre.
13. Leech (see note 1), p.23; Bertha Sokoloff, *Edith and Stepney: The Life of Edith Ramsay* (London: Stepney Books, 1987), p.166. On the Stepney Coloured People's Association, see Michael Banton, *The Coloured Quarter: Negro Immigrants in an English City* (London: Jonathan Cape, 1955), pp.230-34. Kathleen Wrsama's help in this project is acknowledged on p.9. Tower Hamlets Local History Library has one of its newsletters dated 1954.
14. Paul Rich, *Race and Empire in British Politics* (Cambridge: Cambridge University Press, 1986), chapters 5 and 6.
15. Elazar Barkan, *The Retreat of Scientific Racism: Changing Concepts of Race in Britain and the United States Between the World Wars* (Cambridge: Cambridge University Press, 1992).
16. St.John B.Grosser (ed.), *Report on an Investigation into Conditions of the Coloured Population in a Stepney Area* (London: Toynbee Hall, 1944). Of the 400 plus, there were only 12 women but 136 children. West Africans represented over 69 per cent, West Indians 17 per cent and the rest Asians. See p.9 of the report. The tone is indicated on p.13 when discussing the relationship to settlements in the East End such as Toynbee Hall and Bernhard Baron:

> Although the coloured population was not barred] and would be welcomed if they did go, they rarely use them. The difficulties which might arise, such as mixed marriages, the prejudices of the parents of adolescent white girls or of some of the club members, make those responsible for these organisations hesitate before making any special efforts to attract coloured people, while the coloured man has a clear feeling that he is not wanted.

17. Banton (see note 13), pp. 92-3, 116. More relaxed in its approach is the anonymous survey, attributed by Banton to Derek Bamuta, 'Coloured People in Stepney, E1', *Social Work* 7:1 (January 1950), pp.387-95.
18. Caroline Adams, *Across Seven Seas and Thirteen Rivers: Life Stories of Pioneer Sylhetti Settlers in Britain* (London: THAP Books, 1987), pp.54-5, 117.
19. Kenneth Leech, *Struggles in Babylon: Racism in the Cities and Churches of Britain* (London: Sheldon Press, 1988), pp.57-9. See also Chaim Bermant, *Point of Arrival: A Study of London's East End* (London: Eyre Methuen, 1975), pp.251-3.
20. Tony Kushner, 'Heritage and Ethnicity: An Introduction', in idem, (ed.), *The Jewish Heritage in British History: Englishness and Jewishness* (London: Frank Cass, 1992), pp.1-28; The Cable Street Group, *The Battle of Cable Street 1936* (London: Cable Street Group, 1995), end of section 6 refers to 'a forthcoming book on the history of Cable Street'.
21. Doreen Massey, 'Places and Their Pasts', *History Workshop Journal* 39 (Spring 1995), p.13 and idem, 'Double Articulation: A Place in the World', in A.Bammer (ed.), *Displacements: Cultural Identities in Question* (Bloomington, IN: Indiana University

Press, 1994), p.120.
22. Robert Skidelsky, *Oswald Mosley* (London: Papermac, 1981 edition), p.393.
23. For statistics on the East End and a more realistic assessment of Jewish life and identity, see H. Llewellyn Smith, *The New Survey of London Life and Labour* (London, 1934), pp.269-70, 291-3; William Zuckerman, *The Jew in Revolt* (London: Martin Secker and Warburg, 1937), p.70; 'Truth about the Blackshirt March', *Comrade: Newsletter of the Friends of O.M*. No 4 (October-November 1986); Jeffrey Hamm, *Action Replay* (London: Howard Baker, 1983), pp.210-1; *Action*, 10, 17 and 24 October 1936 and Tom Linehan's contribution in this volume.
24. *Jewish Chronicle*, 9 October 1936. See also David Cesarani, *The Jewish Chronicle and Anglo-Jewry, 1841-1991* (Cambridge: Cambridge University Press, 1994), pp.151-2.
25. *Jewish Chronicle*, 16 October 1936.
26. See PRO HO 144/21060 for BUF correspondence on the proposed march.
27. Leaflets in MEPO 3/551.
28. *Daily Worker*, 3 October 1936, four page supplement. This can be found in PRO HO 144/21060 and is partly reproduced in Noreen Branson, *History of the Communist Party of Great Britain 1927-1941* (London: Lawrence & Wishart, 1985), p.165.
29. PRO HO 144/21060/297.
30. *Jewish Chronicle*, 2 October 1936.
31. 'All Out Against Fascism', leaflet with alteration to rally at Aldgate in Communist Party archive, National Labour Museum.
32. Cable Street Group (see note 20), section 2; more generally see Hugh Thomas, *The Spanish Civil War* (Harmondworth: Penguin, 1977, 3rd ed.).
33. *Daily Worker*, 1 October 1936.
34. *Daily Worker*, 6 October 1936. See also Frederic Mullally, *Fascism Inside England* (London: Claude Morris Books, 1946), p.74. For Bramley's speech see Special Branch report, 4 October 1936 in PRO HO 144/21061. See his obituary in *The Guardian*, 8 March 1989.
35. Harold Rosen, 'A Necessary Myth: Cable Street Revisited', *Changing English* 5:1 (1998), p.28.
36. Lazarus Sheridan, letter to the author, 5 January 1999 and in David Cohen, 'Jewish Veterans Remember Cable Street', *Jewish Vanguard*, 11 January 1986.
37. Edmund Frow, founder of the Working Class Movement Library, was arrested and beaten up in this 'battle' of October 1931. See his obituary in *The Guardian*, 21 May 1997.
38. *Daily Worker*, 3 October 1936, special supplement.
39. Full details of all the speeches in the evening event recorded by Special Branch in PRO HO 144/21061.
40. Rosen (see note 35), p.28.
41. Independent Labour Party, *They Did Not Pass* (London: ILP, 1936), pp.3, 11. Copy available at the Wiener Library; *The Star*, 3 October 1936. See also Fenner Brockway, *Inside the Left* (London: George Allen & Unwin, 1942), p.271.
42. Brockway, *Inside the Left*, ibid, pp.271-2; idem, *Outside the Right* (London: Allen & Unwin, 1963), *Towards Tomorrow* (London: Hart-Davis, 1977) and *98 Not Out* (London: Quartet, 1986) but see the interview in *The Guardian*, 3 October 1986 which does refer to the 'Battle'.
43. *Public Order Act, 1936* [1 EDW.8 & 1 GEO.6. CH.6.] (London: HMSO, 1936), p.1.
44. Kingsley Griffith in *Hansard* (HC) Vol.317 Col.1406, 16 November 1936.
45. *Hansard* (HC) Vol.317 Col.1377, 16 November 1936.
46. 'The Fascist March', *Manchester Guardian*, 4 October 1936.
47. Peter Catterall (ed.), 'Witness Seminar: The Battle of Cable Street', *Contemporary Record* 8:1 (Summer 1994), pp.105-32; 'The Battle of Cable Street', *Yesterday's Witness*, 4 January 1970, transcript in Tower Hamlets Local History Library, LP 6899 320.5. As will be shown, three policemen were interviewed for this documentary but those taking part were threatened and subsequently refused to let their testimony be used. See the critical comments relating to the absence of police perspectives of William Fishman, 'The Battle of Cable Street (October 4th 1936)', in Frederick Krantz (ed.), *History from Below: Studies*

in Popular Protest and Popular Ideology in Honour of George Rudé (Montreal: Concordia University, 1985), p.391 and the comments in the introduction to this volume.
48. Fishman, 'A People's Journée', p.391. John Stevenson, 'The BUF, the Metropolitan Police and Public Order', in Kenneth Lunn and Richard Thurlow (eds), *British Fascism: Essays on the Radical Right in Inter-War Britain* (London: Croom Helm, 1980), pp.135-49 is largely based on the 'MEPO' files in the Public Record Office.
49. Skidelsky (see note 22), p.420; Stevenson (see note 48), pp.147-8.
50. C. H. Rolph, *Living Twice: An Autobiography* (London: Victor Gollancz, 1974), p.91.
51. A. G. Ralph report, 5 October 1936 in PRO MEPO 3/551.
52. Ibid., Ralph, memorandum, 23 April 1937 in PRO MEPO 2/3110.
53. In PRO MEPO 3/551 and HO 144/21061.
54. In PRO MEPO 3/551.
55. Special Branch report on 'Jew-baiting', 1 November 1936, in PRO MEPO 2/3043.
56. Game, September 1936 in PRO MEPO 2/3043.
57. See Game, memorandum to the Secretary of State, 12 October 1936, on the causes of anti-semitism and the solution to the problem, in PRO HO 144/20159/155. On poverty and ethnicity in the East End see H. Llewellyn Smith, *The New Survey of London Life and Labour* Vol 6, pp.269-70, 291-3. On police anti-semitism recalled in anti-fascist testimony, see 'They Shall Not Pass', produced and presented by Mark Burman, Student Radio, Hackney, 4 October 1986 and much of this testimony reproduced in 'The Red and the Black', Radio 3, produced by Simon Elmes, 4 March 1994.
58. Crossley to Lloyd, 14 October 1936, PRO MEPO 2/3043/14E.
59. Crossley to Lloyd, 5 October 1936 and idem, 'The Fascist March & The Communist Demonstrations – 4.x.36.' in PRO MEPO 2/3043.
60. Lloyd to Crossley, 16 October 1936 in MEPO 2/3043/14F.
61. A.W. minute, 24 October 1936 in PRO MEPO 3/551.
62. Newsam to Game, 5 October 1936, PRO HO 144/20159.
63. Crossley, 'The Fascist March', PRO MEPO 2/3043.
64. Duncan Campbell, 'Damned Foreigners', *The Guardian*, 2 December 1998.
65. Copy of speech in PRO HO 144/20159/171.
66. *Morning Post*, 10 October 1936 quoted by Robert Benewick, *Political Violence and Public Order* (London: Allen Lane, 1969), p.230.
67. *Morning Post*, 21 October 1936 quoted by Fishman, 'A People's Journée', p.11 note 11.
68. *Daily Sketch*, 14 October 1936 quoted by Benewick (see note 67), pp.230-1; *Morning Post*, 13 October 1936 which significantly found its way into Home Office files: see PRO HO 144/21061/310.
69. For the newsreel see PRO HO 144/20159; *Weekly Illustrated Annual 1936* (London: Odhams Press, 1936), p.49. See also *Illustrated London News*, 10 October 1936: 'Why the Fascist March Was Banned'*; Report of the Commissioner of Police of the Metropolis for the Year 1936* (London: HMSO, 1937 Cmd.5457), pp.25-7.
70. *Morning Post*, 13 October 1936.
71. Horace Thorogood, *East of Aldgate* (London: George Allen & Unwin, 1935), pp.92-3 on reporting of the East End, including Sidney Street, and pp.83-5 and 132-4 on the Jews; Benjamin Lammers, '"Alien Dick Whittingtons": The National Imagination and the Jewish East End'*, Jewish Culture and History* 1:1 (1998), p.49.
72. *The Times*, 20 October 1936.
73. *Daily Express*, 15 October 1936.
74. See, for example, 'Life in a Gangster Atmosphere', *News Chronicle*, 6 August 1936; 'Grim Terror By Night in the East End of London', *John Bull*, 24 October 1936.
75. Skidelsky (see note 22), p.397; Bryan Cheyette, 'Hilaire Belloc and the "Marconi Scandal" 1900-1914: A Reassessment of the Interactionist Model of Racial Hatred', in Tony Kushner and Ken Lunn (eds*), The Politics of Marginality* (London: Frank Cass, 1990), pp.132-3 and p.140 note 23; Dudley Barker, 'East End "Terrorism" – the Truth', *Evening Standard*, 2 November 1936.
76. Sydney Morrell, 'Fear-haunted East End', *Sunday Express*, 11 October 1936; editorial, 'Stop the East End Terror!', *Jewish Chronicle*, 16 October 1936.

77. Frankel in *Hansard* (HC) Vol.317 Col.164 (4 November 1936).
78. Sander Gilman, *The Jew's Body* (London: Routledge, 1991), p.63.
79. *Evening Standard*, 13 November 1936.
80. JPC papers in MS 60/15/53, University of Southampton archive.
81. Marx Memorial Library, 'Cable Street: 60th Anniversary Reminiscences', May 13th 1996; Basil Henriques, *The Indiscretions of a Magistrate* (London: The Non-Fiction Book Club, 1950), pp.45-6.
82. The longest treatment in establishment writing of Anglo-Jewish history is that provided by V. D. Lipman, *A History of the Jews in Britain Since 1858* (Leicester and London: Leicester University Press, 1990), pp.185-6 which deals with the 'Battle' in a matter of sentences. The Jewish East End Education Pack, produced by the Museum in the mid-1980s, gives great prominence in its documents to the 'Battle'.
83. Joyce Goodman quoted in Cable Street Group, *The Battle of Cable Street* (see note 20).
84. Frederic Raphael, *The Limits of Love* (London: Cassell, 1960), p.63. See also Hymie Fagan, 'An Autobiography' (unpublished trs, Brunel University Library), p.105 which calls the 'Battle' the 'high point in the activities of the Party'.
85. *Daily Worker*, 30 September 1937 predicted that 'the opposition will probably be even stronger than that which the Fascists met when they tried to march through the East End a year ago'. For Special Branch responses to the march see PRO MEPO 2/3117; Branson (see note 28), p.171.
86. 'The Communist Way to Make London Gay-Healthy-Happy' (LCC Election Brochure, 1937, Communist Party archive, National Labour Museum); Phil Piratin, *Our Flag Stays Red* (London: Lawrence and Wishart, 1980 edition), chapter 4 on the Stepney Tenants' Defence League.
87. On Blumenfeld, see David Cesarani, 'The East London of Simon Blumenfeld's *Jew Boy*', *London Journal* 13:1 (1987-88), pp.46-53; idem, 'Jew Boy', *The Jewish Quarterly* 34:2 (1987), pp.22-3; Ken Worpole, *Dockers and Detectives* (London: Verso, 1983), pp.93-118; Simon Blumenfeld, *They Won't Let You Live* (London: Nicholson and Watson, 1939), pp.157, 172, 250-1.
88. Lazarus Sheridan, *Twelve a Penny* (London: Azal Press, 1997), chapters 1 and 3, p.88 and chapter 8. On pp.112-3 he relates that he attended meetings at the house of Simon Blumenfeld: 'I suppose merely by associating with them I learned something about the craft of writing and had my horizons widened'; Joseph Leftwich, 'Anglo-Jewish Literature', *The Jewish Quarterly* 1:1 (Spring 1953), p.24. On the influence of Rich see *Twelve a Penny*, chapter 11 and Rich diaries, 14 and 25 October 1939, MS 168/35, University of Southampton archives. Gerry Black, *J.F.S. The History of the Jews' Free School* (London: Tymsder Publishing, 1998), pp.98, 139, 148, 181 and 216 provides very brief glimpses of Rich.
89. Lazar Sheridan, telephone interview with Tony Kushner, 4 January 1999; Sheridan, *Twelve a Penny* (see note 88), pp.146-8.
90. Sheridan, *Twelve a Penny*, ibid, p.154.
91. Sheridan, *Twelve a Penny*, ibid, pp.92-3; telephone interview with Tony Kushner, 4 January 1999.
92. Sheridan, *Twelve a Penny*, ibid, p.183.
93. Barnett Sheridan, *King Sol* (London: Chatto & Windus, 1939), pp.177, 193.
94. Sheridan, *Twelve a Penny* (see note 88), p.91.
95. Sheridan, *Twelve a Penny*, ibid, p.93; Sheridan, *King Sol* (see note 93), p.193.
96. Lazarus Sheridan, telephone interview with Tony Kushner, 4 January 1999. Except for the Jews living in the neighbourhood, Cable Street would have been unfamiliar to many Jews living in other parts of the East End. See the stereotypical construction of gentile drunkenness and violence relating to Cable Street in Maurice Levinson, *The Trouble With Yesterday* (London: Peter Davies, 1946), p.50.
97. Sheridan, *King Sol* (see note 93), p.192. For its favourable reviews see idem, *Twelve a Penny* (see note 88), p.183. The start of the war inevitably affected its success but see the favourable reviews in the *Jewish Chronicle*, 17 November 1939 and *Times Literary Supplement*, 14 October 1939.

98. Meeting reported in *East London Advertiser*, 16 October 1942: 'When Fascists Were Stopped: Street Battle of Stepney Commemorated; Call for United Action'.
99. Ibid.
100. Douglas Hyde, the Communist turned anti-Communist who became during the war the *Daily Worker*'s anti-fascist correspondent, not surprisingly provided a cynical explanation of its 'discovery' of the fascist revival groups in Britain. See his *I Believed* (London: Heinemann, 1951), pp.139-40. For its response in the context of other anti-fascist initiatives in the war see Tony Kushner, *The Persistence of Prejudice: Antisemitism in Britain During the Second World War* (Manchester: Manchester University Press, 1989), chapter 6.
101. Lancashire Communist Party, *13 Years of Anti-Fascist Struggle* (Manchester (?): Lancashire District Communist Party, 1943), p.17. Devine clearly impressed on his son the memory of the 'Battle'. See Phil Cohen, *Children of the Revolution: Communist Childhood in Cold War Britain* (London: Lawrence & Wishart, 1997), p.79.
102. *Daily Worker*, 20 November 1943 quoted by Henry Srebrnik, *London Jews and British Communism 1935-1945* (London: Vallentine Mitchell, 1995), pp.60-1.
103. I. Rennap, *Anti-Semitism and the Jewish Question* (London: Lawrence & Wishart, 1942), p.105.
104. Stepney Branch Communist Party, *A Stepney to be Proud of* (London: Stepney Communist Party, 1944).
105. Srebrnik (see note 102), pp.76, 140. See also the election material in the Zaidman papers, University of Sheffield archive.
106. Srebrnik, *London Jews*, ibid, p.146.
107. Ralph Finn, *No Tears in Aldgate* (London: Robert Hale, 1963), p.121; idem, *Spring in Aldgate* (London: Robert Hale, 1968).
108. Ralph Finn, *Return to Earth* (London: Hutchinson, 1945), p.80. Worpole (see note 87) pp.112-3 does not mention this novel which puts a different gloss on Finn's style.
109. Finn (see note 108), pp.9-10.
110. Ibid, p.96.
111. Angus Calder, *The Myth of the Blitz* (London: Jonathan Cape, 1991); Tony Kushner, 'Wrong War Mate', *Patterns of Prejudice* 29:2/3 (April-July 1995), pp.3-13.
112. Levinson (see note 96), pp.106-11. See also his *Women from Bessarabia* (London: Secker and Warburg, 1964), pp.126-9.
113. Mullally (see note 34), pp.74-5, chapter 6.
114. *Jewish Clarion* No.11 (October 1946).
115. Morris Beckman, *The 43 Group* (London: Centerprise Publications, 1992), pp.4-5, 58.
116. Tony Kushner, *The Holocaust and the Liberal Imagination: A Social and Cultural History* (Oxford: Blackwell, 1994), chapter 7; James E. Young, *Writing and Rewriting the Holocaust: Narrative and the Consequences of Interpretation* (Bloomington and Indianapolis: Indiana University Press 1988).
117. For the quotation on the National Jewish Committee from an ex-Communist, see Dave Renton, 'The Attempted Revival of British Fascism: Fascism and Anti-Fascism in the 1940s' (unpublished PhD dissertation, University of Sheffield, 1998), p.120. The absence of reference to the 'Battle' was true of the successor movement to the 43 Group, the 62 Group and also to another organisation to emerge during the 1960s, the Jewish Aid Committee of Britain. See its *With A Strong Hand: A Policy for Jewish Defence submitted to the Jewish Community for discussion by JACOB* (March 1966, no publisher).
118. 'Bernie Taub' quoted by Mark Burman, 'My God, this was Britain *after* the war?', *The Independent*, 16 October 1990.
119. Beckman (see note 115). See also the obituary of Harry Bidney (1922-84), an influential member of the 43 Group and 'a man who had no time for party politics' in *Searchlight* No.111 (September 1984).
120. Phil Piratin, *Our Flag Stays Red* (London: Lawrence & Wishart, 1978 edn), pp.vii-viii.
121. Ibid, pp.20-1.
122. *Daily Worker*, 'This News Made History', undated cutting, 1948?, in Tower Hamlets Local History Library, press cuttings on the Battle of Cable Street.
123. 'Mosley Plans East End March: Cable Street Battles are Recalled', *Daily Worker*, 1

October 1949.
124. Arnold Wesker, *As Much As I Dare: An Autobiography* (London: Century, 1994), pp.464, 497.
125. Ibid, pp.18-9; Piratin (see note 120), p.ix.
126. Arnold Wesker, 'Chicken Soup with Barley' in *The Wesker Trilogy* (London: Jonathan Cape, 1960), pp.16-7. In Sheridan, *King Sol* (see note 93), p.176, although mention is made of the petition asking for the march to be banned, no mention is made of the fact that it was organised by the Jewish People's Council.
127. Wesker, 'Chicken Soup' (see note 126), p.31; American observer quoted in editorial, *Manchester Guardian*, 5 October 1936.
128. Wesker, 'Chicken Soup' (see note 126), Act III, pp.74-5.
129. Wesker, *As Much As I Dare* (see note 124), pp.496-7.
130. Wesker, 'Chicken Soup' (see note 126), Act III, p.61.
131. Wesker, *As Much As I Dare* (see note 124), pp.497, 527.
132. *New Statesman*, 15 July 1958 quoted in Glenda Leeming, *Wesker on File* (London: Methuen, 1985), p.14; *New Statesman*, 9 October 1936.
133. Max Beloff, 'From the Other Side', *Jewish Chronicle Supplement*, 27 January 1956. See more generally, Tony Kushner, 'The End of the "Anglo-Jewish Progress Show": Representations of the Jewish East End, 1887-1987', in idem, *The Jewish Heritage in British History* (see note 20), pp.88-9.
134. Kops quoted in *A Sense of Belonging*, Channel 4 June and July 1991; Raphael (see note 85), pp.19-21, 63. See also Efraim Sicher, *Beyond Marginality: Anglo-Jewish Literature After the Holocaust* (New York: State University of New York Press, 198), pp.127-8; Jack Pearce, 'The Fascist Threat' in *The Circle Golden Jubilee 1909-1959* (London: Workers' Circle Friendly Society, 1959 [?]), pp.20-1.
135. Hank Janson, *Jack Spot: The Man of a Thousand Cuts* (London: Alexander Moring, 1958), pp.36-7, 55.
136. For further references see Skidelsky (see note 22), p.405 and p.538 note 30, who does not seem to be able to understand the genre in which it was written.
137. 'Ghosts of Cable Street', written by P. Simmonds and the Men They Couldn't Hang, MCA Records, *How Green is the Valley*, 1986.
138. Colin Cross, *The Fascists in Britain* (London: Barrie and Rockliff, 1961), p.159 and chapter 11 of his study also entitled 'The Battle of Cable Street'.
139. Bernard Kops, *The World is a Wedding* (London: Vallentine Mitchell, 1973 edn [originally published in 1963]), p.38.
140. *Stephen Peet: Documentary Film-Maker*, no date; James Cameron, *Yesterday's Witness: A Selection from the BBC Series* (London: BBC, 1979).
141. Cameron, *Yesterday's Witness*, ibid, introduction, no page.
142. Benewick (see note 66).
143. Michael Rabiger, video account of the origins of the documentary, probably made during the 1980s, in the possession of Stephen Peet.
144. Ibid; typescript of 'The Battle of Cable Street', Tower Hamlets Local History Library.
145. Oswald Mosley, *My Life* (London: Nelson & Sons, 1968).
146. The film was transmitted on 4 January 1970.
147. Script of 'The Battle of Cable Street' (see note 144), p.6.
148. Script of 'The Battle of Cable Street', ibid, p.11. Even the comic potential of the 'wrong' lorry having been used 'for overturning purposes' seems to have been lost on Piratin. See Piratin (see note 120), p.ix.
149. Neill Myerd, 'Times change but the real enemy stays', *Morning Star*, 2 October 1976.
150. Ibid, p.10.
151. Rabiger video (see note 143); script, 'The Battle of Cable Street' (see note 144), p.11.
152. Rabiger video (see note 143).
153. Rabiger video, ibid.
154. David Rose, 'You felt the working class could become invincible', *The Guardian*, 3 October 1986.
155. See N. Fielding, *The National Front* (London: Routledge, Kegan Paul, 1981); S. Taylor,

The National Front in English Politics (London: Macmillan, 1982) and C. Husbands, *Racial Exclusion and the City: the Urban Support of the National Front* (London: Allen & Unwin, 1983).
156. This was particularly true of the Anti-Nazi League, formed in 1977, which produced leaflets with the slogan 'Fascism begins like this [alongside a photograph of the National Front marching] 'and ends like this' [with a dead person against the barbed wire of a concentration camp]. The Communist Party archive in the National Labour Museum has a range of early Anti-Nazi League propaganda materials.
157. *They Shall Not Pass: A Poetry Anthology to Celebrate the East Enders Victory over Fascism — October 1936* (London: The Tower Hamlets Movement Against Racism and Fascism, 1975); Leech, *Struggles in Babylon* (see note 19), chapter 5.
158. Quoted in *East End News*, November 1983, cuttings in Tower Hamlets Local History Library.
159. Jim Wolveridge, *'Ain't It Grand' (or 'This Was Stepney')* (London: Stepney Books Publications, 1976); Metz testimony in Jewish Women in London Group, *Generations of Memories: Voices of Jewish Women* (London: The Women's Press, 1989), p.228.
160. See, for example, Sylvia Scaffardi, *Fire Under the Carpet* (London: Lawrence & Wishart, 1986), pp.153-9 which moves from personal accounts of the day at the Royal Mint and then Gardiner's Corner and then becomes totally reliant on Piratin's narrative.
161. Chris Searle (ed.), *The World in a Classroom* (London: Writers and Readers Publishing Cooperative, 1977), p.181. For a review of Searle's work see Andy Beckett, 'Return of a class hero', *The Guardian*, 19 November 1997.
162. Searle, ibid. (see note 161), pp.219-24, 281-3; *The People Marching On: A History of East London 1860-1940* [written and re-lived by the 2nd and 3rd year children of Langdon Park School, Poplar, London E14, 1974-5], pp.54-5.
163. Joe Jacobs, *Out of the Ghetto* (London: Janet Simon, 1978), chapters 11 and 12.
164. See, for example, Dave Landau, 'It takes some front', *Jewish Socialist* No.39 (Winter 1998); JCARP, *From Awareness to Action: Countering Racism and Fascism* (London: JCARP, 1986); David Rosenberg, *Facing Up To Antisemitism: How Jews in Britain Countered the Threats of the 1930s* (London: JCARP, 1985).
165. *The Jewish East End: A Celebration* (1987), organised by Helen Carpenter. See the 1987 Blumenfeld play in this volume and John Cunningham, 'Eastside Story', *The Guardian*, 17 July 1987.
166. See, for example, Branson (see note 28), p.171 note 6.
167. *Searchlight*, February 1975, the cover of which had a photograph of neo-nazis with the slogan 'They Shall Not Pass' superimposed.
168. *Searchlight*, May 1975. See also the profile on Gerry Gable *in Jewish Chronicle*, 23 October 1987.
169. *Searchlight* No.1 (Spring 1965).
170. *Searchlight* No.17 (October 1976).
171. Kate Wesprin, 'Cable Street Beat: A Brief History', *Fighting Talk* No.20 (August 1998).
172. *Fighting Talk* No.1 (September 1991), 'The Battle of Cable Street: Learning the Lessons'.
173. Raphael Samuel, *Theatres of Memory* (London: Verso, 1994).
174. For the available items see *Fighting Talk*. For brief comment on the artifacts available see Roger Mills, 'The Art of Cable Street', *Rising East* 1:1 (1997), pp.172-3.
175. Mills, 'The Art of Cable Street', ibid, pp.166-7.
176. Helen Speir, letter to *Jewish Chronicle*, 17 October 1986.
177. Raymond Kalman, letter to *Jewish Chronicle*, 10 October 1986.
178. Ruah Carlyle, 'Cable Street and the defeat of British fascism', *Workers' Liberty* (October 1996), pp.26-36. See also Colin Sparks, 'Fighting the beast Fascism: the lessons of Cable Street', *International Socialism* (1997), pp.11-4; idem, *Never Again! The Hows and Whys of Stopping Fascism* (London: Bookmarks, 1980), chapter 7 and David Renton's contribution to this volume.
179. The Cable Street Group, *The Battle of Cable Street* (see note 20), section 8; Charles Poulsen, *Scenes from a Stepney Youth* (London: THAP Books, 1988).
180. The Cable Street Group, *The Battle of Cable Street* (see note 20), section 8.

'Long May Its Memory Live' 179

181. Chris Heredge, 'They shall not pass', *The Express*, 14 October 1978.
182. *Hackney Gazette*, 2 October 1979.
183. The Cable Street Group, *The Battle of Cable Street* (see note 20), section 8.
184. Ibid.
185. Desmond Rochfort, 'Ray Walker', in *Ray Walker* (London: Ray Walker Memorial Committee, 1985), p.26.
186. On Berkovitz and the mural, see his obituary in *Jewish Chronicle*, 25 December 1998.
187. I am particularly grateful to Nadia Valman for her thoughts on the mural and its artistic approach; Mills, 'The Art of Cable Street' (see note 174), p.167.
188. Charlie Goodman, oral testimony, London Museum of Jewish Life, 61-1987.
189. In HO 144/21061.
190. *Ray Walker* (see note 185), plate 61 for a full photograph of the mural.
191. Flyer in Tower Hamlets Local History Library Cable Street folder; *Jewish Chronicle*, 17 October 1986, letter from Jeanne Freeman; *Jewish Chronicle*, 6 October 1995.
192. 'Cable Street: The 50th Anniversary October 1936-1986: An Exhibition': exhibition notes, Tower Hamlets Local History Library; 'Cable Street Celebrated', *Searchlight*, November 1986.
193. Anita Dobson, *My East End* (London: Pavilion Books, 1987), p.57.
194. *Searchlight*, November 1986.
195. See *Public Service*, November 1986.
196. *The Independent*, 7 October 1996; *Jewish Chronicle*, 11 October 1996. Mike Hicks of the Communist Party of Britain made the comment on the Asylum Act. See *Morning Star*, 7 October 1996.
197. Copy of poster in Tower Hamlets Local History Library.
198. 'No Pasaran! Stop Fascist Attacks in Turkey', leaflet in possession of author; *The Greater London Pensioner* No.78 (October 1996).
199. There were at least four events devoted to the exploration of the memory and the message of the 'Battle': 'Sixty Years of Fighting Fascism — An East End Tradition', 17 October 1996, organised by Tower Hamlets Militant Labour; 'The Lessons of Cable Street', 16 October 1996, organised by the Jewish Socialist Group; 'Sixty Years On – Cable Street Revisited', 3 October 1996, organised by the Cable Street Group; and 'The Memory of Cable Street', 13 October 1996, organised by the Wiener Library and the basis of the current volume. See also Roger Mills (see note 174); Catterall (see note 47), pp.105-32; Rosen, 'A Necessary Myth' (see note 35), pp.27-34, and Renton (see note 9), pp.189-94..
200. Mills (see note 174), pp.173-4.
201. Tower Hamlets Militant Labour, 'Remember Cable Street', leaflet in possession of the author.
202. Arnold Wesker and John Allin, *Say Goodbye: You May Never See Them Again* (London: Jonathan Cape, 1974).
203. See Paul Gilroy, *There Ain't No Black in the Union Jack: The Cultural Politics of Race and Nation* (London: Hutchinson, 1987).
204. These include David Holman, 'No Pasaran!' (1977); Bernard Kops, 'Simon at Midnight' (1985); Dramatic Events Company, 'You should have been there' (1986); Simon Blumenfeld, 'The Battle of Cable Street' (1987); David Holman's 'No Pasaran!' (1990), Steven Berkoff, *East* (1977) and Alan Gilbey, 'Shattersongs' (late 1980s); Alan Gibbons, *Street of Tall People* (London: Orion Children's Books, 1995). On Gilbey and Searle see *The Guardian*, 19 November 1997 and 'The Fire is in Our Hearts', BBC Radio 4, 20 November 1997.
205. Audrey Willsher, *All Shadows Fly Away* (London: Library Magna Books, 1998 edn), p.326. Other titles by Willsher include *Inherit the Earth, So Shall We Reap, Fruitful Vine, Candle in the Wind* and *Savage Tide*.
206. Willsher (see note 205), pp.359-60.
207. '1936-1986: They Shall Not Pass', leaflet in Tower Hamlets Local History Library.
208. Young (see note 116), p.133.
209. Baron Moss, *Chains* (London: Bachman & Turner, 1978), which owes much to Jeffrey Archer.

210. Renton (see note 117), pp.13-14.
211. The first episode of 'Mosley' was screened on Channel 4, 12 February 1998.
212. Nick Cohen, 'Sympathy for Sir Oswald? Old Nazis, New Dangers', *The Jewish Quarterly* (Autumn 1996), p.28; D. S. Lewis, *Illusions of Grandeur: Mosley, Fascism and British Society, 1931-81* (Manchester: Manchester University Press, 1987).
213. 'Less Than Zero' also appeared on his album *My Aim Is True* (Stiff Records). For analysis see David Gouldstone, *Elvis Costello: God's Comic* (New York: St Martin's Press, 1989), p.19 and Sean O'Hagan 'Kings of America', *The Guardian Weekend*, 19 September 1998. Alan Bennett, *Writing Home* (London: Faber and Faber, 1997), p.336.
214. Nicholas Mosley, *Beyond the Pale: Sir Oswald Mosley 1933-1980* (London: Secker & Warburg, 1983), chapter 12: 'The Battle of Cable Street'.
215. Hamm (see note 23), p.212.
216. Brennan's account of his work is available on http://www.uel.ac.uk/faculties/socsci/culture/cner/inter.htm and also reproduced in *Rising East* 2:1 (1998) and the CNER newsletter, *New Ethnicities* 3 (1998).
217. See those of Ted Bramley, *The Guardian*, 8 March 1989; Phil Piratin, *Jewish Chronicle*, 22 December 1995; Jack Perry, *The Guardian*, 2 January 1997; Jack Wolkind, *The Guardian*, 24 March 1997; Sam Aaronovitch, *The Guardian*, 4 June 1998; Ben Rubner, *The Guardian*, 29 September 1998 and Sam Berkovitz, *Jewish Chronicle*, 25 December 1998.
218. See The Cable Street Group, *The Battle of Cable Street* (see note 21), section 8.2 for the BBC 2 documentary in 1994.
219. Harry Pollitt, *The Nazis Shall Not Pass!* (London: Communist Party of Great Britain, 1952) which, without explicit reference to the 'Battle', constantly warns that 'the Nazis will be marching again'. *Coronation Street*, ITV, 24 December 1998.
220. Lewis (see note 212), p.125.
221. Huw Richards, 'Thanks for the Cable Street memories', *Times Higher Education Supplement*, 31 May 1991.
222. Burns quoted in *Manchester Guardian*, 5 October 1936.

DOCUMENTS

Jewish Girls and the Battle of Cable Street

NADIA VALMAN

Remembering Cable Street as a demonstration of class or multi-cultural solidarity in the East End locality has often tended to obscure questions of gender and generation in the confrontations between fascists and anti-fascists. In contemporary representations, the conflict on the streets was frequently masculinised. Violence at fascist demonstrations was ascribed to 'gangs of youths' and 'Blackshirt ruffians', while fascist speakers claimed they were under attack from 'the brickbats and razors of the Ghetto boys'.[1] A reporter sympathetic to the anti-fascist cause described a Communist meeting in Stoke Newington characterised by 'Youthful speakers – the whole atmosphere was alive with militant, enthusiastic and virile youth.'[2] The imaginative potency of the 'Battle of Cable Street', in contrast, was derived from the remarkable diversity of its crowd, which cut across divisions of age and gender as well as ethnicity. Nevertheless, as Ben Lammers has recently argued, it was a specifically youthful vision that was being endorsed in the demonstration. The diversity of the crowd was a signal of widespread local support for what he describes as a generational 'redefinition of both Jewish and English identity', a notion of Jewishness which 'meant that one could aggressively stand up for one's rights' and a notion of Englishness which 'allowed for ethnic difference'.[3] In this view, the debate within the Anglo-Jewish community about how to respond to the threat of fascism in the East End was prompted not only by the differences of class, politics and location which fractured Anglo-Jewry, but also by differences of generation.

This document – a circular letter and pamphlet sent in the aftermath of the Battle of Cable Street to mothers of girls who had been attending the Oxford and St George's Girls' Club in Berner Street in the East End, by the club's founder, the West End-born and politically conservative Rose

Henriques – presents further evidence that Jewish responses to fascism were mediated by questions of generation and gender as well as class. The distance between working-class East End and elite West End Jewry, which is reflected in the paternalistic structure and rhetoric of the club system, certainly played a key role in shaping Jewish responses to fascism in the months leading up to the 'Battle', but the differences in perspective which it generated persisted long after 4 October. Indeed, such class divisions are reflected in the remembering of the role of women in the Battle of Cable Street, which continues to be contested. In an interview in 1986, Lady Janner, wife of Barnett Janner, Liberal MP for Whitechapel and St George's in the 1930s, claimed that although her husband defied the Board of Deputies ban on Jews attending the demonstration, she herself was not at Cable Street because 'in those days women did not go into demonstrating crowds'.[4]

If women of Lady Janner's class did not go into demonstrating crowds, others certainly did. In the East End, women had not been inviolate from street attacks by fascists nor were they to be exempt from police brutality at the Battle of Cable Street.[5] But women also played a dynamic and important role in anti-fascist activity, from heckling and selling anti-fascist literature at Blackshirt speaker meetings, to whitewashing walls with anti-fascist slogans and street fighting.[6] Women were not only behind the barricades at the Battle of Cable Street but above them. When the police attacked the barricades, women standing at the windows of the tenements threw missiles on them, and when they fled into nearby sheds, the women came down from the buildings and hounded them out.[7] Yet despite – or perhaps because of – the active role that East End women took in responding to the immediate threat of fascism, advice from their West End co-religionists was framed in terms of the Anglo-Jewish philanthropic tradition. At one level Rose Henriques was, in this document, producing a female version of the Anglo-Jewish elite's message to Jewish youth to 'keep off the streets'.[8] But she was also drawing on a older tradition, which viewed Jewish young women and girls as a particular danger to the respectability of the communal public image.

The Oxford and St George's Girls' Club was one of a number of clubs for Jewish working-class girls that were created between the 1890s and the early 1900s by upper middle-class London Jewish women such as Lily Montagu, Emily Marion Harris, and Lady Katie Magnus; among them the West Central Jewish Girls' Club, the Butler Street Girls' Club and the Stepney Girls' Club.[9] The establishment by *fin-de-siècle* social reformers of numerous clubs and uniformed youth movements for working-class young people of both sexes reflected the emergence at this time of 'adolescence' as a distinct social problem requiring urgent solution.[10] In the Victorian liberal tradition of minimalist government, responsibility for social discipline, through institutions such as youth clubs, fell to private or denominational rather than government administration.[11] Jews in particular appear to have considered that 'specialized ethnic needs were not a public responsibility, that immigrants were indeed outsiders requiring socialization and were not legitimate objects of non-sectarian philanthropy'.[12] Jewish clubs were frequently modelled on their Christian counterparts, and similarly sought to inculcate discipline, physical fitness and patriotism, assumed to be dangerously lacking in the youth of poor districts. The Jewish Working Lads' Brigade (later the Jewish Lads' and Girls' Brigade), for example, emulated the Church Lads' Brigade and aimed for 'self-discipline, leadership, punctuality, obedience and hygiene, morality, thrift, social responsibility, self-help and numerous other such desirable aims. All of which would, it was assumed, protect the young from crime and vice and, perhaps more significantly, protect society from delinquency, class conflict and the spread of "dangerous" socialist doctrines.'[13] Through youth clubs the Jewish community 'reminded adolescents not merely of universally shared values and culture, but who belonged where doing what'.[14]

Social work amongst Jewish youth, however, was motivated by the additional concerns of the Anglo-Jewish elite at the rise of anti-alien agitation in the 1890s. The English-born children of Eastern European Jewish immigrants were seen as a key focus for efforts at anglicisation, and institutions such as Jewish schools, religious education classes and youth clubs were developed with a view to encouraging adaptation to English ways of life.[15] Basil Henriques established the Oxford and St George's Club for boys to make worthy citizens of the sons of immigrants 'through the very same methods as were used to achieve that end in the public schools – tradition, the team spirit, athletics and sports on the one hand, educational activities on the other'.[16] Such endeavours were aided, from 1902, by the Education Act, which provided state funding for instruction including English classes and other practical arts.[17] But clubs were essentially dependant on communal financial support, and, as Sharman Kadish has written, the Anglo-Jewish elite 'saw nothing incongruous in seeking to "graft" English public school ideals onto a population which came from an entirely different tradition, with a vibrant cultural life of its own, and which lived under economic and social conditions which were not at all comparable'.[18]

The anglicising origins of the Jewish youth clubs were revived in the 1930s. Vocal public opposition to Blackshirts by the East London Youth Front against Fascism and War was described by Jewish youth workers as 'undermining everything that Englishmen hold as most precious'.[19] The organised Jewish youth movement, on the other hand, believed itself to be clearly aligned with 'English' values, the upholding of which was considered a more appropriate response to provocation in East London. Following the leadership of the Board of Deputies, many of the youth clubs continued to emphasise the importance of good citizenship, physical health and discipline, and thus produced a response to British fascism which resembled their apologetic approach to the anti-alienism of the 1890s. Indeed, Harold Lion, Officer Commanding the London Regiment of the Jewish Lads' Brigade declared in the aftermath of Cable Street that 'ninety per cent of our fellow Jews are as good a type as anyone else. It is that minimum which belongs to no organisation at all who cause trouble. If we can get every member of the Jewish community into the brigade or a club or some similar organization, I am sure that through the training we give them we shall have no anti-Sematism [sic] whatsoever.'[20] Medical facilities at the Oxford and St George's Girls' Club were seen to have 'far reaching effects on the health of the community', while lessons encouraged 'team-work and a high conception of citzenship'.[21] In the same vein, a correspondent to the *Jewish Chronicle* in September 1936 argued that social interaction between Christian and Jewish boys' clubs was one of the most effective means of convincing gentiles 'that we possess the same interest in public affairs; and that we aspire to a complete fulfilment of our duties as citizens'.[22]

The leaders of the club movement were also motivated by the notion of active citizenship. Eugene Black has suggested that the club movement represents one example of the shifting forms and terms of communal authority within Anglo-Jewry: 'Youth clubs were ... one of the more important ways in which the active philanthropic families merged their interests with many among the younger Jewish elite. Fresh from the inspiration of their Jewish mentors at Harrow and Cheltenham, reminded at Oxford or even at Cambridge that young educated gentlemen must take seriously the needs of their world and society, they moved into politics and social activism.'[23] The Oxford and St George's Club was founded in such a spirit. Its mentor, Basil Henriques, became interested in Church social work in East London while at Oxford University. In 1912 he wrote that he wanted to set up what he called a 'Jewish mission on the lines of the Oxford and Bermondsey Mission ... You can organise for the poor pleasant little social evenings ... and keep them thus from temptations and evils.' He was inspired by attending a meeting of the Jewish Association for the Protection of Girls and Women, seeing the potential for 'West End ladies of character and sympathy' to give 'help and advice' to Jewish prostitutes. Henriques' own organisation, the Oxford and St George's Club, sponsored by the Liberal and Reform synagogues in London, was founded in 1914 with the explicit objective of anglicising 'foreign' Jews.[24] At the club, Henriques, a follower of Claude Montefiore's Liberal Judaism, instituted at the end of every evening a brief talk and prayer, often including Christian texts. His own patriotism extended to a militant anti-Zionism.[25] By 1930 the club moved to purpose-built premises provided by Bernhard Baron in Berner Street, where it ran a play centre for children, clubs for different adolescent age-groups, old boys' and old girls' clubs, social and advisory services and a club magazine, *Fratres*.[26] By the 1960s the club was non-denominational and continued to serve the multi-ethnic population of Stepney, where only a small percentage were Jewish. The Club's later history, then, suggests that it can be seen primarily as a local, rather than a specifically Jewish institution.

The Girls' Club at Oxford and St George's, established in 1915 by Henriques' wife-to-be Rose Loewe, must be considered both in terms of the club movement generally and in terms of the gendered history of Jewish youth social work. Historians of youth movements in Britain have tended to marginalise girls' clubs, yet the objectives of the youth club movement were clearly gendered, particularly in the Jewish context.[27] Both boys' and girls' clubs laid a strong emphasis on physical fitness (all clubs ran an annual outdoor summer camp, and often offered drill, gymnastics and exercise every night), and provided religious instruction, a thrift club and job placement services. But girls' clubs also included classes in letter-writing, literature, and singing as well as domestic skills like dressmaking, cookery, embroidery, and basket-making, and were seen to provide for young women in particular 'innocent and wholesome recreation in a district with dangerous attractions and grave temptations'.[28] Indeed, it was for these reasons that the youth club movement began in the Victorian period with provision for Jewish girls rather than boys. Such concerns had particular resonance among British Jews, who saw the susceptibility of immigrant and working girls to prostitution as one of the gravest dangers facing the community, not least for its effect on their own public image. In 1886 the Jewish Association for the Protection of Girls and Women (JAPGW) was established to rescue and reform Jewish prostitutes, 'to cheer and befriend the helpless, the homeless, the struggling and the troubled', but also 'to uphold the honour of the Jewish name, to prove that Jews are no less zealous for purity, no less keenly anxious to "prevent", to shelter and to redeem, than members of any other religious denomination'.[29] By 1915 the cause was seen as still urgent. The Oxford and St George's club reported that 'there are girls who find relaxation and enjoyment in the streets, girls untaught at a mother's knee, innocent of the difficulties of life, ready to have a little sport ... that maybe leads to serious results'.[30] In such a climate the Girls' Club at Oxford and

St George's was established in 1915, and its facilities were seen to be an extension of the work undertaken by the JAPGW.

By the early twentieth century Jewish organisations were serving education and settlement houses and providing clubs for girls and working women. Indeed, Beatrice Webb suggested that she and other social activists had much to learn from Jewish women's organisations.[31] But such proto-feminist successes essentially relied on the social control of other women within the Jewish community. Jewish philanthropy in the East End was highly bureaucratic and coercive to the point of denying charitable relief to those homes which did not obey social workers' prescriptions about domestic hygiene.[32] The increasing participation in the first decades of the twentieth century of middle and upper middle-class Jewish women in welfare agencies such as the Jewish Board of Guardians, as policy-makers as well as workers, certainly signalled their expanding aspirations for communal power. At the same time, however, as Eugene Black has argued,

> Anglo-Jewry organized to impose control upon women, particularly single women. A rhetoric of 'protection' could be invoked wherever family constraints were lacking or seemed insufficient. Thus could the Jewish image of high standards of sexual behaviour and strong family ties be sustained within the community and for the wider public. For those innocent of or impervious to the blandishments of genteel moral persuasion, a vigilance society, with the blessing of the Chief Rabbi and the Bishop of London, helped to enforce community intolerance for moral deviance.[33]

Recent assessments of female philanthropy in Britain in the nineteenth and early twentieth centuries have, like Black, emphasised its conservative character. Victorian women philanthropists, according to F. K. Prochaska, 'held a hierarchical view of society and assumed that distinctions between rich and poor were God-given and likely to persist ... they sought to alleviate the worst abuses of society without undermining their authority'.[34] For Linda Gordon Kuzmack, the rhetoric of 'woman's mission' meant that, 'like their Christian peers, female Anglo-Jewish social workers had a public image as mothers to "their girls"'.[35] Susan Tananbaum also notes a combination of 'the human touch' and 'middle-class assumptions about class, respectability, and notions of the deserving poor' in the rhetoric of Jewish women social workers at the turn of the century, and that 'while middle-class women expanded their voluntary options, they promoted a fairly restrictive domesticity for working-class girls'.[36] Jane Lewis's more nuanced account, however, links philanthropists' implicit refusal to address the structural causes of poverty with gendered notions of middle-class citizenship in the Victorian and Edwardian periods: many women social workers, she argues, were 'strategically located within what was arguably the mainstream of social theory and social action. This linked the solution of social problems firmly to the family and to social work performed voluntarily by middle-class women who thereby fulfilled their citizenship obligations.'[37] Nevertheless, for Lewis 'there remains the issue as to whether [social work] practitioners were effectively little more than the handmaidens of classical political economy, undertaking to discipline the poor'.[38]

In the case of Anglo-Jewish philanthropy the picture is even more complex. Institutions like the Oxford and St George's Club were clearly conceived, like their Christian counterparts, as agencies of social discipline. But in such institutions social discipline operated in an ethnically specific form. The minority status of Anglo-Jewry as a perceived community meant that the politics of Jewish philanthropy did not simply mirror the objectives and assumptions of gentile social work. Anglicisation, as Sharman Kadish has argued, 'was seen as the key to helping young Jews "get on" in society – and *not* to "keeping them down"'.[39] 'Jewish philanthropic endeavours', Susan Tananbaum concludes, 'emerged because of exclusion and were the site of conflict and ambivalence, both among different groups of Jews and between Jews and Gentiles.'[40] A similar argument can be made about the 'social control' of Jewish women. While English gentiles' battle to protect women and girls from prostitution in the early twentieth century 'furnished a basis for political self-assertion by an aspiring, ambitious middle-class group and a launching pad for a new phase in feminist militancy,' the same brand of activism served a different function in the Anglo-Jewish context, as 'the impeccably high bourgeois Jewish elite had no such political needs; its authority was already established. What the campaign offered Anglo-Jewry was an opportunity to display British Jews as staunchly moral, prepared to discharge unpleasant civic duties, standing as peers with the leaders of other religious denominations.'[41]

Concern about what kind of image of Anglo-Jewry was on display – a concern articulated through the protection and surveillance of Jewish women – underpins the code of behaviour promulgated by Rose Henriques in the document under discussion here. The code attempts to refute common fascist accusations against Jews such as dishonesty in business practice, lack of patriotism, disregard for law and order, and association with the Communist Party, yet the bulk of the text in fact constructs Jewish behaviour in terms which were not explicitly part of fascist charges. Despite Rose Henriques' reference to 'accusations of unseemly conduct, ostentation, and vulgarity levelled against Jewish girls and women', such gendered stereotypes were more apparent in literary discourse than in Blackshirt polemic on the East End streets. The Anglo-Jewish leadership nevertheless frequently insisted that such 'failings' needed to be addressed if the fascists were to be resisted.[42] At a public meeting of the Board of Deputies of British Jews in September 1936 in Shoreditch Town Hall, for example, the Board's president, Neville Laski, referred to the 'great deal of ostentation which is unnecessarily displayed in the Community ... They had got to cease to be obtrusive and flamboyant.'[43] A week later a columnist in the *Jewish Chronicle* reiterated the warning that 'when a Jewess makes herself an object of contempt by silly swagger or over-dressing, and a Jew offends by loud conversation and noisiness ... one such thoughtless act, one wrong inflicted on a non-Jew, makes many enemies'.[44] In such expressions, Jews themselves were recognising that 'flamboyance' was a code word for 'foreign'. Moreover, in Rose Henriques' advice to Jewish women and girls, the apologetic concern with reducing Jewish visibility in the public sphere converges with a particular preoccupation with the display of Jewish female sexuality, suggesting that older associations between Jews and prostitution also shaped the barely articulated anxieties of the Club's leadership. In projecting a vision of the body of the Jewish girl which was unadorned, physically fit and chaste, Henriques implicitly reproduces an anti-alienist stereotype of the Jewish woman as oversexualised and physically degenerate.[45]

The internalisation by Anglo-Jewry's leadership of such stereotypes, and the political passivity which it engendered, was precisely one of the reasons why, as Henriques' letter indicates, many young women were abandoning established clubs like the Oxford and St George's in the autumn of 1936. After the confrontation at Cable Street, when thousands of Jews defied the ban on street demonstration imposed by the Board of Deputies and reiterated by communal organisations like the Club, the authority of such institutions – particularly when they continued to insist on the importance of 'working with the authorities' – was severely damaged. The social distance between club leaders and members is all too evident in this document. Although an article in the *Jewish Chronicle* in 1938 insisted that the girls' club movement 'has, in the main, affected women coming originally from two extreme classes of the community and has done an enormous amount to fuse them and to bring about a sisterhood of women imbued with a common ideal of progress and welfare', this document suggests that the club system remained hierarchical and didactic rather than democratic.[46] As Tony Kushner has written, apart from exclusion from synagogue power, 'there was very little else that united the women of Whitechapel with those of Maida Vale'.[47] Rose Henriques' letter, then, reflects the different histories of Anglo-Jewish women of different classes during the 1930s, a period when such differences were particularly intense. Against the background of a widespread return to notions of female domesticity, working-class girls and women were increasingly forced to return to work, while upper and middle-class Jewish women, experiencing increased exclusion from economic and political roles in Anglo-Jewry, began to exert power instead within the voluntary sphere.[48] The Club ethos both reflected and enacted these social changes.

The paternalistic tone of the letter, which confidently offers both reassurance and guidance to its reader, also reflects Rose Henriques' own notoriously dictatorial style of leadership.[49] But its very existence is, at the same time, evidence of the considerable anxiety felt by Anglo-Jewish communal leaders at the signs of their declining credibility in the East End. Expressing a view held widely among Jews in the East End locality, in the labour movement, and in the lower-middle class generally, a correspondent to the *Jewish Chronicle* in August 1936 complained that 'the present Board of Deputies, to my mind, no longer represents the Anglo-Jewish Community, and consequently is out of touch with the rank and file'.[50]

Nevertheless, institutions like the Club, although established in the Edwardian era, persisted even beyond the Second World War, despite the erosion of their substance and the many challenges to their authority.[51] The complicated relationship between generations, social groups and institutions is epitomised in the unevenness of the 'social control' exerted over Jewish youth in the mid 1930s. Young people, in fact, continued to attend establishment clubs while at the same time involving themselves in more radical activities with socialist and Communist organisations. According to Motel Robins, a member of the Jewish Lad's Brigade, 'most youth club members took part in the struggle against Fascism', particularly JLB brass band members who played at street demonstrations.[52] A member of the Oxford and St George's Boys' Club and the Communist Party recalls that 'It was in the days of the Spanish Civil War, and we were very active. We had a little group in the Club, we used to try and raise money for Spain, you know, the International Brigade, and, we used to collect clothing and sell it and all sorts of things going on like that. Food for Spain we used to do. All from the Club. Henriques never knew about it, he'd go mad if he knew about it.'[53] It was certainly true that Basil Henriques took the same conservative line as Rose publicly. In a letter to the *Times* in the week following the Battle of Cable Street, he explained Jewish affiliation with the Communist Party as a desperate measure rather than an ideological sympathy: 'The Jew feels he must do something in self-defence. The only party which is militantly attacking Fascism is the Communist. Thus, contrary to the political views of the vast majority of them, they are being so terrorized as to be forced into the ranks of Communism.'[54] Yet Henriques' private writings suggest a more ambivalent attitude: only a few weeks earlier he had written in his diary that 'the whole of the East End is in a great state of tension on account of a Mosley march. I longed to be out in it, but had instructed the club and synagogue members not to go, so I had to stop in.'[55] Such comments suggest the complex impact of the threat of fascism on existing Anglo-Jewish class and public relations.

As early as 1898 Helen Lucas, a social worker and patron of the welfare organisation the Jewish Board of Guardians, had argued that clubs for girls constituted an urban danger and exacerbated the generation gap in immigrant Anglo-Jewry. Clubs, she argued, served 'to destroy home and family life, and influence, which used to be such a splendid feature among our children ... These clubs teach the girls to seek their pleasures away from their homes and engender the habit of going out at night where dangers await them in every street'.[56] Although her comments were much criticised, Lucas had rightly identified the club system, at an early stage of its development, as a powerful agent of anglicisation that could only intensify the fractures within Anglo-Jewry which were to take on more concrete forms in the twentieth century. In this sense, Lucas saw girls' clubs as a radical, even proto-feminist development, which threatened domestic stability and communal moral values. By the 1930s, a similar opposition was being suggested by Rose Henriques, although now club life was constructed as the respectable alternative to 'rowdy' and unfeminine organised politics. Yet, as Ben Lammers and Elaine Smith have persuasively argued, political activity was becoming for East End Jews in the 1930s 'more than a means of expressing outrage at the activities of the BUF – it was also a means of integration with the national community'.[57] In one sense, political activity served the same need as attending a Jewish youth club had for the previous generation. The possibility that club life and street fighting were *both* ways of identifying with English values was clearly not one that Rose and Basil Henriques wished to entertain. Even so, the Oxford and St George's Club leader himself expressed his feelings of violence in these very terms when he wrote to *The Times* condemning the 'un-English and unsportsmanlike attacks of the Fascist party', and declaring that 'no self-respecting Englishman of the Jewish religion can listen to the [Fascist] speeches without bursting with indignation'.[58]

ACKNOWLEDGEMENTS

I would like to thank Tony Kushner, Susan England and Jo Reilly for helpful advice and comments during the preparation of this article.

NOTES

1. *Jewish Chronicle* 16 October 1936; 4 September 1936; 21 August 1936.
2. *Jewish Chronicle* 28 August 1936.
3. Benjamin Lammers, "A Superior Kind of English": Jewish Ethnicity and English Identity in London's East End, 1905-1939' (unpublished PhD dissertation, Rutgers University, 1997), p.323.
4. Lesley Friedman, 'Cable Street: the day that Mosley's fascists were not allowed to pass', *Jewish Chronicle* 3 October 1986. See also responses by women who did participate in the demonstration, *Jewish Chronicle* 17 October, 1986.
5. *Jewish Chronicle* 17 July 1936; 9 October 1936.
6. *Jewish Chronicle* 7 August 1936; 14 August 1936; Lammers (see note 3), p.311.
7. C.G., interview transcript, cited by Lammers, ibid, p.321.
8. For the Association for Jewish Youth's apprehension at young men speaking at street meetings and attending demonstrations against fascism, see Sidney Bunt, *Jewish Youth Work in Britain. Past, Present and Future* (London: Bedford Square Press, 1975), pp.21-3.
9. Linda Gordon Kuzmack, *Woman's Cause: The Jewish Woman's Movement in England and the United States, 1881-1933* (Columbus: Ohio State University Press, 1990), pp.84-8.
10. Sharman Kadish, *'A Good Jew and a Good Englishman': The Jewish Lads' and Girls' Brigade 1895-1995* (London: Vallentine Mitchell, 1995), p.40.
11. Eugene Black, *The Social Politics of Anglo-Jewry 1880-1920* (Oxford: Basil Blackwell, 1988), pp.236-7.
12. Susan L. Tananbaum, 'Philanthropy and Identity: Gender and Ethnicity in London', *Journal of Social History* 30 (1996-7), p.950.
13. Kadish (see note 10), p.38.
14. Black (see note 11), p.141.
15. For a detailed discussion of these aspects of Anglo-Jewish social history, see Black, ibid, pp.71-193.
16. Tananbaum (see note 12), p.945.
17. Black (see note 11), p.136.
18. Kadish (see note 10), p.44.
19. Association for Jewish Youth, cited by Bunt (see note 8), p.21. There were also efforts in the 1930s to 're-Judaise' youth clubs in order to promote religious values in the face of apparently growing secularisation among young Jews. See Elaine R. Smith, 'Jews and Politics in the East End of London, 1918-1939', in David Cesarani (ed.), *The Making of Modern Anglo-Jewry* (Oxford: Basil Blackwell, 1990), p.144.
20. Kadish (see note 10), p.124.
21. *Jewish Chronicle* 18 March 1938.
22. *Jewish Chronicle* 11 September 1936.
23. Black (see note 11), p.147.
24. L. L. Loewe, *Basil Henriques. A Portrait* (London: Routledge and Kegan Paul, 1976), pp. 14-20.
25. Raphael Loewe, 'The Bernhard Baron Settlement and Oxford & St George's Clubs' in Aubrey Newman, (ed), *The Jewish East End 1840-1939* (London: The Jewish Historical Society of England, 1981), pp.143-4.
26. Loewe, 'Bernhard Baron Settlement', ibid, p.143.
27. See, for example, John Springhall, *Youth, Empire and Society: British Youth Movements 1883-1940* (London: Croom Helm, 1977), which only considers girls' organisations in a brief appendix.
28. Black (see note 11), pp. 140, 136.

29. Cited by Black, ibid, p.234. For a detailed discussion of the overpublicised concerns about Jews and prostitution in this period, see Edward J. Bristow, *Prostitution and Prejudice: the Jewish Fight against White Slavery, 1870-1939* (Oxford: Clarendon, 1982). See also Tony Kushner, 'Sex and Semitism: Jewish Women in Britain in War and Peace', in Panikos Panayi (ed.), *Minorities in Wartime. National and Racial Groupings in Europe, North America and Australia during the Two World Wars* (Oxford: Berg, 1993), pp. 120-32.
30. Bunt (see note 8), p.16.
31. Black (see note 11), p. 223.
32. The Jewish Board of Guardians, which organised welfare provision, adopted the 'scientific' approach to philanthropy developed by the mainstream gentile organisation, the Charity Organisation Society. See Black, ibid, p.231. See also Tananbaum (see note 12), pp.11-12
33. Black, ibid, p.224.
34. F. K. Prochaska, *Women and Philanthropy in Nineteenth-Century England* (Oxford: Clarendon Press, 1980), p.125.
35. Kuzmack (see note 9), p.90.
36. Tananbaum (see note 12), pp.17-18.
37. Jane Lewis, *Women and Social Action in Victorian and Edwardian England* (Aldershot: Edward Elgar, 1991), pp.1-10.
38. Lewis, *Women and Social Action*, ibid, p.13.
39. Kadish (see note 10), p.70.
40. Tananbaum (see note 12), p.26.
41. Black (see note 11), pp.240-1.
42. For the representation of Jewish women as a sexual threat to Gentile men see Kushner (see note 29), pp.142-3.
43. *Jewish Chronicle* 18 September 1936. For Laski's role in other aspects of communal defence policy which also addressed what the Board of Deputies' Defence Committee termed 'the internal causes of antisemitism' like Jewish business practice, see Geoffrey Alderman, *Modern British Jewry* (Oxford: Clarendon, 1992) pp. 282-295.
44. *Jewish Chronicle* 25 September 1936. See also letter of 31 July 1936.
45. For the internalisation of anti-alien discourse by Anglo-Jewry, see David Feldman, *Englishmen and Jews. Social Relations and Political Culture 1840-1914* (New Haven and London: Yale University Press, 1994), chs 11, 12, 15, and Louise London, 'Jewish Refugees, Anglo-Jewry and British Government Policy, 1930-40' in Cesarani (ed), *Modern Anglo-Jewry* (see note 19), pp.163-90.
46. *Jewish Chronicle*, 18 March 1938.
47. Kushner (see note 29), p.124.
48. Kushner, ibid, p.130.
49. Charles Dreyfus, who worked at the Bernhard Baron Settlement as club manager, joint treasurer and chairman of the committee, wrote of Henriques that 'she was very much the boss in her own clubs and it did not matter terribly if she alienated some of her more spirited helpers. What was sad was her inability to keep on close terms with more than a few of her old girls. Their respect and gratitude she retained but very few could give her the almost unquestioning obedience and devotion which they felt she demanded'. See Loewe (see note 24), p.172.
50. *Jewish Chronicle* 7 August 1936. For the crisis in Anglo-Jewish leadership which was exemplified by the Board of Deputies' approach to East End fascism, see David Cesarani, 'The Transformation of Communal Authority in Anglo-Jewry, 1914-1940', in Cesarani, (ed.) (see note 19), pp.126-32.
51. Black (see note 11), p. 6.
52. Cited by Kadish (see note 10), p.127.
53. 'D. R.', interviewed by Benjamin Lammers. Cited in Lammers, 'Superior Kind of English' (see note 3), pp.314-5.
54. Basil L. Q. Henriques, letter, *Times,* 10 October 1936.
55. Cited by Bunt (see note 8), p.21.
56. Helen Lucas, letter, *Jewish Chronicle* 29 March 1898.
57. Lammers (see note 3), p.316. See also Elaine Rosa Smith, 'East End Jews in Politics, 1918-

1939: A Study in Class and Ethnicity' (unpublished PhD dissertation, University of Leicester, 1990).
58. Henriques, letter (see note 54).

DOCUMENTS

Oxford & St George's Girls' Clubs
The Bernhard Baron St George's Jewish Settlement,
Berner Street,
E.1.

28th. October, 1936.

Dear Mrs. [ ]

I find on reference to my register that [ ] has not been coming up to Club lately.

I am writing to you to call your attention to the fact that, since the disturbances of last month a great many Jewish girls have joined Communist clubs, not because they are Communists, but because they feel that the Communists were the only people who were trying to fight the Fascists. I would strongly advise you, in the interests of your daughter, to satisfy yourself as to where she is spending those evenings in which she is not in this Club.

I am sure you will be glad and relieved to hear that the leaders of the Jewish clubs have met together to discuss the position of the Jews in the present situation, and that every effort is being made to work in conjunction with the authorities and our Christian friends to maintain peace and order.

There will be a meeting of all the mothers of our Girls' Clubs and Playcentre members on Monday next, Nov. 2nd., at 3.0 p.m., in order to be able to report to you any plans for the future and to hear from you any suggestions you have to make.

I sincerely hope that you will make every effort to attend and so help the cause we all have so near at heart.

Yours sincerely,

ROSE L. HENRIQUES.

WHAT THE JEWISH WOMAN AND GIRL CAN DO TO COMBAT ANTI-SEMITISM.

In order to uphold the good name of Jewish womanhood, and to show an example of quiet good taste in matters of behaviour, appearance and dress, (thus avoiding the accusations of unseemly conduct, ostentation, and vulgarity levelled against Jewish girls and women,) it is of the utmost urgency that the following code be observed by them.

1). To show loyalty to God, the King, and the State.

2). To join whatever official body is formed and approved by leaders of the Community for the purpose of combating anti-semitism.

3). To avoid taking part in, or being in any way associated with rowdy street meetings, and to help to maintain law and order.

4). To show courteous consideration for all with whom they come in contact and be good neighbours.

5). To uphold the highest moral and ethical standards of Judaism, and to show respect for the religious observances of other Faiths.

6). To keep themselves fit, and to take an active part in the physical, intellectual and social improvement of the nation.

7). To observe the most scrupulous accuracy in dealing with their employers or employees.

8). To avoid behaving in an ostentatious manner, and being noisy in the streets or places of amusement.

9). To patronize only those places of amusement in which a good tone prevails, and to abstain from loitering in the streets at night.

10). To keep the standards of friendship between girls and boys on a high level.

11). To reject extremes of fashion in favour of a middle way.

12). To refrain from excessive painting of the face and dyeing of the hair.

13). To influence other Jewish girls to uphold the same standards of conduct.

14). To give by their whole lives, both at work and socially, the impression to their non-Jewish friends of being LOYAL ENGLISH GENTLEWOMEN OF THE JEWISH FAITH.

Source: Southampton University Library Archives and Manuscripts, reference: MS 60/17/16

A. L. Cohen's
'The Memorable Sunday'

DAVID MAZOWER

'The Memorable Sunday', is a despatch from the frontline of the anti-fascist struggle, a vivid eye-witness account of the tumultuous atmosphere in the East End on the day of the Battle of Cable Street. It is an angry and passionate piece, written by a young Jewish socialist with an unmistakable sense of urgency while the events it describes were still fresh in the author's mind. However, it is also a reminder of the rich history of the British Jewish labour movement, a long and complex story which is still largely unexplored. This neglected area of the Jewish experience in Britain forms the background to A. L. Cohen's sketch.

The piece appeared in a journal distributed to members of the Workers' Circle, or (as it was known in Yiddish), the *Arbeter Ring*. The Circle was a Jewish socialist mutual aid society, founded in Whitechapel in 1909 by immigrant workers and intellectuals.[1] Its early members were almost all Yiddish-speaking radicals – many of them veterans of the revolutionary struggle in Tsarist Russia. In their formative years, many of these men and women had joined strikes or demonstrations, been sent into exile, or spent time in prison. Politically, almost all owed their allegiance either to the Russian anarchist movement, or to the Jewish workers' party, the Bund.

For a contribution of a few pennies a week, members could claim benefits during periods of unemployment, sickness or bereavement. But what gave the Circle its distinctive character was its focus on political and cultural work: organising protests against the Tsarist government, supporting Jewish trade unions, campaigning against restrictive immigration policies, and promoting Yiddish culture.

During the next thirty years, the *Arbeter Ring* became the representative voice of the Jewish labour movement in Britain. By the 1930s, it had about three thousand members representing the entire spectrum of left-wing Jewish opinion, with several branches in London, and others in Manchester, Liverpool, Leeds and Glasgow. Circle House, the organisation's headquarters in Alie Street, was one of the main social and cultural centres of the East End. At almost any hour of the day or night, members might be found playing chess, reading the Yiddish papers, or discussing politics over a glass of lemon tea and a plate of herring. There were evening classes and lectures, a large library, endless committee meetings, fundraising events for left-wing causes, and a left-wing drama group. For a time there was even a radical Sunday school where Circle members sent their children to learn Yiddish and gain an early introduction to left-wing ideas.

The Workers' Circle was also one of the few organisations where two distinct generations of Jewish radicals met and found common ground. On the one hand, there were the older Yiddish-speaking militants, who had founded the society in the early years of the century. The defining political event for this generation was the Russian uprising of 1905; its failure, and the years of counter-revolution that followed, were a bitter disappointment to thousands of activists then in their teens or early twenties. By contrast, the younger members were almost all born in Britain. They attended English schools where they were taught to reject the 'ghetto jargon' of their immigrant parents, and emerged both better educated and less cosmopolitan than their elders. To many of them. the stories of pogroms, clandestine meetings, and anti-Tsarist agitation seemed like faint echoes from a distant era; above all, the old ideologies of anarchism and Bundism seemed to have little relevance to the modern world. By the 1920s and 1930s, younger radicals were far more likely to be attracted to Labour-style socialism, or to Soviet-style communism.

A. L. (Abe) Cohen, the author of this sketch of the Battle of Cable Street, was a lifelong activist in the Workers' Circle, and one of its most dedicated younger members. In 1917, when Abe was a young child, his immigrant father went back to Russia, one of the hundreds of committed radicals who returned in the months following the February revolution, hoping to build a society free from exploitation and oppression. The rest of the family – Abe, his sister and his mother – were taken in by a friend, Rachel Baron, whose husband had also just gone back to Russia, and who lived with her three children in a couple of rooms in Brady Street Buildings.[2] Like dozens of other families in a similar situation, the Cohens and the Barons found themselves facing a future without their main breadwinner. Although most of the men who left had intended that their families would eventually rejoin them, few felt that this was advisable amidst the turmoil that followed the Bolshevik revolution. Eventually, many found themselves trapped inside Russia, and neither Abe's father nor Rachel Baron's husband ever returned.

By the 1930s, A. L. Cohen had found employment as an assistant to the Secretary of the Workers' Circle, working in the main office at Circle House. He took a strong interest in the society's cultural programme, and played a leading role in organising one of its most popular ventures, a series of weekly classical concerts, featuring some of the leading musicians of the day. Cohen was also a regular contributor to the society's journal, *The Circle*, where this sketch was published in October 1936. The journal, then in its third year of publication, came out every few months, with a circulation limited to the several thousand paid-up members. Each issue had two sections, one in Yiddish and another in English, a pragmatic response to the the varying demands of its readers. The content was wide-ranging: polemical articles, features about leading personalities in the Circle, obituaries and reports of Circle activities. There was also the occasional short story or satirical sketch, mostly provided either by the Yiddish writer Katie Brown, or by A. L. Cohen himself.[3]

Inevitably, the pages of *The Circle* also reflect the growing preoccupation of the *Arbeter Ring* with the fascist threat in Britain and abroad. As a grassroots organisation, with a membership overwhelmingly made up of Jewish working men and women, the Workers' Circle was an influential voice among the coalition of anti-fascist forces. In particular, it played an important role in establishing the Jewish People's Council against Fascism and Anti-Semitism (JPC), which mobilised support on the streets of East London and led the campaign against the Mosley march on 'the Memorable Sunday' in October 1936.

The links between the two organisations remained close, and many of the leading officials on the JPC's executive were also members of the Workers' Circle. Cohen's appeal to members of the Workers' Circle to volunteer their services to the JPC would therefore have seemed completely natural, and many did indeed offer assistance. As the JPC's Secretary, Jack Pearce, later recalled, the Workers' Circle was

> a tower of strength. It levied its members to provide the Jewish People's Council with funds, it gave us many able men and women who did yeoman service, speaking, writing, distributing materials, [and] manning meetings in areas where hostility was strong.[4]

'The Memorable Sunday' is a vivid piece of reportage, and an appeal against complacency in the aftermath of an important victory for the left. But perhaps most important of all, its bitter tone underlines the radicalising impact of the anti-fascist struggle on a young generation of British-born Jews. Perhaps for the first time in their lives, British Jews like A. L. Cohen could really understand something of what their parents' generation had experienced in eastern Europe. The heavy-handed behaviour of the mounted police suddenly seems little better than that of Cossack troops under the Tsar, while the references to the Kishinev pogrom and the concentration camps convey a powerful feeling of unease, a sense that Jews could not take their security in Britain for granted.

With the benefit of hindsight, it is tempting to dismiss British fascism as an historical sideshow when set against events in continental Europe. 'The Memorable Sunday' reminds us that, to those caught up in the struggle against Mosley, the threat seemed all too real, and the future far from certain.

THE MEMORABLE SUNDAY – OCTOBER 4TH

By A. L. Cohen

The tension that precedes an electrical thunderstorm hung like a pall over London on Sunday, October 4th. I awoke that day with a heavy heart, for I had had a succession of bad dreams and nightmares all jumbled between the asinine moustache of Sir Oswald, the thick black belts of the Fascists, thousands of signatures to the Jewish People's Council's petitions (the trembling, illiterate hands of poor, old Jewish women tracing their signatures with tears struggling into rheumy eyes), wonder as to whether the "Daily Herald's" and Jewish Board of Deputies' exhortations to "keep off the streets" would be heeded ...

Breakfast stuck in my throat, and food became indigestible patches of torture.

At about one o'clock I boarded a bus towards the East End. We passed a 47 tramcar and saw a Fascist straphanging with his lunch tied neatly with string and dangling from his waist. He looked sheepish, and presented a bank-clerk-cum-tough-guy spectacle. Time and again our bus passed the tram, then fell back, and time and time again my eyes were glued to that Fascist. I am no hero, and physical courage is not one of my principal assets, but the anger and fury that rages through me at that sight will, I suppose, one day burst the bonds of customary control. You know the sort of feeling. You pass a Blackshirt selling the Fascist rag. He sees your Jewish face, and shouts, "Read all about the alien menace." You clench your teeth and breathe hard. And, you mustn't touch him, you mustn't even say anything, for that would be causing a breach of the peace.

And so we reached Liverpool Street, and, after leaving the bus, pushed our way through the seeming ordinary crowd, buying and selling, listening to glib auctioneers, and the happy look of those who think they have bought bargains; until eventually we came to the top of Middlesex Street and Aldgate.

Here things already began to look lively. The crowds became dense, the police force numerous. We pushed our way across Aldgate into Leman Street, and there the crowd was so thick that we could hardly move. Everywhere tremendous crowds of people, a huge mass of humanity, a sea

'The Memorable Sunday'

of faces, with a superficial air of good humour about them, but deep down below an upsurge of hatred for the Fascists; the young bloods, who think that every Yid is stinking wealthy, wears a beard and cringes, and who pretend never to have heard of Jewish workers on the Means Test, or Jewish workers working only one or two days a week and trying to keep a family on 25 bob a week.

They are coming; coming down Whitechapel and the back alleys, breathing fire and thunder against the "alien Jewish financiers." Where are they going to find these "financiers"? Outside the Jewish Board of Guardians? Or, maybe, outside the Settle Street Labour Exchange, where thousands of unemployed Jewish tailors sign on daily? (Haven't they mistaken the day? – Labour Exchanges close on Sundays.) Or perhaps they are going to seek out "Jewish financiers" at the Public Assistance Committee's depots? Or the soup kitchens for the Jewish poor? Or the Jewish Communal Restaurant, where dinners are served to the Jewish equivalent of the Embankment type at 6d. and 10d. a time?

Well, anyway, they are coming, and the mounted police are here to see that they do no damage. We all pay rent and rates, and where income is over £120 per democratic annum, we pay income tax, and, out of these moneys [sic] finance pours into the coffers of the police force for our protection. And look at them upon those handsome horses – tall, well-built, well-fed fellows, with long batons drawn. Proud we are to have these chaps to help us against the black menace.

These inconsequent thoughts tumble through my mind as we push our way through Leman Street. When, suddenly, the crowd commences to heave and surge, and mounted police begin to give chase. Their long batons drawn, the mounties, with eyes flashing and breath hissing through snarling lips, charge the crowd at random, slashing out left and right, blood up, with all the tradition of the Spanish Armada, the Thirty Years' War, Battle of Waterloo (and, yea, verily, Peterloo!) behind them. People run like waves before the mounted police, and I with them. I run like hell towards Circle House, and, with unbelieving eyes, see three mounted police and two afoot spreadeagling a young fellow under arrest. I feel sick at the pit of my stomach as I stumble into the Circle with white face and a feeling as if I had been present at a Kishenev [sic] massacre.[5]

I stand for a moment at the door and then step down to the pavement again. At Leman Street, above the heads of the crowd, mounted policemen wield their batons with sickening regularity. Lorry loads and bus loads of police pass and repass. All London's police are out to protect the Jews against the Blackshirts.

Rumours fly like chaff in the wind. The Fascists are going round Bethnal Green. They have been seen at Cable Street. They are stuck at Royal Mint

Street and can't move. The procession has been banned. The police are determined to hack a way through the crowds. Sir Oswald Mosley has got a black eye.

Meanwhile dozens are being arrested. Men are walking around with bandaged heads. Of course, they do not realise it is for their own good, as they are being protected from the Fascists.

Groups of men with clenched fists trudge along with detemined stride. THEY SHALL NOT PASS is the slogan shouted from the roof-tops; a vast, penetrating chorus, shouted high unto the heavens; a tremendous cascade of sound, heard as clear as a bugle call above the shouting and the fury, above the battle; determined in its stolidity, impervious and impenetrable against the hordes of police; a shout that seems to echo along the stinking back-alleys of Stepney, along the narrow little courts where Jewish "financiers" scrape along at 35s. a week, that gets carried away down to Fascist headquarters at Green Street and Duckett Street and Sanctuary Buildings, S.W.1, a volume of sound that can be heard even down at Whitehall – yes, right inside the Home Office itself.

Suddenly, the clamour seems to subside. THEY HAVE GONE BACK. Everywhere beams of delight, smiles of victory, a chorus of praise. This spontaneous demonstration of hundreds of thousands of working-men – Jews and non-Jews, united in common purpose – has triumphed over the seemingly impenetrable barrier of red-tape and the smirking, hypocritical barrier of the right of "free-speech" for Fascist knuckledusters and pieces of rubber-tubing filled with iron substance.

The knowing ones say, yes, it's a victory all right, but just you wait for Fascist retaliation. And sure enough that night we hear of five small Jewish shops being broken up by Fascist gangs. (Not the alien Jewish banks in Threadneedle Street, mark you.) And, again, the next evening, a poor old Jewish man, drawing a 10s. a week old-age pension, being assaulted at Stepney Green. Crowds of Fascist gangs in Stepney Green, shouting to Jewish unemployed tailors' pressers: "Give us back your jewellery and your money – you've taken it from us, you —— Jews."

And then Herbert Morrison[6] spills the beans by asking, "Where do the Fascists get their money from? From rich people, and, if so, who are these rich people? From foreign governments, if so, which foreign governments?"

All over the East End, one excited topic – the Fascists. In every group on pavement corners, in tramcars and on buses, in workshop and factory, in counting house and warehouse – one topic only – the Blackshirts. A rising tide of clamour – ban the Fascist uniform and let us see these Fascists in their true colours. Where do they come from? Who are they?

In two small rooms on the first floor at 164, Commercial Road, the Jewish People's Council are busy. Two rackety old typewriters, a Gestetner

'The Memorable Sunday'

duplicating machine and a writing table is all they have to fight the Fascist menace with. An eager-eyed Secretary, Jack Pearce,[7] a young fellow with plenty of gumption, rushes about all day answering the 'phone, meeting his Committee, drawing up plans, arranging speakers.

Little do you realise that your fate is being sealed in those two rooms in Commercial Road. Here lies your destiny. It is here, up those rickety stairs, that a stone wall of defence is being mounted for you. With but poor weapons, they are forging a steel chain around which the Fascists will crash to their doom.

As you go about your daily tasks, when Sunday, October 4th, will begin to fade as a glorious memory, do not delude yourself that the Fascists have been completely beaten. It has been a setback for them, but Sir Oswald has been to Berlin to take a few more tips and check up on his translation of "Mein Kampf". Plenty of dough here, boys, to buy uniforms and armoured cars.

Must the Jewish People's Council stand in doorways and plead with you for a dime? Give before it is too late! If you're short of money now, you will be still shorter when the Fascists come strutting along, when William Joyce becomes Chief of Police, and John Beckett Minister of Propaganda. You will have nothing at all to give then. All you members of the Workers' Circle will probably be fleeing to Russia and America (if you have the wherewithal to flee with), or, more probable still, you will be crouching in the Gestapo Depot at Green Street or beaten up by Duckett Street tough guys at Sanctuary (sic) Buildings.

If you have the gift of the gab (come on, you salesmen!) go at once to 164, Commercial Road, and they will give you Mosley coffin-nails to dispose of gratis. If you can typewrite (come on, you "Daily Sketch" shorthand-typists!) make a beeline for 164, Commercial Road. They need you more than ever now, but, on your way down, telephone the Underwood Company to send a typewriter mechanic for the rickety machines they want you to type with. If you are quick at figures, send money to the Jewish People's Council and then go there to help them add it up.

If you are an adept at packing parcels, fix a picture rail, give legal advice, clean a floor, make a fire, or write a poem – go at once to 164, Commercial Road.

Tell your friends not to support the Jewish People's Council if they wish to find themselves within six months at the Itchey Park[8] Concentration Camp.

Source: *The Circle,* official journal of the Workers' Circle Friendly Society, 3:9 (October 1936), 2-3.

NOTES

1. The Circle had its roots in an earlier short-lived society, the *Fraye Arbayter Ring* (Free Workers' Circle) of 1903. The Workers' Circle of 1909 was formed by immigrant workers, most of them cabinet-makers, together with leading Yiddish journalists and political activists. On the early history of the organisation, see Sam Dreen, 'Workers Circle Golden Jubilee', *Jewish Vanguard* 15 April 1960, p.7; and Nathan Weiner, 'Shtrikhen tsu der geshikhte fun arbeter ring in england (Aspects of the history of the Workers' Circle in England)', *Workers Circle Jubilee Publication* (London, 1929)
2. I am grateful to Jack Baron, Rachel Baron's son, for recalling in vivid detail events that happened some eighty years ago; also to Lou Appleton, for information about the Cohen family.
3. Copies of *The Circle* are in the collection of the British Library's Newspaper Library at Colindale.
4. Jack Pearce, 'The Fascist Threat', *The Circle Golden Jubilee 1909-1959* (London: Workers' Circle Friendly Society, 1961), p.21.
5. The city of Kishinev, then the capital of Russian-ruled Bessarabia, gained worldwide notoriety as a result of the pogrom of 1903, in which dozens of Jews were killed and hundreds more seriously injured.
6. Herbert Morrison (1888–1965), a leading Labour politician. In 1936 he was MP for Hackney South, and leader of the London County Council.
7. Jack Pearce (born Jacob Pines) was a member of the Communist Party; after the Second World War he was active in the Workers' Circle and was elected Chairman of the organisation in the 1950s.
8. The garden around Christ Church, Spitalfields, formerly the graveyard, was popularly known as Itchey Park because it was a favourite gathering place for local down-and-outs.

DRAMA

The Battle of Cable Street and *No Pasaran*

SIMON BLUMENFELD

Simon Blumenfeld, author of the bestselling *Jew Boy* (1935), one of the first novels to chronicle East End Jewish life in the 1930s, left school at 14 to work as a cutter and presser in a 'sweatshop'. In his early twenties, he joined the Workers' Theatre who staged several of his plays. His articles were also published by the *Left Review*. With Barnet and Emanuel Litvinoff and William Goldman, Blumenfeld became part of a left-wing Jewish East End literary circle. He later worked as a theatre critic and sports journalist. Blumenfeld himself took part in the 4 October demonstration, but it only entered his writing fifty years later. His play, *The Battle of Cable Street*, draws on the tradition of agitprop theatre, and presents the 4 October rally as a orchestrated, military operation. The play was first performed in Edinburgh and London in 1987.

In 1998, in his nineties, Blumenfeld wrote a sequel to *The Battle of Cable Street*, an extended extract from which is published here for the first time. The second play, *No Pasaran*, considers the changing memory of October 4 from the perspectives of elderly, disillusioned Communists, and the new generation of radicals in the East End under Thatcherism. For the veterans of *No Pasaran*, remembering Cable Street evokes pain and loss as well as pride, while its meaning for contemporary East Enders continues to be contested.

THE BATTLE OF CABLE STREET

Characters:
  Communist Party Cell members:
  Fred Cooper, a cafe owner
  Darkie
  Pearl, a student
  Charles
  Pat Coleman, a docker
May Cooper, Fred's wife
Maxie Birnbaum, a tailor
Father Groser, a priest
Spudsy Murphy, a hanger on

Time: About 11pm. 29 September 1936.

ACT ONE
Scene: Fred's cafe in Manningtree Street, off the Commercial Road in Stepney, an ordinary working men's cafe selling sandwiches, eggs and chips, tea, coffee, soft drinks, cigarettes etc. At centre a wooden counter on which is perched a large tea urn. Several propaganda posters are pinned to the front of the counter. One is in Spanish. It is a picture of a brawny uplifted arm carrying a rifle with the message 'No Pasaran'. Another says 'All Out Trafalgar Square October 4'. Left a pay telephone against the wall. Right a curtain (beaded if possible) covering an exit to the kitchen. There is a large coloured map pinned to a tea chest perched on the counter showing the area. Little coloured pins show state of the confrontation.

When curtain rises, Fred, the owner of the cafe, is reading a book, taking a swig occasionally from a bottle of beer at his elbow and burping. Beside him on the counter is a square utility-type radio set from which is emerging late night dance music by the Savoy Orphans. His wife May has just finished sweeping up. She looks tired. A cigarette end is dangling from her lips.

The October 4 banner has gone. Behind Fred now is a larged curved window bearing the legend 'Cafe' backwards.

MAY: (*tired looking*) You lock up, Fred, or me?

FRED: I'll see to it, May. Leave it to me.

The Battle of Cable Street

(Fred takes a swig from the bottle. Burps gently. May drags her feet to the door, turns, still holding brush and pan.)

MAY: Well, don't hang about. You need to get some sleep. You've got to get up early again in the morning.

FRED: I know ... I know ...

MAY: Like a bloody little boy you are. Can't get you into bed at night. Can't get you out of it in the morning.

FRED: Why, what's up? What's the hurry, May? It's only eleven o'clock. You fancy a bit?

MAY: You'll be lucky! I fancy a bit of shut-eye. That's what I fancy. Get myself nice and warm and comfy, dozing off and you come in fartin' and wheezin' and stinking of beer and fags and drop off like a log and leave me to toss and turn all night till morning.

FRED: Don't worry. I'll be up soon. Promise. I'm going to bed right away. Just finish this chapter.

MAY: Chapter! Always got your nose stuck in a book. Why don't you read a bloody newspaper for a change?

FRED: I do read a newspaper. The *Daily Worker*.

MAY: I mean a real newspaper.

FRED: What for?

MAY: To know what's up in the world.

FRED: I know what's up in the world. The Boss. The Capitalist. And I know what's down in the world. Me. The Worker.

MAY: You don't work in no factory. You're no worker.

FRED: What the hell d'you call what I do in here twenty-five hours a day?

MAY: I don't know what you call it. I know what I call it. A bloody waste of time. You're supposed to be a business man. You've got the brains. You can read and write and reckon. We could be doing all right even here if you ran this place proper. If you wasn't so busy with your politics. Didn't let a lot of scruffy layabouts sit around all day for a cup of tea and a doughnut – and most of that on the slate!

FRED: Come off it, May. What's got into you tonight? They're comrades. Fellow workers.

MAY: Workers my arse! They wouldn't know a worker if he jumped on their backs and pissed in their ears.

FRED: So some of them are unemployed. It's not their fault. They're still comrades. They're workers. Like me.

MAY: I told you before you're no worker. You're what you call petty bourgeoisie. And they're no comrades of yours either. Come the revolution they'll have you up against the wall soon as look at you and shoot you down like dog.

FRED: I wouldn't be at all surprised.

MAY: You wouldn't?

FRED: That's right. I wouldn't. All revolutions consume their children. It's fact. It's a law of nature. It's history. The more successful the revolution the more offspring it devours. Look what happened in the French Revolution. Look what happened to Danton. Almost a god in January. By December the same year, his head is under the guillotine. Take Robespierre ...

MAY: No thanks. Take him yourself. And you know what you can do with him! Along with your Karl Marx and Frederick Engels and Palme Dutt and Sklatvala. I'd swap the whole bloody lot for one Bill Smith talking East End English.

FRED: The trouble with you, May, is you're a cynic.

MAY: I'm a woman.

FRED: Same thing.

MAY: (*exasperated*) Oh, you talk! Now don't forget. Bolt up.

FRED: Yes, ma'am.

MAY: Top and bottom.
FRED: Yes, ma'am.

MAY: And use a bloody ash-tray! (*She plonks ash tray on counter.*) You've burned enough holes in the counter to make a bloomin' golf course. You hear?

FRED: I hear ... You know, May, when you're in one of these moods, you'd make a damned good Commissar.

MAY: Huh! (*Exits right*).

(*Fred continues reading for a moment. Yawns, looks at watch. Closes book, moves to door. Reverses sign to show 'open' inside. Drags chair to door. Bolts bottom. Says as he does so, out loud 'bottom'. Climbs on chair. Shoots top bolt. Says 'top' imitating May's tone. Closes door. Climbs down. Gives a quick glance round the room. His hand reaches for the light switch by the door to turn off the light. The door rattles. Fred turns towards the door but makes no further move. The door rattles more urgently. There is a rapping at the window.*)

VOICE: Fred! ... Fred!...

FRED: Go away. Can't you read? We're closed.

VOICE: Fred! ... It's me ... Darkie.

FRED: We're still closed.

DARKIE: Stop sodding about. Open up, Fred. It's serious.

(*Fred drags chair back, unlocks, grumbling aloud 'bottom' ... 'top' ..., opens door. Enter Darkie, who is tall, slim. Late 20s or early 30s. Could be a light-skinned Negro or a dark Latin type.*)

FRED: I'm supposed to be having an early night tonight.

DARKIE: Not tonight, comrade. We're having a meeting.

FRED: Now?

DARKIE: Soon. The whole cell.

FRED: Who says?

DARKIE: Joe. They've all been contacted.

FRED: So why didn't anyone tell me?

DARKIE: I'm telling you. Now.

FRED: What's up with the phone? (*Points*) Why didn't you ring?

DARKIE: Waffor? We know you're here.

FRED: Too true. Old muggins is always here.

DARKIE: Oh shurrup! From each according to his means.

FRED: Spouting Marx again. Help a bit if you knew what you were talking about.

DARKIE: I know all right. So do you. My brawn. My brains. Those are my means. I offer them all freely to the Party.

FRED: Big deal. So on my behalf you're offering my cafe freely to the Party, as well.

DARKIE: Right. You said it.

FRED: Well, don't let May hear you.

DARKIE: Okay, Fred, I'll keep shtum. It's a secret between ourselves. Now what about some char ... a cuppa.

FRED: I've just turned off the urn.

DARKIE: So turn it on again. Could be a long session.

The Battle of Cable Street

FRED: Better not. Got to be up early in the morning. Been on the go since six.

DARKIE: Fred, this is dead serious. Mosley's definitely got permission.

FRED: Permission? Permission for what?

DARKIE: To march. To march through Stepney.

FRED: No! Well, it's bloody well time we stopped talking and did something about it.

DARKIE: That's what this is all about. – Oh, turn off the bloody wireless. Do we have to listen to that crap?

FRED: *You* don't.

DARKIE: You don't either.

FRED: 'Elps me concentrate on what I'm reading. Aural wallpaper. Shuts out all the crap from you noisy buggers in the cafe.

DARKIE: Can it, Fred. This is serious. I'm telling you. We're getting the official line from the Centre.

FRED: Tonight?

(*He switches off set. Pays attention.*)

DARKIE: Tonight. You know, Fred, it's a shrewd move of Mosley's. Watches us plaster the town with 'Save Spain' posters. 'Rally to Trafalgar Square. Sunday October 4' whitewashed on every pavement. Every hoarding. Every bloody wall. Waits till we've pulled out all the stops for a monster rally then calmly announces he's marching throught the East End himself. On October 4. Meanwhile, we're otherwise engaged in Trafalgar Square. Bloody cheek! But you gotta admit it's caught us on the hop.

FRED: I'll say. Diabolically clever timing.

DARKIE: So now, how's about that cuppa?

FRED: Okay. But sit down, Darkie. You make the place look untidy.

DARKIE: And a packet of Woodbines.

FRED: Twenty, I presume?

DARKIE: No. I won't strain your resources. Five. Just five.

FRED: Tuppence.

DARKIE: Chalk it up.

FRED: That's it. That's your lot. No more tick till you've cleared up what's owing.

(Fred throws over the cigarettes and prepares the tea. Darkie sits at a table left. Enter Pearlie, about 20. Eton cropped. No make up. She nods at Fred. Sits at a centre table. Darkie gets up from his seat to join her.)

DARKIE: Hi, Pearlie!

PEARLIE: Hi!

DARKIE: What are you looking so het up about?

PEARLIE: Had a bit of a tiff with Len. Saw him outside the Help Spain meeting.

DARKIE: Some bit of a tiff. That was hours ago.

PEARLIE: So?

DARKIE: So what was our Len on about?

PEARLIE: Only laying down the law that women are better off out of politics.

DARKIE: He's just kidding you. Pulling your leg, Pearlie.

PEARLIE: Ses you. Len was grinning when he said it but he meant every word seriously. I said, it's alright for Nazi Germany. *Kinder, kuche, kirche.* But we women won't stand for that bloody reactionary rubbish here.

DARKIE: That's telling him.

PEARLIE: That's just what's so galling. That it should be necessary to tell him. An active trades unionist. A leftist. A militant.

DARKIE: Show you, doesn't it. Men! The best of 'em!

PEARLIE: Oh, you shut up too. It's no joking matter.

(*Fred comes over to their table.*)

FRED: What's your pleasure, milady?

DARKIE: Don't you answer that, Pearlie. He'll be trying to take advantage of you next.

FRED: What, with the missus upstairs?

PEARLIE: Wouldn't put it past you, dirty old man.

FRED: Let me put it another way. What would you like to drink? Tea?

PEARLIE: Okay. Tea ... No. Make it coffee for a change. One coffee please, Fred.

(*Fred nods and crosses to his counter where he makes a big show of taking down a bottle of camp coffee, measuring teaspoon of it into a cup. Darkie has noticed Pearlie's bulging carpet bag.*)

DARKIE: What you got there?

(*He pulls out part of a woolly garment bunched round knitting needles.*)

PEARLIE: None of your business, Darkie. Leave it alone!

DARKIE: What the hell's this supposed to be?

(*He unfolds it and takes out part of the garment.*)

PEARLIE: (*snatching it back*) What does it look like?

DARKIE: A skirt ... No. A scarf.

PEARLIE: Ha ha. Very funny. You know very well what it is. It's a cardigan. For Joe.

DARKIE: Still that same one? How long have you been knitting it for God's sake? Seems like years.

PEARLIE: Sometimes feels that way for me, too. But it's only been about nine, ten months, really.

DARKIE: Quicker to 'ave a baby, ain't it?

PEARLIE: You know why, Darkie. I'll tell you. Because I'm not one of those automatic knitters like my mother. To her it comes naturally. Like breathing. Does six other things at the same time.

(*She opens out garment.*)

DARKIE: It's finished, isn't it?

PEARLIE: Not quite. Only the sleeves to sew in, got to tack 'em in first to make sure they hang right.

DARKIE: Want me to try it on? Model it for you?

PEARLIE: No thanks.

DARKIE: No charge!

PEARLIE: Big of you, Darkie. But no. Some other time.

DARKIE: Well, you can't say I didn't offer.

PEARLIE: I won't. It's much appreciated, but I must decline. With thanks.

The Battle of Cable Street

(*Fred comes up.*)

FRED: There you are, Pearlie. One nice cuppa coffee. Milk's inside. Help yourself to sugar. (*Pearlie takes out purse*) No ... no ... that's all right. On the house.

PEARLIE: What do you mean, on the house? Don't you work hard enough to pay for the coffee? And the milk? And I don't suppose you get the sugar for nothing ...

FRED: Yes ... but ...

PEARLIE: Was Darkie's tea on the house too?

DARKIE: (*laughing*) In a pig's ear!

PEARLIE: So why should you treat me any differently? Why behave like those old Victorian hypocrites with their double standards? Especially in the Party, men and women are supposed to be equals. If anything you should charge me double and Darkie nothing. Because I'm working and he's not.

FRED: You're not working. You're a student.

PEARLIE: I've got a part-time job.

FRED: Lady Rothschild! Okay then, fourpence.

PEARLIE: What? Fourpence for a cup of coffee? What d'you take this for, the Savoy Hotel?

FRED: No. This is Fred's Popular Cafe in Manningtree Street. I'm Fred. You're a customer. The customers are always right. You said double so I'm charging double. Darkie's on the house anyway.

DARKIE: On the slate.

FRED: With you, Darkie, same thing. But I tell you what, young lady. If you insist I'll settle for tuppence a cup. One price only for man or beast.

PEARLIE: Beast! Now I'm a beast! Nice way to talk to customers. Wait till I tell May. Here! (*She pretends to throw coppers at him. Puts them on the table.*) Take your filthy lucre.

(*Fred picks up the coins. Moves back to bar. Puts money in till. Enter Charles. He is in his middle thirties, has a thin moustache, carefully trimmed. Wears glasses, carries a briefcase, is neatly dressed. Looks like an accountant.*)

CHARLES: (*looking round*) Joe?

FRED: (*shaking head*) No.

CHARLES: (*shrugging shoulders*) Oh well.

FRED: Wotcher having to drink, Charlie boy?

CHARLES: Nothing, thanks. I've had my supper. Never drink anything after 10 o'clock. I'd be peeing all night. And Fred, my name's not Charlie. It's Charles.

DARKIE: Hear that, Fred. How'd you like us all to start calling you Frederick?

(*Enter Joe. Joe is hatless, casually dressed. He is 21 or 22. He carries a bulging leather satchel crammed with books and papers. Joe looks enquiringly at Fred. Fred shakes his head.*)

JOE: Anything?

FRED: Not a peep. Not a sausage.

JOE: (*looking round*) No Pat?

CHARLES: Whenever it is, Pat's always sure to be late.

(*Charles and Joe move to table, take out documents in preparation for the meeting and pore over them. Joe sits at the head. He takes out documents from his satchel. Enter Max Birnbaum. A tape measure round his neck proclaims his tailor's trade. He speaks with a marked foreign accent.*)

FRED: Hi, Max.

The Battle of Cable Street

MAX: Not interrupting anything?

JOE: It's all right, Max. The meeting hasn't started.

MAX: I saw you pass by, Joe.

JOE: Yeah. I noticed your light was on. Working late?

MAX: Huh! I will still be at it for hours yet.

JOE: Betcha got some little *shiksah* inside as well, eh Max?

MAX: Do me a favour! Who's got time for such foolishness? That should be my last worry – a wedding order. Three suits.

JOE: People still getting married?

MAX: Thank God. And buried.

JOE: Thank God, as well?

MAX: I don't say that. But there's no shortage of funeral orders.

JOE: You get 'em coming and going!

MAX: Lucky I saw you, Joe. I've just taken on a new shop in the City. I will have a dozen pairs of trousers to cut. Can you come round Monday night?

JOE: Why not? I'm anyone's anytime. For one and ninepence an hour.

MAX: You will be round then – whatever happens?

JOE: What do you mean – whatever happens?

MAX: I mean ... You know ... What is going on ... (*drops all pretence and reveals his secret fears*) ... Now, Joe, tell me. What is going to be, Sunday?

JOE: Nothing will be. Trust us. We'll protect you.

MAX: Don't think I'm just a stupid, frightened old man. I am frightened. I have been through this before. I still remember. When I was a child in Russia my parents hid me and my brother Felix in their cellar. Always Easter time when the drunken *pogromchiks* were roaming the streets ... My brother Felix ... I had letters from him in Berlin ... It started there, uniformed ruffians breaking Jewish windows. Beating up old Jewish people ... Now I don't hear from my brother Felix no more ... Nothing! I thought, thank God that Berlin business can't happen here. But it can happen.

DARKIE: (*interrupting*) Dead right. It can. I was in Petticoat Lane last Sunday when that van full with blackshirts drove through, smashing up the market stalls. Hitting people with belts and heavy buckles.

MAX: My best friend Maurice – you know him? He's got a stall with underwear. A real sweet person.

DARKIE: Yeah ... well ...

MAX: A gentleman, wouldn't hurt a fly, that man. They throw him through a plate glass window.

DARKIE: Yeah ... I heard.

MAX: Two weeks ago they wreck his car. They are screaming 'Kill the Yids!' They are not making jokes. They mean it. I see it in their eyes. If a whole army of these savages comes down our streets God alone knows what will happen.

JOE: Nothing will happen. We won't let it. Mosely won't set foot in Whitechapel.

MAX: From your mouth straight in God's ears.

JOE: Go home. Finish off your suits. Sleep tight Saturday night. We'll all be here on Sunday. I promise you. (*salutes*) No pasaran. They shall not pass!

(*Joe rather theatrically raises fist in 'Red Front' salute. Max also half raises a timorous fist obviously unused to the salute and exits*).

The Battle of Cable Street

JOE: Poor old Max!

PEARLIE: He's not the only one. There must be thousands like him here in Stepney.

DARKIE: Can you blame 'em for being scared?

JOE: They're still the old Ghetto types. The cringing stoop-backed Jew. The please-have-pity Jew. The don't-hit-me-too-hard Jew. Lucky we don't have too many of them any more. The breed's dying out, thank God. We're developing a straight-backed Jew. A fight-back Jew. Bolt up if you like, Fred.

CHARLES: What about Prewitt? Our local organiser? Or someone from the Centre? They're bound to send a messenger.

JOE: We'll keep a sharp ear open ... No one's going to come this late. We'll be hearing through the blower. (*phone rings*) I'll lay odds that's it.

FRED: (*at phone*) Avenue 5639 ... Who? ... No. What number do you want? ... This *is* Avenue 5639 ... Fred's Cafe. Three nine! (*hangs up*) Silly bugger. Wrong number.

JOE: Better bolt up now, Fred. We don't want any more interruptions.

FRED: (*moving towards door*) OK, Chief.

CHARLES: Wait a minute.

FRED: What's up now?

CHARLES: Pat.

FRED: Pat?

CHARLES: Pat Coleman. Can't you see? He's not here.

FRED: (*looking round*) That's right. He's not.

JOE: Lock up anyway. He'll knock.

(*Fred locks up grumbling to himself. 'Top ... Bottom'. Moves across to Pearlie and Darkie*).

FRED: Finished your coffee, Pearlie?

PEARLIE: Yes, thank you, Fred.

FRED: (*picking up empties*) Fancy another?

PEARLIE: No. Ta.

DARKIE: I wouldn't mind another tea, Fred.

FRED: Daresay not. 'n I wouldn't mind if you paid me either.

PEARLIE: Oh, don't be so mean. Give him another cuppa.

FRED: Means putting on the urn again.

PEARLIE: So put.

DARKIE: Be a sport, Fred. I'm parched. My throat's dry. As a barrel of sawdust.

FRED: That's because you talk too much.

PEARLIE: Fred. Don't be such a skinflint.

FRED: Sometimes, Pearlie, you also talk too much.

(*Grumbling, Fred takes away the crockery and returns to bar*)

PEARLIE: He's not such a bad old stick, Fred.

DARKIE: Bad? He's a real mate. His handouts keep me alive – But don't tell him I said so for Christ's sake. Stop him grousing at me and you spoil half his fun in life.

PEARLIE: Well, like I was saying, they've really got to beef up our paper. Make it worth reading – if you like, quite apart from the propaganda. Devote more space to things of interest to women. Not all that beauty queen crap guaranteed to make you look like the Queen of Sheba overnight. Print articles with pictures about clothes that don't have to resemble unwrapped paper parcels because they're cheap. Reproduce stylish knitting patterns that don't cost the earth, publish articles that show women as valid comrades in their own right without them having to behave all the time like Rosa Luxembourg.

DARKIE: Couldn't agree more. Same sort of thing goes for men. Half the blokes in the workshops only buy the *Daily Worker* from me for the horse racing tips.

PEARLIE: No! That a fact?

DARKIE: Cross my heart. If we hired a tipster for greyhounds as good as we've got for the gee-gees, our circulation would double – treble. That, to me, makes sound commercial sense.

PEARLIE: Does to me, too. Very much so. But go tell that to the Daily Worker Editorial Board. They seem to be against sound commercial sense on principle. They don't appear to be at all interested in raising the circulation. In reaching more people and keeping those people. Print a few more articles like the full page one by that monumental bore Karl Radek – a whole page for God's sake! – and we won't be able to give the bloody paper away.

(*Knock at door. Fred opens. Enter Pat.*)

PAT: No news at all? Nothing?

(*Joe shakes head. Fred returns to the bar. The others join Joe round the table.*)

JOE: Meeting's open. Only business the Mosley March.

PAT: We go ahead with our counter demo, I propose.

DARKIE: I second.

CHARLES: You're always jumping the gun, Pat. Can't you wait till we get word from the Centre? They promised to let us know tonight, and we'll hear tonight.

PAT: When? It's long gone eleven. We can't stay here till tomorrow. What are we waiting for, anyway? We've canvassed the other wards, the unions, trades councils, party members, fellow travellers, sympathisers, church leaders, ex-servicemen. They're all urging us to make a move. (*holds up his hand as Charles attempts to interrupt*) Let me finish, Charles. I don't see it makes any difference now what the Centre says. If they say stay off the streets while Mosley marches – and somehow I can't see that happening after the reports of mass unrest we've been feeding back from the branches, they'll still have to stage some sort of counter-demonstration. We'll be called upon to get those people out. If they do decide to back us, then we've got everything ready and rolling. Remember, we've got less than a week to mount the biggest demo East London's ever seen.

CHARLES: But...

JOE: No buts, Charles. The motion's been proposed and seconded. The issue's clear. I vote we go ahead regardless. Hands? (*All except Charles signify*). Carried. You're outvoted, Charles. That's the end of that. (*Joe takes out a large piece of paper from his packed satchel and unfolds it on the table. The others crowd round him craning their necks for a better view.*) This is no good; Fred, got such a thing as an old easel?

FRED: What d'you take this for, St Martin's School of Art?

JOE: An empty tea chest? A big box? Anything?

FRED: (*pushing out a tea chest from under the counter*) This do?

(*Instead of tea chests, Joe can press into service Fred's slate with the chalked-on menu hanging from the counter.*)

JOE: Fine. (*He perches tea chest on top of table.*) Got any drawing pins?

FRED: (*reaching up to shelf behind him and throwing over box of pins*) A pound out of the till as well?

JOE: Sure. If you've got it.

FRED: Huh! With you lousy lot of *schnorrers* sitting around all day?

(*Joe pins paper to tea chest. It is a crudely drawn charcoal map of Aldgate and its environs looking rather like the hub of a wheel with three spokes radiating from it. While this is going on there is some rattling unnoticed at the door. A long envelope comes through the letter box landing on the floor. Joe stands before the map like a schoolteacher and jabs at it with a ruler to emphasise the points.*)

JOE: Roughly. This circle here. Aldgate. Whitechapel on the right. Commercial Road here in the middle. Cable Street there, left. (*points*). Minories ... Back of the Minories, Royal Mint Street. That's where the blackshirts parade for der Fuehrer's inspection, two o'clock, kick-off, they hope, two thirty. On Mosley's flank, the river. Can't get at him there. Conversely, he can't get away either. Aldgate we jam right down to Gardiner's Corner with people. No problem. That bars Whitechapel. Roadworks top of Commerical Road. Means he can't march through there. Leaves Cable Street the obvious point of entry. That's the critical sector ... Agreed? (*they nod*) That's you, Pat. The dockers' faction.

PAT: Don't worry about us. We can hold Cable Street.

CHARLES: Enough people?

PAT: Plenty. We've got all Cable Street and St George's. The Bermondsey boys, King George Five Docks, the Limehouse railway sheds. We can call on a heavy mob from Battersea. They've all been alerted. They're all itching to have a go at those fascist bastards, they're ready for anything – on Sunday. All they want to know is where – and when.

JOE: We'll be able to tell 'em soon enough.

PAT: There's a couple of heavy lorries stashed away behind Pell Street. They're loaded with rubble. Upended top of Cable Street they'll take the hell of a lot of shifting. Plenty of loose paving stones knocking around from roadworks. We'll pull up more. Pile 'em high to build barricades. They won't get through. Never! Even if they bloody well bring in tanks.

CHARLES: Don't think they won't if they have to.

PAT: I'm not afraid of tanks. We can deal with them too. We've learnt a lot about street fighting the past few months from our comrades in Spain – And we'll have a couple more East End surprises of our own.

(*Fred has noticed the envelope on the floor. He picks it up and moves towards Joe. They all watch as he tears open the envelope and rapidly skims over the contents in a tense silence.*)

CHARLES: From the Centre?

JOE: (*nodding*) Uh-huh ...

DARKIE: Well, what's it say? Read it, man, read it.

JOE: It's in seven sections.

DARKIE: Only took that many days to create the whole world. Come on, Joe.

JOE: Official. From our local organiser, Tommy Prewitt.

DARKIE: We guessed that already.

PEARLIE: Shut up, Darkie!

CHARLES: Let Joe get on with it.

JOE: (*reads*) The London District Committee has made the following arrangements re Mosley's march. One: a Party meeting at Salmon and Ball. Another at Piggott Street in Poplar, i.e. near to each end of the march. These meetings to be kept orderly and under control. Avoid clashes.

(*Joe pauses. There are whistles. Looks of astonishment, anger and sheer disbelief.*)

PAT: What the hell they nattering about, 'each end of the march'? What march? There ain't going to be no bloody march!

DARKIE: 'Ear! 'Ear!

(*Other murmurs and exclamations of support.*)

CHARLES: Order, comrades, please. Let him continue.

JOE: Two: A loudspeaker van will be touring the area advertising the meetings. There's thousands of leaflets waiting at Carter's Bookshop for immediate distribution ... Four: What Stepney must do is to rally masses to each of these meetings, mostly to Salmon and Ball ... Five:...

DARKIE: For Christ's sake cut the cackle and get to the 'osses. What about our counter demo?

JOE: (*repeating stolidly*) Five: ... Five: ... (*Looks closely at them*) Now, hear this. This is it, comrades. Our instructions as laid down by the District Party Committee.

DARKIE: Holy Writ. We cross ourselves first?

PEARLIE: Do be quiet, Darkie. Joe, please, continue.

JOE: (*reading*) Five: ... Five: ... (*Pauses*) Keep order. Give no excuse for Government to say we, like the British Union of Fascists, are a bunch of hooligans. If Mosley decides to march, let him.

(*Whoops of disgust, dismay, etc.*)

DARKIE: Sure I'll let him. Over my dead body.

JOE: (*holding up hand for silence reads on*) Don't attempt disorder. Time is too short to get a 'They shall not pass' policy across ... (*cries of dissent, Rubbish, No! No! etc.*) ... It would only be a harmful stunt.

DARKIE: What a bloody effin' liberty! Harmful stunt! I'd like to ram that bloody thing down his throat. Let him try calling that a harmful stunt.

JOE: There's more ... Six: ... Six: See there's a good strong meeting at each end of the march. Our biggest trouble on the night will be to keep order and discipline (*More resentful murmurs*) Seven: ... (*Repeats grimly*) Seven: ... Push the Party's leaflets around the crowds. Poplar and Bethnal Green are getting supplies too. Signed Tommy Prewitt. East London Organiser.

DARKIE: Here! – Gimme that! (*Snatches note, tears it in half*) It's going the only place fit for it, flushed down the bloody bog hole.

(*He is about to tear the note again but is restrained by Joe.*)

JOE: No. Leave it. That's history. It goes in with the minutes. Could be useful one day as evidence. (*He recovers the paper and puts it with minutes book on the table.*) Any more comments?

PAT: I think Darkie spoke for all of us.

PEARLIE: Hear! Hear!

CHARLES: They've pointed out before that support for Spain is the key issue. That's still true. even here today. The most urgent, the most pressing problem. Looked at objectively, in a national context, they may well be right. Isn't it possible that our judgement could be clouded by the emotive local issue? Because we're Jews.

PAT: I'm not a Jew. Fred's not a Jew. Darkie's not a Jew. My dockers are not Jews, they're Catholic to a man and there's no one more determined to stop Mosley than my lot.

CHARLES: Nevertheless, we're disciplined Party members. We're pledged to follow the Party line. That's always been our strength. Discipline. What would you do, Joe, as Branch Secretary if a decision reached at Branch level was over-ruled by one of our wards?

JOE: I'd come down on them like a ton of hot bricks.

The Battle of Cable Street

CHARLES: Well, what's so different in what you're doing here? Remember we're the largest and most influential branch in the whole country. Our action could split the whole progressive movement right down the middle.

JOE: It's been done before, and the movement survived. Didn't Lenin split the Social Democrats in Russia? Didn't he support the Bolsheviks against the Mensheviks? Didn't ...

DARKIE: For Christ's sake don't let's get all dialectical. Time's a wasting, comrades. I move we dump the District Committee's directive and go it alone.

PEARLIE: Second.

JOE: Before we vote, Charles, let me say this. There's no question but that our hearts and minds are with the Spanish people. Remember, our own branch members Nat Cohen and Sam Masters are at this moment in the International Brigade, fighting side by side with them against the fascists on Spanish soil. How we here can best help the Spanish people is to stop Mosley marching through Stepney.

(*Murmurs of approval.*)

PEARLIE: Hear! Hear!

DARKIE: Right! Absolutely right!

JOE: (*continues*) Our fight is their fight. It's the same fight. Against Fascism. We say the Fascists shall not pass. Our Spanish comrades are making sure they shall not pass and giving their lives in the process. If Mosley marches here it's a victory for Franco over there. And all we've worked for in the past few years, the trust and supoort for the Party we've built up in Stepney will be utterly destroyed. I'm with Darkie ... We go it alone ... All in favour? (*All hands go up. Charles is last, rather reluctant but firmly in the end.*) ... Unanimous! Now we'd better get cracking. You know what to do. Activate your groups. Fasten on all contacts. Spread by word of mouth 'Rally Aldgate, Sunday'. The District Committee meets tomorrow (*Looks at watch*) today – at four. I'm going down to the Centre in my lunch break. They'll get a full report of what we've decided. We meet here after work tomorrow night – seven o'clock sharp and get down to final details. Times and places. Okay, comrades, goodnight.

PEARLIE: Good morning!

(*Fred puts back tea chest and returns to book. All leave with the exception of Joe and Pearl. Joe sinks down on chair beside Pearl, utterly exhausted. Pearl pulls out a sleeve. Moves closer to him.*)

PEARLIE: Here. Let me measure this for size.

JOE: What are they? Socks?

PEARLIE: Joe. Don't be wicked. (*She measures sleeve against his arm.*) It's a cardigan. For your birthday. A surprise.

JOE: Surprise if you ever finish it.

PEARLIE: Joe!

JOE: Sorry, Pearlie. It's lovely, darling. Just what I need right now ... like a hole in the head.

PEARLIE: Joe! What's the matter with you?

JOE: Take no notice, Pearlie. I'm behaving like a pig ... I know ... Suddenly I feel ... bloody ... awful.

PEARLIE: Why? You should be feeling on top of the world. The way your argument swung Charles round, I thought you were wonderful.

JOE: You're prejudiced. Because of, well ... our relationship.

PEARLIE: Rubbish! I'm sure any East End girl would be ready to follow you. To the furthest barricade.

JOE: Right now, I wouldn't follow me round the corner.

The Battle of Cable Street

PEARLIE: What's up with you, Joe, for heaven's sake? You've got what you wanted. Convinced everyone your tactics are right.

JOE: I wish I could convince myself.

PEARLIE: *You're* not convinced? – What are you saying, Joe?

JOE: Pearlie, darling. I'm only saying this to you. Of course I'm convinced, in my mind, in my heart. But there are so many ... imponderables.

PEARLIE: Imponderables?

JOE: I'm on a hiding to nothing. I'm defying the Party. I don't have to tell you what that makes me – a deviationist. The London District Committee says Sunday's Trafalgar Square rally is on. I say no. They say let Mosley march. Hold street meetings afterwards. I say no. Not on October 4. I know I'm right. In my bones. But they've got the experience of leadership. All I've led is a couple of little workshop strikes. Here I've got, if it blows up, maybe a full scale insurrection on my hands ... I wish Nat Cohen was here, Pearlie, Nat'd know what to do.

PEARLIE: So do you, Joe. You're doing it.

JOE: Defying the Party? It's such an agonising choice. I'm sure I'm right ... Yet I can't help feeling like a traitor ... What happens if there's a poor response? If, say, only 15 or 20 thousand people show up and the police manage to shepherd Mosley safely through our streets?

PEARLIE: Snap out of it, Joe. Never mind deviationist, now you're being a bloody defeatist.

JOE: No ... just a realist.

PEARLIE: 15 to 20 thousand? – You're crazy! The East End's solid behind you. Be more like 400 thousand – half a million!

JOE: Don't let figures run away with you, Pearlie. That's just being childish.

PEARLIE: Well, two hundred thousand at least. According to our last rough canvas. Much more likely three hundred thousand.

JOE: Saturating the streets with three hundred thousand could be just as bad as twenty thousand. Worse. It turns into a classic revolutionary situation. But we're not ready for a revolution. We haven't the organisation. What happens if some take it into their heads to go marching up the West End on their own and start smashing windows? What happens if the police can't cope? If they call in the troops? Declare Martial Law?

PEARLIE: You're talking nonsense, Joe, and you know it. If we are able to collect a crowd, we'll also be able to control it.

JOE: We've just got to. Otherwise, God knows what will happen.

PEARLIE: You'll know, Joe. That's what counts.

JOE: I hope so, Pearlie, I hope so ... I know I talk tough. I believe what I say when I'm saying it. I'm pretty sure I've thought out every move. Then it hits me. I'm so young.

PEARLIE: Phooey! You're over 21.

JOE: That may be so. But I'm a babe in arms compared with those seasoned politicians on the London District Committee. They're the brains of the movement. After all, I'm only 22.

PEARLIE: 23.

JOE: 23 when my cardigan's finished.

PEARLIE: Alexander conquered half the known world before he was 23.

JOE: Look who she's comparing me with. I'm a lousy little trousers cutter in a Whitechapel sweatshop. Alexander had an empire behind him – an an army.

PEARLIE: (*gives clenched fist salute*) You've got an army too, bigger than Alexander's. They're waiting outside.

JOE: (*kisses her fist*) Thank you, darling.

PEARLIE: What for?

JOE: For the cardigan ... for everything.

(*He moves closer to her. They embrace and kiss. By this time Fred is fast asleep over his book, arms folded. May enters, her hair in curlers. She takes in the situation immediately.*)

MAY: 'At'll be enough!

(*They disengage self-consciously.*)

PEARLIE: Hello, May.

MAY: 'Op it, you two. Go and do yer spooning somewhere else!

(*Pearlie and Joe stand up.*)

PEARLIE: Here, May. Let's give you a hand.

MAY: Now bugger off before I lose my temper!

(*Joe packs his papers away in his satchel. He exits with Pearlie giving a passing glance at Fred. May watches grumpily, looks round the room with distaste.*)

MAY: Fred!

(*No reply. She shifts chair to door, climbs on it, bolts top, climbs down, bolts bottom, puts chair back and switches off light. The comatose Fred is illumined solely by the light that comes from the open kitchen door right, whence May has entered. She moves behind the counter, grabs him by the shoulder and shakes him.*)

MAY: Fred! Fred! Wake up! Come to sleep!

(*Fred lifts up his head. looks at her drowsily, scratches his head and rises as the curtain falls.*)

END OF ACT ONE.

ACT TWO SCENE ONE

Music: The Battle of Gandzha.

Scene: Fred's cafe in Manningtree Street, the next day, Wednesday September 30 about 7 pm. The cafe is closed. Fred is behind the bar reading as usual. The handle of the door rattles. A rapping at the window. Fred leaves book and opens the door. A priest stands outside.

FRED: Evening, Father Groser.

GROSER: Early closing night?

FRED: No. There's a meeting later on. Come in.

GROSER: (*looking round*) Joe not arrived?

FRED: (*looks at watch*) Any minute now. Can I get you something while you're waiting?

GROSER: Well, if it's no trouble.

FRED: No trouble at all.

GROSER: (*sitting*) Tea then, please.

FRED: Something with it?

GROSER: No, thank you. Tea will do very nicely.

(*Fred goes to counter. Makes tea*)

FRED: What's it like out – quiet?

GROSER: On the surface, yes. Underneath, no. In all my years in the East End, I've never known such suppressed excitement on the streets.

FRED: If it's like this today, Father, what's it going to be like when it all bursts out Sunday?

(*Groser shrugs shoulders, raises hands in an unhappy gesture. Fred puts tray on table. Groser put hand in pocket.*)

GROSER: How much?

FRED: Oh, that's all right ... Here's Joe.

(*Joe enters.*)

JOE: Any messages?

FRED: Not a peep. Nothing.

(*Groser rises. They shake hands.*)

GROSER: Joe.

JOE: Father Groser. Good of you to call.

GROSER: Missed you by this much in the vestry this afternoon (*gestures with hands*).

JOE: Sorry. Couldn't wait. It was my dinner break. I had another appointment.

GROSER: Sounds like you're a busy young man.

JOE: You can say that again. Rushed off my blooming feet. But I'm taking the rest of the week off. Got to.

GROSER: Without pay, I presume?

JOE: No. That's the remarkable part. With my boss's blessing.

GROSER: Amazing.

JOE: A miracle. Or maybe not. Shows you even money doesn't count when survival's at stake.

GROSER: Well, here I am. How can I be of help?

JOE: First let me put the situation in a nutshell as of now. Everything we've done, petitions, letters, personal approaches locally and to the Home Office have failed.

GROSER: And the police?

JOE: The police. Ah. The police won't ban the march. They won't re-route it. The chips are down.

GROSER: Looks like it, Joe.

JOE: It's up to us. We've got to get so many East Enders on the streets Mosley won't be able to move out of the Minories.

GROSER: Then what?

JOE: I don't know, yet. Let's get that far first. Bottle the bugger up – if you'll excuse the expression.

GROSER: And that's the official Party line?

JOE: I have to tell you, no. The word from the Centre is 'let him march – don't interfere'.

GROSER: No! I can't believe it.

JOE: I can show you the evidence in black and white. The official Party directive.

GROSER: How could they?

JOE: Well, they could. They did. 'Let him march' is what they say. We, the Stepney branch of the Communist party say no. We won't let him march. We won't let him pass through our streets. The trades councils are with us. The unions are with us. The ex-servicemen, the dockers, the railwaymen, even some rabbis are with us. I know you are, too.

GROSER: I am indeed. You have my wholehearted moral support – for what it's worth.

JOE: We're very grateful. I've never underestimated the value of moral support.

GROSER: Something practical I can do now? Speak at a meeting?

JOE: Would you?

GROSER: With pleasure. It's an honour. A duty.

JOE: Thanks. We'll take you up on that.

GROSER: Please. It'll be the subject of my sermon on Sunday morning. Most of my congregation will have made up their minds, anyway. On Sunday afternoon we'll be with you. But where?

JOE: Ah ... That's what we settle this evening, I gave the Centre an ultimatum.

GROSER: You did what?

JOE: Gave them an ultimatum. Back us or we act alone.

GROSER: And?

JOE: We've been promised a yea or nay for certain tonight.

GROSER: Well, you know exactly where I stand. Where the whole Christian Socialist Church stands.

JOE: It's only what we expected. But we had to make sure.

GROSER: (*dismissing thanks*) Please ...

JOE: Every single person of influence counts.

GROSER: (*giving card*) If you need me, ring. Any time. This number. Day or night, doesn't matter (*Rises*). Bless you, my son. I know you don't believe in Christ, our Messiah, but in protecting the poor and innocent, Joe, you are also doing the work of Jesus.

JOE: Well, we Jews have got to stick together ... Bit of a surprise though, a priest following the Communist party line.

GROSER: You've just been at pains to point out it isn't the Party line at all – quite the reverse.

JOE: I apologise, Father. You're absolutely right.

GROSER: Let me tell you something. Christians and communists have more in common than perhaps you realise. Jesus himself was probably a member of the Essene sect. They, as you may, or may not know, practised a primitive form of communism.

JOE: Good for them – and Him!

GROSER: Well, keep in touch, close touch, the next couple of days, Joe. And good luck!

JOE: Thanks, Father. We certainly need it.

(*Exit Groser. Joe goes to counter.*)

JOE: Cold drink, please, Fred.

FRED: Lemonade, orangeade, Cola, Tizer? What?

JOE: Lemonade please.

(*Fred pours drink from a bottle. Joe puts coins on counter. May appears in doorway backstage right. She moves to counter.*)

FRED: See who was just here? – Father Groser.

(*May nods.*)

JOE: Getting a better class of trade, May. You'll have to up your prices.

MAY: Fat chance Fred doing that. Besides, real priests never have any money. They're not givers – they just take. Like some of your lousy comrades.

JOE: Which comrades? Who? If anyone's taking liberties, tell me. I'll soon put a stop to it.

FRED: Never mind the comrades. What do you mean real priests? Isn't Father Groser?

MAY: 'Course not. He's like all those High Churchers. Walk about all the time in flowing robes like monks. Our priests only wear vestments at Mass on Sundays. All week they go about in jacket and trousers. From the back you can't tell 'em from rent collectors. (*To Joe*) Now you, Joe, take notice, if you're 'avin' one of your Party meetings tonight, for Christ's sake try and keep the place a bit tidy.

JOE: Promise, May. (*salutes*) Scout's honour.

MAY: Huh!

(*She exits. Enter Darkie.*)

DARKIE: Anything?

(*Joe shakes head.*)

JOE: No.

DARKIE: Well, what the hell are we waiting for? The District meeting was at four. It's nearly seven. We should have heard something by now.

FRED: Got to go through channels, I suppose. We'll probably get a visit from our esteemed East London organiser.

DARKIE: Prewitt?

FRED: Uh-huh.

DARKIE: You'll be lucky. I don't believe there's any such bloke as Prewitt – it's a ghost. Only materialises to shit notes.

FRED: Darkie's right. We'll just get another chit from that twit, Prewitt. I say, let's forget it. Go ahead with our own plans. I say we don't wait.

JOE: We won't. We can't. Events have overtaken us. Party members have always prided themselves on being the vanguard of the working class. The pace setters. The leaders. Now ordinary people are leading us.

They're raring to go.

DARKIE: So let's go with 'em.

JOE: Hold your horses, Darkie. We'll make it official when the others come.

(*Enter Pearlie*).

DARKIE: Hi Pearlie.

PEARLIE: Any news?

DARKIE: No. But let me tell you right away, before you tell me. We're not going to wait.

PEARLIE: Ah ... about time too!

JOE: We start our counterdemo plan tonight.

PEARLIE: The ex-servicemen have started already.

JOE: They have? What the hell's your brother Harold been up to, Pearlie?

PEARLIE: They're going to rally in Aldgate Sunday afternoon no matter what.

JOE: (*explodes*) The silly sod!

PEARLIE: You should have heard *his* language! Now, calm down, Joe, the anti-fascist branches and the British Legion are all getting on to him. They say, you're the secretary, Harold. Tell us when we meet, where we meet ... For Christ's sake, Joe. It's Wednesday – Wednesday! There's only three days to go. Thursday, Friday, Saturday. We've got to organise a monster on Sunday or we'll be in the shit all round. With the Party *and* the people.

JOE: Point taken, Pearlie. But listen to me. We don't want the ex-servicemen to go off half cock on their own. We've got to synchronise our strategy. Act in unison. As soon as our meeting's over, you'll contact Harold before he sends out any official directives. Tell him what's been decided. Get him to meet me here tonight.

(*Pearlie nods. She sit on high stool by counter and takes out her knitting.*)

PEARLIE: Give us a drink, Fred ... anything.

FRED: Hot? Cold?

PEARLIE: Anything.

FRED: Tea all right? Just made some fresh.

PEARLIE: Tea then, thanks. You know, Fred, this cafe's an oasis of calm in the mouth of a volcano that's about to belch molten lava any minute.

DARKIE: Marvellous the way everybody's starting to talk poetry all of a sudden.

FRED: Some oasis – Maningtree Street! But it won't be calm much longer. Now we're moving.

PEARLIE: The whole area's sizzling. I've just come from Great Garden Street, the Ladies Tailors Union. They're solid behind us. The Gents trade, one hundred per cent. The Capmakers' Union, Michaelson's lot, with us all the way. Even the tiny Bakers' Union's a hundred per cent solid. (*Slight pause*) Anyone know what's happened about old Father Groser's Christian Socialists?

FRED: In the bag. He was here just before.

PEARLIE: Himself?

FRED: In person.

PEARLIE: Good old Father Groser. You know, Fred, this situation – the whole atmosphere. It makes me feel quite – I don't know – peculiar. You can't hear it. You can't see it. Yet somehow you can sense it. A sort of underground rumbling. A heaviness in the air. Like a thunderstorm waiting to explode. Flashes of forked lightning that you can't see, only feel.

(*Enter Charles.*)

JOE: Glad you've arrived, Charles. Pat may be late. Got a bit of a problem at home. His missus. Thinks she's ill.

CHARLES: Nothing else to report?

JOE: Who from?

CHARLES: The Centre.

JOE: No.

CHARLES: Nothing?

JOE: Not a bloody dicky bird.

CHARLES: Odd.

JOE: Odd or not, we're not waiting, we're going it alone.

CHARLES: Who says?

JOE: Us. We do. The cell. It's unanimous. A quorum's here. Me, Pearlie, Darkie, Fred, you. It's what Pat Coleman's been advocating right from scratch.

CHARLES: Well, it's a democratic decision. I'll go along. But I must say, I'm not happy.

JOE: Why not? Have you heard what's going on in the streets?

CHARLES: I've heard. I've seen. It's staggering. But it's an unknown quantity unless it's controlled and directed, otherwise come Sunday and it rains all their enthusiasm evaporates.

DARKIE: Come off it, Charlie. It'll take a tidal wave to sweep all that bottled-up anger away!

The Battle of Cable Street

CHARLES: I don't know. I'm not so sure ... I'm an accountant. In the commercial world you just can't take such chances. You've got to be a bit more pragmatic. Look at the logistics of the situation. What is, and is not possible with the material at hand in the time at our disposal. I'd say that even with the Party's approval and backing, it would be terribly difficult to get the numbers we want to rally at Aldgate. If the Party comes out in direct opposition, I'd say it was quite impossible.

JOE: Quite impossible or just terribly difficult, the die's been cast. That's our unanimous decision. We're going to make the impossible possible. Let's move round the table and get this thing started.

CHARLES: Very well. Come on comrade. You heard.

(*Darkie and Pearlie are still at the counter and talk as they move down to take their places at the table. Darkie notes knitting sticking out of bag.*)

DARKIE: Still knitting? I thought you'd finished.

PEARLIE: So did I. Sewed the sleeves in. Then I remembered the pockets. You know Joe. He's got to have pockets with everything. Big pockets. (*she shows knitted squares.*) Think these'll do?

DARKIE: Do?

PEARLIE: I mean big enough?

DARKIE: Big? I should say. Any bigger you could use 'em for blankets.

(*They laugh. The phone rings. Fred answers.*)

FRED: Avenue 5639 ... Yes ... He's here. Who's calling? ... Ah. (*Turns to Joe. Holds out earpiece*). Pat.

JOE: Christ! I hope it's nothing serious. That's all we're short of. Our key man kaput!

(*Joe crosses heavily to phone. The others watch. He takes phone, obviously filled with foreboding.*)

JOE: Hi, Pat ... Oh ... No, no ... Go on ... Yes ... right ... we'll be there ... All night if necessary.

(*He hangs up with a bemused expression on his face. The others seem puzzled, maybe also apprehensive. The door opens to admit Pat Coleman.*)

DARKIE: Pat! Blimey! That's quick!

PAT: Quick?

DARKIE: Where you bin? – Call box 'cross the road, I'll bet.

PAT: Me?

DARKIE: Suppose it wasn't you just on the blower?

PAT: You jokers daft or something? Off yer bleeding rockers?

JOE: (*moving towards counter*) It was Pat Devine.

DARKIE: From the Centre?

(*Joe nods.*)

DARKIE: Well? Spit it out. Come on Joe. What's the good word?

JOE: They've called off Trafalgar Square!

PEARLIE: That's wonderful! Great!

DARKIE: Boy! oh boy! oh boy!

JOE: Seems it's only today the District Committee quote 'really appreciated the depth of feeling about the fascist march in the East End of London' unquote.

FRED: Well, better late than never.

The Battle of Cable Street

DARKIE: We appreciate their appreciation. But what the hell are they doin' about it?

JOE: They're instructing all branches to rally at Aldgate East instead of Trafalgar Square on October fourth.

DARKIE: Blimey! Instructions! No shilly-shallying there. Instructions. That's marvellous. Watcher say now, Charlie boy? Comrades, this is a cause for jubilation. I'm ordering drinks all round. Okay, Fred?

FRED: Okay. Tea and doughnuts coming up.

DARKIE: Who said doughnuts?

FRED: I did. On me ... May as well be hanged for a sheep ...

DARKIE: Well, let's be proper devils. Make it coffee and damn the expense!

JOE: Later. There's not time for celebrations.

DARKIE: Not even for a lousy cup of coffee?

FRED: Hey! Who's calling my coffee lousy?

JOE: No coffee.

DARKIE: Aw! C'mon Joe!

JOE: No. There's not a second to waste. We've got to get down to work right away. There's too much to do.

(They settle themselves round the table and come to order.)

JOE: Devine's coming down.

CHARLES: When?

JOE: Later.

DARKIE: Where?

JOE: Here.

CHARLES: He's bound to have some suggestions.

DARKIE: Joe said instructions.

JOE: Whatever. But there's a lot we can do till he shows up.

DARKIE: Such as?

PAT: Never mind. Joe, shoot.

JOE: Okay. First things first. Slogans. All messages on pavements and hoardings have got to be altered. Right away.

DARKIE: (*whistles*) Phew! Some job, Joe.

JOE: Right away. And I mean that. Right away. It's a must. We've got to alert all our squads for whitewashing. Now.

DARKIE: Now?

JOE: Not tomorrow. Now. Right now.

CHARLES: What's the whitewash situation, Fred?

FRED: Enough down in the cellar to whitewash the House of Commons.

DARKIE: They don't need it. They manufacture enough of their own.

CHARLES: What's the new slogan, Joe?

JOE: No change. That stays the same. NO PASARAN. They shall not pass. It can even be underlined. Leave the words 'All out October 4' but scrub Trafalgar Square. Instead 'Rally Aldgate East two o'clock'.

DARKIE: Why not be more specific? Gardiner's Corner?

JOE: That'll do too. Or Leman Street.

CHARLES: That's moving into Pat Coleman's bailliewick. What do you say, Pat?

PAT: Leman Street's fine. Gardiner's Corner's fine. So's Cable Street. Leave that to me. I'll get the lads on the job tonight.

JOE: Tonight's too late. Now.

PAT: (*rising*) You bloody slave driver. I suppose you'd like it done yesterday?

JOE: Too true. – You still here?

CHARLES: Got enough whitewash down the docks, Pat? Brushes?

PAT: Plenty. Where d'you think you got 'em from in the first place? Remember?

JOE: Report back on the blower.

(*Pat nods and exits. Others get ready to leave.*)

FRED: I'll get some more stuff up from the cellar.

DARKIE: Need a hand?

FRED: No, that's all right. There's some buckets in the kitchen as well. I'll get May if I want any help.

(*Fred exits right through kitchen.*)

CHARLES: Now then, what about leaflets?

JOE: (*groans*) We've got stacks of 'em.

CHARLES: How many?

JOE: 200,000 'All Out Trafalgar Square'.

CHARLES: 200,000 – Phew! Fat lot of use they are now.

JOE: You can say that again.

CHARLES: Hope they're soft paper.

JOE: You've said it!

(*Fred brings in buckets and brushes. Darkie picks his up*).

JOE: Don't suppose I've got to tell you old sweats where to go.

DARKIE: St Mary's Ward. Spitalfields.

JOE: Right. Make sure all your squads carry the same message. 'Rally Aldgate East 2 o'clock'.

DARKIE: Okay.

(*He exits. Fred brings over buckets to Pearlie*).

FRED: Here you are, comrade.

PEARLIE: (*indignant*) Who asked you to bring up my…

JOE: All right, all right, Pearlie. No time for that now. Just get cracking. Go over your old art work. Same streets as last week. Got the message?

PEARLIE: Trafalgar Square scrubbed. 'Rally Aldgate East 2 o'clock' written in.

JOE: Right, Pearlie. And grab brother Harold. I must see him tonight. Urgent.

PEARLIE: I'll find him. I'll tell him.

JOE: Tonight. Without fail.

PEARLIE: All right. All right. Don't worry (*exits*).

JOE: (*to Charles*) Those leaflets … .

CHARLES: I've told you. All they're good for now is toilet paper.

JOE: Pity to dump 'em … But we still need some leaflets. Urgent, Charles. We've got to get more somehow.

CHARLES: No time to print another batch.

JOE: Do we have to?

CHARLES: What d'you mean? Ah! I get you. Alter them somehow?

JOE: That's the ticket – I mean the leaflet. Can do?

CHARLES: It could be possible. Overprint. But not too many words.

JOE: Only the message. In red. Big, bold. Trafalgar Square cancelled. Rally Aldgate East 2 o'clock.

CHARLES: Could do the trick – I'll knock up the printers.

JOE: On your way, Charles. You haven't forgotten loudspeaker vans?

CHARLES: (*looking at diary*) They're on my inventory. Two at least.

JOE: Not just for a couple of hours. We need 'em all day. Every day. Including Sunday – specially Sunday morning – covering every inch of the place.

CHARLES: That was the general idea. I haven't forgotten anything. First aid posts. Couriers, messengers, transport. All well in hand. Anything else.

JOE: No. Not for the moment.

CHARLES: You'll think of something. Be seeing you then. If I can't make it tonight I'll ring back (*exit*).

JOE: Where's our easel, Fred?

(*Fred drags out tea chest – mounts it on table*).

FRED: There you are, maestro.

(*Joe takes out large map and unrolls it. This could be played simply by laying a large map across the table.*)

FRED: The real McCoy, eh?

JOE: Ordnance Survey. Large scale.

FRED: Where'd you get it?

JOE: Borough Council Surveyor's office. On loan.

FRED: Hope they know.

JOE: They will when someone tells them. On Monday.

FRED: Suppose now you need drawing pins as well (*reaches up behind him for box*).

JOE: No thanks. Got my own. Coloured flags as well.

FRED: Where'd they come from? All right, I won't ask ...

(*Phone rings. Fred answers.*)

FRED: Avenue 5639 ... Who? ... Hold on, Father. (*Covers mouthpiece*) ... Groser ... for you.

JOE: He was just here. Wonder what he wants?

FRED: Might have forgotten something.

JOE: (*at phone*) Hello Father ... Yes ... That's right — we've only just heard ourselves ... thanks ... Who told you? ... Er ... Oh ... Yes ... yes. You do that. Thanks (*hangs up*).

FRED: He knows eh?

JOE: Ah-hah.

FRED: Who told him?

JOE: He wouldn't say. 'My son, you know I can't divulge the sources of my information.' Made it sound like the secrets of the confessional box.

The Battle of Cable Street

FRED: Must have been someone pretty high up then. Pat Devine?

JOE: No. Higher.

FRED: Can't be Stalin. Must have been the Holy Ghost!

JOE: Well, here we go, Fred. Better lay on some grub. It's going to be a long, long session. (*Starts sticking flags in map*) ... Aldgate ... Whitechapel ... Commercial Road ... Leman Street ... Cable Street ... Ah ... Cable Street (*surveys map thoughtfully*) ... Cable Street.

(*Slow curtain. Music before scene 2: Vilna Ghetto Song*)

ACT TWO SCENE TWO

(*Late afternoon. When door opens one must be conscious of the press of a vast multitude outside. There must also be snatches of songs and slogans. 'The Internationale' ... 'they shall not pass' ... cheers ... boos etc. There could be constantly moving shadows across the large cafe windows. Inside Charles and Joe are studying the map. Fred is behind bar. Joe breaks off and walks up and down impatiently. The phone rings. Fred makes a pounce at it, but it stops before he can quite get there. He bangs hook up and down in frustration. The tension is so palpable one could cut it with a knife*).

FRED: Not a bloody thing!

JOE: They must be trying to get through. Been no message for how long?

CHARLES: (*consulting watch*) ... Seven ... eight minutes. How about the wireless? Any news?

(*Fred switches it on. A garbled sound of voices and static emerges. Fred bashes it frustratedly with his fist.*)

JOE: Still on the blink. Christ almighty, Fred. Not a blind bit of use these new-fangled sets. Would 'ave done better with the old cat's whiskers. Try the exchange again.

FRED: (*he has been putting money in box and banging hook up and down*) ... No use ... Nobody's answering.

CHARLES: Line dead?

FRED: No. It's alive all right.

JOE: Someone's interfering with the bloody thing. Must be. .. must be ...

CHARLES: Could also be the lines are overloaded. It's Sunday. They're always short staffed weekends ... The whole world must be trying to get through to the East End.

(*There is a movement at the cafe door. A young woman pushes past. Enter Pearlie. She flops down on a chair*).

PEARLIE: Phew! I'm whacked!

JOE: Well? ... Still holding?

PEARLIE: I'll say. It's wonderful. Unbelievable. It's like a dream. There must be a quarter of a million people out there. Aldgate right down to Gardiner's Corner. It's jam-packed solid. Couldn't squeeze a mouse through.

JOE: Good ... good ... Anything else to report? More casualties?

PEARLIE: Bertie Harris.

JOE: What about Bertie?

PEARLIE: He's been arrested. We tried to get him away, but there were too many cops around.

JOE: Well, if it's no worse than that ...

PEARLIE: (*sombrely*) 'Fraid it is. Darkie's injured.

JOE: Bad?

PEARLIE: Very. I believe they took him to the London Hospital.

The Battle of Cable Street

JOE: Hospital! You believe! Hell! Couldn't you get him to one of our first aid posts?

PEARLIE: Not a chance. He was out like a light. Bleeding like a stuck pig. Before we could organise anything he disappeared in the crowd.

JOE: Disappeared!

PEARLIE: Got swept away. Someone told me he'd been carted off to the London in an ambulance.

JOE: Who's this someone? Who told you? Reliable? A comrade? Someone we know?

PEARLIE: Sure. I know the face. Can't put a name to it. Remember the circumstances, Joe.

JOE: (*groans*) Oh God! Now he'll be charged. They'll cook up something. Those bastards won't let him go. It's jail for sure!

CHARLES: If he survives.

JOE: He'll survive. They can't kill our Darkie. He's got more lives than a cat. He'll survive.

PEARLIE: What about Cable Street?

JOE: Not so good.

PEARLIE: Why? Last I heard outside, Mosley was still holed up. In the Minories.

JOE: Still is. Doesn't dare poke his nose out. It's the police, trying to bash a way through for him. The sods have rushed the barricades three times. Three times we've pushed them back.

PEARLIE: But now. Now. Still holding?

JOE: Hope so. I hope so.

CHARLES: Last runner left about fifteen minutes ago.

PEARLIE: Nothing since?

CHARLES: Last phone report ten minutes back. Still holding.

PEARLIE: Casualties?

JOE: Shocking! Dozens. Dozens and dozens of 'em — Not all on our side, I'm happy to say ... Your medical students are working like Trojans (*looks at watch*). Getting on for four.

CHARLES: We've had Mosley bottled up an hour and a half.

JOE: Fine. So far, so good. But not good enough if we start to crack up now.

CHARLES: All our reserves are committed, Joe. Bermondsey, Battersea, the lot. All we can do now is wait.

JOE: And pray.

CHARLES: That's Father Groser's department.

JOE: Where'd we send those two coachloads, the latecomers?

(*Charles consults the map and points.*)

CHARLES: Top of Brick Lane.

JOE: With Mitchell's crowd?

CHARLES: That's right.

JOE: We don't need them there any more. Pearlie, on your feet. You've got to get moving again. Mitchell must be rushed down to Cable Street through the back doubles (*pokes finger at map*) with as many people as he can get to follow him ... Spread some sort of rumour ... The fascists have broken through the barricades ... okay?

PEARLIE: Okay, I get the picture, Joe. (*exits*)

CHARLES: I hope it *is* only a rumour.

JOE: (*pacing about agitatedly*) Why doesn't the phone ring? – Where are all our bloody runners? ... Ring, ring! ... For Christ's sake, ring! ... . (*quietening down a bit*) Think I'm taking a chance weakening the Brick Lane sector, Charles?

CHARLES: No. Nowhere Mosley can move now in that direction. Supposed to be a military man. He's just a big twit. One little push through Houndsditch here (*points at map*) down behind Petticoat Lane to Valance Road, New Road, Cannon Street Road, Cable Street and he's got the whole lot of us outflanked.

JOE: You're right, Charles. It's shit or bust for him now! Cable Street or nowhere.

(*There is a scuffling sound from the door and some urgent rapping.*)

JOE: See what that is, Charles.

(*Charles crosses to door, opens it slightly, seems to be talking to someone outside. He closes the door and comes back in.*)

CHARLES: Know a chap comes in the cafe – name Murphy?

FRED: Murphy? There's a million Murphys round here.

CHARLES: Spudsy? – Spudsy Murphy?

FRED: That only brings it down to around 500,000.

CHARLES: Says he's been in here with Pat Coleman.

FRED: No ... wait a minute. What's he look like?

CHARLES: Skinny. Shabby. Needs a shave. Sixty-ish.

FRED: Wears a sailor's peaked cap?

CHARLES: Ah-hah.

FRED: Dirty donkey jacket? (*Charles nods*) Ah! *That* Spudsy. Sounds like him alright. Been in a couple of times looking for Pat. Their folks came from the same bog. Always trying to cadge some Woodbines or a few coppers. – Tell him to sling his hook.

CHARLES: He says he's been with Pat. Says he's come straight from Cable Street.

JOE: Maybe he's got some message.

FRED: Maybe. But I have my doubts. Not that old scrounger. I know the type.

CHARLES: Under extreme pressure, you can't go by types. Ordinary blokes, who'd run a mile rather than risk a punch on the nose, are fighting like lions outside. I say let's have him in.

JOE: Okay. What can we lose? Maybe he does have a message. Let him in, Charles.

(*Charles goes to door, lets Murphy in and closes door behind him. Murphy stands to attention and makes a military salute.*)

JOE: So you were in Cable Street with Pat Coleman?

MURPHY: Uh-huh.

JOE: He sent you?

MURPHY: Not exactly ...

JOE: He sent you? Yes or no. Exactly.

MURPHY: Er ... no ... 'Tis like this. I hear him sending runner here to Fred's cafe. Bits of kids. They can't get through. They can't get back. Ses to meself, Spudsy, you old rebel, youse got the experience. You can do it. So here I am. A soldier of the republic. At your service, commandant. (*He stands to attention and salutes.*)

JOE: What's it like down there, Spudsy? Rough?

The Battle of Cable Street

MURPHY: Worse than rough. It's terrible. So it is. Wounded lying about groaning on the pavement. In the road, holding their heads. Like the Easter Day massacre round the Four Courts in 1916. Three times them cossacks rushed the barricades. Three times we pushed the blue bastards back ... But the boys is getting tired. What they're going through is more than flesh and blood can stand. If the cops bring up more reinforcements, next time they'll break through for sure. (*Shivers.*)

JOE: All right, man. Take it easy.

MURPHY: Can't help it, sorr. It was the firing reminded me.

JOE: Firing? – you sure?

MURPHY: Sure I'm sure. Ain't I heard the black and tans popping off them big pistols a score of times. And didn't I see just now with me own two eyes a couple of dead corpses collapsed at me feet? On me bloody boots, so help me!

(*Phone rings. Fred answers.*)

FRED: Pat. For you.

JOE: (*rushing off*) Pat! Thank God! At last. What's happening? ... Ah-hah ... ah-hah ... yes ... yes ... I know ... line's been busy ... or out of order ... no ... nobody arrived ... nobody I said. Not since we spoke last ... (*looks across at Murphy*) ... Oh, we've got Spudsy Murphy here ... you know him? ... Yeah ... yeah ... . He told us about the police opening fire ... yeah .. two dead!... Uh-huh ... ah-hah ...Okay, Pat. Keep punching.

(*Joe returns to Murphy, looks at him curiously.*)

JOE: That was Pat Coleman.

MURPHY: Me old buddy Patsy. See, I told you he knows me.

JOE: He knows you all right. (*He writes on a piece of paper, folds it small and gives it to Murphy.*) Now, get back to Cable Street right away. Take him this message. Important. Top secret. For Pat's eyes only.

MURPHY: Okay, commandant. With your permission could I wet me whistle first? Can I have a drink sorr?

JOE: Sure. Fred, give him a cuppa. Tea or coffee?

MURPHY: Couldn't you stretch to a bottle of stout maybe, or a wee drop of the hard stuff to settle me nerves a bit?

JOE: No time now. When you come back. Get cracking, man. There's a war outside.

MURPHY: Very good, sorr. (*puts paper in pocket*) I'll get this through to Patsy if I have to crawl there on me hands and knees.

JOE: That's the spirit. On your way, soldier!

(*Spudsy draws himself up proudly, salutes and exits.*)

CHARLES: You got rid of him pretty smartish, Joe.

JOE: Poor old sod. Just another loudmouth. Bit drunk as well. Stank, close to, like a brewery. Knew Pat's folks back home in Ireland.

CHARLES: And the shooting?

JOE: Firecrackers. Some silly buggers chucked them in the road to frighten the horses.

FRED: Don't know if they frightened the horses; they sure made our Easter hero do a bunk.

CHARLES: So no collapsing corpses bleeding at his feet?

JOE: Not in Cable Street. Not yet.

FRED: Can't remember where I heard it before. Must have read it. Sounds straight out of O'Casey.

CHARLES: So what *is* going on out there?

JOE: Something very funny. There's a lull. Regrouping, Pat thinks. Senior officers moving around having conferences.

The Battle of Cable Street

FRED: Must be planning an all-out attack.

CHARLES: Could be thinking of calling it off.

JOE: Could be. We'll know soon, either way. Just have to sweat it out, that's all.

(*Joe paces about impatiently. Enter May carrying a huge tray of sandwiches.*)

MAY: Now what about some food, you boys? You'll be dropping down dead from exhaustion. I keep bringing you in sandwiches and takin' 'em out again, absolutely untouched. Come on now, Fred, Joe, Charles – have a bite.

JOE: Who can eat now? Good of you, May, but I'm too tense. Too worked up.

FRED: The lad's right. It'd only make him sick.

MAY: Bloody cheek! My grub never made anyone sick!

JOE: You know, you'd make a good Yiddisher Momma, May. You're just like my old lady. I come home late at night, tired, shagged out after a long day in the workshop and maybe a couple of Party meetings and the minute I step in the house the first thing she'll say is 'Ess apess' – eat something. Like now, who's got the appetite?

MAY: Well, I'll leave them on the counter. God help you if you let this lot go stale as well!

CHARLES: Thanks, May. You really are a good sort.

MAY: Huh!

FRED: My missus may not have too much up here (*taps head*) but her heart's in the right place.

MAY: You should know. You've felt it often enough ... jokin' apart, boys, it wouldn't 'urt you to relax for a couple of minutes. You look bloody awful, the lot of you ... Sit down, Joe, you're not helping any wearing out the lino.

CHARLES: Sit down, Joe. Take the weight off your feet for a bit.

JOE: I'll sit down later, Charles. Not now, I can't. Things are happening ... It's coming to the boil.

CHARLES: It's coming to what our Spanish comrades call 'the moment of truth'. When the bull stands in the ring, bleeding. Barbed ribbons streaming down his back. His head's drooping, he's weakened, confused. He doesn't know which way to turn. The crowd's yelling 'Ole, Ole' with every pass. (*mimes matador with cape*) Ole, Ole ... then the matador takes the sword (*Picks up ruler from table*) Stands on tiptoe right between the horns. Takes aim like this (*starts to lunge in mime*) and suddenly it's quiet ... not a sound ... that's their moment of truth.

(*They stand silent, transfixed. There is a sudden loud roar from outside. At the same moment the door bursts open and Pearlie comes in, leans for a second as the door closes behind her then erupts.*).

PEARLIE: We've won! Listen! It's all over. (*moves downstage*) Joe, we've won! We've won!

(*She cries hysterically, hugs him tightly.*)

JOE: Okay, okay, okay, take it easy, kid.

PEARLIE: (*wiping eyes*) True. It's true I tell you. They've called it off.

CHARLES: What exactly's happened?

PEARLIE: Like I'm telling you. Police with loudhailers kept repeating 'Go home – the march has been abandoned. Go home. Go home.'

FRED: This calls for a celebration. First orders, please!

(*He brings out a bottle of whisky and glasses.*)

PEARLIE: They're celebrating already outside. Going dotty. Dancing, cheering, kissing each other. It's wonderful, marvellous. It's a dream come true. It's like New Year's Eve in Trafalgar Square.

FRED: Have a drop of this. Soon make you feel like New Year's yourself.

PEARLIE: Not for me. I'm too light headed already.

FRED: Joe?

(*Before he can reply the door opens admitting a gush of noise and Darkie. He is wearing a huge plaster dressing across his forehead. He holds his arms in the air, his fists clenched like a boxer taking a bow in the ring.*)

DARKIE: Tara-boom! Comrades, we've made it!

PEARLIE: Darkie!

FRED: You're supposed to be dead.

DARKIE: (*laughing*) So why didn't someone tell me? (*does a few vigorous dance steps*) Does that look like I'm dead?

CHARLES: No. Only decayed.

JOE: We heard the cops carted you off to hospital in an ambulance.

DARKIE: Yeah, that's right. Got patched up in casualty. I used to be a porter there. Know the hospital like the back of my hand. Stepped straight out the window. Magic. Allez-oop. Dead there – alive here – what's that in your hand, Fred?

FRED: What's it look like? Johnnie Walker. (*Pours out a large measure*) Have a drink, Darkie.

DARKIE: Thought you'd never ask. (*hesitates jokingly*) On the slate?

FRED: On the house.

(*The semi-hysterical atmosphere pervades the scene. They are all on a high. They start a combination 'Knees Up Mother Brown' dance to the tune and words of 'The Internationale'. The sound of the phone breaks through the noise. Fred goes to the phone, picks it up with his right hand, pokes a finger of his left in his ear and tries to carry on a conversation.*)

FRED: Joe – it's for you. Devine.

(*Joe walks to phone. Yells to make himself heard above the hullaballoo.*)

JOE: Simmer down a bit, chums. This could be important ... (*at phone*) Pat ... Yeah ... We just heard ... Yes ... okay. See you soon. (*hangs up, crosses to group*) Official. It's over. The big police boss himself, Sir Philip Game and the Home Secretary no less, they were both in Royal Mint Street. They ordered Mosley to call it off. The blackshirts are slinking off with their tails between their legs. It really is all over! (*collapses on chair*) Now I could go for that drink, Fred.

(*The atmosphere has suddenly sobered.*)

FRED: (*pours drink for Joe*) You, Pearlie? Have a drop of this scotch. It's a bit of all right.

PEARLIE: No thanks. I'm sticking with lemonade.

FRED: Go on. Have a shot. Put hairs on your chest.

PEARLIE: Be most becoming, I'm sure. I'll be able to join a circus.

JOE: (*drinking*) Lechaim!

FRED: Bottoms up!

DARKIE: Cheers!

JOE: Now, we need clear heads. All of us. There's a lot to do. We've got to follow up this victory. After all, we've only won a battle. We haven't won the war. They're still out there. The enemy. Blackshirts, brownshirts, blueshirts, National Socialists – whatever shirts they wear, whatever they bloody well call themselves –they're still out there!

(*Door opens. Pat enters with plasters on his face. The sleeve of his jacket is almost ripped off.*)

CHARLES: (*ribbing him*) Pat ... Late as usual.

JOE: You all right?

PAT: Sure ...

PEARLIE: What happened to your jacket?

PAT: Oh – just on my way to the tailor's for a second fitting.

FRED: Drink? We're celebrating.

PAT: Ta. (*Fred pours*). We've sure got something to celebrate, comrades. (*Drinks. Fred refills. Pat sinks on chair*) ... Phew! ... I'm clobbered.

JOE: Pat, you and your boys have done us all proud.

PAT: We've all done ourselves proud. Funny, now it's over, I feel like a returned empty Guiness bottle. I was superman in the fighting. Now I'm a dead mouse. All I want to do now is have a good kip. I feel as if I could sleep for a week.

JOE: There'll be plenty of time for sleep afterwards. We've got to decide on our next move, now.

CHARLES: The moment of triumph is the hour for consolidation.

FRED: Who said that?

CHARLES: I did. Just now.

(*Phone rings. Fred answers.*)

FRED: Yeah ... Joe – Devine again.

JOE: (*at phone*) Yeah ... yeah ... We're all here – you know about Bertie Harris? Ahah. Well, can't be helped. Charles'll fix up bail. Eh? Good idea, yes ... Very good ... Thanks. See you.

JOE: (*rejoining others*) Devine on the blower. He suggests a victory march.

PEARLIE: Great! I'll drink to that!

JOE: I think so too.

CHARLES: When?

JOE: Now. This evening. Five thirty-six o'clock as ever was. We've got to strike while the iron's hot. While there are still people milling around ... all in favour? (*all hands go up*) ... We'll rustle up a bit of a band. Drums and fife. (*moves over to map*) Meet top of Brick Lane. Bloom's corner. March down Bethnal Green.

PEARLIE: Have a short meeting in Victoria Square!

JOE: Right! March through Mosley's hot spots ... End up in Duckett Street. Feel up to it, Darkie?

DARKIE: You try an' stop me!

(*Pat rises and slowly moves to door.*)

JOE: Hey Pat! We're not ready yet. Where are you going?

PAT: Where do you think I'm going? – Home.

JOE: Home? What about the victory march? You voted in favour.

PAT: I *am* in favour.

JOE: So?

PAT: *You* march.

JOE: But you and your dockers should lead it.

PAT: Lead it yourself. My lads have done enough. All they want to do just now is to get pissed. They've earned it. The only place I'll lead them to is the boozer. Today they've saved Stepney. Tonight you'll have to save Spain on your own. (*exits*).

JOE: (*calling after him unavailingly*) Pat! – (*bitterly*) Anyone else want to go home?

CHARLES: Don't you start playing prima donnas as well, Joe. You heard from Devine. Let's march.

JOE: Right, everybody. (*gathers papers in briefcase*) Bloom's Corner. Same marshals. We've got to keep it disciplined. Instructions: Don't break rank whatever the provocation – come on Pearlie, let's go (*grabs her arm*).

PEARLIE: No. I've got to give May a hand. Just look at this place.

FRED: No, lovey. 'Op it with Joe. The pair of you. I've volunteered. Right? (*looks round*) So where do we start?

(*The others begin to leave.*)

MAY: (*by door*) You start by taking a broom in your hand, and so! (*shoves broom in fist*) Then you push it around, so ... and so ... And you can sing the bloody Red Flag all night while you're doing it.

CHARLES: (*looks back*) So long as you keep your mind on your work.

Lights dim to final spot. Door opens, burst of music from outside: 'Internationale'. Lights up. Curtain.

NO PASARAN (EXTRACT)

The play is set on October 4 1993 in a cafe on the Whitechapel Road, as in 'The Battle of Cable Street'. A middle-aged grey-haired Bangladeshi, Jahalal Verma, is seated behind a counter reading an Asian newspaper. Four or five tables are scattered about. A smooth Bangladeshi melody is playing on a tape recorder. Posters advertising Indian concerts hang round the walls. In the first part of the play Darkie, a light-skinned Negro or Indian in his 70s but vigorous, well-preserved and outgoing, enters the cafe and begins a conversation with Verma about the disappearance of the Jews from the East End. Verma shows him a poster with an arm holding a rifle aloft and the slogan 'No Pasaran', which he recognises from 4 October 1936.

This extract begins with the entry of an elderly blind man, Joe. Later Darkie talks to Verma's son Rahji, a medical student.

VERMA: My friend, Mister Joe. What am I doing for you?

JOE: The usual. I don't feel up to making a return trip to the betting shop.

VERMA: Is a pleasure my friend to be taking your bet there. You are having very special information? Yes?

JOE: Sure. Direct from the Aga Khan.

(Darkie has joined them at the counter. Watches Joe curiously. Joe hands over slip.)

JOE: You'll write it for me, please?

VERMA: Is not too complicated?

JOE: No. Just like always. Write on top Hackney. Saturday.

VERMA: *(nods, writing)* Saturday.

JOE: First five races ...

VERMA: ... five races.

JOE: Five 20p straight forecast ...

VERMA: Straight forecast ...

JOE: Traps six and two ...

VERMA: And two ...

JOE: One pound exactly.

(*Joe hands over coin to Verma.*)

DARKIE: 100p. Last of the big spenders, hey?

JOE: Who're you? From the way you talk you're not from round here.

DARKIE: Neither are you. You're the first white man I've seen since Aldgate pump.

JOE: Didn't you know? I'm the last of the Mohicans.

DARKIE: Me too, in a way. Can't you recognise my voice, Joe?

JOE: Say that again. Slow.

DARKIE: (*slowly*) Can't you recognise my voice, Joe?

JOE: (*still unsure*) Darkie?

DARKIE: The very same. Old loudmouth.

JOE: Knew all the answers.

DARKIE: Right. But I knew all the questions, as well.

JOE: Sometimes even better than the answers.

DARKIE: Because I knew my Karl Marx. Because I actually read *Das Kapital* from cover to cover.

JOE: Much good it did you – or me for that matter.

DARKIE: Too true my sainted Joseph.

JOE: So what now? God almighty. How long's it been since last we met? Forty years ago? Fifty?

DARKIE: More like sixty.

JOE: Anyway, good to hear your voice again. How've you been keeping, mate?

DARKIE: Can't complain. I'm keeping the wolves from the door now – just about. I'm in the music business.

JOE: You know, Darkie, I often used to think about you. Suddenly you disappeared from the East End. Nobody knew where you'd got to. I said you don't have to worry about Darkie. I'll lay odds that boy ends up a millionaire or a jailbird.

DARKIE: Pity you had no takers. I've been a bit of both, and I'm not through yet. In the music business, especially records, you can get rich quick and very poor even quicker.

JOE: At least you've settled down?

DARKIE: Like a sailor. Wife in every port.

JOE: Time you hung up your bell bottoms for good, then.

DARKIE: Did that a long time ago. Got a nice flat in Highbury, steady girlfriend, a room and a phone in a top publisher's suite.

JOE: Must be a bit of luck, that.

DARKIE: Luck had nothing to do with it. He owed me. I did the same for him when his business was in *shtook* and I was well away ... But why are we standing in front of the counter yacking? We're interfering with Mr Verma's business.

VERMA: No, no. It's quite all right. Please to continue.

DARKIE: (*grabbing Joe's arm*) Come on. We're sitting down. What are you having? Coffee? Something to eat?

JOE: Nothing. No thanks.

DARKIE: At least a cold drink. For old time's sake.

JOE: All right. A lemonade.

DARKIE: (*over his shoulder, leading Joe to a table*) Mr Verma, a double lemonade for my friend, please. With extra lemons – and damn the expense. (*Seating Joe solicitously*) Ah, that's better ... Don't you find it strange living among all these Asian people?

JOE: Not at all strange. They're very nice. Very kind and helpful.

DARKIE: Of course. You've got your lovely Dolores.

JOE: (*glumly*) Dolores ... well ...

DARKIE: Hope I've not spoken out of turn ... She was much younger than you, wasn't she?

JOE: Ten years.

DARKIE: Sorry, Joe ... Not dead, is she?

JOE: As good as. She's got rheumatoid arthritis. Bad.

DARKIE: (*gives sympathetic whistle*) The lovely Dolores. What was it they called her? The second Passionara, Mascot of the International Brigade?

JOE: She was always getting her picture in the papers.

DARKIE: Some girl! I've still got a few cuttings myself somewhere. Showed her in uniform at the front. I can tell you, Joe, when you first brought her home after Franco's war, the lads in the party used to fancy her something chronic.

JOE: You too?

DARKIE: Course, me too.

JOE: Well, you wouldn't now. Our blazing Spanish beauty's a gnarled, bent old wreck. Can hardly move. She hasn't left the house for months.

DARKIE: (*sympathetically*) Ah ... Joe ...

JOE: (*shrugging shoulders resignedly*) That's the way it goes, Darkie.

(*Verma brings glass of lemonade to table. Darkie reaches in pocket for cash. Verma reproves him.*)

VERMA: Mister Joe is my friend, also, no? Besides, you are already paying for this drink twice over with your tip.

DARKIE: Okay. Ta. You're a good fellow, Verma.

(*Verma returns to bar.*)

Drink up, Joe ... *Gesundheit*!

(*Joe takes a sip of drink.*)

JOE: So ... You're a born-again Highbury Yuppie. Watcha doing in Banglatown? That's what they call it now. What brings you to our neck of the woods?

DARKIE: I had some business in the city, Bishopsgate. Negotiating a contract. Then I remembered the date. And I thought I must see if any of the old faces were still about.

JOE: Date, you said? What date?

DARKIE: You must be joking?

JOE: Honestly, Darkie. I'm not kidding. What date? Gimme a clue.

DARKIE: You once took me to your house when we were kids. It was one of your Jew Festivals. I must say, I only went for the nosh. After a few prayers you had to ask your father about the exodus of the Jews from Egypt. As I recall, your first

	question was wherefore is this night different from all other nights? – I'm asking you, Joe, wherefore?
JOE:	Wherefore what? You've got your dates mixed up. You're thinking of the Passover festival. That's in April. We're in October.
DARKIE:	You're getting closer.
JOE:	Not so sure about that, but I am getting older, by the minute. I still don't know what the hell you're talking about.
DARKIE:	I'm talking about today, Joe. Today is October the fourth.
JOE:	So it's October the fourth. So ...?
DARKIE:	October the fourth ... 'No Pasaran!' (*lifts fist in a salute*) 'No Pasaran!' Joe! (*almost pleading*).

(*Joe sits back almost in shock. With a shaking hand he upsets his lemonade*).

JOE: Good God! – I forgot all about it.

(*Verma comes rushing over with a towel to clean the table.*)

VERMA: Not to worry, Mister Joe. I am bringing you another.

JOE: No ... No, thanks. Just a glass of water. Feeling a bit faint, that's all.

(*Verma nods, takes empty glass back and returns a moment later with water.*)

VERMA: Is a piece ice in it also...

JOE: Thanks ...

DARKIE: (*solicitously*) ... Better? Joe?

JOE: Didn't half give me a turn, Darkie. Fancy forgetting October the fourth!

DARKIE: Forgetting happens to all of us. I'm always going to the bathroom for something or other, and can't remember what the hell it was by the time I get there.

JOE: Hardly the same thing, is it? Me forgetting October the fourth is like a Rabbi forgetting to fast on *Yom Kippur*.

DARKIE: Don't worry – you'll get over it.

JOE: Let me tell you what happened at the fiftieth anniversary celebration of October the fourth.

DARKIE: Was there a celebration?

JOE: A handful of Jews turned up in St George's Town Hall in Cable Street. Maybe because it actually was *Yom Kippur* that day. The banners and the couple of hundred strong crowd were all Bangladeshi. Half could barely speak English and weren't born when it happened. The other half were still kids in India.

DARKIE: Bit of a liberty, Bangladeshis taking over our victory celebrations?

JOE: Not really. It's logical. Historically, we were the immigrants then, and the sons of immigrants. When it happened, the East End was ours. Now it belongs to them. So does the celebration. What hurt me most was the jeers from some young hecklers along the route reminding us it was the Day of Atonement, *Yom Kippur*, and we ought to be praying in *shul*. To my mind we *were* praying, saying in our hearts like the Jews in Babylon, 'if I forget thee, O fourth of October' – and here it is, October the fourth, only a year or so later, and Darkie, – I've forgotten.

DARKIE: If it's any consolation, from what I've heard round here, even our Bangladeshis have forgotten, as well.

JOE: But so quickly, and me here, in Fred's cafe where so much of it began.

DARKIE: Let's put things in perspective, shall we? It's not Fred's cafe any more. Hasn't been for 25 years. It's Mr Verma's cafe.

The Battle of Cable Street 269

               The Mosley business was in 1936, so the fiftieth celebration was in 1986, which, since we're now in 1993, makes that seven years and not just a year or two ago as you're suggesting.

JOE: Of course you're right, Darkie – I've lost my marbles – Doctor Alzheimer come and get me!

DARKIE: And save a corner for old Darkie – I won't be far behind.

JOE: That's the way our world ends. In the nut house. Not even with a whimper. Just a slap and a shove. We deserved better, Darkie. We were the foot soldiers. We were the ones who got our skulls cracked on the barricades. We did the fighting. All our leaders did was thinking – and talking.

DARKIE: They pointed the way. We followed. Then they renegued. We're the betrayed generation, Joe.

JOE: They're all liars and cheats. From your Marx and Engels downwards, Keir Hardy, Ramsay Macdonald, Bernard Shaw, H. G. Wells, Professor Keynes, Roosevelt, J. F. Kennedy, Stalin, Gorbachev.

DARKIE: You've missed out Sigmund Freud.

JOE: Him too.

DARKIE: And genetic engineering.

JOE: (*laughs*) Her as well ... Joking apart they've brought us to such a pitch at the end of the twentieth century. We don't know who we are, what we are. We don't know any more what's Left. What's Right. At the last General Election, I'm ashamed to say I voted Conservative for the first time in my life.

DARKIE: Well at least they rewarded you handsomely.

JOE: Rewarded?

DARKIE: They cut Social Services benefits, didn't they?

JOE: Because this lot have no principles. Why should we expect principles from local politicians when all the world leaders are finally exposed with feet of clay.

DARKIE: I remember when Stalin died. I cried like a baby. And the bastard turned out to have been a bloody monster. Yet it gripped me like a deep personal loss. Closer than any living relative.

JOE: Maybe that was the trouble. We had no real relatives. Socialism and the Party were our family while we were busy building up our brave new world. And our family let us down. Our family betrayed us. But what the hell am I rabbitting on about? None of this is news to you, Darkie. Forgive me, old pal.

DARKIE: Oh – forget it! It does a power of good to let off steam occasionally.

JOE: Never mind occasionally, I get no chance at all to let off steam, as you call it.

DARKIE: Not at all? How come?

JOE: I've only got Dolores to talk to at home. We've long exhausted the Spanish Civil War. The only public place I visit these days is the betting shop. And that's not a place to excite any conversation between blokes like us who've lived a bit and read a bit and travelled and thought a bit.

DARKIE: Joe, I'm sorry. You can guess how I feel – genuinely. If there's anything I can do? ... Anything you need?

JOE: Well, I can do with a new pair of eyes, for a start. And a whole new body for Dolores. Apart from those little items, there's nothing anyone can do for me.

DARKIE: Sure? ... If you could use a few quid? (*goes to take out his wallet. Joe reaches out restraining hand.*)

JOE: (*reproachfully*) Darkie! Don't!

DARKIE: (*puts wallet back*) Oh all right – if you say so.

JOE: Well, no more time for tears, Darkie. Let's look on the bright side.

DARKIE: What bright side?

JOE: I've still got Dolores ...

DARKIE: But when she's gone?
JOE: I'll go too. That's all arranged. And good riddance. That's the bright side.

DARKIE: Oh ... could be a long time yet for both of you.

JOE: Sure. She'll go back to ballet dancing and I'll join the Foreign Legion ... Well, I gotta go. Dolores gets worried when she's left on her own too long.

DARKIE: You still live in that crappy old flat?

JOE: Crappy's right. Three damp, paper-peeling rooms. Been there fifty years.

DARKIE: Controlled rent, I suppose? About tuppence a week?

JOE: By today's values, tuppence a week is right.

DARKIE: So what you moaning about, matey?

JOE: Who's moaning? Just being realistic. It isn't *worth* tuppence. (*attempts to rise*) Well, really must push off this time. It's been a tonic – I nearly said 'seeing you' – (*laughs*) But you know ...

DARKIE: Let me see you home, Joe. I'd love to see Dolores again.

JOE: Nothing to see – literally six and a half stone of suffering skin and bones on someone you've never met before.

DARKIE: (*sympathetically*) Ah ...

JOE: But she still remembers who she was. Best if no one else reminds her.

DARKIE: Okay. But I know where you are. I'll keep in touch.

JOE: (*knowing nothing of the sort will happen*) Sure ... sure. You do that, Darkie. (*Darkie helps him up from the table and they walk over to Verma at the counter.*)

JOE: Thanks for putting on the bet, chum.
VERMA: Is nothing. Any time.

(*Doorbell rings admitting Rahji. Tall, slim, 22, smartly but casually dressed in jeans and sports jacket.*)

RAHJI: Hi, Pop! (*looks at Joe*) Hey! Look who's here! Mister Joe, the Wandering Jew.

JOE: Well, I'm just about to wander off again, Rahji. (*turns to Darkie*). Verma's son. Nice lad. He rescued me once. I was collecting my books from Whitechapel Library and he found me walking around in circles fifty yards from my flat.

RAHJI: Think nothing of it, Mister Joe.

JOE: This is Darkie. I can't remember his real name. A comrade from the old days.

RAHJI: Hi!

(*Darkie nods. Joe shuffles towards door.*)

DARKIE: Sure you won't let me see you home?

JOE: Please!

DARKIE: Well if you're sure you'll be alright.

JOE: Sure I'm sure.

(*Rahji opens door for him. Darkie makes obvious preparations for leaving. Rahji sits*).

DARKIE: I'd better be off as well, before it gets dark.

VERMA: My friend, you are not yet leaving. You have some business with my son. Yes?

DARKIE: Business?

(*Darkie doesn't catch on. Rahji is equally perplexed. Verma takes out the poster and places it prominently in the centre of the counter*).
Oh ... the poster ... 'No Pasaran'...

RAHJI: It's not for sale.

DARKIE: You don't know how much I've offered.

RAHJI: I don't care. It's still not for sale. It's a bit of working-class history.

DARKIE: Sounds familiar ... So what you going to do with it?

RAHJI: Have it framed and hang it up in the shop, I suppose.

DARKIE: Not the best place in the world.

RAHJI: Only temporarily. We're turning part of St George's Arts Centre into a Bangladeshi exhibition in the London Museum. Along the lines of the Jews in the East End exhibition in Finchley.

VERMA: (*leaving counter and moving to door*) I am going to the betting shop. Not for long. I am coming back in a few minutes.

RAHJI: Don't worry, Pop. I'll look after any rush of customers.

VERMA: Is no need. Say we are closed. Yes?

(*Exit Verma. Rahji and Darkie are left together. Darkie soon recognises in Rahji himself as a young man, dreaming of a better life for his fellow and ready to devote himself wholeheartedly to the cause.*)

RAHJI: Yes. We can learn a lot from the Jews. Especially the way they killed that Mosley march.

DARKIE: It wasn't only the Jews. It was the Dockers who tore up the paving stones for the barricades in Cable Street. Roman Catholics to a man – like me, though I'm probably as much Catholic these days as you are Muslim. Can't remember the last time I went to confession – down the road actually in Watney Street. But as they say in showbiz I'll be alright on the night. Bound to be a priest around. There usually are. If not, God will forgive me. It's his speciality, according to Heine.

RAHJI: You certainly sound like my sort of Muslim. But even if I don't go to the Mosque, or pray five times a day, that's not to say there aren't many good things in our culture and the Koran. Things well worth preserving.

DARKIE: There are also good things in the Talmud and St Augustine and Karl Marx and in the philosophy of Zen Buddhists and Epicurus. In every religion and none. The point is they were all represented on the streets on October the fourth. Not as Jews or Catholic, Zoroastrians or whatever, but as East Enders.

RAHJI: I suppose you were there.

DARKIE: I'm proud to say I was.

RAHJI: Leelah's grandfather was there too.

DARKIE: Ted Gershom? Red Ted? You couldn't bribe him away from a fight.

RAHJI: I tried to talk to him about it once, but he was already gaga. Alzheimer's. He died not long after. But he did harp on one name a couple of times. A local hero so far as I could make out. Fought in the International Brigade. Joe Jacobs. You know him?

DARKIE: (*nods affirmatively*) So do you.

(*Rahji jerks thumb looking towards the door. Darkie nods in agreement*).

RAHJI: (*Amazed*) Mr Joe! That pathetic old wreck, Joe Jacobs? How are the mighty fallen!

DARKIE: Tell me about it when *you* are pushing 80.

RAHJI: Sorry. Shouldn't have said that. Wasn't he supposed to have written a book about the whole affair?

DARKIE: That's right. It's in the library.

RAHJI: It was. A long time ago. I tried to get it. No luck.

DARKIE: Someone must've nicked the bloody thing.

RAHJI: So they said. But they couldn't get another copy, it was out of print.

(*Rahji shows he is in pain. He gets up and walks about a bit.*)

DARKIE: What's up, Rahji?

RAHJI: A little accident.

DARKIE: ... Oh! ... How?

RAHJI: Just happened. Nothing serious. Got it patched up in casualty. Feels better when I move about a bit.

(*Rahji lifts up shirt, shows a large bandaged patch on abdomen*).

DARKIE: That looks nasty.

RAHJI: Looks worse than it is. Luckily.

DARKIE: Dad know?

RAHJI: Not yet. He will eventually. Just the fortunes of war.

DARKIE: You said accident ...

RAHJI: Simply a figure of speech. But we *are* in a war – a perpetual war on our streets. We've always got to be on our guard. As you can see, not only our property's liable to be damaged.

DARKIE: I noticed. Your windows are boarded up outside. Same war?

RAHJI: Skinheads.

DARKIE: Cheeky sods!

RAHJI: Paid us a visit couple of weeks ago, after dark. Been quiet for a bit since then. Now it's starting up again. Every time they hear about Turks being burned to death in Germany, it inspires them to have a go at us. My fault. I really should have been more careful.

DARKIE: If you say so, chum.

RAHJI: But after all – in broad daylight? Took a short cut home through one of those narrow little alleys opposite the hospital. Can't walk more than two abreast. Found the way blocked by a couple of yobs. They looked harmless enough. Bit drunk. Made a chirpy little song and dance about letting me pass. One of them – big fellow – gave me a beery bear hug before they let me go. Then I found I'd been stabbed just below the left rib cage by some sharp object. I was bruising there, too. Popped across the road to casualty. Got cleaned up and bandaged in no time. Now good as new.

DARKIE: Didn't they teach you in school classics lessons to beware Greeks bearing gifts?

RAHJI: Yes. I learned it then. Trouble is, I forgot it this afternoon. But praise be to Allah, the wound wasn't a couple of inches higher. I wouldn't be talking here with you. I'd be just another fatal Asian statistic.

DARKIE: Well, touch wood you're a pretty alive one now, Rahji.

RAHJI: Amazing how quick and effective the new techniques for treating walking wounded have become.

DARKIE: Probably because there are always so many little wars around these days. I hear they're great places for developing Do-It-Yourself surgery.

RAHJI: No DIY about the Royal London, my friend. We've got the best, the most up-to-date, the most expensive equipment in the world. We've even got our own helicopter.

DARKIE: I don't ever recall anything about helicopters at the London hospital.

RAHJI: It's only a couple of years old. Lands on top of the roof. Wafts patients into intensive care in a matter of minutes.

DARKIE: Great for the patients, I dare say, but how about the street market across the road, Mile End Waste? Crowded with customers like a Bombay souk – what happens if there's an accident?

RAHJI: Most unlikely. The 'copter's checked thoroughly before and after every flight. Using it for emergencies means many lives hanging on a hair can be saved. And every possible precaution on the journey is taken.

DARKIE: But if it's the will of Allah? Say it suddenly blows up?

RAHJI: Depends where it lands. Could be a couple of dozen casualties. But they'd all be Bangladeshis, so I expect nobody's unduly disturbed. There are plenty more of us.

DARKIE: I know the bitterness you feel, Rahji. I've gone through it myself. But ethnic minorities have always been second-rate citizens – work fodder in modern industrialised societies. It was like that when the Irish followed refugee Huguenots at the time of the potato famine, settled in Stepney as dock labourers and were put to digging canals and building all the new railroads. After the Irish came the Jews fleeing the pogroms in Russia and the Nazis in Hitler's Germany, becoming absorbed into the booming *schmutter* business. Now, it's the Asians who are the city's work horses.

RAHJI: I've heard all that before, Darkie – you don't mind if I call you that? (*Darkie shakes head and brushes the term aside*). I heard it from old Ted in his saner moments – often.

DARKIE: So who's next in our East End immigrant world? Who's left to follow the Asians?

RAHJI: When they've been thoroughly ground down to third world standards – how about the Scots? (*both laugh*).

DARKIE: Well, at least you've got a British sense of humour.

RAHJI: After 22 years, man and baby, in Whitechapel, I should hope so.

DARKIE: Now, let's be serious. Come back to the real world. It's the same East End it was fifty years ago when we stopped Mosley in his tracks.

RAHJI: Is it, though?

DARKIE: Where's the difference? There are still whole foreign-speaking families in backroom sweatshops sewing dresses, suits and imitation suede leathers for a pittance. So they're not Jews. They're Pakistanis, Bangladeshis. They're still exploited by their own richer compatriots, still in danger from our own neo-Nazis. It's exactly the same – only the colour of their skin has changed.

RAHJI: A lot more than that has changed. Your thesis is good as far as it goes. But it doesn't go far enough. It's now a whole new ball game.

DARKIE: It's your over, so bowl. Give me a for instance.

RAHJI: For instance: how many Jews, Asians or blacks were killed in unprovoked racial attacks in 1936? In what the Queen would call your *annus mirabilis*, the miracle year of your East End uprising?

DARKIE: Well ... I'd say one ... possibly two.

RAHJI: And how many injured?

DARKIE: There were dozens badly injured on the Mosley march alone. Country-wide it must have run into hundreds.

RAHJI: Well, listen to this. In 1992, last year, nine Asians were killed in unprovoked racial assaults. Eight thousand were seriously injured.

DARKIE: Phew!

The Battle of Cable Street

RAHJI: That's official Home Office statistics. But our own monitors found that only one in ten attacks were actually reported to the police. That makes, as far as we're concerned, a total of eighty thousand. How do you account for the disproportionate casualty figures between 1936 and 1992?

DARKIE: Well ... for a start there are four more, must be six times as many Asians here now as there were Jews then.

RAHJI: Too right. That's the whole point. That's what makes 1992 different from 1936. It's not just a few hundred thousand Jews at risk, but more than two million Asians. Add to them another million or so blacks and people of mixed race and it means that by the end of the century one in twenty Britons will have skin of a different colour.

DARKIE: Oh, I don't think there's any doubt we'll have a multi-racial society by then.

RAHJI: We're not waiting till the year 2001. For us, 1992 was a watershed. We won't be treated any longer as second-class citizens. We respect the law and we demand that the law respect us and protect us. We demand an end to the wanton racial murdering and injuring. Enough is enough. If the law won't defend us, we'll have to defend ourselves.

Conclusion

TONY KUSHNER and NADIA VALMAN

It has become fashionable amongst historians and others to debunk the significance of the 'Battle of Cable Street'. Bernard Wasserstein, in his waspish account of post-war Jewish communists, suggests that they survive in their 'English version ... as a pub bore reminiscing about street battles against fascism'.[1] The sad disappearance of the 'veterans', but the respect that those who took part on 4 October 1936 have received at least since the 1970s, suggests that Wasserstein's comments are somewhat misplaced (although it cannot be long, in these days of almost instant heritage, before a theme pub named 'The No Pasaran and Parrot' opens up in Cable Street). More seriously it has become almost orthodoxy now to point out that rather than destroy East End fascism, the 'Battle' actually provided a stimulus. Membership figures did, indeed, increase for the BUF in late 1936, proving that there is rarely such a thing as bad publicity. Nevertheless, most of the evidence for the post-4 October 1936 resurgence comes from sources which need to be severely queried – the fascists themselves and Special Branch. On a psychological level, the 'Battle' was disastrous for the BUF. Mosley desperately tried to claim it as a victory after the war. Other fascists have denied it ever happened or have attempted, as with the defacement of the Cable Street mural, to obliterate its memory. Special Branch also had particular reason to downplay the significance of 4 October 1936. The day itself was, as we have seen, one of general humiliation for the police, and Special Branch especially wanted to counter Communist Party claims that it represented a 'tremendous victory over Fascism'. Their post-October 1936 reports have formed the basis for recent revisionism about the impact of the 'Battle'. Ultimately, however, they tell us more about the anti-Communism of Special Branch than about the growth, or decline, of the BUF. Indeed, the Public Order Act of 1936, which was the most direct state response to the 'Battle', was aimed as much at the anti-fascists as their opponents. Ironically, the decline in the overall fortunes of the BUF after the 'Battle' went alongside intensified anti-semitism in the East End, which continued to concern the local Jewish community, at least in the weeks immediately following 4 October 1936 if not beyond. It is salient, however, that governments turned down requests made in the late 1930s and during the Second World War to provide legislation to protect its ethnic minorities from specific attack. The rather half-hearted attempts to do so since 1945 have, it could be argued, facilitated the racist murders which have more than tarnished Britain's liberal reputation in recent years, most notoriously in the case of Stephen Lawrence.[2]

'The Battle of Cable Street' mattered to those tens of thousands of anti-fascists who were present. For many, it was a life shaping day. Whether or not the BUF went into terminal decline after October 1936 it remains that the *fear* of British fascism, if not its reality, was perceived, after the initial intensification of anti-semitism, as less of a threat by Jews (and local non-Jews) thereafter. The 'Battle' has subsequently been romanticised and shaped to fit later struggles. But in spite of any distortion that has occurred, it remains a special moment in the people's history of the twentieth century, worthy of detailed consideration. The sociologist Robert Miles has pointed out that in much academic and popular writing there is a 'one-sided emphasis on racism and associated practices of exclusion in the absence of an analysis of resistance'.[3] It is to be hoped that the essays in this collection have started the process of achieving the balance Miles calls for as well as acting as a memorial in itself to all those anti-fascists who took part in that remarkable day. As those first commemorating the 'Battle' during the Second World War put it: 'Long May Its Memory Live!'[4]

NOTES

1. Bernard Wasserstein, *Vanishing Diaspora: The Jews in Europe since 1945* (London: Hamish Hamilton, 1996), p.57.
2. Special Branch report, 1 November 1936 and subsequent reports in PRO MEPO 2/3043. It does not follow, however, that these reports indicate that 'the Special Branch in particular was sympathetically inclined towards the fascists', as suggested by Scaffardi, *Fire Under the Carpet: Working for Civil Liberties in the 1930s* (London: Lawrence and Wishart, 1986). p.161. For state responses and the protection of minorities see Richard Thurlow's contribution to this volume. The *Jewish Chronicle* in the last months of 1936 gives ample evidence of the continuation of BUF anti-semitism in the East End. For more recent racist violence see *The Report of the Stephen Lawrence Inquiry*, released on 24 February 1999.
3. Robert Miles quoted by John Solomos and Les Back, *Racism and Society* (Basingstoke: Macmillan, 1996), p.105. One important exception which looks at anti-alienism and resistance to it within the East End is Nicholas Deakin, 'The Vitality of a Tradition', in Colin Holmes (ed), *Immigrants and Minorities in British Society* (London: Allen & Unwin, 1978), pp.158-85.
4. Quoted in *East London Advertiser*, 10 October 1942.

Abstracts to Articles

Fascist Perceptions of Cable Street
Thomas P. Linehan

The 'Cable Street' events have been interpreted by many as a major victory for anti-fascism, yet immediately after 4 October 1936 support for the British Union of Fascists increased substantially. Fascist writers and speakers represented the anti-fascist demonstration in a number of ways, as deliberately seditious, as orchestrated by outside forces, as irrationally violent and as ungodly. An analysis of the images and metaphors deployed to describe the demonstrating crowd indicates the ways in which the BUF appealed to East End audiences by rhetorically recasting the defeat they had suffered at Cable Street.

Women and Fascism in the East End
Julie Gottlieb

By examining women's participation in fascist activities in London's East End, the British Union of Fascist's policies towards working-class women, and the feminisation of British fascist discourses concerning race and otherness, this article argues that women played a critical role in the successes and failures of the BUF's campaigns in the East End. Women members were certainly visible and ready for action on the now legendary 4 October 1936. Ironically, however, it was the absence of one woman, Diana Guinness, that might well have been responsible for Sir Oswald Mosley's decision to abandon his position before the Battle of Cable Street.

But What Did They Do?
Contemporary Jewish Responses to Cable Street
Elaine R. Smith

Jewish responses to the Battle of Cable Street and indeed to fascist anti-semitism in general were varied and complex. At one level, there were the obvious divisions between East End Jews and the Anglo-Jewish leadership. At another level, there were the numerous opinions and strategies which emanated from East End Jews themselves. This article looks at both the conflict between the East End Jewish community and the Jewish leadership, and at the various divisions within the East End Jewish community itself. It also examines the practical and theoretical consequences of these divisions – in other words what they meant in terms of the action which Jews took at the time of the Cable Street disturbances.

The Threat of the British Union of Fascists in Manchester
Neil Barrett

This article highlights the congruence of response to the BUF by the Jewish elite nationally and in Manchester, focusing on the Laski family. The moderate responses of the communal leadership to BUF slanders and the reasoning which lay behind such responses is considered, as is the failure to engage with the BUF in a more proactive way. Such responses, it is argued, were grounded in the traditional norms of collective communal action which stressed the importance of established principles of moderation, toleration and fair play. But this line of defence came uncomfortably close to asking Jews to accept second-class social status in order that the fiction of communal unity and acceptance within the wider society be maintained.

The Straw that Broke the Camel's Back: Public Order, Civil Liberties and the Battle of Cable Street

Richard C. Thurlow

The problem of fascist-communist violence and the growth of political anti-semitism in east London was the background to both the Battle of Cable Street and the passing of the Public Order Act in 1936. Although it increased the powers of the authorities to deal with general problems of law and order, the Act was specifically targeted at the BUF, whose meetings, processions and demonstrations were seen by the authorities as provocations and attempts to intimidate the Jewish community. Somewhat ironically, its use was mainly directed at anti-fascists, particularly in relation to abusive words and behaviour, the original cause of the problem.

Docker and Garment Worker, Railwayman and Cabinet Maker: The Class Memory of Cable Street

David Renton

The dominant memory of 4 October 1936 has emphasised class conflict and class unity. Anti-fascism has been widely represented as a movement of working-class solidarity against what has been seen as the predominantly middle-class and capitalist character of British fascism. Recent research suggests a more nuanced analysis, both of the membership of the British Union of Fascists and of the interaction between ethnic and class identities in the resistance to fascism. Nevertheless, the class model, if used in a dynamic way, remains the most compelling approach to interpreting the Battle of Cable Street.

'Long May Its Memory Live!': Writing and Rewriting 'the Battle of Cable Street'

Tony Kushner

The Battle of Cable Street is, excluding events connected to the Royal family and world wars, the most remembered day in twentieth century Britain. This article explores how the memory of 4 October 1936 was contested initially by contemporaries and then by subsequent generations in attempts to make it a 'usable past'. The pattern of remembering has been uneven, with periods of intense interest and then decline, but the 'Battle' has now gained mythical status and is represented in a wide range of artistic and cultural forms. The major argument of this article, following the general approach of Jonathan Boyarin, is that the processes of remembering and forgetting the 'Battle' are inseparable and cannot be seen as simple opposites. Indeed, as the century comes to a close there is a danger that the increasing commemoration of 4 October 1936 will be at the expense of remembering the specific events of the day itself.

Notes on Contributors

Neil Barrett completed a PhD which examined responses to the BUF in south Lancashire in the context of political stability in inter-war Britain. He is an Associate Lecturer in the School of Politics and Communication Studies at the University of Liverpool, and he also works in industry. He has published widely on anti-fascism and the history of the BUF.

Simon Blumenfeld left school at 14 to work as a cutter and presser in a 'sweatshop'. He joined the Worker's Theatre and wrote plays and novels, including the bestselling *Jew Boy* (1935). He later worked as a sports journalist and theatre critic. Now in his nineties, Blumenfeld continues to write for *The Stage*.

Julie V. Gottlieb is a post-doctoral fellow at the University of Toronto. She was awarded her doctorate from the University of Cambridge in 1998 and her book on women and fascism in inter-war Britain is forthcoming from I. B. Tauris in 2000. She is currently researching feminist anti-fascism in Britain during the 1930s.

Tony Kushner is Marcus Sieff Professor in the Department of History at the University of Southampton. He is the author of *The Persistence of Prejudice: Antisemitism in British Society During the Second World War* (Manchester University Press, 1989), *The Holocaust and the Liberal Imagination* (Blackwell, 1994) and, with Katharine Knox, *Refugees in an Age of Genocide* (Frank Cass, 1999).

Thomas P. Linehan was awarded his PhD by Royal Holloway and Bedford New College, University of London and now lectures in Modern History at Brunel University. He is the author of *East London for Mosley: The BUF in East London and South West Essex, 1933-40*, published by Frank Cass in 1996.

David Mazower is a senior journalist with BBC World Service, where he works on international current affairs programmes. In his spare time, he researches and writes about Yiddish culture in Britain and the Jewish East End. He is the author of *Yiddish Theatre in London* (1987; 2nd ed 1996).

David Renton is the author of *Fascism: Theory and Practice* (Pluto, 1999). He has taught at Nottingham Trent and Rhodes Universities, and is currently researching fascism and anti-fascism in Britain, 1945–51.

Elaine R. Smith completed her Leicester University doctorate on the subject of 'East End Jews in Politics 1918-1939: A Study in Class and Ethnicity'. She worked in adult education at the Faculty of Continuing Education, Birkbeck College, University of London, until the birth of her son, Daniel Eliezer.

Richard C. Thurlow is Senior Lecturer in History at the University of Sheffield. He is the author of *Fascism in Britain* (rev. edition, I. B. Tauris, 1998), *Fascism* (Cambridge University Press, 1999) and *The Secret State* (Blackwell, 1994). His current research is on the surveillance of political extremism in Britain.

Nadia Valman is Ian Karten Research Fellow at the Parkes Centre for Jewish/non-Jewish relations, University of Southampton. She has published articles on Victorian Jewish culture and is currently researching questions of gender in Victorian Jewish literature. She is editor of *Jewish Culture and History*.

Index

Anti-fascism 2, 82-3, 116-20, 123
   and class 101-6
   and communism 101-4
   effect of Public Order Act 91-3
   Jewish 63-7, 68-70, 82-3, 123-4, 197 *see also* Jewish People's Council
   modern 152-3
   post-war 137-8, 141-3
Anti-Fascist Action 157
anti-semitism 39-40, 123-5
   in BUF 37-8, 79, 81, 90
   in East End 81-2
   of police 7-11
Arbeter Ring see Workers' Circle
Association for Jewish Youth 6
Association of Jewish Friendly Societies 53

Battle of Cable Street 87, 89-90, 92
   aftermath 104-6
   as class struggle 95-7, 101-6
   as myth 109-11, 118
   commemorations of 134-6, 155, 157, 162-4, 169-70
   Communist Party and 130-1, 142-3
   contemporary perspectives of 120-40
   development of memory of 152-70
   documentary on 149-52
   eyewitness account of 198-201
   Jewish memory of 128-30, 146-8
   mural of 158-62
   naming of 148
   participants in 101-4
   post-war perspectives of 140-6, 166-71
   and the press 125-7
Beckett, John 25, 105
Beckman, Morris 96-7
Becow, Barnett 123
Bellamy, Richard Reynell 56
Bloomfield, Alte 103
Blumenfeld, Simon 3, 131, 203
Board of Deputies of British Jews 1, 18-19, 129
   communal defence 51-4, 57-70
   criticisms of 59, 61, 68
British Fascists 32-3
British Lion 32-3
British Union of Fascists (BUF) 2, 79-82, 87-9
   anti-semitism in 37-8, 79, 81, 90

   consequences of Cable Street 23-4, 104-6, 280-1
   effect of Public Order Act 91-2
   in Manchester 56
   Jewish responses to 49-54, 57-70
   membership of 98-101
   policy on women 35
   political surveillance of 77
   women in 31-45
Brock Griggs, Anne 34-8, 40-2
Brockway, Fenner 119-20
BUF *see* British Union of Fascists
Butler Street Girls' Club 182

Cable Street 111-15 *see also* Battle of Cable Street
Cable Street Group 114-15, 158
Cameron, James 151
Chesterton, A.K. 26, 81, 88-9
children 15-18
The Circle 197
class 2, 28-9, 95-7, 101-6, 181-2
Cohen, A.L. 3, 4, 196-7
   account of Cable Street 198-201
Cohen, Hannah 53
communism 82-3, 101-4, 142-3
Communist Party 2, 14, 77, 82
   and Cable Street 118-19, 142-4
   and Jews 82-3, 102-4
   role in anti-fascism 49-51, 58, 86-7, 101-4
   and women 12-15
Council of Manchester and Salford Jews (CMSJ) 57, 63-70 passim
Crossley, Sir Anthony 43, 86, 124-5
crowd, images of the 24-8
Cutmore, Anne 41

Daily Worker 12, 95, 117-19
Davis, Morry 48-9, 53-4
Devine, Pat 119, 136-7
dockers 18, 101-2

East End of London 81-2, 85, 86
   anti-fascism in 82-4
   confrontations in 77-9, 87-9
   Jewish 20, 48, 50, 53-4
East London Youth Front Against Fascism and War 183
Elam, Norah 38

Index

ethnic minorities and the police 4-5
ethnicity 2, 102-4
Eveson, Inspector Thomas 6-7
Ex-Servicemen's Movement Against Fascism and Anti-semitism 51, 116-17

Fascism 2, 79-82, 88-9
  and class 97-101
  Jews and 49-54, 127-8
  post-war 140-1, 143-4
  propaganda 2, 24-8, 34-40
  women in 3, 31-45
Fascist Children's Clubs 33
Faulkner, William 150-1
Fine, J.L. 117
Finn, Ralph 103, 138-9
Fishman, Bill 7, 18, 150, 151
43 Group 16-17, 96, 141
Frankel, Dan 48-9, 53-4, 127-8
Freeman, Jeanne 11

Game, Sir Philip 84-5, 88, 89, 90, 92, 123
Gardiner's Corner 13, 14, 16, 95, 118-19
gender 3, 11, 15, 181-2 *see also* women
Glasgow 20
Goldman, Willy 18
Gollancz, Victor 56-7
Goodman, Charlie 8, 14, 134, 162
Goodman, Joyce 14, 16, 129
Grant, Hannah 11
Greenberg, Ivan 58

Hawks, Olive 35-6, 41
Henriques, Basil 49, 183-5, 189-90
Henriques, Rose 12, 15, 49, 182, 185, 187-90
Home Office 92
  and public order 83-4
Hunger Marches 75-6, 89, 90

Independent Labour Party (ILP) 119-20

Jacobs, Joe 49, 50, 104, 110-11, 155
Janner, Barnett 68
Janner, Lady 11, 182
Jewish anti-fascism 82-3, 123-4, 197
  in Manchester 63-7, 68-70 *see also* Jewish People's Council
Jewish Association for the Protection of Girls and Women 184, 185
Jewish Chronicle 56-7, 58, 68, 116
Jewish communism 82-3, 102-4
Jewish councillors 48-9
Jewish Defence Committee 60
Jewish East End Project 6
Jewish Ex-Servicemen's Legion 2, 51

Jewish girls 181-3, 185-90
Jewish girls' clubs 181-3, 185-6, 190
Jewish Historical Society of England (JHSE) 5-6
Jewish historiography 5-6, 15
Jewish Labour Council 2, 51
Jewish organisations 51-3
Jewish People's Council against Fascism and Anti-semitism (JPC) 2, 51-3, 58, 61, 86, 117, 129, 147, 197
Jewish Standard 141
Jewish stereotypes 39-40, 187-8
Jewish Working Lads' Brigade 183, 184
Jewish youth 15-19, 183
Jewish youth clubs 181-90
Jews 2, 6
  and class 181-2, 186-7
  communal defence 5, 48, 49-54, 65-7
  of East End 20, 48, 50, 53-4
  of Manchester 56-70
  responses to BUF 49-54, 57-70
  responses to fascism 2, 63-7, 68-70, 82-3, 197
Joyce, William 25, 28

Kidd, Ronald 13
King Sol 132-4
Kops, Bernard 7, 15-16, 18

Laski, Harold 56, 68-9
Laski, Nathan 57, 63, 66
Laski, Neville 49, 53, 57, 61-2, 63, 67-8
Lawrence, Stephen 4-5, 281
League of Ex-Servicemen 140
Leech, Kenneth 109, 111-12
Leese, Arnold 79, 88
Levinson, Maurice 139-40
Lintorn-Orman, Rotha 32-3
Litvinoff, Emmanuel 103
local studies 153-5

McShane, Yolande 34, 39
Manchester 56-70
memory 110, 111, 128-30, 146-8, 152-70
Morgan, Joe 109-10
Morrison, Herbert 61-2
Mosley, Cynthia 34
Mosley, Diana 43-5
Mosley, Nicholas 44
Mosley, Oswald 24, 32, 79-82
  in documentary 150
  on women 31, 37-8
  second marriage 43-5
  views on 167-8
Mullally, Frederic 140-1
multi-culturalism 155-6, 164

National Council for Civil Liberties 67, 68, 70, 82, 83, 88
National Jewish Committee of the Communist Party (NJC) 142
National Unemployed Workers' Movement 75-6
Nordic League 61

Oxford and St George's Club 183, 184-5, 187
Oxford and St George's Girls' Club 12, 181, 182, 184, 185-6

Pakistan Welfare Association 114
Pearce, Jack 52, 197
Piratin, Phil 12-13, 48, 50, 82, 138, 142-3
　in documentary 150-2
　on fascism 95-6, 100-101, 104
police 4-5, 10-11, 77-9, 83-7
　and Cable Street 121-3
　in Manchester 63-4
　and Jewish community 6-11
　racism in 85
political violence 77-9
Pollitt, Harry 61-2
popular front policy 49
propaganda 2, 24-9, 34-40
public order 3-4, 75
　and civil liberties 78, 89-90, 92-3
　threats to 76-9, 83-6, 89
Public Order Act 1936 4, 79, 89-93, 120-1

Rabiger, Michael 149-51
racism 4-5, 10, 85
Ralph, A.G. 122-3
Ramsay, Edith 14, 17, 112, 150, 151
Ravensdale, Baroness 33-4
Rocker, Rudolph 18
Rockman, Alf 134-5
Rolph, C.H. 8-9, 121-2
Rosen, Harold 95, 118
Rosen, Michael 102
Rothermere, Lord 80

Sanitt, Leonard 17

Sassoon, Vidal 141-2
Scaffardi, Sylvia 13
Scottish Protestant League 20
Searchlight 156
Shaw, Jack 8
Sheridan (Shrensky), Lazar 118, 132-4
Simon, Sir John 63, 90
Skidelsky, Robert 115-16, 121, 127
Smith, May 163
Sokoloff, Bertha 14, 18
Spanish Civil War 28, 117-18
Special Branch 11-12, 75
　expansion of 77
　reports on Cable Street 123
Spector, Cyril 17
Spot, Jack 147-8
Stepney Girls' Club 182
Stepney Labour Council 48-9

They Won't Let You Live 131
trade unions 51
Trenchard, Lord 83-4
Turney, Bob 8

Union Movement 143

Vigilance Committees 59

Walsh, Gladys 42
Warshaw, Jack 152-3
Wesker, Arnold 144-6
West Central Jewish Girls' Club 182
White, Jack 63-5
Willsher, Audrey 165-7
Wolveridge, Jim 153, 154
women 3, 11-15, 186-8
　anti-fascism and 32, 182
　anti-semitism and 38-40
　in BUF 31-45
Workers' Circle 3, 17, 51-2, 82, 147, 195-7
Wrsama, Kathleen 112

Yesterday's Witness 9, 17, 149
Zuckerman, William 20